Ancient Menippean Satire

JOEL C. RELIHAN

Ancient Menippean Satire

The Johns Hopkins University Press

Baltimore and London

© 1993 The Johns Hopkins University Press
All rights reserved
Printed in the United States of America on acid-free paper

The Johns Hopkins University Press
2715 North Charles Street
Baltimore, Maryland 21218-4139
The Johns Hopkins Press Ltd., London

Library of Congress Cataloging-in-Publication Data
Relihan, Joel C.
    Ancient Menippean satire / Joel C. Relihan.
      p. cm.
    Includes bibliographical references and index.
    ISBN 0-8018-4524-6 (alk. paper)
    1. Classical literature—History and criticism.   2. Satire, Greek—History and
criticism.   3. Satire, Latin—Greek influences.   4. Satire—Classical
influences.   5. Rhetoric, Ancient.   6. Literary form.   7. Parody.   I. Title.
PA3033.R44   1993
887'.0109—dc20   92-36271

A catalog record for this book is available from
the British Library.

für Elise

Contents

THE PERSONIFIED Dialogue of Lucian's *Bis Accusatus* ("The Author Twice on Trial") states a fundamental truth about Menippean satire: he says that the author has so compounded him of contrasting elements, of which the mixture of prose and verse is the strangest, that he appears to the audience as a paradoxical hybrid and a centaur.[1] Yet the truth is a critical embarrassment: a mixture of incompatible elements will hardly do as a rigorous definition of a genre, and in fact this genre has coughed up quite a few idiosyncratic works that are often taken as sui generis. One could collect critical sentiments on this topic: C. S. Lewis's view of one of our texts has achieved some notoriety ("This universe, which has produced the bee-orchid and the giraffe, has produced nothing stranger than Martianus Capella");[2] the *Satyricon* has been seen as a unique cross-fertilization of genres; and the *Consolation of Philosophy* has given rise to similar wonderment. It is a pardonable exasperation that asks whether generic labels have any value at all in discussing these works. It is my claim that these and other works do form a genre; that the genre's characteristics logically result from the consideration of a certain set of themes; and that the genre has a history that may be traced from Hellenistic times through late antiquity. I present here a study in the history of classical literature, documenting the rise of a genre, its bifurcation into Greek and Roman traditions, and the Christianization of these traditions in late antiquity. It is not a handbook but a critical attempt to save the phenomena of a genre that has not yet found its true niche in handbooks.

My studies began with the *Mythologies* of Fulgentius. I was surprised to discover in its prologue an account of a scholarly narrator who hoped to demonstrate that classical mythology was bogus, and who was himself in turn surprised to discover that the pagan Muses were alive and well; they, in contempt of the incompetent narrator and his theory of interpretation, were going on to dictate the rest of the book. It was pleasant enough to see that one of the more despised authors of late antiquity was capable of academic self-parody; but more remarkable was the realization that the theory that the narrator had hoped to use to prove the triviality of mythology was Christian. A Christian scholar (at least he thought of himself as such) depicted his faith as incapable of understanding a past that was intransigent in its error. The prologue is written in a mixture of prose and verse, and this traditional Menippean shibboleth led me to Varro, in whose *Menippean Satires* I became convinced was the origin of a comic form in which scholars were abused for mastery of a learning that was insufficient to explain or to control the irrational and human world. I ultimately concluded that Varro had turned Menippus's parody of philosophical certainties into what I would call the parody of encyclopedic knowledge; and that the late classical authors, including Martianus Capella and Boethius, were not contaminating Varro the satirist and Varro the encyclopedist but were, in their own literary renaissance, returning to its original Roman intent (though with a greatly augmented factual content) a genre that, in the hands of Seneca and Petronius, had been more of a parody of the traditions of verse satire.

In what follows I present the theoretical and analytical ramifications of this view. The theoretical chapters, which take Frye and Bakhtin as their starting point, attempt to minimize critical jargon and are in many respects a condensation of the interpretative chapters of practical criticism that follow them. The interpretative chapters, however, are not all written on the same model. When dealing with well-known works, such as the *Apocolocyntosis* or the *Satyricon,* I am more concerned to trace a trajectory through them than to describe them entire, and hope to give to contemporary critical conclusions a Menippean orientation. For example, Niall Slater's *Reading Petronius* treats the *Satyricon* as a novel; but its conclusions, about a narrator who cannot make sense of the world around him, and about a text that continually invokes the possibility of meaning only to dash these expectations, are fair descriptions of Menippean satire as a whole. For less well known works I attempt fuller outlines of the progress of the action and give a reading of the text; for the least familiar texts I have provided annotated translations in the appendixes.

Rather than treat the authors from Lucian on as afterthoughts in the history of Menippean satire, I give them full rein. Not only are the later works the only unfragmented ones in this genre to reach us (the *Apocolocyntosis* has a sizable lacuna at its center), but the Christianization of a self-parodic genre is a wonderful aspect of the literary world of late antiquity. A number of my interpretations will seem strange, especially to those who know how boring and awful the works of a Fulgentius or an Ennodius can be. It no longer surprises us, perhaps, that a Seneca can make fun of himself; but even those whose claims to academic competence are more slim can make the attempt. In the Menippean world, the modest topoi of an author's ignorance come to life: Martianus names one of Philology's escorts Agrypnia (Insomnia or "I was working on this late last night"); Ennodius's bashful deprecation of his learning is dramatized when the Liberal Arts he recommends say things that he does not want them to say. These posturings may be clumsy and infuriating, or weird and fascinating, depending on how charitably you are prepared to view the dancing of late antique dinosaurs. But these experiments in literary revival and transformation will culminate in the sublimely ironic *Consolation*.

Some disclaimer might be expected at the outset of this work—that its broad scope will necessarily dissatisfy specialists in the eras and authors that I survey, and that its claims to usefulness hope to outweigh its inevitable omissions. Yet this is trite; it would be more novel to invoke a Menippean Muse and say that this book is true to its topic, corroborating in and of itself the Menippean theme that any attempt to reduce the strange phenomena of this world to rule and theory can lead only to the embarrassment of the theorist. But I would rather quote Sir Thomas Browne: "We hope it will not be unconsidered, that we finde no open tract, or constant manuduction in this Labyrinth; but are oft-times fain to wander in the America and untravelled parts of Truth."[3]

I AM GLAD to admit my deep and abiding gratitude to my advisor Fannie LeMoine, who first introduced me to the topic of Menippean satire, and whose support, both scriptural and spiritual, has been invaluable over the long period of the germination of this work. I am fortunate also to be able to thank Danuta Shanzer for her careful reading of a large draft, for encouragement and keen insight, as the project drew to a close; and R. Bracht Branham, who was especially helpful in matters concerning Menippus and Cynicism. The anonymous reader for the press was also lavish with informative criticism. That all of their suggestions are not followed is merely an indictment of a stiff-necked and froward nature. Whatever merits this book may possess I hope will be accepted as some satisfaction of enormous debts. The dedication records the one to whom I owe an even greater debt than these.

THIS IS a good time for the study of Menippean satire: many of the important texts are now available in new or revised editions, though we wait for Marcovich's edition of Diogenes Laertius. The following editions are the sources of the quotations used in this study; other useful editions of these authors are cited in the Bibliography. I have not thought it necessary to give space in the Bibliography to standard editions of well-known texts, but I have included here some particular texts of importance to individual Menippean authors, as well as references to important editions of fragmentary authors and to collections known primarily by abbreviations. I have referred to Menippean texts by the titles under which they most frequently travel, preferring English translations but having little choice but to retain *Apocolocyntosis* and *Satyricon;* the possible meanings of these titles are discussed at appropriate places. These conventional titles are listed here, followed when necessary by their originals or by translations; for the title of an individual Menippean satire of Varro or a dialogue of Lucian, a translation is given at its first appearance in the text; both the original titles and their translations will be found in the Index.

The lowercase *u* and uppercase *V* have been regularized throughout the Latin quotations. Transliterations from the Greek follow the older conventions (*catascopia, catascopus*), though *mythos* is unavoidable. All translations, unless otherwise indicated, are my own. Verse passages have been translated as prose, as I make no pretense to being a poet; but an exception has been made for the text of Ennodius, whose polymetric exercises have been printed in their various and identifiable shapes: Sapphic strophe, distich, hexameter, and so on.

Boethius, *The Consolation of Philosophy*
> Ludwig Bieler, ed., *Anicii Manlii Seuerini Boethii Philosophiae Consolatio,* 2nd ed., Corpus Christianorum, Series Latina 94 (Turnhout, 1984).

Ennodius, *Paraenesis Didascalica* ("An Educational Address")
> Rosalba A. Rallo Freni, ed., *Magno Felice Ennodio, La "Paraenesis Didascalica"* (Messina, 1970): valuable for its introduction and Italian translation. The text varies only slightly from the standard

edition of F. Vogel, *Magni Felicis Ennodi Opera*, Monumenta Germaniae Historica, Auctores Antiquissimi 7 (1885; reprint Munich, 1981), 310–15.

Fulgentius, *Mythologies* (*Mitologiae*)

Rudolf Helm, ed., *Fabii Planciadis Fulgentii V. C. Opera* (1898; reprint, with addenda by J. Préaux, Stuttgart, 1970).

Julian, *Caesars* ("Symposium, or The Saturnalia")

Christian Lacombrade, ed., *L'Empereur Julien: Oeuvres complètes*, vol. 2, part 2 (Paris, 1964).

Lucian, *Necyomantia* ("Menippus, or The Consultation of the Dead") and *Icaromenippus* ("Menippus the New Icarus, or Over the Rainbow")

M. D. MacLeod, ed., *Luciani Opera*, vols. 1–4 (Oxford, 1972–87). The Oxford text of the *Necyomantia*, with facing translation and brief notes, may be found in MacLeod's *Lucian: A Selection* (Warminster, 1991). All references to the *Dialogues of the Dead* are by MacLeod's numbers alone.

Martianus Capella, *De Nuptiis* (in full, *De Nuptiis Philologiae et Mercurii*, "The Marriage of Philology and Mercury")

James Willis, ed., *Martianus Capella* (Leipzig, 1983).

Menippus, *Necyia* ("In the Land of the Dead")

For the fragments of and testimonia concerning Menippus, the following are of greatest importance:

Athenaeus: G. Kaibel, ed., *Athenaei Naucratitae Dipnosophistarum Libri XV*, 3 vols. (1887–90; reprint Stuttgart, 1961–62).

Diogenes Laertius: H. S. Long, ed., *Diogenis Laertii Vitae Philosophorum*, 2 vols. (Oxford, 1964).

Greek Anthology: W. R. Paton, ed., trans., *The Greek Anthology*, 5 vols. (Cambridge, Mass., 1916–18; frequently reprinted).

Lucian: see the previous entry under Lucian.

Lucian, scholia: H. Rabe, ed., *Scholia in Lucianum* (1906; reprint Stuttgart, 1971).

Marcus Aurelius: Joachim Dalfen, ed., *Marci Aurelii Antonini ad se ipsum Libri XII* (Leipzig, 1976).

Pseudo-Probus, *Commentary on Vergil's Eclogues and Georgics:* H. Hagen, ed., *Appendix Serviana* (Leipzig, 1902), 321–91 [= G. Thilo and H. Hagen, eds., *Seruii Grammatici Qui Feruntur in Vergilii Carmina Commentarii*, vol. 3, part 2; reprint Hildesheim, 1961].

Stobaeus as cited in Photius: R. Henry, ed., *Photius: Bibliothèque*, vol. 2 (Paris, 1960).

The *Suda:* A. Adler, ed., *Suidae Lexicon*, 5 vols. (1928–37; reprint Stuttgart, 1967–71).

Petronius, *Satyricon*

 Konrad Müller, ed., and Wilhelm Ehlers, trans., *Petronius: Satyrica: Schelmenszenen*, 3rd ed. (Munich, 1983).

Seneca, *Apocolocyntosis*

 P. T. Eden, ed., *Seneca, Apocolocyntosis* (Cambridge, 1984). The Teubner edition of R. Roncali, *L. Annaei Senecae* Ἀποκολοκύντωσις (Leipzig, 1990), has also been consulted.

Varro, *Menippean Satires* (*Saturae Menippeae*)

 Raymond Astbury, ed., *M. Terentii Varronis Saturarum Menippearum Fragmenta* (Leipzig, 1985). The massive and ongoing edition of J.-P. Cèbe, *Varron: Satires ménippées*, Collection de l'École Française de Rome 9 (Paris, 1972–), has now passed the halfway point with its eighth volume, *Marcopolis—Mysteria*. Also important for Varro are:

 Cicero, *Posterior Academics:* O. Plasberg, ed., *Academicorum Reliquiae cum Lucullo*, M. Tulli Ciceronis Scripta Quae Manserunt Omnia, fasc. 42 (1922; reprint Stuttgart, 1961).

 Aulus Gellius: P. K. Marshall, ed., *A. Gellii Noctes Atticae*, 2 vols. (Oxford, 1968).

 Keil, *Grammatici Latini:* H. Keil, ed., *Grammatici Latini*, 7 vols. (Leipzig, 1855–79; reprint Hildesheim, 1961).

General: editions of fragments, abbreviations

 Ennius, *Annals:* Otto Skutsch, ed., *The Annals of Q. Ennius* (Oxford, 1985).

 Ennius, tragedies: H. D. Jocelyn, ed., *The Tragedies of Ennius* (Cambridge, 1967).

 Euripides: A. Nauck, ed., *Tragicorum Graecorum Fragmenta*, 2nd ed. (1889; reprint with addenda by Bruno Snell, Hildesheim, 1964).

 FPL: W. Morel, ed., *Fragmenta Poetarum Latinarum*, 2nd ed. (1927; reprint Stuttgart, 1975).

 Hesiod: R. Merkelbach and M. L. West, eds., *Fragmenta Hesiodea* (Oxford, 1967).

 Lucilius: Werner Krenkel, ed., trans., *Lucilius: Satiren*, 2 vols. (Leiden, 1970).

 PLRE II: J. R. Martindale, ed., *The Prosopography of the Later Roman Empire*, Vol. II, *A.D. 395–527* (Cambridge, 1980).

 PMG: Denys Page, ed., *Poetae Melici Graeci* (Oxford, 1962).

 Sophocles: S. Radt, ed., *Tragicorum Graecorum Fragmenta*, vol. 4 (Göttingen, 1977).

 SVF: J. von Arnim, ed., *Stoicorum Veterum Fragmenta*, 3 vols. (Leipzig, 1903–5); vol. 4, *Indices*, M. Adler (Leipzig, 1924).

I.

THEORY AND PRACTICE

 *Chapter One*

SOME MODERN APPROACHES

TRADITIONAL classical studies have treated Menippean satire in one of three ways: as the task of reconstructing or understanding Menippus himself, which task considers the genre a subdivision of the diatribe; as a stylistic phenomenon known as prosimetrum; and as a variation on the traditions of Roman verse satire. The last is most frequent: handbooks of Roman satire discuss the social outlook of Varro, Seneca, and Petronius and dismiss the claims of the Greeks (Lucian, Julian) and the late Romans (Martianus Capella, Fulgentius, Ennodius, Boethius). Treatment of purely literary aspects of the genre is comparatively rare in classical circles, although brief considerations of its history are a staple commodity in the introductions to studies of individual authors. There is in general an unwillingness among classicists to treat Menippean satire as a genre in and of itself which spans both Greek and Latin literature, and this is perhaps due to the pervasive influence of Quintilian's dictum that satire is entirely, or at least preeminently, a Roman genre. The present work intends to separate classical Menippean satire from the confines of Cynicism and verse satire, cautiously following the lead of critics from other literary disciplines.[1]

Outside of classical circles Menippean satire has become a critical term used to discuss a vast genre of world literature, comprising practically the full range of seriocomic and learned fiction, and denotes, in very general terms, an unsettling or subversive combination of fantasy, learning, and philosophy. Within its categories are included, with varying degrees of persuasiveness, Erasmus and humanistic literature, Rabelais and Burton and Swift, *Tristram Shandy, Moby Dick, Alice in Wonderland,* and *Ulysses.*[2] The genre is invoked both to explain the origins of the modern novel and to categorize forms of prose fiction which are not essentially novelistic. Consequently, the bloom is off the rose of Menippean satire. What was once novel is now a somewhat discredited commonplace; the term has been long enough in vogue that it has been expanded beyond what many would consider its reasonable bounds, and its usefulness has justly been questioned.[3] I am not primarily concerned with modern literature or the propriety of such attributions, but the theoretical

3

interests of modern Menippean studies can still provide a basis for the understanding of the definition and the historical development of the genre in antiquity. They are a luxuriant growth and require some pruning.

The deans of the study of modern Menippean satire are Northrop Frye and Mikhail Bakhtin. As Bakhtin has only recently been discovered by the West, Frye is the earlier in terms of the development of modern attitudes toward the genre. In his *Anatomy of Criticism,* Frye, with his accustomed brilliance, distinguishes four types of fiction that may occur in pure forms (though rarely) or in various combinations with each other: novel, confession, anatomy, and romance. Of these, anatomy is the preferred term for Menippean satire, which is considered misleading:

> The Menippean satire deals less with people as such than with mental attitudes. Pedants, bigots, cranks, parvenus, virtuosi, enthusiasts, rapacious and incompetent professional men of all kinds, are handled in terms of their occupational approach to life as distinct from their social behavior. The Menippean satire thus resembles the confession in its ability to handle abstract ideas and theories, and differs from the novel in its characterization, which is stylized rather than naturalistic, and presents people as mouthpieces of the ideas they represent. . . . The novelist sees evil and folly as social diseases, but the Menippean satirist sees them as diseases of the intellect, as a kind of maddened pedantry which the *philosophus gloriosus* at once symbolizes and defines.[4]

Menippean satire does not concentrate on plot and action, nor does it set out to observe the real workings of society. Frye is quite right to say that "at its most concentrated the Menippean satire presents us with a vision of the world in terms of a single intellectual pattern." Within this framework, a Menippean satire can be purely fantastic (Frye's example is Carroll's Alice books) or purely moral, as in utopian fiction.[5] This concept of intellectual satire will be most useful when dealing with the *Apocolocyntosis* and *Satyricon,* works whose intentions, I shall argue, are not to be confused with those of verse satire's social criticism. And it will be of great importance in treating Boethius's *Consolation of Philosophy,* which is characterized by its "contemplative irony." Frye rightly notes that Varro is probably responsible for making Menippean satire a genre apt for encyclopedic displays of learning: this tendency, which explains the generic affiliations of such a work as Burton's *Anatomy of Melancholy* (the origin of Frye's renaming of the genre as "anatomy"), is a work in Martianus Capella and Boethius, and in the Greek Julian as well.

Frye's anatomy is not a genre in the classical sense but a much broader classification, and his sensible renaming of the genre indicates that we ought not to identify it immediately with the peculiarities of specific ancient texts, which are, as it were, a subset of it.[6] Anatomy therefore tends to blur distinctions that classical literary criticism would prefer to maintain; similarly, Frye's romance is a fictional pattern that can include New Comedy as well as Heliodorus.[7] For example, Frye sees a long and a short form of Menippean satire, the latter being the dialogue that focuses on "conflict of ideas rather than of character," and which may be satiric in character, but often simply fantastic or simply moral.[8] When this dialogue is itself expanded, it becomes the symposium. But there are many types of dialogue, and Lucian's comic dialogues are best thought of as a separate genre of literature, one of Lucian's own invention, conceived of as a parody of the Socratic dialogue. Further, while some symposia are, or are contained in, Menippean satires (the *Cena Trimalchionis*, Julian's *Caesars*), others are not (the *Saturnalia* of Macrobius and the *Deipnosophists* of Athenaeus, or Methodius's *Symposium of the Ten Virgins*). Lucian's *Symposium, or The Lapiths* is a parody of Plato's *Symposium* without actually being a Menippean satire. Frye is right that Macrobius and Athenaeus embody the same principle of anatomy that Menippean satire feeds on, and Athenaeus even has some of the academic humor that we require; but I think that Macrobius and Petronius are best relegated to different genres.[9] The various elements of anatomy that Frye catalogs—dialogue, stylization of character, fantasy, intellectual satire, and so on—are separable, and I would allow that only particular combinations of them denominate essential Menippean satire, while other combinations result in other related comic, or noncomic, genres.

In current studies of Menippean satire the theories of Mikhail Bakhtin are in the ascendant. He too is most interested in creating a broad classification of the totality of literature. In his *Problems of Dostoevsky's Poetics* he documents the rise of the modern, "polyphonic" novel; crucial to its development is the genre that he calls "menippea" (a singular noun; note again the creation of new name).[10] In this genre the centrality of the author to the interpretation of the work breaks down. The narrator discovers that he "means more than one thing," and truth comes as a possibility that arises from the conflict of ideas. The genre is essentially dialogic and seriocomic, and opposed to the monologic and serious genres (tragedy, epic, history, rhetoric, the epistle), which take for granted "an integrated and stable universe of discourse."[11] The world that it describes is the world of carnival, in which everything is upside-down. Socrates and Plato are of great importance here, and Bakhtin postulates a prehistory of Menippean satire in which Menippus appears only as one who gave it a fixed form; Antisthenes, Heraclides Ponticus, and Bion are said to have written Menippean satires.[12] Bakhtin casts his net very wide: the diatribe, the soliloquy, the symposium, the novel, utopian literature, and others, all develop under its influence.[13]

Again, we may object that the classification is too broad to be a useful guide to the genre's classical origins and its specific texts. Sometimes Bakhtin is careful to distinguish between the genre and things merely influenced by it, but often he is not. It seems that the menippea can be viewed as an intellectual attitude adopted toward the value of truth and the possibility of meaning, a particular world view, that may show up in a number of different genres (the pseudo-Hippocratic *Letters,* the logistoricus, the aretalogy). More important for this study is his attempt to define the genre in terms of a number of interrelated structural and thematic elements, most of which are relevant to our more restricted study of the Menippean genre in antiquity. These fourteen elements prove to be a very useful supplement to Frye's discussion, and they can be summarized as follows:

1. A greater importance given to the comic element, in contrast to the Socratic dialogue. The humor may be exaggerated (as in Varro) or greatly reduced (as in Boethius).

2. An independence from plausibility in its depictions, and an extraordinary freedom of plot and philosophical invention.

3. The creation of extraordinary situations in which to test a truth or philosophical idea, itself embodied in the person of the wise man. This accounts for the frequent journeys to heaven and hell in menippea, whose real content is the adventures of an idea in the world.

4. Slum naturalism—the organic combination of fantastic, elevated, and even mystical or religious elements with the dregs of earthly life: robbers' dens, brothels, prisons, and so on. Bakhtin points out that this is present in its fullest degree in the works of Petronius and Apuleius, menippea expanded into novels; we should note that it is present in the ideal romance as well.

5. A genre of ultimate questions, it contemplates the world on the broadest possible scale. Fantasy and free invention allow this.

6. A construction on three levels (Olympus, earth, the underworld), a consequence of its philosophical universalism. Riikonen points out that Seneca's *Apocolocyntosis* is the primary example of this sort of structure.[14]

7. Experimental fantasticality, observation from an unusual point of view, typically from on high, as when Menippus looks down on the earth from the moon in Lucian's *Icaromenippus*. The Greek word for such an observation is *catascopia*.

8. Moral-psychological experimentation and a representation of abnormal psychic states: insanity, split personality, and so on. This breaks down the unity of the person and suggests another person within, and raises the possibility that characters do not coincide with themselves.

9. Violations of the established norms of behavior, including habits of speech. Such breaks in the normal order of the world free human behavior from the presuppositions that predetermine it.

10. A love of sharp and oxymoronic contrast and abrupt transitions: "unexpected comings together of distant and disunited things, mésalliances of all sorts."

11. Elements of social utopias, usually present in the form of a voyage to an unknown land.

12. A wide use of inserted genres: "novellas, letters, oratorical speeches, symposia, and so on," with varying degrees of distance from an authorial point of view, or parody. Bakhtin here alludes to the mixture of prose and verse, and adds that verse insertions are almost always parodic.

13. A mixture of styles and tones, consistent with the preceding element. "What is coalescing here is a new relationship to the word as the material of literature."

14. A concern with social and topical issues. Bakhtin speaks of journalistic overtones to the genre; and refers tendentiously to the satires of Lucian as an "encyclopedia of his times," a sort of *Diary of a Writer*.[15]

Bakhtin speaks of the logic behind these elements in terms of an epoch in which all ancient ideas of seemliness and order have passed away, in which the proliferation of philosophical and religious

groups has made arguing over ultimate questions a function of the
marketplace, and in which the wise man rises to prominence in society. Yet it is an epoch in which the individual seems to play a role
assigned by a blind fate, which thus sponsors an alienation and despair that lead to "the destruction of the epic and tragic wholeness of
a man and his fate." In short, Bakhtin invokes the all-elastic Hellenistic zeitgeist, whose chronological limits may be extended to include
Marcus Aurelius and even the Christian Augustine. This sociological
explanation, which asserts the essential unity of over six hundred
years of history, is as unsatisfactory here as it is in explanations of the
origins and popularity of the ancient romance. Bakhtin makes the
intriguing claim that the menippea provides in this vast era a stable
form into which to pour these inexplicable and contradictory ideas
and feelings, a form that creates a link among them, a unity and a
sort of meaning. Unfortunately, he does not consider the different
ways in which the various seriocomic genres attack the myth of the
epic and tragic wholeness of life, and this stable form seems a Pro-
crustean thing. Nevertheless, Bakhtin does create an impressive series of relations between structural elements (fantasy, multileveled
construction, voyages, *catascopia*, mad characters, variations in style
and tone, subsumed genres, use of verse) and thematic ones (the
breakdown of old notions of truth and order, the search for new
truths, the possibility that truth may be anywhere). These interrelations will be of crucial importance.

Both Frye and Bakhtin attend more to modern than to ancient
literature and use Varro, Seneca, Petronius, and Apuleius as a
springboard from which to leap into modern times. They are careful
(generally) to adopt new names for their supergenres, more careful
than those who follow them. Both make the excellent point that
much of what is strange in modern fiction has an excellent and antique pedigree. Both claim that Menippean satire, however it is to be
named, has a profound influence on a wide range of other works.
They agree that a new relation of author to work is the issue, and the
elimination of the word *satire* from their names for the genre avoids
the glib associations of social criticism that that word normally entails. But a serious and unfortunate consequence of these brilliant
schemes of modern discourse is that the ancient texts are themselves
deprived of a history and are presented as a unity, and our individual
works are not so much subjected to analysis as used to exemplify
elements important to the development of later literary traditions.
When Bakhtin speaks of a "powerful and multi-branched generic
tradition," he does not contemplate the change of the classical genre

through time, except to posit a prehistory for what he sees as a stable form.[16]

The application of Frye's and Bakhtin's constructs to specific ancient texts has proved difficult. Riikonen presents not an interpretation of the *Apocolocyntosis* but an identification of elements within it which correspond to Bakhtin's fourteen categories. Payne has more success, relating Lucian and Boethius to a tradition that reaches to Chaucer, but is concerned primarily with the subversive and intellectual implications of Menippean fantasy.[17] Some studies have pursued the function of the seriocomic in ancient literature, but *spoudogeloion* is hardly a generic term, and Branham's study of Lucian demonstrates admirably that individual authors must be studied for the particular ways in which they are seriocomic.[18] What is clear to me is that Menippean satire has not in effect been invoked in modern discussions of classical texts as often as anatomy, menippea, prosimetrum, and *spoudogeloion*. It is just as hazardous to equate such all-embracing categories with the specific form of any individual ancient work as it is to confuse "the satiric" and "a satire."

By calling this work *Ancient Menippean Satire* I mean to speak of the specific relations among a limited number of texts, and to confine myself to the practical criticism of a genre that changes through time. "Menippean satire" has no ancient sanction as a generic term; as I shall detail in the next chapter, there is no use of the term to label a genre of literature until the sixteenth century, and I am free to attempt to make a meaningful term of it. My own definition of a genre of ancient Menippean satire, discussion of its origins, and explanation of the relations between its particular forms and the themes that are typical to it are, to a certain and inevitable extent, arbitrary procedures. There is a need both to select the works that define the normal characteristics of the genre and to decide which characteristics will isolate the normative works. The circular argument is an inescapable component of the creation of a classification and its definition and it need not be apologized for, but it does require some caution.[19] What will be achieved in Chapter 2 is a definition of what I think may be viewed as the epicenter of the phenomena discussed by Frye and Bakhtin; I will then chart the fortunes and influence of this narrowly conceived genre through time.

My starting point is what may be plausibly labeled, on ancient evidence, the Menippean satires of antiquity. I proceed to distinguish, in what we may loosely call Aristotelian terms, between what is essential and what is accidental to the genre; to separate the genre from other seriocomic genres; to document how the conception of the genre changed through time; and to explain how the genre that culminates in Boethius's *Consolation* lives on in the Middle Ages. In all of this Frye and Bakhtin are most useful. But I urge that the genre is primarily a parody of philosophical thought and forms of writing, a parody of the habits of civilized discourse in general, and that it ultimately turns into the parody of the author who has dared to write in such an unorthodox way. What I see as essential to Menippean satire is a continuous narrative, subsuming a number of parodies of other literary forms along the way, of a fantastic voyage to a source of truth that is itself highly questionable, a voyage that mocks both the traveler who desires the truth and the world that is the traveler's goal, related by an unreliable narrator in a form that abuses all the proprieties of literature and authorship. In this genre, fantasy is rarely liberating: in insisting on the value of what is commonplace and commonsensical, Menippean satire creates fantastic worlds that are suspiciously like the flawed real world, which the voyager has foolishly left behind. From such a vantage point we will be able to see, for example, that Claudius in the *Apocolocyntosis* is the typical naïf of Menippean satire who observes a wholly ridiculous other world; and that the point of the *Satyricon* is not merely criticism of declining standards of taste and learning and of the nouveau riche as typified by Trimalchio, but the parody of the dissolute narrator who in his wanderings pretends to be a social and literary critic. Later antiquity will on occasion find less dramatic ways to represent this voyage, but *catascopia* and *catabasis* are never very far below the surface of a Menippean satire.

I view a genre as a body of conventions, in structure and in style, to which certain themes are more appropriate than others. The reader, aware of the conventions of the genre, pays attention to variations on these conventions, deviations from them, or simple compliance with them. The point of the work is revealed in large part through the use of these conventions.[20] The conventions themselves have a life of their own, obey an inner logic, and may be said to have a history independent of the text. One must therefore look outside, to the genre as a whole, in order to understand an individual work; by virtue of its generic affiliations, a text is not self-sufficient but makes sense in the context of its tradition. I accept Frye's view that literary structures and conventions have primacy over ostensible subject matter: I am not as concerned with, say, Julian's "real" feelings toward his imperial predecessors as with the implications of encapsulating a history of the Roman Empire in a heavenly banquet. Yet for practical criticism one cannot be entirely ahistorical and synchronic. My claim

is that as the nature of the genre which I abstract from ancient literature itself changes through time, it reflects both specific innovations
by specific authors in the tradition and the reinterpretation of specific themes and elements in different historical and social settings.
And for the meanings of the words themselves in any text we need
reference to various historical and social phenomena, not because
the age explains the work (rather the opposite—the works we possess
may define and explain their ages) but because the age can explain
the word, and these texts are written in many different ages.

Menippean satire could be viewed as a parasitical genre that feeds
on other authors and the *corpora;* it cannot be understood except as a
reaction against, or a toying with, the authority that people invest in
certain texts. In the Conclusion I argue that the primary impulse for
Menippean satire, the force that both motivates and encircles the
genre in its eight-hundred-year history, is Book 10 of Plato's *Republic,*
which prefaces the Myth of Er, itself in most of its elements a Menippean satire, with a statement doubting the ability of words to express
anything other than the lowest level of phenomenal reality. Menippean satire accepts this caveat and takes the Myth of Er, and Platonic
mythologizing in general, as perfect demonstrations of how *not* to go
about proclaiming truth and defining reality. Menippean satire, one
may say, opposes the word-centered view of the universe, and is a
genre that, in words, denies the possibility of expressing the truth in
words. The genre further frustrates the reader's search for truth in
words by following the *Odyssey*'s lead in making its hero a master of
lies, whose tales of the fantastic are never certainly true, and who
ultimately passes by all sources of extravagant wisdom to live the
simple life, apart and at home. This is a pleasantly intoxicating point
of view, but I am unwilling to make the theory the essence of this
work. Or, to borrow the moral from Lucian's *Charon, or Those Who
Look Down from a Great Height* 5, in which the paradoxical nature of
the *catascopia* is stressed: "You can't be both secure and contemplative
at the same time." The definition of Menippean satire that follows
this chapter is the logical culmination of the study, the other chapters
being the material on which it is based. These latter chapters show, I
hope, the practical advantages of reading these strange works as part
of a long and vital, if eccentric, literary tradition.

 *Chapter Two*

A DEFINITION OF ANCIENT MENIPPEAN SATIRE

Menippean satire is not an ancient generic term. The only formal definition of satire preserved from antiquity, that of the fourth-century A.D. grammarian Diomedes, speaks only of morally corrective poems (citing Lucilius and Horace) and an earlier satire consisting of poems in different meters (citing Pacuvius and Ennius).[1] There are many references to Varro's *Saturae Menippeae* and to Varro's nickname "Menippeus," but these do not suggest that Varro's title was a generic designation, or anything other than the collective title of 150 short pieces.[2] The popular belief that Menippean satire was acknowledged in antiquity by this name as an "alternative convention" of satire is based on a misreading of Quintilian, who only admits to the same categories as Diomedes: the hexameter, in the tradition of Lucilius; and the mixed meter, in the tradition of Ennius.[3] Quintilian believes that Varro's *Menippeans*, written in a mixture of prose and verse, represent merely a variation on the Ennian model. *Menippean satire* is not used as a generic term until 1581, when Justus Lipsius writes his *Satyra Menippea. Somnium. Lusus in nostri aevi criticos.*[4] The French *Satyre ménippé* of the 1590s follows suit, but Casaubon does not, preferring the term *Varronian satire* in his *De Satyrica Graecorum Poesi & Romanorum Satira* of 1605.[5] The volubility of the name is thus not merely a modern phenomenon (Frye's *anatomy*, Bakhtin's *menippea*); and Gellius reports that even Varro's works were occasionally known under the name of *Cynic satires* (2.18.7, 13.31.1).

The genre, like many others, has evaded the grammarians' notice. But there are a number of important pieces of evidence as to how this sort of *satura* was viewed. A manuscript of the *Apocolocyntosis* of the tenth or eleventh century calls the work *Ludus de Morte Claudii per saturam;*[6] similarly, an anonymous ninth-century commentary on the *Consolation* says that Boethius wrote it *per saturam*, "evidently in imitation of Martianus Capella." This evidence would suggest that we are dealing purely with the phenomenon of prosimetrum; but medieval sources are careful to distinguish between *prosimetrum,* a term reserved for medieval works, and *satire,* which is reserved for ancient works.[7] Further, the titles of some of the Roman works speak, I think, of a polemical relation to traditional verse satire. Varro's title is complex and allusive: van Rooy takes it to mean "satiric medleys in the (Cynic) manner of the Greek Menippus," in which we may allow that the strong mixture of things Greek and Cynical and things Roman and moral, attested by the alternative ancient label for these works, creates something of a paradox.[8] And the *Satyricon,* whatever the proper form of that title may be, similarly conjures up associations of Roman satire in a Greek context: satire and satyr, the moral and the erotic.[9] Satire as a formally recognized literary genre may be entirely Roman, as Quintilian says, but these satires align themselves with the Greeks. To a certain extent, the promise of Greek satire held out by Varro and Petronius reminds us of the Greek kalends, and it seems that a Roman (Macrobius is a convenient witness) would have difficulty accepting the *Satyricon* as a work in the spirit of Horace.[10] Yet even the Romans can accept that satire in the sense of a jumble of things, particularly of prose and verse, is a phenomenon of Greek literature as well, attached to the name of Menippus: "Probus," commenting on Vergil's *Eclogues* (6.39), explains Varro's nickname "Menippeus" as denoting "a similarity of literary expression, for Menippus too adorned his satires with poems of every sort."[11]

What the above evidence suggests is that *satura* is somehow an appropriate term for a mixture of prose and verse, that this Menippean mixture is first found in a Greek author, and that it toys with the expectations of Roman verse satire. What confirms these suspicions is the evidence of two late Menippean satirists, Martianus Capella and Fulgentius, who introduce Satura (Satyra in Fulgentius) as an allegorical character in their works; their testimony may be supplemented by that of Lucian. Martianus Capella is the more important, for his Satura engages in a debate with the narrator of the *De Nuptiis Philologiae et Mercurii* ("The Marriage of Philology and Mercury") on certain vital questions: how the work is to mean what it means, and whether its evident lack of literary and thematic propriety advances or hinders this meaning. The details of the debate are given in the appropriate chapter; most important for us here is the concluding poem, in which Satura, who dictates the work to an author described as a doddering and incompetent old man, abandons the work as a disgrace. This crucial text must be given in full; the topic is who is responsible for the mess that is the *De Nuptiis* (9.997–1000):

Habes anilem,[12] Martiane, fabulam,   997
miscillo lusit quam lucernis flamine
Satura, Pelasgos dum docere nititur
artes †cagris uix amicas Atticis.
sic in nouena decidit uolumina;
haec quippe loquax docta indoctis[13] aggerans   998
fandis tacenda farcinat, immiscuit
Musas deosque, disciplinas cyclicas
garrire agresti cruda finxit plasmate.
haec ipsa namque rupta conscientia   999
turgensque felle ac bili, "multa chlamyde
prodire doctis approbanda cultibus
possemque comis utque e Martis curia;
Felicis" inquit "sed Capellae flamine,
indocta rabidum quem uidere saecula
iurgis caninos blateratos pendere
proconsulari uerba dantem culmini
†ipsoque dudum bobinatore flosculo
decertum fulquem iam canescenti rota,†
beata alumnum urbs Elissae quem uidet
iugariorum murcidam uiciniam
paruo obsidentem uixque respersum lucro
nictante cura somnolentum lucibus—
ab hoc creatum Pegaseum gurgitem   1,000
decente quando possem haurire poculo?"
testem ergo nostrum quae ueternum prodidit
secute nugis, nate, ignosce lectitans.

The following translation, owing to the frustrating cruces, can hope
to be no more than an inspired guess:

> You have, my son, an old woman's fiction, Satura's playful
> creation by the lamplight with its hodgepodge flame,[14] while
> she strove to teach Greek disciplines barely friendly to At-
> tic . . . ; thus does she end after the ninth book. For she, too
> talkative, piled together the learned on the unlearned,
> stuffed together the trite and the ineffable, mixed together
> the Muses and the gods and, undigested, made the Liberal
> Arts to chatter in a rude concoction. For she herself, shat-
> tered by knowledge of this and swelling with gall and bile,
> said "I could have come forth in a great philosopher's cloak,
> praiseworthy for my learned elegance, and could have done
> so decently, as if from the court of Mars himself. But, in-

spired by Martianus Capella, whom the present ignorant
generation sees as a rabid dog, paying out his canine nonsense onto judicial disputes while deceiving the proconsular
glory . . . whom the prosperous city of Dido sees as its foster
son, settling on slender means in a lazy neighborhood of
oxen, hardly crowned by wealth, groggy at sunrise with
blinking anxiety—when am I ever to be able to drink from a
fitting cup the waters of the Muses when he has created
them?" My son, you have followed the witness who has revealed my own ineptitude; as you read, pardon the nonsense.

What is obvious is the insistence on *satura* as mixture, medley: *miscillo, aggerans, farcinat, immiscuit*. But note also the mixture of opposites: *fandis tacenda*, gods and Muses with textbook Arts, *docta indoctis*.[15] The mixture is playful, jejune, or incompetent: *anilem fabulam, lusit, loquax, garrire agresti cruda finxit plasmate*. Insofar as *satura* is
a culinary term (*farcinat* suggests the etymology of *satura* as a stuffed
sausage), it is uncooked (*cruda*).[16] The mixture of prose and verse is
not mentioned, unless it lies behind the "hodgepodge flame," in a
sense of "inspiration from all literary genres." But the *satura* which is
the *De Nuptiis* is to be seen as a mixture of a great number of opposites of which the combination of prose and verse is only a part, and it
is a mixture that frustrates sense and the possibility of instruction.
Satura objects that the presentation of the matter of the work has
made it seem absurd. The narrator blames Satura, or his genre, for
the resulting absurdity; Satura blames the narrator, who in the closing lines accepts ultimate responsibility.

The closing poem is self-parodic: the author makes fun of himself,
his learning, and the form in which he has chosen to reveal what he
knows. As a fictional encyclopedia, the work is described as fundamentally ridiculous. Literary impropriety, self-parody, and the mockery of standards of judgment are all intertwined. And note that even
in the *De Nuptiis* the author alludes to the Cynic origins of his genre:
the author is *rabidus*, his words are *caninos blateratus*.[17] The senseless
mad dog ultimately points to Menippus, and a famous passage of
Lucian describing the perverse nature of Menippus's literary influence supplements the passage from Martianus.

In the dialogue *Bis Accusatus*, Lucian presents himself, under the
name of Syrus, as an author made to face charges of evil intent,
brought by Rhetoric, and of hybris, brought by Dialogue. At issue is
the impropriety of the genre of the comic dialogue, which is Lucian's

creation. Dialogue complains that he was once august and exalted in the hands of philosophers but is now made laughable; once upright, he now endures insult, lampoon, Cynic influence, Eupolis, and Aristophanes (*Bis Acc.* 33). Nor was this mixture of noble form and degrading content enough, for Menippus was added as well, a dog with a loud bark and a vicious bite, the bite made all the worse because it comes with a smile. This is the seriocomic Menippus, practically the only Cynic to whom the epithet ὁ σπουδογέλοιος adheres;[18] he is viewed here as inimical to philosophical instruction. Dialogue's greatest complaint, however, is still to come: Lucian's mixture of prose and verse, not specifically said to be an importation from Menippus's writings, makes Dialogue a misshapen thing (*Bis Acc.* 33): "For, strangest of all, I am mixed up into a paradoxical mixture and neither march on foot nor ride on meter, but, like a centaur, seem to the listeners to be some kind of hybrid and an outlandish monster."[19] Lucian's knowledge of the Roman world is, I think, sufficient for us to see an allusion to the word *satura* in the terms "paradoxical mixture" and "hybrid" (κρᾶσίν τινα παράδοξον κέκραμαι, σύνθετόν τι). Lucian here makes clear that a mixture of prose and verse will, in a dialogue at least, strike a conservative ancient audience as paradoxical, and that Menippean influence contributes to make a genre (the comic dialogue, not Menippean satire in this case) that is opposed to traditional teaching.[20] Further, it is plausible that Menippus and his writings are the ones ultimately guilty of the mixture of prose and verse for which Dialogue condemns Lucian: Menippus was said to have written in a mixture of prose and verse, he seems to have been one of the poets excerpted by Stobaeus, and the amount of verse in Lucian's own dialogues is so small as to make Dialogue's statements seem to be a definite overreaction.[21]

In Fulgentius's *Mythologies*, Satyra joins Calliope and two other Muses to take over the work that the narrator had intended to write: Urania and Philosophia seem to denominate the intellectual substance of what will follow, but Satyra is more of the critical spirit (14.2–6):

> . . . a comely maiden wanton in floral luxuriance, circled in abundant ivy, with a shameless face and a mouth pregnant with a bundle of insults; her ironic eye darted about with such a penetrating native wit that she could have described even the meanings deeply hidden in drunken writings.[22]

She is both erotic and insightful, crowned with bacchic ivy and capable of understanding inebriated texts, her shamelessness and insults suggesting both satyr and satire. Like Martianus's Satura, she comes to proclaim the author's work madness, for as I shall argue in its proper place the drunken writings alluded to are not just classical myths, but the *Mythologies* itself; at the point at which the maidens enter, the narrator has just been blurting out meaningless poetry in his sleep "like a mad poet" (13.18: "sicut insanus uates"). The Menippean satire is a work presented as a provocative mixture of things which its author does not understand.

In Horace's classic formulation, Roman verse satire combines humor and truth (*S.* 1.1.25–26): "ridentem dicere uerum / quid uetat?" But Menippean satire is not merely a pleasant form for the statement of ethical truth. The form of Menippean satire works against the reader's ability to understand its purpose. In the *De Nuptiis*, the reader is of uncertain vantage point: the author and his genre are at war over what to say and how to say it, and they express doubts that the form is adequate for the expression of a coherent point of view.[23] Verse satire is hardly so uncertain, despite the self-parody that is obvious in Horace. Menippean satire, which parodies preaching, is, on Roman soil at least, in many ways a parody of traditional satire. The loss of central authority in Menippean satire, of the author's presentation of a single point of view, has been noted by Bakhtin, who relates it to his dialogical principle. But Menippean satire, which plays with the word *satura* and the presuppositions of traditional satire, is militant in its denial of authority. We shall see that we have to deal with an intellectual joke, which in its origins is not concerned with finding new ways to truth but only with making fun of those who would claim to have found it, or who would try to preach it. Menippus is a mocker, and those who follow in his steps mock themselves and their own works: the creation of a work of literature is itself a violation of the cardinal principle that there can be no authoritative point of view about anything important.

PROSE AND VERSE

The evidence just presented suggests that the most obvious *formal* characteristic of the *satura* which is Menippean satire is its mixture of prose and verse. A precise definition of the nature of this phenomenon and its generic implications is in order. It is not simply a matter of quoting poets in a prose narration: this habit, very common in the romance, for example, may simply reflect a desire to vary the narrative.[24] It is true that such citations may have ironic overtones in the romance when they import the atmosphere of epic or tragedy into a

much less elevated situation;[25] but the discovery of fragments of so-
called Greek prosimetric romances (see Appendix A), in which characters speak in original verses of exotic metrical shape, brings us
much closer to the world of Menippean satire. The poetics of quotation and reference (intertextuality) crosses generic boundaries. The
question becomes, How is the use of verse in Menippean satire distinctive?[26]

Menippean satire's use of prose and verse cannot pass by the insufficient generic label of prosimetrum.[27] This is a medieval term, applied to a wide range of texts, some of which take some inspiration
from classical models, some not. Like the diatribe in which it is originally exploited, it is a style appropriate to a number of possible com-
positions.[28] Eckhardt distinguishes four categories of medieval prosimetra: philosophical works involving personification and allegory
(the legacy of Martianus Capella and Boethius); historiographic
works and the *uitae* of saints and kings; letter collections (for which
the letters of Sidonius are a model); and fictional works primarily in
the vernacular, including the chantefable.[29] Prose works in which
characters quote poetry in learned discussions of poetry (Athenaeus,
Macrobius), or in which an *aduersarius fictiuus* cites poets to make
moral arguments that the main speaker will quickly disprove (as in
the diatribe), are quite different in nature from works like the *Satyricon* or the *Apocolocyntosis*.[30] What is crucial to Menippean satire is the
creation of characters who do not merely quote but actually speak in
verse, and of a narrative whose action is advanced through separate
verse passages.[31] When verse ceases to be illustration and becomes
integral to the progress of a plot, it transcends the diatribe to create a
genre of fiction that is unclassifiable by ancient standards, which
insist on fairly rigid boundaries between prose and verse genres.[32]
The author, who usually begs to be identified with his narrator,
makes fun of his own standards of literary taste by writing in this
bizarre fashion. Impropriety of form is closely linked to themes of
the inadequacy of preaching and of truth, for speaking in verse is
itself a parody of the conventions of rational and civilized discourse.

The self-parodying author/narrator is a fixed feature of Menippean satire, and Lucian provides some good examples of how speaking in verse contributes to this self-parody. The opening passages of
Icaromenippus, Necyomantia, and *Juppiter Tragoedus* ("Zeus the Tragic
Actor," this last not a true Menippean satire but a recasting of one
into dialogue form) exploit the same motif: an unpretentious character listens with amazement or impatience to the principals of the
scene who are wrapped up in some fantastic narration or dialogue.

In *Icaromenippus,* Menippus's friend interrupts him as he is lost in thought and babbling in prose about astronomical calculations (Menippus has just returned from a flight to the moon); in *Necyomantia,* Menippus's friend finds him recently returned from Hades and speaking in tags from Homer and Euripides, but by his questioning he finally brings Menippus around to speaking in prose; in *Juppiter Tragoedus,* Hermes, Athena, and Zeus are involved in a metrical discussion of what is ailing the king of the gods until Hera, who cannot speak in meter, asks them to speak in prose. The interlocutor as straight man makes the other characters look ridiculous, and it is part of their comic characterization in *Necyomantia* and *Juppiter Tragoedus* that they speak in verse.[33]

Another weapon in the arsenal of Menippean satire is the creation of amusing verse parodies, put in the mouths of people who are ridiculous because they speak in verse. Petronius provides an example of this in the poems of Eumolpus. The *Troiae Halosis* ("The Capture of Troy") and *Bellum Ciuile* ("The Civil War") are parodies of Vergil and Lucan respectively; I do not see in them any grand theories of how Petronius thinks epic ought to be written, merely humor at the expense of well-known authors.[34] But the larger target is Eumolpus: as he does not view them as parodies but obliviously delivers them to unappreciative audiences, he is nothing but a fool for his poetic presumptions.[35]

Ennodius is the only Menippean satirist to spell out a theory of verse, and describes its virtues in ironic terms.[36] The *Paraenesis Didascalica* (translated in Appendix C) is a comic textbook of moral and scholastic virtues presented to two of the author's young friends. Ennodius first says that the verse insertions will relieve the burden of instruction, but then presents a poem (section 3) "In Praise of Poetry," in the course of which poetry is consistently downgraded until its presence is said to be a corrupting influence ("We suffer the inborn toughness of the soldier of Christ / to be on guard against effeminate composition"). When the narrator resumes in prose, he seems to have rejected poetry (4): "We shall therefore run from the pleasantries of words now and then and proclaim solid stuff from our own mouth, lest this virile work suffer the setbacks of impotent speech." Yet the persistent use of verse will remind the reader that it is at odds with the instruction that the narrator, who shows himself to be confused, wants to offer.

Seneca provides a further example of the humor and impropriety inherent in a narrator who speaks in verse parodies. The time of Claudius's death is described in a parody of epic periphrasis, which is promptly deflated when the narrator resumes in prose (2.1–2): "I think that I'll be better understood if I say it was October, three days before the Ides of October. I can't tell you the hour for certain, though."[37]

> Already had Phoebus on a shorter course contracted his bow of light, and the time of darkling Sleep was growing; already had conquering Cynthia extended her rule, and hideous Winter was plucking the pleasing benefices of wealthy Autumn; and with Bacchus under orders to mature, the vintager was plucking sparse grapes, late in the season.

He continues to argue with an imaginary interlocutor who professes amazement that the narrator does not know the hour of Claudius's death. The narrator (details in Chapter 5) yields to pressure and makes up a poem on the time of day that is as oblique as his first, and which in fact adds nothing to what he says in prose, that it was between the sixth and seventh hour (the first hour after noon).

We may generalize: Menippean satires whose introductions are extant include poems that serve to underline the ridiculousness of speaking or writing in verse, and thus the ridiculousness of the character who does the speaking, this narrator frequently being associated with the author himself. Note how the opening poem in the *Consolation* serves to show how confused and far from the truth Boethius is; Martianus's son makes fun of his old father's poem on divine Love which begins the *De Nuptiis;* Fulgentius, in a passage directly modeled on the Senecan one just quoted (13.6–7), tells us that he was composing dreadful verses in his sleep when the Muses finally came to take over the task of the interpretation of classical mythology, which has proved to be too much for him. These considerations will, I trust, serve to separate Menippean satire from the literary categories with which it is now confused. It is a satire in the sense of a mixture of opposites, of things that do not belong together, not in the sense of a censuring of morally or socially undesirable behavior.[38] It is not a genial *spoudogeloion* of gentle instruction, but a playing with the possibility of instruction. It is not an artistically varied prosimetrum, in which verse serves to relieve the weight of instruction or buoy up the narrative, but is so fashioned of warring components as to make it a literary anomaly and a form that appears inappropriate for edification. It is not a genre of Cynic instruction, but a fantastic tale that calls into question the intelligence and perception of its author/narrator.

Consequently, some texts that may be included in the ambit of Menippean satire, on prosimetric or thematic grounds, are here excluded. Apuleius's *Golden Ass,* with only an oracle to represent verse mixed with prose, is best left to picaresque fiction. Lucian's comic dialogues represent Menippean influence but are not Menippean satires. *Testamentum Porcelli* ("The Piglet's Last Will and Testament") is merely a comic parody of a soldier's will.[39] The problematic Greek prosimetrical romances are discussed in Appendix A. Prosimetric epistles, such as those of Sidonius Apollinaris, deserve a separate study; most interesting is Ausonius's *Epistle* 19, which contains, in the manner of Seneca, a parodic poem whose meaning the author professes not to know. Two tantalizing late texts could illumine the history of our genre if we knew of them in full. Jerome (*De Vir. Ill.* 111) mentions a prosimetric and autobiographical work of one Acilius Severus, otherwise unknown (died before 376 A.D.). It is styled a *hodoeporicon,* or guidebook; the author seems to have given it a double title, *Catastrophe* ("The Calamity"), or *Peira* ("The Trial"). It seems a parallel to the *Consolation;* it is curious to note that after Boethius's example autobiography is squeezed out of Menippean satire. The second text is a conjecture of Alan Cameron: if Tiberianus (whom Cameron would date to the beginning of the fourth century) wrote prosimetra, and if the poems assigned to him are excerpts from it, we could posit him as the philosophical and poetic reviver of Varro, from which source Martianus, Fulgentius (who cites him), and Boethius (who alludes to him) all flow.[40] Although our genre has many fragmentary texts, these notices and conjectures cannot detain us here. In the remaining portion of this chapter, I will present a number of further considerations that cement the interrelations of the works in this study: certain common motifs and the themes related to them, and certain arguments about the historical development and transformation of the genre. These, I hope, will demonstrate the integrity and logical cohesion of the genre both as a theory and as a series of related texts, both early and late, and Greek and Roman.

FANTASTIC NARRATIVE

The setting of a Menippean satire is typically fantastic: the *Satyricon* is grotesque, and the only possible exception is Ennodius's *Paraenesis,* in which we may allow that the author's abstractions refuse to remain abstract but insist on having lives of their own. Such settings have been cataloged: posthumous judgments, dialogues of the dead, divine assemblies, heavenly symposia, sojourns in heaven or Hades.[41] The notion that such fantasy is merely one of the comic components of *spoudogeloion* is naive, for fantasy is part of the meaning of the piece. A Menippean satire travesties important things (epic, myth, religion, etc.); humor at the expense of such literary and cultural authority is much more the message than the medium.[42] Some critics early in this century suspected that serious instruction was not Menippus's goal and that fantasy is an element in a confusing whole.[43] It is not a great leap from this position to the enumeration of the characteristics of Menippean satire as set forth by Bakhtin.

But it is important to see that fantasy serves not only to undermine other forms of cultural and literary authority, but also to undermine the importance of the particular Menippean satire itself. It is a genre that desires that nothing be taken too seriously. We have seen this in the conventional Menippean opening, in which the narrator/author's intelligence is drawn into question by the form that he has chosen for his presentation, the mixture of prose and verse. There is also a conventional Menippean ending, bearing some similarity to conventions of verse satire, in which the lessons preached and learned in the body of the text are negated.[44] A good first example is the end of Lucian's *Necyomantia*. Menippus has gone to the underworld to learn the truth about life from the seer Teiresias (21): "Take care of the business before you and run on, laughing at most things and caring about nothing." Menippus decides that he must go preach this truth to the living; he takes a shortcut out of the underworld, and reappears through the oracular hole of the false prophet Trophonius.[45] At this point we remember the ridiculous appearance of Menippus from the beginning of the work: the narrative is a long reminiscence of one just returned from the underworld, wearing Odysseus's hat and Heracles' lion-skin, and carrying Orpheus's lyre. The preacher is himself mocked.[46] Further, the lesson learned at great expense is that which the narrator knew before his journey: the simple life is best.

Consider also the end of the *Apocolocyntosis*. When Claudius is judged in the underworld, popular demand requires that a new and eternal punishment be fashioned to suit the enormity of his crimes, but Aeacus and Caligula conspire to overturn their verdict and make Claudius merely a freedman's slave in Hades (14.3–15.2). The condemnation of Claudius is effectively subverted, for the corruption of the underworld assures that there will be no justice, and Claudius is allowed to be as much a tool of his freedmen as he ever was when alive. The end of Julian's *Caesars* is, I argue, directly modeled on that of the *Apocolocyntosis*. Julian presents a contest among dead emperors, the best of them to be elevated to heaven as Romulus's companion. Though there was to be only one winner, all gain access to heaven, including the vile Constantine. Constantine faces eternal punishment for the slaughter of his family but receives an unexpected and wholly undeserved pardon from Jesus, notorious for easy absolution (336A–B).[47] Constantine cheats justice as Claudius does; the narrator ends the *Caesars* by saying that he has an assurance that if he obeys the commandments of Mithras he will avoid this ridiculous heaven altogether.

Menippean satire tends to pull the rug out from under the reader. The end of the *De Nuptiis* does so by having a personification of the genre of the work abandon it as a disgrace because it did not adhere to that genre's conventions. The reader cannot reasonably evaluate the competing charges of generic impropriety and authorial incompetence. The *Mythologies* has mythical abstractions take over the reasoning behind and the writing of Fulgentius's allegorical handbook of mythology. Calliope introduces Philosophia as the chief allegorist, and in the *Story of the Nine Muses* (25.1–27.11) Philosophia, if literally understood, will define the characters of the prologue as only allegorical realities by the middle of the first book. The point Menippean satires seem to make, often very effectively in particular scenes (the joy of the simple life in the *Necyomantia*, Seneca's hatred of Claudius and Julian's of Constantine, the value of the Liberal Arts in Martianus, the meaninglessness of mythology in Fulgentius), is devalued by its foundation on this quicksand.

As Bakhtin points out, there is no consistent authorial point of view in a Menippean satire. But he does not add that the author's self-parody is its necessary adjunct. Menippean satire creates a narrator who is a fantastic experimenter, a naïf who travels to impossible places and sees impossible sights. But his speaking and writing in a mixture of prose and verse makes the reader doubt his intelligence and taste; and the very fantasy in which he participates troubles the conclusions that he would reach and preach. Menippean satire is true to the simplicity of its Cynic origins: the simple life is best, and fantastic journeys to impossible places (as in the *Necyomantia*) are a pursuit of wind, a search for truth where it is not to be found. Fantasy in Menippean satire, unlike fantasy in Old Comedy, is self-destructive and does not accomplish good and useful ends. A Menippean satire is not a comedy, and it has no happy ending (though we cannot judge the *Satyricon* in this regard); the argument turns inward and collapses on itself in an ironic, not satiric, ending.[48] Fantasy serves to show that the lesson being preached is not true or, at best, inadequate.

Therefore, Menippean satire creates an unreliable narrator, incapable of understanding all that he sees. He is oblivious to his own inadequacies and contradictions as he strives toward his goal. Modern theories take this obliviousness as a positive thing, a quest for truth unhampered by convention.[49] But I think that in ancient Menippean satire (as I delimit it here) it is treated as a joke; the narrator himself presents to the reader a series of theories and interpretations that the reader can see do not square with the facts of the narrative. The prime example of this is Encolpius in the *Satyricon,* whom we first meet delivering a declamation against declamation.[50] He changes chameleonlike from scene to scene, decrying the decline of contemporary morality despite his own perversions, and lamenting the loss of ancient literary standards even though he speaks in (and is trapped in a work of) a mixture of prose and verse. His preaching, theorizing, and criticism are perpetually contradicted by his own person; he is a parodied satirist, whom we come to dislike more than the objects of his scorn—Trimalchio, for example, who for all his shortcomings is a rather likable character. The unreliable narrator appears in different ways in Menippean satire: for example, Seneca and Julian quote doubtful sources for their stories (the man who saw the apotheosis of the scandalous Drusilla, and the trickster god Hermes, respectively), and Fulgentius at first denies the existence of the mythical creatures who physically appear before him.

Menippean satire may create an innocent, or a fantastic experimenter, to observe a topsy-turvy world. Such narrators allow us to see by their own ad hoc and inadequate theories both the ridiculousness of the fantastic world and of those who try to understand it. Behind the confusion is the basic assumption that no world can be understood, that language is inadequate to express or confine reality, and that the act of analysis is the work of a fool. This becomes particularly evident in the late Latin authors whose works present a narrator who cannot reach the conclusion he so ardently desires, and whose great efforts therefore seem somewhat ineffectual and comic. Martianus's Liberal Arts are the vomit of Philology; mythological creatures cannot be allegorized away in Fulgentius; Ennodius cannot teach his friends but must recommend them to others for instruction; and Philosophy never does take Boethius to his true home.

Menippean satire has another remarkable feature related to this comic narrator: the author frequently identifies with his narrator in a first-person narrative. Only the calculating Lucian, who hides behind the character of Menippus in the *Necyomantia* and *Icaromenippus*, fails to suggest he is to be related directly to the narrator or principal character of his works.[51] There is never a great gulf between the parody of literature and language which is at the heart of the genre and the parody of the author who writes in such a way. The author cannot logically preach against the inadequacy of preaching. As a parody of all things noble in literature, the genre draws the narrator and author into self-parody as surely as it draws its action into fantasy and its matter and style into incoherence. It is to this question of parody in Menippean satire that I now turn.

BURLESQUE OF LANGUAGE AND LITERATURE

The parodied verses of Homer and Euripides found in various Menippean satires (Seneca, Lucian, Julian) do not define the extent of parody within the genre, but only a particular and limited manifestation of a much larger condition. Menippean satire is a parody of literature in general because it plays with the traditional assumption of the author's control of a coherent work. We could speak broadly of this belligerent genre as a vast burlesque in which specific parodies are found; by the general term *burlesque* we avoid the implications of unintentional literary structures, or of intellectual profundities, frequently present in the word *parody*.

Menippean satires are often constructed in their broadest outlines as parodies of other genres of literature or types of discourse. Menippus parodies the conventions of Cynic preaching, and in much of Varro we can infer the parody of the Cynic diatribe. The *Satyricon* is still plausibly viewed as a parody of the romance. The *De Nuptiis* and the *Paraenesis* are parodies of Roman father-son instructional literature; and it is in Boethius, not Lucian, that we find a parody of the philosophical dialogue in Menippean dress, expressed in Frye's "contemplative irony." Within the various satires are parodies in passing of other distinguished authors, authoritative works, and sober modes of discourse. The parodies of Vergil and Lucan in Petronius's *Troiae Halosis* and *Bellum Ciuile* have already been mentioned; on a smaller scale of epic parody, there is the bombastic description of the time of day at the beginning of the *Apocolocyntosis*. Parodies of Platonic myth and writing are rampant in Menippean satire: the Myth of Er seems to be the ultimate ancestor of Lucian's *Necyomantia;* Julian constructs his tale of heavenly lies in Platonic form; parodies of the *Symposium* are very popular (in Menippus, Varro, Julian, and even Martianus).

Literature and its authors are a vehicle of authority; a Menippean satirist makes fun of the idea of deriving *auctoritas* from an *auctor*. This may be at heart a very conservative (or, depending on your point of view, adolescent) comic interpretation of literature, one that claims that fiction cannot be truth. The modern and reasonable desire to see fiction as more real than nonfiction should not impose itself too heavily on an ancient genre that is making a joke at the expense of literature with all the means available to it: authorship, unity, genre, and style. This latter is very important. Bakhtin notes the multiplicity of styles in a Menippean satire and connects it to the multiplicity of inserted genres in a given work. This is a parody of another literary propriety, the expectation that a topic be given a unified treatment. Vocabulary and grammar are allowed to be as fantastic as the action that they describe, and are suffered to alternate in the wildest swings from grand to low style, from fustian to textbook simplicity, from the recherché to the banal. Parallel to this is the juxtaposition of relevant and irrelevant material which keeps a work from marching uninterrupted to its appointed ends; the genre is very tolerant of digressions.[52]

Readers who expect the classical unities find a work like the *De Nuptiis* tasteless; the usual view of the educational defects of the author and his age takes his style as a childish and exasperating straining after effect. But there is a purpose to Martianus's joining of the learned and the simple, of the sublime and the ridiculous, of the abstruse and convoluted allegorical opening books and the dry-as-dust treatments of the Arts in Books 3–9.[53] As the closing poem shows, it is a device intended to shock bookish sensibilities and question the importance of the textbook material presented: is rhetoric divine, and can one scale heaven by a ladder whose rungs are the Seven Liberal Arts? There is a similar disjunction between the tortured vocabulary of the introduction to Fulgentius's *Mythologies* and the actual allegories that follow it. This use of languages is not degenerate, for it is in the tradition of the language of Varro's *Menippeans*. No doubt in the lesser authors of late antiquity this style can be used merely for the unreflective vain display of erudition, but Menippean satirists realize the comic potential of an aesthetic that, in Palmer's elegant phrase, "sanctioned the simultaneous application of lipstick and woad."[54] The lack of taste and artistic unity is an integral part of a genre whose essence is the shocking juxtaposition of irreconcilable opposites.

Unfortunately, the fragments of Varro's *Menippeans* are almost entirely preserved by grammarians for their linguistic oddities, and we cannot tell therefore to what extent Varro's linguistic excesses alternated with passages of sober prose. But we can see that the inflated language was used for comic effect. Consider F 375 of the *Papia Papae* περὶ ἐγκωμίων ("Tut-tut!, or On Encomia") whose topic seems to be excessive praise:

> ante auris modo ex subolibus paruuli intorti demittebantur sex cincinni; oculis suppaetulis nigelli pupuli quam hilaritatem significantes animi! rictus paruissimus, ut refrenato risu roseo[55]

> Just before her ears were six ringlets dependent, dainty, plaited into shoots; what gaiety of soul portended the dusky little pupils in her squinty little eyes! Her mouth only slightly open, as if her rosy smile were bridled . . .

The passage mocks the fulsome praise that is directed to a beautiful woman, and the language itself, with its strange combination of cute diminutives and overspecific nouns, is condemned for its excesses. Yet the passage is not really distinguishable from many of the other fragments of the *Menippeans*, and it seems that Varro's learned language is itself a source of humor. This is playful language, not designed to impress by sophistication but to amuse by misapplication of sophistication; it is perfectly represented by Apuleius's *Golden Ass*. For a modern American example of such Varronian tendencies toward recherché vocabulary, polyglot invention, combination of archaism and neologism, variation in style and tone, and sheer delight in language which combine to present a self-parodic author/narrator, one may consider the comic essays of S. J. Perelman.[56]

Digressions with a life of their own are also at home in Menippean satire. The recitations of Eumolpus in Petronius are digressions in the cause of parody; the listing of the emperors in Julian's *Caesars* and their places at the heavenly banquet is a digression that is a sort of comic encapsulation of Roman history. The handbook material in Martianus is presented in a series of vast digressions in the story of the marriage of Mercury and Philology; and the joke is frequently made that the learned disquisitions of the Arts are a frustration of and an impediment to the consummation of the marriage. The lectures of Philosophy in the *Consolation*, particularly Books 4 and 5, do not reach either Philosophy's or the narrator's desired end of homecoming, no matter how well they actually present Neoplatonic learning. Such digressions serve, among other things, to frustrate the reader's (and the narrator's) sense of the development of plot or point, and in a work of moral proportions they tend to subvert that moral by distraction. Frye sees anatomy at work here, the ruthless compilation of facts and information observed with an ironic eye, and an attempt to get all of life between the covers of the book. I would only add that this tendency is more obvious in Varro and his late Roman followers than, say, in Seneca and Petronius; and that the philosophical importance of such digressions is an element that grows as the genre develops through time. In origin, digressions cohere with the pervasive aesthetic of incoherence and literary impropriety.[57] At the end of antiquity, the sum total of the digressions is a view of a universe which cannot quite be understood; but it waits for Bernardus Silvestris and the twelfth century to turn such matters into a *philosophical* contemplation of the disjunction between mortals and their universe, between Microcosm and Macrocosm.

Finally in this regard consider a fragment of Varro's *Testamentum* περὶ διαθηκῶν ("The Last Will, or On Testaments"). It seems that the speaker here is Varro himself, represented as on his deathbed and referring to his *Menippeans* when he speaks of his children (F 543):

> If one or more sons are born to me within nine months, if they are mere "asses at the lyre," let them be disinherited; but if one is born in the tenth month (as Aristotle says can happen), let him have his rights from me regardless.[58]

The speaker seems to be making arrangements for after his death: the child who risks seeming illegitimate is to be accepted as his own, whereas the legitimate but dull child is disowned. So too does Martianus ultimately claim his bastard offspring at the end of the *De Nuptiis*. Menippean satire is abnormal in all of its aspects. It is an antigenre; insofar as it is a satire, it is ultimately a satire on literature itself and all its pretensions to meaning, though burlesque would remain the better term. All is parody in a Menippean jeu d'esprit: the genre presents a battle of form and content, where all claims to perception, knowledge, and truth are negated by fantasy, form, style, language, and self-parody.

JOKES AT THE EXPENSE OF LEARNING

There are of course thematic implications of this war against meaning. Menippean satires mean something too. We may apply Branham's description of Lucian's intentions in *How to Write History:*

like Diogenes the Cynic's pointless rolling of his tub, they are "a vain reproof to idle efforts."[59] It is too modern to say that Menippean satire champions the eternal search for truth by a refusal to be limited by the straitjacket of reason and propriety, though certainly the genre is refreshing for its indulgence in fantasy and its general lack of the trappings of persuasion that seek to steer the audience of a diatribe or a verse satire. Menippean satire rises through time to philosophical formulations of the inadequacy of human knowledge and the existence of a reality that transcends reason, but in its origins the genre merely thumbs its nose at pretenders to the truth by a denial that anything other than common sense is valuable or apprehensible.

This is most remarkable because the Menippean satirists of Greece and Rome are almost all academics of one sort or another. Menippus is a renegade Cynic; Boethius is the only true philosopher of their number. Varro the antiquarian is the immediate inspiration for the bookworms Martianus, Fulgentius, and Ennodius. Julian is the author of numerous abstruse philosophical and religious treatises; Seneca is prominent as an unpalatable Stoic. Petronius and Lucian, the authors perhaps most to the modern taste, are on the fringes of such a group. Further, when a Menippean satirist has left behind a body of works that we can evaluate, the Menippean satire stands in stark contrast to its more conservative relations. Seneca's view of Claudius in the *Apocolocyntosis* is difficult to reconcile with that found in his pitiful letters from exile, the effusions of a toady; the relation between Boethius's *Consolation* and his Christian works is a notorious problem. The idea that an author's views as expressed elsewhere ought to be consistent with the views expressed in a Menippean satire has sponsored a great misunderstanding of Varro's *Menippeans,* in which he makes fun of his antiquarianism and old-fashioned patriotism and morality. Fulgentius's view of the allegorical truth to be derived from ancient literature is quite different in the *Mythologies* and the *Allegorical Content of Vergil.* Menippus himself is the paradigm of such self-mockery: he dressed as a bearded Fury, visiting the land of the living as an emissary from the lords of the dead, no doubt to make the point that the classical underworld with all its terrors cannot possibly exist. As he is depicted at the end of Lucian's *Necyomantia,* so may he have been in real life: a preacher with a true message who cannot be trusted, not so much a Cassandra, doomed not to be believed, but a catechizer catechized.

Parody of those who claim to possess the truth, combined with self-parody, creates in the scholars who write in the genre a parody of encyclopedic knowledge. Cicero has Varro say that he made a special point of adding his erudition and humor to the form he inherited from Menippus, to which Cicero adds that the philosophical content was insufficient for philosophical instruction.[60] Varro's massive erudition, displayed in abstruse vocabulary, technical lists, etymologies, learned allusion, and philosophical argumentation, may be serious in the *Antiquitates* or the *De Lingua Latina* but is turned to self-parody in his *Menippeans*. The *Menippeans* frequently seem to show the author/narrator embarrassed by a comic reliance on and misapplication of his learning. This interpretation of Varro, which will be argued in Chapter 4, is crucial to our understanding of the development of the genre, for it establishes that Martianus Capella was not the first to unify Varro the satirist and Varro the encyclopedist, but that Varro himself made that combination in his own *Menippeans*. Varro provided a model for a type of Menippean satire of greater intellectual content that, while not a great influence on Seneca and Petronius, who took their cue from Varro's parody of moralists, had great repercussions in the late classical and medieval periods.

The genre creates characters who have achieved wisdom through impossible means. The *catascopus,* who, like Plato's Er, views human folly from some great height, is one of the genre's most important comic conventions. In Lucian's *Icaromenippus,* Menippus tells of how he sat on the moon and learned from the religious and philosophical fraud Empedocles how to see the world below. His interlocutor exclaims (19): "O wonderful Menippus, what a paradoxical vision!" Philosophical theory (θεωρία) is literally a vision; but Platonic vision of things invisible becomes a running Menippean joke. A position from which one can contemplate all of the world is too far removed from it to allow for understanding; the critics themselves, the ones who try to make sense of what they see and draw an appropriate moral from it, despite their good intentions and even their plausible conclusions, emerge as more or less ridiculous. The world is, to the Cynic, irrational and incomprehensible; the anatomy of folly can only be ironically performed, and the patient on the table is never so much the world as the preacher or author who thinks that he can understand it and reduce it to rule.

THE THREE SUBTEXTS OF MENIPPEAN SATIRE

As I shall attempt to show in the following chapter, not all of Menippus's own writings can be said to be in the same genre. This should not surprise us in a comic author (consider Lucian) or in an ironic one (even the *Symposium* is numbered among Plato's dialogues); and we should not be misled by the modern generic term to believe that Varro in his *Menippeans* confined himself to a single genre. We may be sure that Menippus composed parodies of letters, wills, and decrees, which may be classed generically as parodies of their respective genres; but his masterwork was the *Necyia*, and if Lucian's *Necyomantia* is any sort of guide to its contents, we may say that it is the subsuming of a number of parodies into a fictional narrative that identifies the structural presence of parody in Menippean satire. There are latent within the genre as a whole, and present within any given Menippean satire in different proportions and degrees, three essential parodies, all of which are to be related to the theme of the fantastic voyager in the land of ultimate answers, whose experience champions the values of common sense. The parody of the diatribe is important as well, but it offers no specific character or plot lines to the Menippean mill. An awareness of these subtexts will do much to explain the texture of such different works as the *Satyricon* and the *Consolation*, and to explain their ultimate consanguinity. I will give them in chronological order, not of their importation into the genre (an insoluble question) but of their existence independent of Menippean satire.

The Odyssey. The *Odyssey*, especially in the wanderings of Books 9 through 12, is an account of a man who travels at great length through a fantastic world, often learning of supernatural truths (in the underworld), and tempted by immortality (on the island of Calypso). He chooses to reject all of this in a search for his mortal home, and life with his family. Yet Odysseus is not Everyman: he is a master of lies and deception, a thoroughly unreliable narrator of his own adventures, and is part charlatan, part shaman. He comes back from the other world to tell his deceitful tales to gullible audiences, and the truth he knows he presents as lies. Menippus seems to take Odysseus as a model in his own account of his voyage to the land of the dead, the ultimate ancestor of texts as diverse as Horace's *Sermones* (2.5) and Lucian's *Necyomantia;* and in the *Necyomantia* we see Menippus dressed up as Odysseus, though with the attributes of Orpheus and Heracles as well. Menippus as a shaman does not take on the form of an animal (dog though he may be) but is dressed as it were in the pages of a book. Thus the genre owes quite a different debt to the *Odyssey* than the romance does: in the latter's clever tales of lovers separated and reunited the *Odyssey* is present as a text full of dangers and cliff-hangers.[61] Further, romance relies heavily on a deceitful heroine or hero whose machinations can convolute the plot;[62] plot is simple in Menippean satire. In Menippean satire, the *Odyssey* is a series of more metaphysical quests, a tale of truth and where it may be found, and what may be learned by those who choose not to live at the ends of the earth where truth may dwell.

Old Comedy. The heroes of Old Comedy travel to heaven and hell to find simple answers; the genre champions common sense over charlatans, quacks, and frauds.[63] Pretenders to truth are humiliated, for the genre is essentially conservative, distrusting philosophers and all dogmatic systems. Further, it relies on strange language and a great variety of styles; it deals freely with personifications and abstractions; and in it the sublime may be heard in the midst of the obscene. In all of this, we see the interests of Menippean satire. Yet there are great differences. When earthly problems prove insoluble in Old Comedy, the fantastic is invoked as a source of solutions, and in the happy endings of comedy these solutions are found. Menippean satire has no happy endings, and no solutions; in this sense, one should not speak of Menippean satire as a comic genre at all.

But Old Comedy is not just present in Menippean satire as a linguistic model and a thematic source for tales of the triumph of simple common sense over the dogmatic. It is also a source of specific plots. Consider the flight of Trygaeus to heaven on a dung beetle in *Peace,* and Menippus's flight to the moon with the wings of an eagle and a vulture in Lucian's *Icaromenippus;* the lament of Musica over her maltreatment at the hands of moderns in Pherecrates' *Chiron,* and the complaints of Calliope in Fulgentius and of Philosophy in Boethius's *Consolation;* the arraignment of a drunken author by his genre in Cratinus's *Pytine* and the castigation of Fulgentius by Calliope and Martianus by Satura and his son.[64] Even Ennodius participates in this, whose Rhetoric is a reanimation of the Unjust Argument of Aristophanes' *Clouds.*[65] Further, it is in Old Comedy that we see the question of the composition of poetry made a topic of poetry; consider Dionysus's journey to Hades in *Frogs* to find a good author, and the debate on poetry and the weighing of words of Euripides and Aeschylus. Varro must have been a great repository of such plots, and some of his works are reminiscent of comedy, with personified abstractions of genres on stage, and a debate between the two halves of his authorial personality dramatized in the *Bimarcus.* Old Comedy is the comedy of words, and comedy at the expense of words.

Platonic Myth, Especially the Myth of Er. A full appreciation of the purely literary influence of Plato's writings may never be achieved; suffice it to say here that much of Plato reappears in Menippean satire, as much a source of plot and device as an emblem of philosophical sophistication itself, in all its suspicious appeal. The *Symposium* has been mentioned; the myths of Plato also appear as taking-off points for a comic treatment of the utility of suprarational appeals to truth. The Conclusion of the present volume will document the importance of the Myth of Er in the creation and the history of the Menippean genre, and only a few points about this crucial text need to be mentioned here. The apocalyptic vision is present in Menippean satire from its inception.[66] Er observes the folly of humans from some lofty vantage point; as a *catascopus*, he says that one would laugh to see the choices made by souls about to reenter the world. But note that, as a soldier turned philosopher on an impossible journey (his soul departs and then returns on the twelfth day, at the point of his imminent cremation), he is the passive recipient of this strange vision and not the wise man on a quest. His conclusion, that those who spend ten thousand years in the realms of truth are not necessarily edified by it but continue to make horrible choices, again advocates common sense by questioning the utility of the vision of the eternal realm. Metaphysical theory here is quietly mocked. We who hear the story may hope to be better instructed than those who saw the truth. Menippean satire too puts the burden of meaning on the listener, and not on the author and the source.

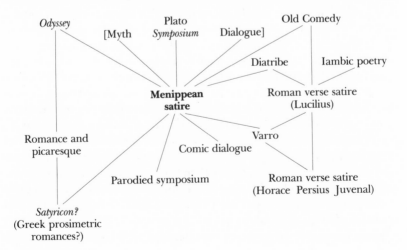

WE MAY SAY that Menippean satire is compounded of the *Odyssey*'s tale of a liar shaman and his battle against both death and immortality; Old Comedy's exaltation of common humanity over charlatans; and Plato's apocalyptic dramatization of the relative values of philosopher and theory. Lucian's *Necyomantia* illustrates perfectly the confluence of all these traditions; we may allow that the *Odyssey* dominates in the *Satyricon* and Plato in the *Consolation*. These subtextual works and genres may also be allowed to create or inspire other comic genres; and Menippean satire may work its influence as well, in conjunction with its constituents, in creating further comic genres. The accompanying diagram may illustrate the literary and logical connections among some of the comic genres usually discussed in connection with Menippean satire.

CONCLUSION

I submit then that the various strange features of Menippean satire are consistent with, and logically derived from, an aesthetic that approves of the organic mixture of prose and verse in a single work. The genre is an indecorous mixture of disparate elements, of forms, styles, and themes that exist uneasily side by side, and from which no coherent intellectual, moral, or aesthetic appreciation may be drawn. Consistent with the mixture of prose and verse is the juxtaposition of seemingly serious material and a comic, fantastic setting; the alternation of passages in wildly different styles; the toleration of digression; the combination of the moral and the erotic. This would seem to be a description of Old Comedy, were it not for the presence of prose, and Old Comedy is certainly a tremendous influence in the creation of Menippean satire. But the crucial differences are that there are morals unequivocally pronounced in the parabasis that do not seem to be negated by the fantasy, which in general moves toward productive goals and happy endings; its commonsense heroes triumph over charlatans and frauds; it has clear aims of social satire; and there is little in the way of self-parody or parody of philosophical thought (except in *Clouds*). The conventions of Old Comedy are obscene, but there is little if any sense that a fantastic story told in this manner cannot tell the truth. What transform Old Comedy into Menippean satire are the parody of the narrator and the narrator's quest (a gift of the *Odyssey*) and the parody of philosophical thought and philosophical genres, particularly those of Plato.

By its insistence on such a form, Menippean satire is essentially an antigenre, a burlesque of literature at large. It falls between the cracks of traditional literary categories. It plays with the underpinning of all ancient literature, the connection of *auctor* and *auctoritas:* in it the author is not a teacher, and it assumes no stable moral or didactic purpose. Thus the genre can be turned to specific parodies of those genres that are explicitly instructive: the diatribe in Menippus and Varro; the encyclopedia in Varro (embryonically) and the late Romans; formal verse satire in Seneca and Petronius; the philosophical dialogue or symposium in Menippus, Varro, Lucian, Julian, and Boethius.

In a Menippean satire, fantasy undermines interpretation and is but another example of form fighting content, of the frustration of reasonable expectations, of irony. There is an unreliable narrator or source, no driving unity of purpose (whence the digressions), and no fixed point of view. Such plot as there is is very simple; rhetoric and persuasion are minimal. Because the genre strives for effect through impropriety, the author of a Menippean satire accuses himself of a lack of respect for taste, tradition, and decorum, and this is usually translated into self-parody when the author identifies himself with his narrator. Self-parody extends to the parody of the author's own knowledge, and the rejection of all dogma which the form implies leads to the rejection of the author's ability to preach, or even to understand. The narrator is central to the work only as the nexus of confusion.

This definition is an abstraction from texts that seemed at first to be united by a significant use of prosimetrum. They represent a set of thematically and structurally linked conventions that are manipulated by an author to an end; the reader's awareness of the conventions conditions the response to what is present in any given text. Some elements are pointedly omitted in a Menippean satire; an example is the absence of independent verse composition in Lucian. This does not invalidate the affiliation of *Necyomantia* and *Icaromenippus* to the Menippean genre; it is possible, after all, to write a murder mystery in which there is no murder. Some elements lose or gain in significance over time; note the increasing and regular use of verse in the late Latin authors, an increasing philosophical content, and a framed serious passage (for example, the prayer to the Unknown Father in Martianus and the pivotal poem in the *Consolation*, 3 m. 9, *o qui perpetua*), coupled with a decline in fantastic plot (there being only a fantastic mise-en-scène in the *Consolation*, and no plot at all in the *Paraenesis*). Any genre is elastic, and admits to individual interpretations of the genre's constituent elements among its practitioners. But the range of a genre's possibilities is also defined by specific reactions to what are viewed as authoritative models. Even Menippean satirists look back to specific authorities within their genre (Varro to Menippus, Julian to Seneca and Lucian, Boethius to Martianus and Fulgentius, Martianus to Varro and possibly Lucian) and feel an author's usual schizophrenic desires to follow and to distance himself from some master's influence.

With these considerations we can see that there is a coherent Menippean tradition from Menippus into the Middle Ages. Menippus parodies the diatribe and the preacher of the diatribe; this is interpreted by Varro as a parody of Roman satire (itself influenced by the diatribe) and a parody of learning. Lucian represents a different interpretation of the Menippean model, one that concentrates on the parody of Cynicism and Cynic preachers in stories that deal with Menippus himself; his comic dialogue is an idiosyncratic mixture of Aristophanes and Plato, whose primary difference is the exclusion of authorial self-parody. Seneca and Petronius, perhaps with an eye on Menippus, borrow from Varro the parody of Roman satire; Julian follows Lucian, Seneca, and Varro to write a digressive but proper self-destructive political fantasy. The late Roman authors take Varro's encyclopedic self-parody to heart, and not his social concerns; and from the models provided by Martianus and Boethius, the writers of the twelfth-century Renaissance write the philosophical treatises that mock Christian Platonism and assert that only faith, not reason and theory, can understand the bizarre and frustrating multiplicities of this world. Christian faith will ultimately transcend the opposites that the Menippean genre brings together. The genre relies for its meaning on silence, for the truth that appears between the lines, that emerges from the spectacle of inconclusive debate. The real heaven and hell of the author's imagination never appear. To the Hellenistic Menippus, truth is Cynic common sense, which cannot be preached directly because preaching is dogma and dogma is lies; but in the history of Menippean satire we watch the nature of that unstated truth change, through the mysticism of Martianus to the Christianity of Boethius and the authors beyond.

II. FRAGMENTS

Chapter Three

MENIPPUS

MENIPPUS (of the first half of the third century B.C.) must be considered one of the most influential Hellenistic authors, even though his meager fragments cannot really establish his relation to his predecessors, and his many literary descendants cannot be used to reconstruct any of his works.[1] He is a literary innovator who has faded away not, as Duff would have it, to the Cheshire Cat's grin but, more faithfully to Carroll's otherworldly fictions, to a *risus sardonicus*. The primary source of information about what is essential to the Menippus of Menippean satire is not a collection of fragments but his appearance as a character in fictional works, primarily Lucian's: *Icaromenippus, Necyomantia,* and especially the *Dialogues of the Dead.*[2] This is supplemented by a rich body of testimonia also connecting him with the Land of the Dead. We can learn what Menippus means to the tradition not so much by looking to the body of generic characteristics of Menippean satire as it has been defined here (such a projection of details onto Menippus would add nothing to this study, to say nothing of the logical problems involved) but by considering the reaction of his genre to his personality. The founder of the genre, or rather its Muse, if such an antigenre may claim one for itself, becomes himself a crucial element in the vocabulary of the genre, and by consideration of his semantic range we can distinguish him from the welter of Cynics and Hellenistic authors of philosophical fantasy. We can define what made him worthy of emulation in literary circles and the object of scorn in philosophical circles; we shall see that they are equally plausible reactions to the same thing, a self-parodic mocker of philosophy and of Cynic preaching.

WORKS AND FRAGMENTS

Diogenes Laertius's *Life of Menippus* (6.99–101) is a hostile collection of scandalous and denigrating details which concludes with a list of Menippus's works. It is impossible to disentangle titles and descriptions with confidence, and some corruption has surely crept into the Epicurean works that Laertius names. Adding to the confusion is the fact that Laertius himself elsewhere quotes from a work not on his list. We must proceed with caution: "The Cynic's works number thirteen: *Necyia, Wills, Letters* imagined to be from the gods' presence, *Against the Natural Scientists and Mathematicians and Grammarians, The Herd* (or *Birth*) *of Epicurus* and their reverence for the *Twentieth Day*, and other works."[3] The list, corruptions and all, points to three things. First, the *Necyia* ("In the Land of the Dead") is given pride of place. Second, Menippus seems to have a generic range: the *Wills* and the *Letters from the Gods* seem to be of much more limited scope than the narrative *Necyia*.[4] If we follow Dörrie's argument, Menippus is also the creator of the genre of the heroic epistle.[5] Third, the playful and allusive titles, a possible source of the text's confusions, foreshadow those of Varro's *Menippeans*.

From a variety of sources we have a few quotations from Menippus's works. They reveal two things: first, that the philosophical tradition knows practically nothing about Menippus's works, as every certain quotation that we have derives not from the works in Laertius's list but from others; second, that Menippus is cited for anecdote, not instruction. Laertius himself cites Menippus's *Sale of Diogenes* in his own *Life of Diogenes* (6.29): when captured, put on the auction block, and asked what he knew how to do, Diogenes the Cynic answered, "Rule men."[6] Laertius refers to Menippus for the paradox, but to Eubulus for details of the educational program to which Diogenes subjected the buyer and his sons. True to his interests, Athenaeus at 664E gives a culinary rather than a philosophical fragment of Menippus's *Arcesilaus,* possibly a learned funeral banquet.[7] More suggestive is another fragment preserved by Athenaeus (629E): "And there is another dance called 'The Conflagration of the World,' which Menippus the Cynic mentions in his *Symposium.*" If someone danced this dance, there must have been playful abuse of Stoic notions in a parody of a Platonic genre; but nothing more definite may be said. Athenaeus gives us a final unassigned fragment, whose value lies in its being a piece of a hexameter, an independent poetic creation complete with a neologism (32E): "At any rate, Menippus says 'the brine-drinking city of Myndos.'"[8] To these scanty remains we may assign to Menippus an interesting quotation put in the mouth of Diogenes at the beginning of the first of Lucian's *Dialogues of the Dead*. Diogenes tells Pollux to fetch Menippus and tell him that the real laughter is to be found below, for laughter above is a doubtful thing, and "Who really knows the things that come after this life?" is much too frequent a question.[9]

Ancient reaction to Menippus's literary qualities is exiguous but interesting. That Menippus wrote in a mixture of prose and verse is not a matter of prime importance, and the external form of his works is not discussed.[10] Literary judgments passed upon his work are concerned more with the humor of his presentation than with anything else, pointing to the conflict of thought and form which is part of Menippean satire. The poet Meleager, a native of Menippus's Gadara who began his literary life as a Cynic and, perhaps, as a Menippean satirist, records his debt to "Menippean Graces" in two autobiographical poems.[11] Athenaeus informs us that Meleager wrote Cynic works called Χάριτες (157A), and it may be that Meleager is referring to his early works as Menippean instead of labeling Menippus's style as graceful. "Menippean Graces" at any event seems an oxymoron, as "Menippean Satires" is in Varro's title. Lastly, Laertius himself preserves a backhanded indication of the literary excellence, as opposed to the philosophical bankruptcy, of Menippus's works. He records a story that Dionysius and Zopyrus of Colophon had written them as a joke and had handed them over to Menippus as to some sort of a literary broker.[12] The story is clearly a slur, yet there is no need to deny to a disliked author the authorship of bad books; the implication is that the works in question are too good, for all their lack of proper philosophical *spoudogeloion*, to be by Menippus.

A number of points must be stressed. Our creation of the generic term Menippean satire does not retroactively compel all of Menippus's works into a single genre. Nor is there any reason to limit Menippus's generic innovations to the one genre of Menippean satire. His creation of the heroic epistle has already been mentioned; the Menippean symposium has many descendants and may be considered a genre unto itself;[13] and the *Sale of Diogenes*, of which Lucian's *Philosophers for Sale* may be a travesty, may have been more in the realm of hagiography than anything else. We certainly have attested parodies of symposia, wills, and letters; although all of these appear as elements in later Menippean satires, it is reasonable to assume that Menippus wrote both specific parodies of literary genres as well as Menippean satires per se. Works such as Lucian's *Icaromenippus* and *Necyomantia* show such parodies integrated into a fantastic narrative; it is this storytelling that distinguishes our genre. Lucian affords us caution: literary experimentation, even within a fairly narrow thematic range, can produce works in quite a number of genres.

We are safest in assuming this much: that the *Necyia* is Menippus's most important work, his most "Menippean" satire, and the most accessible paradigm for his literary followers of what makes him unique, even if other works betray similar comic and intellectual attitudes, and even if other works by Menippus were directly to influence later Menippean satires. His comedy is at the expense of, not the service of, philosophy; it expresses itself in a number of forms. There is a suggestion of elegance of expression and love of anecdote and paradox. For the questions of content, presentation, and style in the *Necyia*, we need to turn to the testimonia.

DIOGENES AND MENIPPUS

The most important observation to make about the reputation of Menippus in antiquity is that he is always referred to the example of Diogenes the Cynic. There are two distinct points of view: one, that Menippus is the true follower of Diogenes; the other, that Menippus does not deserve to glory in this association. Biographical details are similar: both are said to have been slaves and then philosophers;[14] both are associated at some time with Sinope in Pontus;[15] Lucian represents them as kindred spirits in the *Dialogues of the Dead* (a crucial qualification will be given later);[16] both are accused of shady financial dealings;[17] and both are said to have committed suicide or to have died eating raw food.[18] Lucian's description in the *Dialogues of the Dead* of Menippus as an old bald man in rags is probably more accurately a description of Diogenes himself.[19]

We get the impression that Menippus was eager to follow the example of the master; the *Sale of Diogenes* suggests an allegiance. It is entirely possible that the popularity of the *Sale* accounts for some of the confusion between these two personalities.[20] But it is remarkable that philosophical and literary traditions deny to Menippus any real connection to Diogenes, or to the succession of Cynic philosophers. I believe that this is not out of an attempt to correct a mistaken impression of the biographical tradition but is a reaction to, or an attempt to counter, Menippus's specific claims to the mantle of Diogenes and the Cynic creed. Laertius tells no stories of Menippus's relations with the other Cynics, although such details often bulk up the rest of the Cynic *Lives*. He is grouped among the followers of Crates at 6.95, but is said only to have become notable (ἐπιφανής) among them; this is vague, and lacks the usual vocabulary of discipleship (μαθητής, ἤκου-σεν, διήκουσεν).[21] Laertius quotes no wise sayings of Menippus, no Cynic *chreiae*, though the *Life of Diogenes* bristles with such material; and even Lucian, though he depicts a special relation between Menippus and Diogenes in the *Dialogues of the Dead*, attributes to Menip-

pus merely mocking statements, and never shows Menippus in the
company of the other Cynics.[22] Only one problematic passage in
Lucian seems to place Menippus within the Cynic succession.[23]

Cynicism is not just a debunking philosophical movement but has
much positive instruction to impart in the way of morality and common sense; Laertius's *Life of Diogenes* is ample proof of this. There is
no indication that Menippus followed Diogenes in this important
aspect; the distinction between Menippus's and Eubulus's account of
Diogenes' sale has already been mentioned. We are nowhere given
the impression that Menippus was a Socratic ironist; even though
Lucian often creates such characters, he does not make one of Menippus (further in Chapter 7). And Varro's claim that he had to add
both *hilaritas* and philosophical matter to his Menippean model to
achieve his own brand of *spoudogeloion* in his *Menippean Satires* suggests that the effect of Menippus's works was not so much ironic
as mocking, and not so much instructional as narrative and fantastic.

Laertius's *Life of Menippus* is hostile not just because Menippus's
actions did not fit his beliefs (there is much room for criticism of
Diogenes on this score);[24] nor is it indignant at Menippus's uncom-
promising censure; rather, it belittles him for the triviality of his
writings and the shallowness of his thought. According to Laertius,
Menippus is no Cynic at all. The poem Laertius composes on Menippus's life and character accuses him of not knowing what it means to
be a Cynic because he was a usurer and committed suicide in despair
when he lost his money.[25] Laertius calls Menippus a "Cretan cur,"
which seems to label Menippus not as a Cynic but as a cynanthrope or
werewolf; by dying Menippus returns to the tombs where he belongs.[26] Both halves of the traditional epithet for Menippus as a
Cynic author, *spoudogeloios,* are specifically denied to him: his works
have no seriousness and are full of derision, not laughter.[27] There
are no other indications that Menippus was not primarily seen as a
Cynic. Dialogue speaks of Cynicism and Menippus as two separate
degradations that he endures in Lucian's comic dialogue (*Bis Acc.*
33); Photius mentions Menippus among the poets, not the Cynics,
that Stobaeus excerpted;[28] Varro speaks of how he needed to add
philosophical content to his Menippean model and does not mention
Menippus's Cynicism; "Probus" speaks of Menippus as purely a literary influence on Varro; Marcus Aurelius, in a gloomy meditation on
how death overtakes kings and counselors, gives examples of dead
philosophers but belittles Menippus as a mocker to whose strident

truths Death was ultimately indifferent.[29] In Lucian's *Piscator* ("Fishing for Philosophers"), Diogenes complains that Menippus, at least as he has been compelled by Lucian, has turned traitor to philosophy as a whole, Diogenes and Cynicism included.[30]

True Cynicism is denied to Menippus in other ways as well. It is a trite witticism to call a Cynic a dog, but it attaches to Menippus with a peculiar insistence as a paradox: because he is so much the dog, he is not a Cynic. Lucian has Dialogue complain that Menippus is truly fearsome because he bites while he laughs; this implies more than Menippus *spoudogeloios*.[31] Varro's Ταφὴ Μενίππου ("The Funeral of Menippus") seems to refer to him as a *nobilis canis* and a *canis sine coda* (F 516, 517); a tailless dog is one that bites all the time, as dogs proverbially do not bite when they wag their tails.[32] He is always called a dog in the *Dialogues of the Dead*, where he speaks to Cerberus as a relative (4.1). Allied with this is the presentation of Menippus purely as a mocker of philosophers and not a philosopher himself. So Diogenes describes him to Pollux in the first of the *Dialogues of the Dead* (1.2): "he laughs all the time and for the most part ridicules those damn braggart philosophers." Lucian has Demonax suffer the same accusation from an unsympathetic source: too much humor may cancel one's claim to Cynicism.[33]

We may see Menippus as a radical interpreter of Cynicism, one who pushes the teaching and example of Diogenes to what none of his contemporaries would call a *logical* extreme. Many of Diogenes' *chreiae* are destructive rather than constructive; yet it is Menippus who is criticized for an unremitting negation. Writing the *Sale of Diogenes* is not sufficient to make him a philosopher in the eyes of the ancients.[34] Menippus gained no respect, and his claims to philosophy are rigorously rejected. Menippus must be seen as a lone wolf on the fringes of the Cynic movement. The two Cynics are complementary opposites: Menippus is the dog of the underworld, whereas Diogenes, according to the famous epitaph composed about him and preserved in the *Greek Anthology*, is the dog who lives in heaven.[35] Diogenes is a mad Socrates; Menippus, a mad Diogenes. As far as antiquity is concerned, he is not to be confused with the Cynics; if we require a milder Cynicism we must look to Bion of Borysthenes.[36] Menippus's opposition to the bugbears of Cynicism, to pride and self-importance, to fraud and deception, to philosophical culture at large, leads him to repudiate both philosophy as a whole and the antiphilosophy of Cynicism. He rejects all dogma and all certainties, and has nothing positive with which to replace it.

MENIPPUS THE PREACHER

Menippus is responsible to some extent for the confusion of Diogenes and himself. I believe it may be shown that the vehicle for some of this confusion is Menippus's self-presentation in his own works, particularly the *Necyia*. Menippus made himself a character in a fantastic work and parodied himself in doing so. His ridiculous, autobiographical account of a journey to the underworld, and of his return from there, is the source of what makes him anathema to philosophers and acceptable to comic authors.[37] We could explain the similarity in the stories told about Menippus's and Diogenes' suicides (particularly that of dying by eating raw food) by assuming that the charlatan Menippus made a production out of his death (the examples of Empedocles and Peregrinus come to mind); if the similar details are not just due to the confusion by other sources, the simpler expedient, that Menippus described his own death in a literary work, is more pleasant to assume. And there is evidence that he did so, and in the *Necyia*.

For Menippus's self-presentation we are fortunate to have explicit evidence outside of the pages of Lucian in a very important testimonium in the *Suda*, which says that he went about pretending to be an emissary from the underworld, an observer of human sins who will report them to the proper authorities below. He is said to have dressed like a figure from tragedy, wearing boots and a robe, but he made this posture even more ridiculous by making himself a bearded Fury:

> Menippus the Cynic went so far in his hocus-pocus that he took on the appearance of a Fury and said that he had come from Hades as an observer of sins and would go back down again to report them to the divinities there. This was his attire: a grey, ankle-length cloak with a purple belt around it; an Arcadian cap with the twelve signs of the Zodiac woven into it on his head; tragic boots; an immense beard; and an ashen staff in his hand.[38]

It is a Cynic commonplace that the world is a stage and people are actors, and Menippus's wild excess toys with this commonplace, making hell the stage on which he acts.[39] We have various confirmations of this picture of Menippus the bogeyman. Varro's Ταφὴ Μενίππου seems to speak of Menippus (F 539): "but an underworld lurker-in-the-shadows, an evil spirit, and let him keep people anxious, for they have worse fear of him than the fuller does of the owl."[40] Lucian (if we leave aside the principal role that Menippus plays in the *Dialogues of the Dead*) has Dialogue complain that Lucian "exhumed" Menippus.[41] This implies not just the fact that Menippus died before Lucian's time but also that the Land of the Dead is Menippus's true home.

Lucian's *Necyomantia,* in which Menippus makes a trip to the underworld dressed in Odysseus's hat and Heracles' lion-skin, carrying Orpheus's lyre (all to ensure a safe return), certainly implies that Menippus the Fury existed in Menippus's *Necyia,* not in real life. We cannot be absolutely sure; Lucian is quite capable of making fun of Menippus and his reputation. But Menippus in his *Necyia* would claim to be able to decry human vanity because of direct experience of the underworld, and his comic presentation of himself as one who now lives below allows us to infer that Menippus in the *Necyia* depicted himself *as dead.* To be sure, a Fury is not dead; but it no longer lives in the upper air, and as an agent of the infernal powers it could represent a commissioning of the dead Menippus as a soldier in the fight against human vanities. He does not return to life as Er does, in his old human form, but has been transformed, rather as great sinners like Ardiaeus are, into something from which we may take a valuable lesson.

The conjecture explains much of the self-parody and many of the themes of the genre that develops from the *Necyia;* Menippus may have depicted himself as one who learns, by dying and journeying through the Land of the Dead, of the emptiness of human endeavor and of the judgments that await the proud; as a *catascopus,* he could enjoy his laughter at the sight of human error now made abundantly clear; but he would come back not to live his human life in accordance with the truth, but as the absurd actor, the bearded Fury, the spy of the lords of the Dead.[42] Truth would be bought at the cost of his life, and he could not put it to use; nor could he, in his ridiculous attire, expect anyone to profit by it either. Menippus could fashion for himself a personality compounded of equal parts sinner, shaman, and Er; and as the bogeyman he preaches a wisdom that comes too late. The underworld that coughs up a bearded Fury cannot deserve our respect, and the fantastic journey to learn the simple truth in an impossible place is an expense of effort for a doubtful cause, and such preachers cannot be trusted. Menippus's *Necyia* is an elaborate dramatization that Cynic truths have no absolute authority. Again, it is a "vain reproof of idle effort." Lucian's *Dialogues of the Dead* plays with this theme by making Menippus die and then keeping him in that absurd afterworld which he cannot believe in; there is no return from the *Dialogues* as there is from the *Necyomantia,* and Menippus must take his place among the bones and lie down.[43]

Death itself is the answer, we may imagine, that the *Necyia* offers to the questions of philosophy: those who want to know the truth may go to hell for it.[44] It is worth noting that the *Dialogues of the Dead* does not present the spectacle of wrangling philosophers, and that the actual philosophical content is quite low. Menippus and Lucian do not need to criticize the particular dogmas of rival sects, given the overriding importance of the fact of death. More important than their technical disputes, or even their proud and disputatious natures, is the fact that the lives of the philosophers make them all hypocrites. In this regard, the contrast to the *Silli* of Timon of Phlius is instructive. The *Silli* too are cast in the form of a verse *necyia,* in which the author observes the dead philosophers arguing philosophical points in parodies of Homeric language and descriptions of battle. The fragmentary remains allow only for plausible conjecture, but it seems that, to Timon, the underworld provides an opportunity to break the barriers of time and space and thus allow all the wise men of antiquity to meet and discover that they do not like each other. It is a different sort of humor from that of the *Necyia,* which Timon may have had in front of him.[45] Such a *situation* could of course be at home in a Menippean satire, and it is in evidence in the *Caesars* of Julian; but there is no evidence that Timon himself participated in the humor of the *Silli* or in any way made his own person the focus of the descent or of the lessons learned.

CONCLUSION

Menippus wrote about his own death and return from the dead. This has some later repercussions. Claudius is a dead fool and traveling naïf in the underworld; Philology rises to the Homeric heaven never to return, though evidently as an immortalized rather than a dead being; Boethius has as a guide to his true home a Philosophy who seems to come to him from the Land of the Dead.[46] But later Menippean satire strives in general not so much to recreate the plot of the Menippean original as to reinterpret its self-parodic preaching and fantastic journey. One way is to write Menippean satires that are about Menippus, making fun of the founder of the genre with an irreverence quite in keeping with the genre's nature. Varro's Ταφὴ Μενίππου tells of Menippus's death from another angle; Lucian keeps Menippus alive in his *Necyomantia* (though preserving his appearance as false prophet) and the *Icaromenippus,* only to kill him off in the *Dialogues of the Dead.* Here, Menippus learns in the underworld that even his own Cynic detachment and self-parody are insufficient to distinguish him from any of the other shades: the democracy of Hades treats Menippus like anyone else.[47] Lucian here accomplishes the rare feat of mocking a self-parodic mocker. But there are other ways to motivate a Menippean satire. Narrators return alive from the dead and from heaven, and awake from dreams and visions; certain proprieties may be maintained even in an anarchic genre. Of course, this picture of the history of Menippean satire as a series of recastings of the *Necyia* depends upon viewing it as Menippus's only Menippean satire, a decision that may still seem arbitrary. Menippus's symposia, wills, letters, and auctions may well be among the models for later Menippean satirists, but these most likely did not contain this extreme of self-parodic involvement in fantasy. But Menippus's association with the Land of the Dead is undeniable, and what we have seen of the probable nature of humor, preaching, and self-presentation in the *Necyia,* coupled with the fame of the work, is sufficient to proclaim it as Menippus's signature work and the generic font of all later Menippean satire.

Chapter Four

VARRO

MENIPPUS'S *Necyia* may be imagined as antiphilosophical parody in the most general terms: humor at the expense of the idea of an absolute good, the search for it, and the proclamation of it. Menippus is the Cynic who burlesques the persona, the teachings, and the certainties of the Cynic preacher. Varro supplies to this burlesque the parody of various dogmatic systems in their particulars, details that were superfluous to Menippus. Varro puts his own encyclopedic knowledge to self-parodic use in his *Menippeans*, frequently abusing the ideas that we know he held elsewhere, and depicting himself as a ridiculous reformer to whom no one pays any attention. I hope to present here a Varro who is not the social satirist of the handbooks, but a Menippean satirist who crosses Menippus and Lucilius to create a strange hybrid whose focus is the failure of the academic pedant to understand and improve the world about him. Because of this, the *Menippeans* are to be seen as both the ancestor of the parody of verse satire that we see in Seneca and Petronius, and of the parody of encyclopedic knowledge that we see in the late classical Menippean satirists, Greek (Julian) as well as Latin (from Martianus Capella to Boethius).

BETWEEN 80 and 67 B.C., Marcus Terentius Varro, the greatest scholar of republican Rome, wrote 150 books of what he called *Saturae Menippeae*.[1] If the proportions of the *Apocolocyntosis* and the prologue of the *Mythologies* are any guide to the length of an average *Menippean*, we gasp to reckon that these occasional pieces could have filled well over 1,500 Teubner pages.[2] This is a comic collection of extravagant length, but not wholly out of place in the ambit of Menippean satire, which may inspire vast works often to leave only fragments. Lucian's lifework rivals it; the extremist theories of the length of the *Satyricon* surpass it.[3] These numbers command awe and respect, for not only are the *Menippeans* enormous, but they are absolutely atypical of Varro as well.

I wish to establish here a few guiding principles for my examination, not of the *Menippeans* per se, but of the place of the *Menippeans* in the history of the genre that we name after them.

1. The text of nearly every fragment is debatable. The very length of the collection guaranteed that the *Menippeans* would not survive.[4] The nearly six hundred fragments and ninety titles preserved for us, largely by the fourth-century grammarian Nonius Marcellus, represent primarily oddities of vocabulary and syntax very poorly transmitted; a few continuous passages are preserved elsewhere.[5] It is very sobering to contemplate the tortured apparatus of a critical edition of the *Menippeans;* realistically, there are very few pieces of solid evidence upon which to base any theory at all.

2. Very few fragments can be definitely assigned to a speaker. We know that philosophers speak but cannot be certain when that philosopher is Varro; Varro is sometimes addressed (as Marcus), but we are not sure what are his responses; fantastic stories are told, but we usually know neither speaker nor audience. A valuable piece of evidence about Varro's self-presentation comes in a piece to which Bakhtin draws our attention, the *Bimarcus,* or "The Author Split in Two," but we can hardly extend these observations to the other satires. The *Marcipor* ("Varro's Servant"), with its comic voyage to heaven, and the *Marcopolis* ("Varro's City"), which describes a city's founding in scenes that remind one of Aristophanes' *Birds,* certainly depict Varro as the chief actor in fantastic tales that result in the narrator's embarrassment. But these are exceptional, and we are compelled to speak more of the potential and the possible than of the real and actual in the collection as a whole.

3. It is inconceivable that all of the *Menippeans* would formally belong to the same genre. If our concern were the *Menippeans* alone, we could reasonably speak of the intellectual and thematic unity they possess; but as we speak here of the ancestor of a genre of literature, whose participants, to the exception of Lucian, confine themselves to a single Menippean satire apiece, we must be careful to separate theme and genre. Some *Menippeans* may have resembled diatribe; some, parodies of the symposium; others, fantastic narratives. The περὶ ἐξαγωγῆς ("On Suicide") involves a *necyia;* Hannibal is asked why he committed suicide (F 407). The mythical subjects of the *Hercules Tuam Fidem* ("Hercules, Help!"), the *Prometheus Liber,* and the *Tithonus* all speak, and these satires may represent their musings on the state of human affairs.[6] In what must have been a philosopher's nightmare, F 582 (an unassigned fragment) speaks of three hundred headless Jupiters on stage. Nor are all of the *Menippeans* confined to one book; the Περίπλους ("Circumnavigation") has a second book subtitled περὶ φιλοσοφίας, and should make us cautious about drawing general conclusions.[7] As argued in the previous chapter, Menip-

pean satire likes to appropriate various genres of literature as grist
for its mill, and what appears to be the origin of Menippean satire as
a genre is the incorporation of such parodies into a fantastic narrative, exemplified by Menippus's *Necyia*. An author who writes 150
pieces under the rubric of *Saturae Menippeae* may well break down
this unity into its component parts on occasion without violating the
thematic integrity of the whole.[8] In practical terms, we must treat
Varro as we treat Menippus—not as a historical person whose views
of genre and literature we may recapture, but as an icon worshiped
by his followers.

4. Reconstruction of individual Menippeans is therefore hazardous, and largely dependent on plot lines known from other authors,
primarily Lucian.[9] The loss of the *Menippeans* is a frustrating and
inestimable handicap on the study of Seneca, Petronius, and the late
Roman authors; and one cannot simply reason backward from early
and late successors of Varro to define the nature of the source, for
innovation is always a possibility, and the late Romans are often accused of contaminating two distinct Varros, the satirist and the encyclopedist.

5. Testimonia are ultimately more valuable than fragments in
evaluating the *Menippeans*. The reaction of intelligent readers to
Varro's texts is worth more than the random fragments offered by
the grammarians. The second-century A.D. belletrist Aulus Gellius is
an important and greatly undervalued source of information about
the nature of Varro's humor and its relation to the moral and philosophical content of the *Menippeans;* I shall come to him shortly. But
consider here the introduction to Cicero's *Academica Posteriora,* to
which I have already referred, and which may be pressed into service
one last time. Varro claims (1.8) that he added philosophy and humor
to the model offered by Menippus, in what seems an attempt to
create his own variety of *spoudogeloion*. Cicero objects (1.9):

> You have brought much light to our poets and to Latin
> literature and language as well, and have yourself made a
> multiform and elegant poetic work in nearly every meter,
> and have in many places embarked upon philosophical top-
> ics, sufficient for inspiring your readers, but insufficient for
> their instruction.[10]

Cicero stresses Varro's poetic and literary achievements against his
philosophical inadequacy. Cicero is, no doubt, on his best behavior in
this description of what he thinks is the shortcoming in the works of
the dedicatee of his dialogue, and his dissatisfaction with Varro's

philosophical substance is very politely put.[11] If Varro's goals were protreptic and didactic, he would seem to be a failure. I conclude that Varro never intended the doctrinal matter of his *Menippeans* to be instructive in any real sense, and that Cicero is not being so much provocative and offensive as stating an obvious fact.

6. It is certainly true that the *Menippeans* have philosophical interests, content, and debate far in excess of what may be imagined of Menippus's *Necyia*. The titles alone make this clear.[12] But critics who have studied the philosophical content of the fragments expand Cicero's conclusion: Varro's interest is not in philosophizing but in moralizing.[13] But this raises another question: why did Varro feel the need to infuse works of no true philosophical import with philosophical sophistication? Is Varro more like Timon of Phlius than Menippus, setting ridiculous philosophers against each other, offering by the way bits of philosophical lore for the satisfaction of the less learned? It is often claimed that Varro, an adept at philosophy, is careful not to make fun of philosophical speculation per se but concentrates instead on making fun of philosophers in general.[14] I think otherwise, and suggest a twofold motivation for this. First, philosophizing as an activity is a dubious occupation, more Greek than Roman and inimical to the ways of simple and ancient Rome. Philosophical hairsplitting is a comic example of modern and unacceptable behavior.[15] Second, and more important, the philosophical content allows Varro to display his own learning. Varro the pedant appears in the *Menippeans,* but the critics who dismiss these intrusions as embarrassments have rarely seen the self-parody implied by them,[16] though Riese took it for granted that in most of the *Menippeans* Varro presented himself as a failed preacher.[17] Philosophers endure much comic criticism in the fragments, but a pedant is susceptible to the same sort of criticism, of relying too much on abstraction and of living a life inconsistent with theory. One who knows the intricacies of the philosophical sects can easily convict himself of knowing too much.

7. It is certainly true that many of the fragments speak of topics common to verse satire. The conclusions usually reached about this aspect of the *Menippeans* are as follows.[18] Varro borrows only the form of his works from Menippus, for the concerns of a Roman, landowning patriot must be different from those of a Hellenistic, cosmopolitan nihilist.[19] Varro favors the techniques of the diatribe to enforce moral preaching.[20] He is a true Roman satirist, and champions the cause of the old, patriotic, religious, rustic Roman life over

the decadence, indulgence, and impiety of modern sensual Rome;[21] his theme is the contrast of then and now, *tunc* and *nunc*.[22] His strange language (a mad mixture of Latin and Greek, archaism and neologism, everyday speech and rhetorical prose, homely proverbs and technical terms of art) and his peculiar titles (which are playful and typically obscure the topic of any given satire)[23] are to some extent in the tradition of Lucilius and to some extent the legacy of Menippus, and form the humorous side of Varro's *spoudogeloion:* they sweeten his philosophical instruction and serve the end of the moral preaching of patriotic sentiment. These conclusions rest on the assumption that Varro in his *Menippeans* expresses opinions coherent with what we know of him elsewhere; yet wherever we can evaluate a Menippean satire against an author's other works, there is always a great difference. The presence of social and patriotic topics does not necessarily imply that they are successfully advocated.

8. A history of the genre of Menippean satire must be most concerned with the ways in which these evident philosophical and social interests are interrelated. It cannot be denied that the topics of the *Menippeans* seem to be those of antique virtue defended against contemporary sensuality, decay, and vice. But how do the obvious humorous aspects of the composition affect the reader's appreciation of their validity and application? If the arguments concerning Menippus and his writings in the previous chapter are accepted, we must be willing to see Varro, a follower of Menippus, in a new light as well.

THE EVIDENCE therefore is quite voluble, and by itself would not yield more than tantalizing possibilities. The fragments must be aligned with a particular tradition to yield some sort of sense. But presupposition more than hard evidence determines which tradition allows us to interpret these remains. To those who consider that the main influence on them is the diatribe and that Varro must be true here to the principles which he holds in other works, the *Menippeans* are in the tradition of verse satire. But the fragments do not themselves prove that the *Menippeans* pursue, in a different form, the same moral and social goals as verse satire does. I think it more plausible to assign Varro primarily to the tradition that stretches from Menippus to Boethius, and not to that which ranges from Lucilius to Juvenal, but in doing so I am not merely reasoning backward. I hope to show that it is primarily the testimonia that entitle us to read the fragments as proof of the continuity of Menippean satire from Menippus through Varro to late antiquity.

AULUS GELLIUS

The suspicions raised concerning Varro as a self-parodying pedant by the passage of Cicero's *Academics* can be largely confirmed in the pages of Aulus Gellius. From him we learn that the elegance that Cicero ascribes to Varro can be plausibly related to the artful and comic presentation of encyclopedic knowledge which frustrates a reader looking for unequivocal instruction.[24] It is hard to imagine Cicero admiring the language of the *Menippeans*, given its lack of stylistic purity and the tendency toward Asiatic, not Attic, habits of speech.[25] What pleases Cicero is not matter per se or language, but the witty exploitation of technical material for ends other than instruction.

Beyond the half-dozen passages in which Gellius merely cites the *Saturae Menippeae* for illustration of a Latin idiom, a Greek proverb, a grammatical anomaly, proper vowel lengths, or a definition of a technical term,[26] he has many things to say about Varro and these works. He tells us that Varro imitated but did not copy Menippus (2.18.7) and thus confirms Cicero's account of Varro's dependence. He mentions that others dubbed the *Menippeans* "Cynic Satires" (2.18.7, 13.31.1); further, through an amusing account of an inept scholar who claimed to be the only one who could interpret the *Menippeans*, but who faltered when asked to explain the words *prandium caninum* or "dog's lunch" (13.31.1–13), Gellius leads us to believe that the *Menippeans* were, on the average, hard to understand, at least in the second century.[27] If the difficulty of the *Menippeans* is Varro's conscious creation, born of strange language and abstruse material, as the fragments suggest, then the *Menippeans* can have little to do with the diatribe, which is nothing if not clear and accessible to its audience. The Cynic presence in these satires, suggested by the alternate title, can only stand in contrast to its matter and style.[28]

Gellius also provides three discussions, of varying length and detail, of parts of the *Menippeans* which allow us to appreciate what he thought was the source of Varro's humor. The first and most important of these is a synopsis of part of the *Nescis Quid Vesper Serus Vehat*, "You Know Not What Late Evening May Bring" (13.11.1ff. = F 333–41). To Gellius, the whole satire is a most witty work (*lepidissimus liber*, 13.11.1; *lepidus* and its relations constitute Gellius's stock description of Varro *Menippeus*), "in which he discourses upon the right number of guests for a symposium and on its constitution and cultivation."[29] This disquisition must have formed only a part of the satire, as the title would imply that something unexpected happened at the end of a symposium over which Varro (if Gellius's words are literally correct; otherwise, Varro's narrator) presided and for which he developed his regulations.[30] But the rules that are established are themselves comic in form and in reference, and seem to belong to a Menippean tradition of comic laws and regulations.[31] Varro toys with this tradition, abusing not actual and existing decrees but the academic love of laying down rules and definitions.

Gellius begins with views on the ideal number of guests (13.11.2 = F 333):

> Now he says that the number of the guests ought to begin with the number of the Graces and proceed to the number of the Muses so that, when there are few guests, they be no fewer than three, and when there are many, they be no more than nine.

This is comic: not only is it prolix, but it labors to explain its own allusiveness. We may relate this inflationary rhetoric to the traditions of the panegyric, yet the comparison of guests to Graces and Muses would be remembered with chagrin if the symposium ends in the uproar that the title promises. It is promptly deflated by the next citation (13.11.3 = F 334):

> For, he says, it will not do to have many, for a crowd is for the most part uncontrollable: it stands at Rome, sits at Athens, but nowhere reclines to eat.

Any number greater than nine is an audience for oratory, either in the forum or on the Pnyx. Varro moves from the fanciful to an exaggerated and practical analogy. This exaggeration is quite witty in itself, but it also tends to undermine what has gone before by trying to justify its modest numerical limits by pointing to the behavior of huge crowds.

The next citation also draws our attention to comic and unnecessary corroborative detail (13.11.3 = F 335):

> Then he says that a symposium consists of four things and is at that point perfect in all of its numbers [i.e., "proportions"]: if witty fellows are collected, if the place is elected, if the time is selected, if the paraphernalia are not neglected.

This is a list of distinctions without differences (*conlecti, electus, lectum, non neglectus*) which turns the reader's attention away from its commonsense aspects (see to your guests, your location, the time for dinner, and the place settings) to etymological play.[32] Form triumphs over content at the expense of the speaker, and while we cannot know if the speaker is Varro, it is Varronian interest in language that is made fun of here.

In this light, the subsequent list of bland prescriptions participates in the humor of meaningless academic distinctions. Guests should neither be garrulous (*loquaces*) nor dumb (*mutos*) (11.13.3 = F 336); *eloquentia* belongs in the forum and *silentium* in the bedroom. This qualification not only expresses the curious notion that proper conversation is a mean between silence and oratory, but equates the normally positive *eloquentia* and the normally negative *loquaces*. This belittling of eloquence is self-parodic, given the narrator's attention to rhetoric in these balanced prescriptions; one feels that this sort of speech is precisely the sort of thing inappropriate for a symposium and pleasant conversation.

Both in Gellius's summary and in direct quotation we hear of topics for conversation (13.11.4–5 = F 337–38). These should be not involved but pleasant, not on matters of state but on daily life, and may risk some moral impropriety. The goal of such conversation is to make the wit more pleasant and provocative ("uenustius . . . et amoenius") by means of delight and enticement ("cum quadam illecebra et uoluptate"). The master of ceremonies need not be so much polished as not vulgar ("non tam lautum quam sine sordibus," 13.11.5 = F 339); this too will be humor at the speaker's expense if he conducts the symposium that the title implies. This is then summarized (13.11.5 = F 340):

> Not all topics ought to be chosen for a symposium, but those in particular which are both of practical value and which delight.[33]

In another place, Gellius gives this quotation in fuller form, adding these words (1.22.5): "but in such a way that that element as well seems not to be absent rather than present in overabundance."[34] This mincing distinction falls in line with other etymological jokes and pieces of noninformation. Gellius's failure to relate this last clause in his larger synopsis may reflect an exhaustion with this kind of humor, and an eagerness to shift away from convivial rules to a final and impressive joke on the subject of second courses (desserts) (13.11.6 = F 341):

> bellaria *inquit* ea maxime sunt mellita quae mellita non sunt, πέμμασιν enim cum πέψει societas infida.

Those desserts, he says, are especially sweet which are un-
sweetened, for there is an untrustworthy connection between pastry and digestion.

There are two puns in one sentence, and the effect is overpowering.
The first is Latin and an oxymoron, the second is Greek and etymological (both πέμμα, "pastry," and πέψις, "digestion," derive from
πέπτω, "to cook").[35] The speaker carries on like Polonius; the humor
of these pronouncements is ultimately invested in the character of
the pedant who speaks them.

Gellius's reaction to the *Nescis Quid* is the most valuable piece of
primary evidence we have for the nature of Varro's *Menippeans*. Gellius seems to find its elegance in puns and comic lists, in an academic
parade of dogmatic opinion that for all of its wit turns the humor
ultimately toward the speaker, who may be Varro himself. The same
impression is recorded in Gellius's account of another of the *Menippeans*, the περὶ ἐδεσμάτων (6.16.1–5 = F 403):

> Varro, in the satire he entitled "On Gourmet Food," in fairly
> elegant and cleverly composed verses [*lepide admodum et scite
> factis uersibus*] made a list of the far-fetched delicacies of the
> table and kitchen. For he put forward, and enclosed in se-
> narians, most of the sorts of things that the gourmands seek
> on land and sea. He who has the leisure may read the verses
> which are to be found in the book I mentioned; but, insofar
> as memory serves, these are approximately the species and
> names of the delicacies and the locations of the foods that
> are better than all the rest, things that insatiable maws have
> found out, and which Varro pursued out of derision: the
> peacock from Samos, the Phrygian heath cock, the cranes of
> Media, the kid of Ambracia, the yearling tuna from Chal-
> cedon, the eel of Tartessus, the haddock of Pessinus, the
> oysters of Tarentum, the scallop . . . , the swordfish of
> Rhodes, the wrasse of Cilicia, the nuts of Thasos, the dates
> of Egypt, the acorns of Spain.

Gellius's attitude toward Varro's poem is not easy to decipher. He
praises the senarians for their elegance and seems to appreciate the
fact that such unlikely material has found its way into clever verse.
But while he notes that Varro's purpose in the satire was moralistic,
the delicacies "pursued out of derision," he does not quote Varro for
anything other than technical matters. Gellius 6.16 is itself a moral
work condemning gluttony; after referring to the *Menippean*, Gellius

says that we shall reject such misplaced industry all the more forcefully (6.16.6: "indagines . . . maiore detestatione dignas censebimus")
if we remember the words of Euripides on the subject (frag. 892
Nauck[2]), here said to be a favorite text of the philosopher Chrysippus.[36] It is an unnecessary conjecture that Gellius derived this
quotation from Varro's satire.[37] For the moral, Gellius relies on Chrysippus; for details, Varro.

As can be reconstructed easily from Gellius's prose synopsis, one
portion of Varro's satire is a poetic list of delicacies and locations.[38]
The poem seems not to be a sermon against gluttony with examples,
such as is found in the poem assigned to Publilius Syrus and quoted
by Trimalchio at *Satyricon* 55.6.[39] Despite the context of the discussion which introduced it, the poem would seem to resemble a patter
song in academic dress.[40] The example of Ennius's *Hedyphagetica*
(roughly "Epic Eating") preserved in part by Apuleius, *Apologia* 39,
offers a precedent: in his parody of the epic, the list of foods parodies
epic lists of warriors and ships. Further, the sheer verbal ingenuity of
such a versified shopping list inevitably draws the reader's attention
away from substance to an artistic appreciation of unlikely words in
an unlikely form. There is no doubt that the general thrust of the
περὶ ἐδεσμάτων was a condemnation of the excesses of the table, and
elsewhere Gellius quotes with approval another fragment of the satire which is unequivocally moral.[41] But the passage that Gellius singles out here is notable for its elegance only, and is ultimately frustrating to Gellius, who seeks to moralize against gluttony but who has
to turn to authors other than Varro for pointed condemnation of the
excesses of gourmets and gourmands.

Gellius's judgment of elegance in Varro's satire is not necessarily a
claim of accuracy or approval, as a final example will make clear. At
1.17.4 (F 83) Gellius gives the following quotation from another of
Varro's *Menippeans*, the *De Officio Mariti* ("The Husband's Duty"):

> uitium *inquit* uxoris aut tollendum aut ferendum est. Qui
> tollit uitium, uxorem commodiorem praestat; qui fert, sese
> meliorem facit.
>
> He says that a wife's faults ought to be removed or endured.
> He who removes the faults makes his wife more acceptable;
> he who endures them makes himself better.

Gellius thinks that the contrast of *tollere* and *ferre* (both meaning "to
carry") is a clever pun (1.17.5: "lepide quidem composita sunt"), but
adds that it seems to him that *tollere* here has the meaning of *corrigere*,

"to correct." His explanation of the pun suggests that he thinks that it obscures Varro's moral meaning, which he then produces, saying "it seems that Varro thought that, if they cannot be corrected, a wife's faults ought to be endured if they are of the sort that can be endured by an upright man, for faults are less serious than scandals [*flagitiis*]." Here, elegance frustrates Gellius's search for the truth, as it does also in some opinions of Varro which Gellius quotes on the meaning of the word *indutiae*, "cease-fires" (1.25.3):

> But both definitions seem to be more elegant and of pleasant brevity than unequivocal or correct.[42]

Gellius is interested in moral maxims in all of these discussions and throughout the *Noctes Atticae*. The *Nescis Quid*, περὶ ἐδεσμάτων, and *De Officio Mariti* all contain advice that Gellius would recommend. But he brings these works to our attention for the clever ways in which Varro expresses opinions that are morally ambiguous, and which require Gellius to explain Varro's intended meaning. Gellius appreciates comic lists and the self-parodic presentation of preacher and pedant in puns that detract from matter by means of odd form and suspicious information. Gellius provides a new point of departure for the study of the *Menippeans*. He allows us to proceed to two further points crucial to an understanding of later Menippean satire: first, the dramatization of the writing of a Menippean satire as a proper topic of a Menippean satire; second, Varro's burlesque of Cynic diatribe in the service of a parody of an intellectual with a theory to preach.

THE CRITICISM OF THE MENIPPEANS IN THE MENIPPEANS

Varro's interest in literary matters goes far beyond the parodic citation of authors which is fundamental to Menippean satire and is probably one of his own additions to the genre. Here too we may imagine that he follows Lucilius's lead, as he did in creating the strange language of the *Menippeans*. He discusses the technical aspects of writing, discourses on the nature of poetry and the quality of poets, responds to critics, attacks authors whom he does not like, explains the nature of his works, and writes in a bewildering variety of meters that allows us to associate him with the Alexandrian poets. This last demonstrates Varro's considerable interest in the purely literary, and he is no hack poet keeping an eye on handbooks of composition.[43] Only in Petronius will we find a similar range of liter-

ary preoccupations, although the innovation of dramatizing the process of composition as a fit topic for a satire exerts much influence on
the late Roman authors.

The act of writing appears in a number of contexts, often simply as
hard work.[44] But some satires devoted themselves, in whole or in
part, to the subject of writing. The *Cynodidascalicus* ("The Cynic's
Handbook") included a technical discussion of metrics, even though
it seems incongruous that a book of Cynic instruction would include
such things.[45] The *Desultorius* περὶ τοῦ γράφειν ("The Trick Horse, or
On Writing") seems to have dealt entirely with writing;[46] given the
ancient metaphors of marching for prose writing and riding for
verse (cf. Lucian *Bis Acc.* 33), a trick horse (or trick rider) may allude
to the Menippean form. The *Deuicti* περὶ φιλονικίας ("The Con-
quered, or On the Love of Victory") speaks of Varro's refusal to
name names and implies his fear of prosecution, a common and
reasonable fear after the days of Lucilius (F 90):[47]

> I like to write epigrams, and since I remember no names, I'll
> put down whatever comes to me.

The title of this *Menippean* may indicate that Varro's own love of
literary triumph came to naught. The same desire for success is
found elsewhere. Consider a fragment from another comic prologue, that of the *Gloria* περὶ φθόνου ("Glory, or On Envy," F 218):

> and you in the theater, who have run here together from
> your homes to capture pleasure with your ears, approach
> and learn from me what I have to offer, so that you may take
> literature home with you from the theater.

The topic is literature, not morality.

The *Testamentum* preserves two fragments that relate to the
strangeness of the *Menippeans* as literature and the difficulty of their
interpretation. The first has already been discussed (F 543; see
Chapter 2): even those children of Varro's who are asses at the lyre
are his true descendants so long as they are born, contrary to all
expectation, in the tenth month. The second is commonly quoted as
proof of Varro's patriotic concerns (F 542):

> to those born of my Love of Envy, whom the Menippean
> sect has raised, I give as guardians "you who wish the Ro-
> man state and Latium to increase."[48]

Here, as in the *Deuicti* and the *Gloria,* love of fame and envy is the
expressed motivation for Varro's writing of the *Menippeans.* The Me-

nippean sect, which fosters what this love of envy has created, is not a philosophical system but a literary entity, and his desire for fame is tied to the strangeness of his chosen form. The appeal to patriots to watch over these works does not mean that the *Menippeans* are whole-heartedly in praise of ancient Rome, but only that Varro wants those who desire the best for Rome to see to their interpretation. Varro claims in F 543 that his works are definitely strange, and possibly stupid (asses at the lyre); if these are recommended to those who love ancient Rome, it may well be because such people are predisposed to interpret Varro's works in ways that would please their frustrated author. At any event, Varro does say that his works need protectors, and this should indicate that they can stand on their own only with difficulty.

An intriguing illustration of the embarrassment the narrator can suffer by being a man of letters is the *Manius* ("Mr. Early-to-Rise," F 247–68). The satire seems to involve a chest of Numa's sacred writings, discovered during the digging of a grave (F 255–56):

> while they were looking after this, they found a chest while digging a grave . . .

> then they brought it to me, because they knew that I was a litterateur.

Varro is the narrator, and refers to himself comically (*libellionem*). He seems to have a servant who also knows literature, and who offers unwanted opinions (F 257):

> my servant Automedon: what he bellowed like an ox driver in the school of the rhetorician Plotius added to his master's grief.

Perhaps Automedon, playing Davus to Varro's Horace as in *Sermones* 2.7, pretended to be as learned as his master.[49] But the parody of the narrator extends beyond this. The theme of the *Manius* is the contrast of ancient virtue and modern decadence,[50] but if the discovery of a chest of writings sparked such a discussion, then the narrator is very likely succumbing to fraud. The ruse of burying philosophical-religious works attributed to Numa in order to have them discovered to foment social change is well attested before Varro's day.[51] Varro the author must have known of such imposture, but as a narrator in a *Menippean* he allows himself to succumb to it, thereby convicting himself of simplemindedness and providing a doubtful framework for the praise of ancient times.

A number of *Menippeans* speak of poetry and inspiration in comic terms, contrasting city sophistication and country simplicity. The rooster on the dung heap is associated with the Muses in two places.[52] The *Parmeno* (F 385–99) involves both a discussion of the art of poetry and a rustic scene of hunting and the chopping down of trees. The topic of this *Menippean* seems to be art as imitation: a farmer with a squealing piglet concealed under his cloak is said to sneer at the tastes of city folk who preferred Parmeno's imitation to the real thing.[53] The *Parmeno* appears to present the urban Muses in a confrontation of rustic and sophisticated theories of poetry (F 395):

> I am ashamed of you and your Muses. . . . I am exhausted at running and following along.[54]

Pedantic and handbook definitions of poetic terms appear (F 398):

> *poema* is rhythmic speech; that is, a number of words cast into a certain form obeying certain proprieties [or does *modice* mean "according to *modus*," or proper rhythm?]. Thus even a distich they call an epigrammatic poem. *poesis* is a continuous narrative in rhythm, like Homer's *Iliad* and Ennius's *Annales*. *poetice* is the art of such things.[55]

Surely a pedant speaks, one who shares Varro's views: the formula may derive from Posidonius, although a similar discussion is to be found in Lucilius;[56] the list of the relative merits of the comic poets found at F 399 may represent Varro's considered opinions on these authors.[57] But such learning is in pointed contrast to the other praise of poetry preserved from this satire (F 394, an Aristophanean):

> you [pl.] take away bitter cares from the heart with song and holy poetry.

If our knowledge of it were more certain, the most important of the *Menippeans* for an understanding of Varro's own opinion of them would be the *Bimarcus* (F 45–70), which seems to involve a fantastic discussion between two halves of Varro's personality, that of the moralist and that of the litterateur.[58] Yet there are other speakers besides the possible twin Varros (F 66 addresses a Manius); and while Varro makes fun of himself by presenting himself in this schizophrenic fashion and by making public his internal worries about the way in which he writes, we do not know the extent of this fantasy or its relation to the whole. Very little can be said with certainty concerning the order of the fragments.[59] We must content ourselves with some general observations.

The topic of the satire is τρόποι, in the rhetorical sense of "figures of speech" and the ethical sense of "ways of life." Someone accuses Varro of confusion (F 60):

> ebrius es, Marce; Odyssian enim Homeri ruminari incipis, cum περὶ τρόπων scripturum te Seio receperis.

> You're drunk, Varro! You're starting to ponder Homer's *Odyssey*, although you had taken yourself to Seius's house to write about tropes.

The pedant (*ruminari* is a verb used elsewhere of Varro the pedant narrator)[60] had gotten himself involved in a discussion of Odysseus's epithet πολύτροπος (from the first line of the *Odyssey*) and had forgotten his real intention of treating tropes. Etymological explanation plays a role (F 61):

> thus the rout of the enemy is called in Greek a τροπή, whence captured spoils set up on stakes are called trophies.[61]

And someone is frustrated that his knowledge of tropes has been called into question (F 45):

> not only does he exclaim that I am ignorant of the "ways of ways," but he absolutely denies that I know heroes at all.[62]

Here the humor lies in the depiction of a literary man whose literary interests are academic and pedantic, and who finds himself on an irrelevant tangent from an argument his audience is not willing to accept in the first place.[63]

The author makes a self-effacing plea (F 59):

> since Quintipor Clodius wrote so many comedies without a single Muse, can I not "hew out," as Ennius says, a single little book?[64]

The pedant wants to write only one little book (*libellum*), and this contemptuous diminutive makes an amusing contrast to the Ennian epic verb *edolare*, "to hew out, to embellish." But the defense is somewhat belligerent as well, for Ennius is a stock example of simple and compelling writing, committed to the praise of Roman ways. As elsewhere in the *Menippeans*, Ennius can be cited as precedent for questionable and modern behavior.[65] Moralists cannot be pleased with these justifications.

In two very difficult fragments, the *Bimarcus* addresses the signifi-

cance of prose and verse, the first in choliambics, the second in prose
(F 57–58):

> ne me pedatus . . . uersuum tardor
> refrenet †tarte cum† rhythmon certum

> lest the slowness of verses with their metrical feet restrain
> me, a certain rhythm . . .

> mihique †diuidum stilo nostro† papyri inpleui scapos [capi-
> tio] nouo partu poetico

> for me, . . . I have filled the pages of papyrus, with a new
> birth of things poetic.

Both fragments have very troubled texts.[66] Whatever the proper
form, the first describes the limitations of verse in verse, the second
praises verse in prose. This is sufficient to suggest that the Menippean form itself is under discussion, and that prose and verse are
seen as appropriate to different inclinations; presumably, prose is a
moralist's medium, poetry a stylist's. A contrast is implied between
literary sophistication and moral purpose; further, with sophistication comes pedantry in the eyes of the moralist, and with the aban-
donment of moral purpose a rejection of the ethos of ancient Rome.

Praise of the past and criticism of the present are attempted, and
we hear of the moral excellence of the Roman ancestors.[67] But consider the following indignant criticisms of modern Rome (F 53–54,
trochaic septenarian and octonarians):

> magna uti tremescat Roma et magnae mandonum gulae

> that great Rome may tremble, and the great maws of the
> gluttons . . .

> et pàter diuum trisulcum fulmen igni feruido actum
> mittat in tholum macelli

> and let the father of the gods cast his thrice-forked light-
> ning bolt, driven by blazing fire, into the dome of the meat
> market.

The grandiloquent poetry accords ill with its subjects; moral rage is
rendered comic by bombast and exaggeration. The parallel between
"great Rome" and "great maws of the gluttons" is striking, and the
deflation of the description of the mighty lightning bolt by its humble
object is similarly absurd. The *Bimarcus* suggests that the union of
old-fashioned morality and Varro's modern literary preoccupations

is itself the object of much of the humor of the *Menippeans,* and that his moral and poetic impulses work at cross-purposes.

The equation of author and pedant in the *Bimarcus,* which suggests that learned sophistication is allied to dullness and is alien to moral purposes, delineates a type of self-parody akin to that which Aulus Gellius describes in his analysis of the *Nescis Quid.* Although its fantastic action, Varro actually arguing with himself, is quite singular in the body of the *Menippeans,* it seems thematically to cohere with the other inferences we have drawn from the testimonia and the fragments. This presentation of Varro in the *Menippeans* as a professional writer, worried about literary fame, not achieving the respect of his audience, and depicting parodically both the effort of his production and the erudition that lies behind it, is sufficiently frequent to allow us to conclude that part of the personal involvement of the author in the action of his stories is as a writer of the *Menippeans* themselves. The *Menippeans* reveal a conflict of stylistic and moralistic concerns; Varro as a pedant narrator embodies this contradiction in his own person, and he makes fun not only of his intellectual and moral interests, but also of his position as a writer of works that betray a confusion of the two. By making the difficulty of expressing his ideas in print a proper topic for Menippean satire, Varro inspires the introspective authors of the late Roman period, for whom the struggle to write a meaningful book is part of their self-parodic presentation.[68]

THE PARODIC EXPLOITATION OF THE DIATRIBE AND CYNICISM

Much of the humor of the *Menippeans* depends upon the comic embarrassment of philosophers. The symposium, exploited by Menippus, is frequently encountered in the *Menippeans* as a scene of absurd debate: *Agatho, Est Modus Matulae, Eumenides, Manius, Meleagri,* Ταφὴ Μενίππου. Had Varro restricted his philosophical pieces to symposia and parodied debate, we might acquiesce to the view that Varro made fun only of philosophers in the *Menippeans,* but never of philosophical speculation itself.[69] But I think that a distinction between parody of philosophers and parody of philosophy in the *Menippeans* cannot be drawn. The antiphilosophical Cynical presence in the Menippeans urges this conclusion on us.

According to Aulus Gellius, some referred to the *Menippeans* as *Cynic Satires* (2.18.7, 13.31.1). Tertullian, who calls Varro a *Romanus Cynicus* (*Apol.* 14.9) and a *Romani stili Diogenes* (*Ad Nat.* 1.10.43 =

F 582a), understands the comic nature of this Cynicism: "But even
Diogenes made some fun of Hercules, and Varro, the Diogenes with
the Roman pen, brought on stage three hundred headless Joves (or
perhaps one should say Jupiters?)." Mras's investigations into the
Cynicism of the *Menippeans* remain the fundamental study of this
question, and he identifies the following as Cynic elements in Varro:
the transience of earthly goods and possessions; the championing of
the poor against the rich (although he notes that Varro is quite different from Menippus in this, and lacks any true invective on the topic,
preferring to advocate mere self-sufficiency); polemic against unworthy and foreign gods; attacks against the dogmas and lives of the
various philosophers; the contrast of the Cynic bugbears τῦφος and
κενοδοξία (vainglory) to true self-knowledge (although Varro is supposed not to make fun of any of the particular theories of the philosophers because of his personal interest in philosophy); a special dislike of Stoics and Epicureans; the belief in the Cynic life as a shortcut
to virtue; a comparison of Cynic sages to Heracles; the contrast of
τροφή (nourishment) and τρυφή (luxury); the advocacy of water
drinking; the use of the phrase *non uides?* ("Can't you see?") from the
diatribe; the use of the *catascopia*.[70] He thinks that the main differences between Varro and Menippus in particular, and the Cynics in
general, are an insistence on positive instruction, a cultivation of
patriotic themes, and a refusal to limit the material of his *Menippeans*
to ethics: this results in the great range of philosophical interests that
are attested.[71]

I believe that these conclusions are in need of qualification, for
they do not take into account the way in which such themes are
presented and the ways in which Cynicism as a philosophy is treated
in those *Menippeans* which feature Cynic characters. I submit that
Cynicism is itself exploited for humorous effect, and that Varro, who
casts himself as a Cynic and a preacher, is aware of the incongruity of
his being simultaneously an advocate of Cynic simplicity and Roman
patriotism. A Roman Cynic is a contradiction in terms; certainly pure
Cynicism, mendicant and antiinstitutional, ought not be espoused by
a lover of Roman traditions.[72] By juxtaposing a Cynic stance and a
Roman outlook, Varro follows the lead of Menippus in making the
trappings of preaching undercut the things preached.

A number of titles refer specifically to Cynicism but in a provocative manner, drawing attention to the opposition of Cynicism to the
topics under discussion. The *Cynodidascalicus* includes a technical discussion of metrics. The Cynic opposition to such formalities suggests
that the title is an oxymoron, and that the satire presented a conflict

between Cynic impulses and Varro's own handbook tendencies. The Κυνορήτωρ ("The Cynic Orator") may just mean "The Diatribist," but if the implications of the second half of the compound are stressed, it draws attention to the strange combination of Cynic and rhetorician, for the laws and proprieties of oratory (especially Roman forensic oratory) are quite alien to a Cynic. The Ἱπποκύων ("The Cynic Senator") deals with the intricacies of the Roman senate, among other things,[73] but one suspects that a Cynic senator is not a real senator at all. The Ὑδροκύων ("The Water-drinking Cynic") embodies no such contradiction, but, as we shall see, the Cynic in favor of water drinking misrepresents a medical authority about the nature of wine to make his point and cannot command our respect as an instructor; it is tempting to think that part of the comic characterization of a Cynic preacher in the *Menippeans* is just this sort of attempt to prove a simple and Cynic point of view by reference to a body of technical knowledge over which he has no competent control owing to his Cynic bias.[74]

The host of the banquet that is given in the *Eumenides* is a Cynic who hangs over his door a placard reading *caue canem* when he is expecting guests (F 143); Trimalchio has the same in Petronius (29.1).[75] He is thought mad, and his intellectual wanderings are related at length (F 146). Mosca offers the interesting opinion that in the *Eumenides* all of the philosophers who are gathered for this feast seem as mad to the common people as the common people do to them.[76] It is certain that the Cynic host does not preach his particular opinions (though he no doubt ridicules the opinions of his various guests); rather, he lays bare his own scandalous past and talks of his own madness, detailing his youthful devotion to the various philosophical sects, to pleasure, to the priests of Cybele, and so on.[77] The piece may end with a scene like that which concludes Lucian's *Piscator,* in which certain philosophical abstractions (Veritas, F 141; Existimatio, F 147) appear and vindicate the narrator and pronounce him sane (or possibly insane). But this is still the fantastic story of a very human Cynic who is not above relating his own distress for comic as well as instructional purposes; we may compare Menippus's fantastic journey in Lucian's *Icaromenippus,* which ridicules both the narrator and the philosophers whose opinions he rejects.

If we accept Cèbe's arguments about the *Endymiones,*[78] a Varronian narrator speaks in F 105:

> I sent my soul to search the city, to tell me what people do
> when they are awake; and to tell me who makes a better use

of his time, so that I might better keep myself awake, relying on his advice. What else (?) did it see but one laboring in the middle of the night. . . .

This is a use of the Cynic *catascopia;* the attempt to spy on human life resembles the end of Lucian's *Gallus.* It is contrasted with a philosopher's journey to heaven, which took place in his sleep (F 107), and whose failure is described (F 108):

thus did I miserably fall spinning down to you, quicker than I expected.

The narrator's *catascopia* is superior to the philosopher's, as the latter's interest is scientific and dogmatic, whereas the former's is ethical.[79] But the narrator's quest is not without its self-parody. The phrase "so that I might better keep myself awake" implies that he might fall asleep; the words "to tell me who makes a better use of his time" suggest that someone might be doing something better than investigating the city. The politest interpretation that can be put on this fragment is that the narrator's soul is taking on outside help in its search for human frailty, which is in itself a comic abuse of a Cynic convention. A less polite interpretation would render him an insomniac and his whole *catascopia* a waste of time.

The speaker in the *Synephebus* περὶ ἐμμονῆς ("My Fellow Ephebe, or On Stick-to-itiveness") mangles a Cynic exemplum, possibly used by Menippus himself (F 513):

Believe me, more servants than dogs have eaten their masters. If Actaeon had seized on this and had himself eaten his own dogs first, he would not now be a divertissement for dancers in the theater.

The speaker has twisted the import of this: according to Dio Chrysostom in a Cynic oration, bad people are worse than animals, and Actaeon is the lone counterexample of people killed by dogs.[80] But for Actaeon to eat his own dogs and so not make a spectacle of himself is simple foolishness, and the speaker quickly wanders from his Cynic and moral path to dyspeptic commentary on the contemporary stage.

A final point of formal parody of the diatribe is the use of the tag *non uides?* to introduce an exemplum. There is no need to deny that some of the *non uides?* questions have no obvious comic or parodic intent.[81] But a number of misapplications may be noted. In the *Flax-tabula* περὶ ἐπαρχιῶν (the main title, which excited the praise of the elder Pliny for its inventiveness,[82] cannot now be understood; the subtitle means "On Provinces"), the plot seems to revolve around sexual passion and the ability of a country wife to seduce even an honest and upstanding man (F 176–177).[83] Passion is explained in pedantic terms (F 177), to which discussion the following seems to belong (F 179):

> quid? tu non uides in uineis quod tria pala habeant tripales dici?

> What? Can't you see that in vineyards the term *tripales* is used when they have three stakes [*pala*]?

This seems to be an attempt to explain the obscene term τριφάλλος, "triple phallus," a word with good Aristophanic connections and which also appears as the title of another *Menippean*.[84] Etymology seems to be pressed into the service of obscenity with diatribic insistence.[85]

Aulus Gellius tells a story of a braggart scholar who claimed to be able to understand Varro's *Menippeans* (13.31.1–13). He is tripped up by someone who demanded an explanation of the phrase *caninum prandium* ("dog's lunch"). The passage in question comes from the Ὑδροκύων, F 575:

> Don't you see that it is written in the works of the doctor Mnesitheus that there are three types of wine, the black, the white, and the middle one which they call tawny [κιρρόν], and the old, the new, and the middle? And that the black makes semen, the white makes urine, and the middle good digestion [πέψιν]; that the new makes you cold, the old makes you hot, and the middle is a dog's lunch?[86]

The reference to Mnesitheus may come from Menippus himself,[87] but the crucial point is that the reference is perverted by the speaker and must be spoken tongue-in-cheek. Mnesitheus says in Athenaeus that the wine that is κιρρός is dry and an aid to digestion, and this accords with our fragment.[88] But Gellius explains that a dog's lunch is a meal without wine. The speaker would have it that as wine is either new or old, there is no such thing a middle-aged wine (Gellius 13.31.16–17), and that the middle wine ought not to be considered a wine at all. The speaker misrepresents Mnesitheus's opinions and seeks to justify his own point of view that one should only drink water by couching an unwarranted conclusion in a list of elements most of which readily command assent.

Another exemplum in Cynic discourse shows how the writings of the patriotic Ennius could be quoted *in favor* of modern decadence. From the Γεροντοδιδάσκαλος ("The Aged Teacher" or possibly "The Teacher of Old Men," F 189):

> non uides apud ⟨Ennium⟩ esse scriptum:
> "ter sub armis malim uitam cernere
> quam semel modo parere"?

> Don't you see that it is written in the works of Ennius, "I would rather risk my life three times in battle than give birth just once"?

The quotation is from the *Medea Exul* (frag. 109 Jocelyn). The speaker attributes to no less an authority than Ennius himself the famous words of Euripides' *Medea*, in justification of not having children. A final example comes from the *Est Modus Matulae* ("The Chamber Pot Has Its Limits," F 115):

> Don't you see that when the gods themselves want to taste wine they slink off to the temples of men, and that liquor is offered in a sacrificial bowl to Liber himself?

The speaker appeals to his audience to see the invisible; no one has seen gods slinking into temples. Whether the passage intends to attack anthropomorphic deities or to justify drunken behavior, the involvement of an element of Roman religion suggests that praise of the old Roman ways can be turned to comic ends. Other fragments show a similar appeal to the invisible or the impossible to make a point in a diatribe as well.[89]

It is impossible that all of the argumentation of the *Menippeans* is to be assigned to the fictive adversaries of the diatribe.[90] The narrator himself or certain of the characters that he encounters may take on the role of a preacher and to this extent deal in diatribe, but the diatribe is a suspicious form of argumentation in the *Menippeans*. What we see is the use of Cynicism, both as a form of discourse and a source of moral argumentation, used to comic ends both by Varro or his narrators and by the philosophers who argue against the point of view that we presume is preferred. Cynicism is a form of argumentation that stands in uneasy relation to the philosophical and moral aims of the *Menippeans*. It can easily be put into the service of doubtful debate, for its fervor can be used to support erroneous conclusions. Cynicism in the *Menippeans* represents a paradox: not only is it impossible to be a Cynic and a Roman patriot, but it is also impossible to be a Cynic diatribist and an advocate of philosophical sophistication. The moral and intellectual concerns that Varro imported into his Menippean model are in fact inimical to this chosen form. Varro elects to make of himself, or his narrators, Cynic preachers of most un-Cynical attitudes: respect for the past, for the state, and for patriotism; devotion to the intricacies of philosophical debate; and positive instruction in general. The self-parody observable in the *Menippeans* in the comic treatment of encyclopedic knowledge is inseparably related to Varro's posture as a Cynic who preaches the virtue of Rome. The contrast of form and content is readily seen, and parallel to the contrast of stylistic and moral interests demonstrated previously. Varro and his narrators are failed preachers, not entirely because of the indifference of the audience to which they preach but more importantly because of their hypocritical stance as Cynics who extol Rome and philosophy.

CONCLUSION

To summarize: Aulus Gellius, who found the *Menippeans* to be elegant and witty, describes their author as a Roman Polonius who speaks moral truths in a self-parodic manner. The sophistication of Varro's presentation of his material—versified technicalities, puns and etymological play, and so on—blunts his moral fervor, and Gellius, who also wishes in his essays to preach simple virtues, finds that he must often explain Varro's meaning and cast his words into a more accessible form, or supplement Varro's text, in order to convey to his readers a sense of moral urgency. From Gellius's testimony we suspect that the extreme difficulty of the *Menippeans* cannot consist with a desire to advocate the commonsense virtues; neither diatribe nor traditional Roman satire can endure being incomprehensible. The *Menippeans* adopt satiric, protreptic, and didactic poses, and abuse those who strike those poses.

Cicero, who makes Varro speak in the *Academics,* can claim that the *Menippeans* were insufficient for the teaching of philosophy; Varro does not deny this lack. There is a good deal of philosophical sophistication in the *Menippeans,* but it is reasonable to assume that the prominence granted to philosophical topics and argumentation in these pieces derives from a desire to abuse the technicalities of philosophy and philosophers. Varro, a student of philosophy if not a philosopher, makes fun of matters dear to his own heart as he follows the lead of Menippus, who abused all dogmatic systems and even the Cynicism that presumed to criticize these systems. The self-parody of

Menippean satire becomes in Varro's hands the parody of encyclopedic knowledge. The parody of erudition is found in the use of etymology for comic effect, in the creation of lists of technical and descriptive terms that have a sort of poetic life of their own, in the abuse of the praise of ancient times. I do not deny that Varro wants the *Menippeans* to tell of the difference between an ideal past and a corrupt present, to contrast *tunc* and *nunc;* but he presents himself as a questionable teacher and belittles the morals that he would preach through the comedy of misapplied learning. One who declaims against the evils of modern times is himself one of those evils; philosophizing is itself unacceptable to the virtuous old Romans whose era Varro praises, and Varro the scholar and pedant is seen to be a modern and unpleasant phenomenon. Petronius will best carry on this particular tradition; his narrator Encolpius, who is himself a moral affront narrating a work that is a literary outrage, takes it upon himself to decry the moral and literary degeneration of his own times.

VARRO's *Menippeans* are fantastically innovative and are the primary source for Roman Menippean satire. But there are two important qualifications. First, the *Menippeans* may allow Varro's followers now and then to glimpse and to imitate the simpler postures of Menippus: the *Apocolocyntosis* is effectively halfway between Menippus and Varro's reinterpretation of him. Second, not all of his imitators adopt Varro's model in all its fullness, but pick and choose elements of style, content, and form that they find congenial. For example, the *Menippeans* constitute an amazing collection of poems in various and experimental meters, and Varro surely takes Alexandrian poetic interests far beyond Menippus's own practice.[91] Petronius, Martianus Capella, Ennodius (to a lesser degree), and Boethius (to a greater) embrace this polymetry; Seneca and his student Fulgentius are much more restrained in their use of verse types; Julian, a Roman who writes in Greek, cleverly manipulates his verse citations in ways that suggest that Varro shows him the way to independence from Lucian's example. As a prose stylist, Varro has little influence on Seneca and Petronius, but his self-parodic purple prose lives on in the late Latin authors, Boethius excluded. His encyclopedic content is revived in late antiquity, Julian again attaching himself to Roman rather than Greek traditions in this regard. Only Seneca and Julian fail to follow Varro's lead in the dramatization of the process of writing Menippean satire and in his great concern with literary matters. The story of the scholar's fall waits for the late antique revival. Menippus's head was never so full as Varro's was, and Seneca, who makes very little of

Claudius the antiquarian bookworm, has something else in mind when he has Claudius journey to the farthest reaches of the Roman afterlife.

This study began with the question whether anything found in Fulgentius's prologue could not be plausibly assigned to Varro's *Menippeans*. I hope that I have avoided purely circular reasoning in these arguments, although it is true that the assertion of a direct link between the two influences the weight that I give to the difficult evidence of the fragments of Varro. But I do think that Fulgentius is an excellent illustration of the possibilities latent in the fragments, and may serve as a guide to the essence of a Varronian Menippean satire. I give here a synopsis of the prologue of the *Mythologies;* the reader is referred to Chapter 10 and Appendix B for fuller treatment.

THE INTRODUCTION (3.1–4.7) speaks of the work's similarity to comedy (3.11–13) and of its being a strange mixture of wit and erudition which shows the triviality of the author (3.17–20):

> a tale . . . which recently I concocted from pungent Attic wit and the midnight guiding lamp, a tale tricked out in the fantasies of dreams in such a way that you will see in me no mad poet, but rather observe an interpreter of dreams who divines meanings from the trifles of sleep.

In a long passage (4.6–6.18) he describes the devastation of his native land during the Vandal invasions and his joy at being able to roam free again after order is restored; but this commentary on the social order is merely a device to get the narrator to rest under a tree and drift off into fantasy (6.18–7.4). He sings a song to summon the Muses (7.5–8.5). After these abstractions arrive, we overhear a debate on the nature of myth and poetry. In this central portion (8.6–13.5) the narrator promises to reveal a new theory of myth that will deny the existence of the creatures before him; it ends when Calliope promises to come again with Philosofia, Urania, and Satyra in order to help the narrator explain his theories. After a bad and self-parodic poem recited in his sleep (13.6–16), the narrator wakes in confusion when these three arrive (13.17–14.20). These four mythical creatures assume the burden of the exposition and replace the narrator as exegetes (14.20–end): Calliope will deliver the first allegory, and Philosophy will take up the torch from that point. The three books of allegories which follow are not written in the mixture of bombastic prose and verse of the prologue but in sober and simple prose; they indicate not the narrator's literary theorizings but those of the mythical helpers whom he had hoped to allegorize away.

We note in this a number of themes and treatments which derive from Varro: the comparison of the work to comedy; the paradoxical mixture of wit and study; the odd mixture of commentary on the real world and its troubles and indulgence in fantasy; the use of prose and verse to create a comic narrator; bombastic, "learned" prose as an element of self-parodic humor; a topic that is, in effect, how to write a Menippean satire; theorizing on the nature of poetry and art; the inclusion of abstractions; the failure of the theorist who tries to proclaim a new theory of moral and intellectual dimensions; and a radical break between the encyclopedic matter that the author wants the reader to understand and the narrator's own ability to comprehend or present such material. The prologue creates an ironic framework for the material that is to follow: there must be a new approach to secular learning in a Christian age, but the author shows that such learning is trivial by describing the embarrassment of one who tries in vain to subject it to the scrutiny of faith. Fulgentius does not proclaim the inanity of myth directly; he merely shows how comic it is for someone to take myth seriously. The *Mythologies* presents an unresolved opposition of *nunc* and *tunc;* the message of the piece lies only in the reader's contemplation of the failure of the preacher, not in anything positively asserted. That Fulgentius should Christianize Varro's self-parody demonstrates how vital Varro's genre is.

Chapter Five

SENECA

SENECA's *Apocolocyntosis* tells of the death of the despised Roman emperor Claudius (in A.D. 54) and of his postmortem humiliations in heaven, on earth, and in hell, to use the shorthand terms. In brief, he is rejected in his attempt to become a god, passes down though earth just long enough to witness his own funeral procession and be captivated by the sound of his own dirge, and finds himself before the tribunal of Aeacus, where he is condemned for his crimes, although the very end of the work makes it fairly certain that he is not punished for them. Consequently, the three-tiered *Apocolocyntosis* is schematically the most complicated of the Menippean satires; it is therefore not a generic paradigm, but represents many Menippean possibilities rolled into one.[1] Unfortunately, the search for the political motivations of its composition tends to push to one side the details of the Menippean plot, which becomes a series of pegs on which to hang anti-Claudian insults. I think that the questions of what Seneca ought to have said about Agrippina, and what lesson he intended for Nero, are insoluble until the plot is understood;[2] similarly the *Aeneid* cannot be reduced to what Vergil ought to have said, or what Augustus wanted him to say. Further, and I shall return to this point, even if we wish to consider the question of its actual audience and the circumstances of its performance, we must be restricted by the nature of the text. A good case has been made that the *Apocolocyntosis* is a work designed to be read at the feast of the Saturnalia, and that Claudius is present within it as a Saturnalian lord of misrule whose rule has come to an end so that Augustus's Golden Age may return in Nero.[3] Yet there remains the fact that Claudius the fool reveals the foolishness of the worlds that presume to judge him, and that there is some sympathy for this Claudius caught in these ridiculous worlds. I reach this conclusion not through any loyalty to Robert Graves but out of the conviction that Menippean satire, a genre that makes fun of the quest for otherworldly knowledge, is alive and well in this tale of Claudius.

The complexity of the work's structure deserves more respect than it has received. The combination of a voyage to heaven and a voyage to hell, very rare in ancient literature, creates an observer of the whole of the world. Menippean satire offers the example of the character of Menippus in Lucian's *Icaromenippus* (with its voyage to heaven) and the *Necyomantia* (with its voyage to hell), but only if the two works are viewed as a diptych, as is the rule in the Renaissance. The sailors in Lucian's *True History* spend seven months at the Islands of the Blessed and later visit briefly the Island of the Damned, where one of their own number is punished.[4] There are also some early Christian visions, like that of Paul, in which the soul is taken on a guided tour of heaven and hell.[5] Much more important is Plato's Er, who sees both heaven and hell; and Alexander the Great, who flies toward heaven, descends to the depths of Ocean, wanders in the realms of eternal night, and is cheated of a chance to drink the waters of eternal life at the end of the second book of the *Romance*.[6] Beyond these few there is only Claudius.

Both Er and Alexander have much to do with the physical world as well as with the supernatural ones. Alexander is not content with his physical limits but is compelled largely to stay within them, and Er's vision of the machinery of the universe is almost as important as the description of the souls choosing their new lives. Claudius passes through this world on his downward journey, rather as Dante passes through Purgatory, located on the surface of the earth, in his ascent. The tripartite structure of the *Apocolocyntosis* should therefore be seen as a sensible extension of the desire to see both heaven and hell. This world is part of the universal order; it takes the Christianity of the late classical era to assert that there is heaven and hell and nothing between.[7]

The question remains: of what sorts of stories about heaven and hell is the *Apocolocyntosis* compounded? In Menippean satire and the literature in its ambit there are a number of ways to journey toward a laughable afterlife. Menippean satire describes two permanent ascents to a comic heaven: in Julian's *Caesars* and Martianus's *De Nuptiis*, our heroes and heroine rise to a corrupt heaven. The celestial bitterness of Erasmus's *Julius Exclusus,* itself inspired by the *Apocolocyntosis*, should not require us to think that the only point of our fantasy is that an unworthy applicant for godhead has been rejected; Lucian shows us heavenly assemblies in which it is decided that no further poor excuses should clutter heaven (especially the *Concilium Deorum*), and Menippean satire in general is content to let a poor heaven grow even poorer (as in the *Caesars*). But it is also in the Menippean tradition to allow a character to rise to heaven only to have a look around. Either heaven affords a place from which to view the smallness of the world below (Menippus sitting on the Moon in

Lucian's *Icaromenippus* affords a less noble vision than that of Cicero's *Dream of Scipio*) or we see the workings of heaven itself. This may be serious in Christian authors who have John's *Apocalypse* to draw on, but it is comic in pagan literature. This is a staple of Lucianic comedy and its assemblies of the gods; the hero proves embarrassing to the powers above and is removed.[8] It is to this category of views of heaven itself that I assign Claudius's ascent to heaven in the *Apocolocyntosis*.

In tales of voyages to the underworld, the main character either returns or does not. If not, the story is about finding a place among the creatures below. This is the story of Lucian's *Dialogues of the Dead*, which concerns the descent of the dead rationalist Menippus into a ridiculous underworld from which he cannot escape. If a narrator does return, there has only been a dream vision, or else a physical descent. It may be for knowledge (following the lead of Odysseus in Book 11 of the *Odyssey*); or to reclaim the dead (this is the tradition of Orpheus, and of Dionysus's descent in Aristophanes' *Frogs,* and also of Christ's harrowing of hell). Return can be uneventful, or comic; Menippus in Lucian's *Necyomantia* comes back to the light by scrabbling up through the oracular cave of a false prophet. Our fool Claudius is dead and is not searching for knowledge; he must take his place.

In assigning the *Apocolocyntosis* to the genre of Menippean satire I assert more than humor in a mixture of prose and verse. I would claim that even the fool Claudius can be a universal observer and that the real emphasis of the work is not the foolishness of Claudius, which is viewed as a sort of birth defect and beyond anyone's control, but the foolishness of the supernatural apparatus that sits in judgment upon him, that tries to explain and find room for an inhuman monster that it hopes will never be seen again. The following analysis attempts to take into account the structures of Menippean satire: unreliable source, fantastic journey, serious interlude, and comic reprieve. Much of what is unique about the *Apocolocyntosis* as regards the Menippean genre derives from the fact that our hero is actually dead and is not able either to return or to narrate his adventures in his own person. I take Senecan authorship as a given; I delay consideration of the meaning of the title and the political import of the work.[9] The *Apocolocyntosis* is not an attack on Claudius pure and simple, but an account of an occasionally sympathetic wanderer who is caught in a comic afterworld whose right to judge and condemn him is at least as questionable as his own right to become a god.

PROLOGUE

The prologue of the *Apocolocyntosis* announces the impending fantasy with tongue in cheek (1.1–3). It is well known and much imitated; it belongs here as an excellent example of the devices that Menippean satire may marshall at its beginning to draw into question the significance of the story that is to follow.

> I wish to preserve for posterity what happened in heaven on October 13 of the new year, of the beginning of this most blessed age. No quarter shall be given to calumny or to partiality. These things are true as they stand. If someone wants to know how I know—first, if I don't want to, I won't answer. Who will compel me? I know that I have been made a free man after the passing of him who proved the adage true that one ought to be born either a king or a fool. If it does please me to answer, I'll say whatever comes into my mouth. Who ever demanded sworn witnesses from a historian? Nevertheless, should it be necessary to produce a witness—ask the man who saw Drusilla going to heaven: the same man will say that he saw Claudius making his journey "with unequal steps." Whether he wants to or not, he has to see everything that happens in heaven, for he is the magistrate in charge of the Appian Way, the very road by which you know the Divine Augustus and Tiberius Caesar went to the gods. If you question this man, he'll speak to you alone; he'll never make a sound in the presence of a crowd. For ever since the day when he swore in the senate that he saw Drusilla ascending the heavens and despite such good news no one believed what he saw, he has sworn a solemn oath that he will not give evidence even should he see a man murdered in the middle of the forum. What I heard from him then I give to you now, definite and unquestionable; long may he live and prosper![10]

This conflation of parodies of historiography and aretalogy is Seneca's happy innovation; the presence of a *iurator* usually signifies not history but tales of miracles.[11] The narrator does not want to have the story subjected to verification, and the witness who is ultimately produced is highly untrustworthy. The apotheosis of Drusilla was itself a scandal; the sister and lover of Caligula, she received divine honors only after one Livius Geminius attested to her ascent to heaven. This same man is now said to vouch nervously for Claudius's assault on heaven; if we press this fiction, Claudius's experience there will eventually give Livius his first chance to observe a journey to the regions below.

Rather like the beginning of Lucian's *True History*, this prologue proclaims that all that follows is a lie. This may seem harmless, introducing a fantasy because Claudius of course did not go to heaven. But a crucial lie is buried within it: Tiberius was never granted divine honors.[12] This narrator wants to condemn Claudius and his apotheosis but, like some of Varro's narrators, he is not quite in control of his Roman history, which he views as seriously tainted. In the present context, the proverb that one should be born a king or a fool equates Roman emperors and idiots;[13] later, in a speech before the divine assembly, Augustus will refer to one of Claudius's victims as "stupid enough to be emperor" (11.2; "Crassum uero tam fatuum ut etiam regnare posset"). The presence in heaven of Drusilla, who did not deserve such honors, and of the hated Tiberius, who never gained them, shows that the heaven to which Claudius will apply for divinity already has quite a few unworthy inhabitants. Current opinion correctly rejects the older theories that took the *Apocolocyntosis* as a *philosopher's* criticism of apotheosis,[14] but it is nevertheless clear that the presentation of this Roman custom is a comic one, and that the narrator simultaneously misunderstands its workings and reviles them. We shall see that the Roman heaven of the *Apocolocyntosis* is venal and corrupt, and that the inadequacy of Claudius as a candidate for divine honors finds its comic counterpart in the silly heaven to which he applies for them. Tiberius, Drusilla, and Claudius stand in opposition to Augustus, whose divinity was deserved and whose characterization in the *Apocolocyntosis* is as respectful as a Menippean satire will allow; this contrast of *tunc* and *nunc*, couched in morally ambiguous terms (Augustus inhabits a comic heaven), is in the best Varronian tradition.

The text continues with a poem on the time of year when Claudius died. This passage has already been discussed in Chapter 2: the bombastic verses parody the conventions of epic poetry in true Menippean fashion (neoteric poets will be bidden to mourn Claudius's death in the funeral dirge at 12.29). The narrator's source, who seems to speak these lines, then devolves to prose (2.2):

> I think I'll be better understood if I say: it was in the month of October, on October 13. I can't tell you the exact hour;

agreement is easier among philosophers than among clocks, but it was between the sixth and the seventh.

Lucian offers parallel examples of the comic deflation of a comic style by a nervous speaker who wants to be better understood;[15] such a speech is obviously not just a piece of literary parody but also an element of the comic characterization of its declaimer. He continues (2.3–4):

> "Much too crude! All the poets yield so often to such requests that, not satisfied merely to describe the risings and the settings of the sun, they even make the middle of the day nervous; will you pass over such a fine hour in this way?"

> Now had Phoebus split the middle of the circle with his chariot and, nearer to night, he was shaking weary reins as he drew the light oblique on path convex:

> Claudius began to stir his soul nor yet could it find release.

Whether the narrator made such a demand of his tight-lipped source, or whether he now is responding to the audience's desire for less matter and more art, the interruption of the narrative breaks the illusion that the narrator is just reporting the source's story; he is making himself personally untrustworthy as a willing accomplice to the fraud of his source. Similar intrusions appear later in the narrative as well, recording certain scruples in reporting fantastic action; they will serve to remind the reader of Seneca's witness and to shift the weight of the parody from Claudius's shoulders and transfer it to those of a presumptuous source.[16]

The introduction, therefore, presents a comic and self-parodying narrator who acknowledges that he is going to tell lies and that his source is unreliable. The parodies of history and epic poetry contribute not just to literary wit but also to the ironic framing of what the narrator and his source have to say. The introduction is in the tradition of Varro, even to the inclusion of the fictive interlocutor of the diatribe for comic rather than instructive purposes. Nor is all of this mere lighthearted humor, for the references to the apotheoses of Drusilla and Tiberius suggest a certain bitterness. Claudius is not the only despicable applicant for divine honors; rather, Seneca suggests that he is a Roman type and that what will follow will not be just personal invective.

THE CRIMINAL AS FANTASTIC EXPERIMENTER

Seneca presents his Roman topic in Greek form. Ascent to heaven, application for deification, council of unworthy gods, journey to Hades, judgment and reprieve: these owe more to Menippus than to Varro.[17] Seneca's innovation in the *Apocolocyntosis* lies not in populating a Greek landscape with Roman characters but in interlarding traditional scenes with some of his own device, through which moves the dead Claudius, who is a much more specific character than the genre prefers. After the two chapters of the introduction, the *Apocolocyntosis* may be divided into seven scenes:[18] Claudius's death, including the praise of Nero (chaps. 3–4); Claudius's arrival at the gate of heaven (5–6); his conversation with Hercules in which the two become friends (7 and the lacuna);[19] the council of the gods and Augustus's condemnation of Claudius (8–11); the scene on earth with Claudius's funeral dirge (12); the judgment in Hades and Claudius's punishment by Aeacus (13–15.1); and Claudius's rescue by Caligula, who substitutes a different punishment (15.2). The death scene, the reconciliation of Claudius and Hercules, the funeral dirge, and the exchange of punishments are all Senecan innovations, and they uniformly present Claudius in a sympathetic light.[20]

Claudius is therefore not unrelievedly hideous but is occasionally a pathetic character. Consider first his death, a parody of Vergil's description of the end of Dido in *Aeneid* 4.693ff.[21] Mercury convinces one of the Parcae to take pity on Claudius's death throes (3.1):

> quid, femina crudelissima, hominem miserum torqueri pateris? nec umquam tam diu cruciatus cesset? annus sexagesimus et quartus est, ex quo *cum anima luctatur.* quid huic et reipublicae inuides?

> You most unfeeling woman, why do you let the poor man be wracked so? Shall he never stop, he who has so long been tortured? This is now the sixty-fourth year since he has struggled with his soul. Why hold a grudge against him and the state?

Claudius finally dies, possibly expelling his soul as a fart (4.3). In Vergil, Juno takes pity on the dying ruler (*Aen.* 4.693–95, 704–5):

> tum Iuno omnipotens, *longum miserata dolorem*
> *difficilesque obitus,* Irim demisit Olympo,
> quae *luctantem animam* nexosque resolueret artus. . . .

sic ait, et dextra crinem secat, omnis et una
dilapsus calor, *atque in uentos uita recessit.*

Then all-powerful Juno, having taken pity on Dido's long
sorrow and painful death throes, sent Iris down from
Olympus to release her struggling soul and her fettered
limbs. . . . So Iris spoke, and cut Dido's hair with her right
hand, and the body's warmth all dissipated at once, and her
life receded into the winds.

The ruler in both passages is dispatched by a pitying god for the sake
of the Roman Empire. The praise of Nero in epic hexameters at 4.1 is
the focal point of the entire scene. The poem, while certainly lavish,
is not obviously parodic.[22] We witness not the death of a monster but
of an embarrassing fool; Claudius is more belittled than condemned.

We again feel sympathy for Claudius during his interview with
Hercules. When Hercules first sees this crippled and babbling thing,
more resembling a sea monster than the beasts of his other labors, he
thinks that his thirteenth labor has come (5.2–3).[23] The goddess Fe-
bris reveals Claudius's Gallic origins, and Hercules imperiously demands, in good Senecan senarians, that Claudius tell the truth about
himself (7.1–2). But Claudius makes a clever move to bring Hercules
over to his side; he says that the two of them are actually very much
alike (7.4–5):

"I had hoped, Hercules, bravest of the gods, that you would
come to my rescue before the other gods, and if anyone
asked me for a character witness I was going to name you,
for you know me very well. If you remember, I was the one
who decided law cases all day long before your temple during July and August. You know how much suffering I endured there, when I was listening to lawyers day and night.
If you had fallen afoul of them, even though you think you
are very tough, you would have preferred to cleanse the
Augean stables; I swallowed much more bullshit than you
did. But since I want . . ." [here the text breaks off].

Claudius is abused here and in the funeral dirge (12.3.19–23) for his
fondness for hearing judicial disputes and for the efficiency that
came from hearing only a single side. Yet his self-imposed misery is
real enough, and had the text not been damaged, we would have
seen how these *ad hominem* (*ad deum?*) arguments win Hercules'
friendship. Although it is to Claudius's discredit that his new-found

patron and friend is a fool, his sufferings and the trust he puts in a fool like himself gain our bemused sympathy.

In the third of Seneca's original scenes, Claudius, led by Mercury, goes down the Via Sacra and sees his own exequies and hears his own dirge. This is chanted not by the lawyers who mourn his passing but by everyone else; the Roman people are rejoicing at his death. Claudius nevertheless likes what he hears and wants to watch longer (13.1). Part of the humor lies in Claudius's blindness to the chorus's irony. In the dirge we hear that Claudius is the bravest man in the world; he could outrun the swiftest warriors and draw the bow with a steady hand; he was the swiftest judge, hearing only one side of the case; Minos should yield his place to him in the underworld; lawyers, new poets, and crapshooters shall mourn his loss. Claudius's encounter with Aeacus and his torture with the bottomless dice cup at the end of the *Apocolocyntosis* give these last details their point. But in the midst of this is praise of Claudius's victories in Britain, betraying only mild irony and expressed in language entirely suited to and typical of imperial praise (12.3.13–18):[24]

> He commanded the Britons, beyond the shores of the known sea, and the Brigantes with their blue shields, to submit their necks to the chains of Romulus; and commanded the Ocean itself to tremble before the new laws of the Roman fasces.

No wonder then that Claudius was pleased. The dirge seems to represent the best possible praise that can be accorded the dead emperor; the fact that his enemies, not his friends, pronounce such praises assures us that it can be taken in some measure to his credit. The mixture of ironic and sincere praise in a single poem is Menippean, and the ironic frame certainly muddies the praise at the center. But Claudius is at any rate a fool whose flaws are ambiguously presented. This is what we would expect of the antihero of a Menippean satire. He is much more closely related to Encolpius in the *Satyricon* and Menippus in the *Icaromenippus* than to the recipients of political lampoons.

Claudius in the *Apocolocyntosis* is cast in the role of the fantastic voyager of Menippean satire. But Claudius does not undertake this journey of his own accord. Death, not curiosity or the desire to grind some philosophical ax, propels him forward; he is led about, largely passive. This passivity is crucial to the nature of the action, for the *Apocolocyntosis* is not a joke about what Claudius does (he speaks his dying words, converses with Hercules, hears his own funeral dirge, plays dice) but about what happens to him. This imparts an aura of innocence about Claudius. Death has made him an unwilling observer of things beyond his comprehension.

I defer discussion of the final scene of the work, which is to be understood in the light of the two judgments that precede it. Claudius's two trials show that the afterlife is not really competent to try his case. Before the formal debate on Claudius's apotheosis, a god (whose identity is unknown because of the lacuna) asks Hercules what sort of god he wants Claudius to be; before Hercules can answer, this god rejects the possibility that Claudius could become a Stoic or Epicurean divinity (8.1).[25] He then turns to Claudius's pretensions as a moralist: he had his prospective son-in-law Silanus killed after accusing him of incest with his sister, and this is an obvious insult to Jupiter's relations to Juno.[26] Evidently Claudius has been running for godhood on the reform ticket, for the unknown speaker can then exclaim indignantly (8.3): "hic nobis curua corriget?" ("Shall this one make our crooked paths straight?"). The god has thus managed both to suggest that heaven needs correction, by reference to Jupiter's incest, and to Claudius's inability to improve it, by reference to the murder of Silanus on trumped-up charges. Jupiter soon realizes that the attack on Claudius is becoming embarrassing to himself and to the other gods (9.1):

> "Conscript fathers, I had allowed you to question him, but you have made a complete mess of things. Please, preserve the dignity of the court! Whatever he is, what has he now thought about us?"

The criticism of Claudius has only served to point out ways in which the gods themselves may be criticized.

Claudius is then removed from the council chamber. Janus speaks and complains that in the case of Claudius apotheosis has gotten out of hand; it used to be a great honor to be a god, but now such honor is lightly bestowed. But his objections are theoretical, and he refuses to discuss Claudius personally (9.3).[27] He concludes not that Claudius should be denied divine status but that no mortal *after this day* should be thus transformed. Janus would allow Claudius's deification; he seems to wish to preserve the dignity of this Roman heaven by not publicizing its shortcomings through the rejection of even an unworthy applicant.

Diespiter is next to speak and takes a similar approach. Since Claudius is related to the divine Augustus, and since he is himself responsible for the deification of Livia, Augustus's wife and Claudius's grandmother, he has the right connections; his great intelligence (ironically meant) and his similarity to Romulus, with whom he can "eat boiled beets" (9.5: "feruentia rapa uorare"), provide the right qualifications. Therefore Claudius should be made a god, just as anyone else who was made a god before his time *in perfect accordance with the law* (9.5: "ita uti ante eum quis optimo iure factus sit"), and the whole affair should be added to Ovid's *Metamorphoses*.[28] In other words, the already excessive granting of divine honors and Claudius's questionable intelligence make him an ideal citizen of this heaven.

This is all comically intended, and Weinreich has pointed out the similarities between this scene and various divine councils in the works of Lucian.[29] But the crucial point is that, in fact, Claudius is thoroughly worthy of this heaven, as these Roman divinities are all sorry excuses for godhead themselves. Janus is an equivocator, looking both forward and backward (9.2: "homo, quantum uia sua fert, qui semper videt ἅμα πρόσσω καὶ ὀπίσσω"); Diespiter is a usurer and a seller of citizenship perks (9.4: "nummulariolus. hoc quaestu se sustinebat: uendere ciuitatulas solebat"); Romulus is not the great founder of Rome but a country bumpkin who eats boiled beets.[30] As the voting proceeds, Claudius seems to be on the point of victory (9.6); the active support of Hercules nearly wins the day, as he promises to return the favor of ballots cast on behalf of his protégé.[31] But this Hercules is the Hercules found in Greek comedy and in the divine councils of Lucian;[32] his own well-being depends upon Claudius's apotheosis, and this can only imply that if Claudius is denied a place in heaven, Hercules' own right to be there will be drawn into question. They are both fools, and as a fool Claudius has every right to expect deification.

Augustus's long speech (10–11) is the centerpiece of the *Apocolocyntosis* and records in indignant detail the various outrages, most of which touch on the members of Augustus' family, which make Claudius's deification an insult to heaven.[33] The criticism is deserved. But note the comedy in having a deified mortal (whose own right to heaven has been tacitly called into question through its association with that of Tiberius [1.2] and Livia [9.4]) reject the opinion of bona fide gods in the name of divinity and oppose the solicitations of another deified mortal (Hercules) to prevent yet another apotheosis. Augustus is more noble than the gods. The humor of the entire sequence lies in this double view of Claudius: according to divine standards, he should be divine; according to mortal standards, he should be banished from heaven; the most elevated view of divinity is put in the mouth of an ex-mortal, while the basest view is that of gods who have always been in heaven.

A similar double vision holds in Claudius's punishment in Hades. Two things act to diminish the moral force of the condemnation that Claudius deserves and receives for his crimes. The first is the manner in which he is convicted. Pedo Pompeius attacks Claudius before Aeacus's tribunal, but Claudius's counsel is given no chance to respond (14.2):

> Counsel for the defense was just about to begin to respond. Aeacus, a most just man, forbade him and condemned Claudius after hearing only one side of the case. He said: "If you suffer what you have yourself done, it would be straight justice." A great silence followed. All were amazed at the strangeness of the thing; they denied that such a thing had ever been done before.[34]

Claudius is condemned as he himself condemned others; this is poetic justice, but the fact remains that the most just judge of the underworld acts unjustly to secure justice, and that the denizens of Hades are shocked at his actions. It is hard not to feel some sympathy for Claudius, both because of his unfair trial and because Claudius realizes his own guilt in such matters (14.3): "Claudio magis iniquum uidebatur quam nouum" ("To Claudius it seemed more unjust than unparalleled").[35]

Second, the manner of Claudius's punishment reveals another division between corrupt, divine sentiments and upright, mortal ones. A debate on Claudius's punishment follows the brief trial: some think that Claudius should take the place of Tantalus or Ixion, but the idea is rejected, for thus Claudius too could hope for eventual release. Claudius is finally condemned to play dice with a bottomless dice cup; his fruitless labor is to remind us of the Danaids and of Sisyphus (cf. 15.1.7, in the poem describing Claudius playing dice in this fashion), and the appearance of unattainable pleasure is reminiscent of Tantalus.[36] We expect then that Claudius will remain eternally punished in this travesty of eternal torment.

But this is not the case. After only a brief time at his dice cup, Claudius remarkably becomes a contested piece of property rather than a condemned sinner. He is claimed as a slave by Caligula, who had often beaten him in he world above; if we follow Eden's text, Aeacus then remands Claudius to Caligula's custody, and Caligula proceeds to hand him over to his freedman Menander, to serve as his law clerk (15.2).[37] Claudius does not serve in this capacity during intermissions from his other punishment;[38] rather, Claudius's sentence has been commuted, despite the popular desire that Claudius never be given a reprieve. Commentators speak hopefully of the final punishment as a sort of ultimate debasement, appropriate in that Claudius is the slave of his freedmen in Hades as he was on earth,[39] but Claudius is clearly receiving a lighter sentence. The collusion of Caligula, worst of emperors, and of Aeacus, the just judge who operates by unjust means, suggests that justice is not being served.

Just as Claudius was deemed unworthy of heaven, so too is he unworthy of hell. In both places, the human population operates with a higher standard of decency than the divine one. Claudius does and does not belong in heaven and hell. Because Claudius does not fit in, because the divine apparatus is not capable of handling his peculiarities, because his example points out the absurdity of this very Roman afterworld, we see in Claudius the fantastic experimenter of Menippean satire. Through his experiences, we see the corruption of the places that ponder his merits and his destiny. This shifts the force of the criticism in the *Apocolocyntosis* away from Claudius himself and toward the system that allowed the apotheosis of such a fool. Claudius proves the inadequacy of apotheosis as practiced and approved by Roman political convention because he is a fool and not a hero or a criminal; the fool that reveals the defect of theories that try to encompass and define the entirety of life is the Menippean hero much more than the lampoonist's villain.

CLAUDIUS THE COLOCYNTH

As the Greek proverb has it, kings and fools obey unwritten laws, meaning that neither is accountable to higher authorities for his actions.[40] Seneca alludes to this at the beginning of the *Apocolocyntosis* when he says that Claudius proved the adage true that one ought to be born a king or a fool (1.1). Seneca suppresses the reason behind the saying,[41] but it underlies all of the subsequent narration. As a king, Claudius enjoyed unlimited power; as a fool, he avoids the consequences of his crimes, ultimately finding himself in a queer sort of limbo as a freedman's clerk. But Claudius has not escaped scot-free, and limbo is an unsatisfying place. How has Claudius proved the rule that one should be a king *or* a fool when he is a king *and* a fool? We cannot say that he reaps a double reward, for the reward is hard to find in the *Apocolocyntosis*.[42] I suggest that Claudius proves it negatively. The afterworld in the *Apocolocyntosis* seems to treat heroes and villains fairly equally: we hear of Tiberius, Drusilla, Livia, and Augustus in heaven, while Caligula, denied heavenly honors, is a friend of the judge Aeacus below. Had Claudius just been a murderous king, he might have enjoyed the freedom that Caligula obviously enjoys in the underworld; had he been just a fool, he might have found a niche in heaven. But by being a king and a fool, a murderer and an innocent, he can find no place at all.

What then are we to make of the title *Apocolocyntosis?* Claudius has been transformed, not literally but figuratively, into a bottle gourd.[43] It should in some way point to his unique status in the next world; after all, he is the only one ever to be removed from heaven, "from where they say no one returns" (11.6), a phrase that for anyone else would be applied to the world below.[44] The bottle gourd is not to be taken as an emblem of foolishness, for Claudius was already a fool and is not transformed into one; I see no application for possible sexual overtones.[45] Eden considers the emptiness of the dried bottle gourd its most salient characteristic; but Claudius is not transformed into something empty-headed, which would only be foolishness again. I think that Claudius, rejected by earth, heaven, and hell, has been turned into nothing, into an emptiness. We may call the work *The Nullification of Claudius,* though we may gain something in theological indecency were we to translate, *The Exinanition.*[46]

It is at this point that we may make our claims for the political implications of the *Apocolocyntosis.*[47] When Menippean satire seeks to devalue the extravagant search for truth, it makes its fantasies reveal what was known all along on earth. Fantasy and the imagination do not describe unusual worlds; the Roman heaven and Roman hell of the *Apocolocyntosis* look surprisingly like the Roman real world, where virtue and vice exist side by side. The real interest of the *Apocolocyntosis* is not in finding an appropriate punishment for Claudius, and the claim could be made that he is in fact not doing anything significantly different in Hades from what he did all along while alive. He acts as a petty bureaucrat, under the thumb of his freedmen. The point is that he is now out of the way and out of sight; the Saturnalia are over, and the world returns to normal with the death of Claudius and breathes a collective sigh of relief.[48] What is celebrated here is a very small sort of utopian longing: the world does not require justice to improve it, only the death of the anomalous Claudius. There is a celebration of a flawed status quo, for the monster's reign can now be safely viewed as a comedy of horrors, and the simple fact of Death is the only answer needed to the problem that was Claudius. The impending reign of Nero seems to be a promise of better things, but we are assured only of a return to normalcy.

In this light, the *Apocolocyntosis* stakes out for itself very little political ground; what it says of the nature of Roman society, politics, and real life is depressingly limited; there is more of resignation than enthusiasm.[49] The great example of proper political behavior is Augustus, the ruler whom the awful Claudius claimed to emulate while alive; but Wolf concludes that Augustus's disgust with Claudius, expressed in the phrase "I am ashamed of empire," (10.2: "pudet imperii") has much wider applications as well, and that Nero's future reign is painted here in blood-red colors.[50] Skepticism is evident in its very plot: Claudius does not deserve deification, yet deification means very little, and there is no respect for true justice in the Roman afterworld. There is no need to claim that this is a savage indictment of the Roman order; Seneca's self-parody—expressed in fun had at the expense of his own tragedies and of Hercules, that paradigm of Stoic virtue—ensures a wider scope of playful humor.[51]

What makes the *Apocolocyntosis* difficult to pin down is its double perspective. From one point of view, fictional and severe, the *Apocolocyntosis* tells of Claudius's unworthiness of heaven (cf. the speech of Augustus); from another, factual and lighthearted, it takes Claudius's apotheosis as a fact and examines what sort of heaven and hell would be consistent with such a deity (cf. the speeches of Janus and Diespiter). The latter view is ultimately prominent, and with good reason. Claudius was responsible neither for his foolishness nor for his death nor for his apotheosis. Nero and his court conferred divine honors upon Claudius as a sort of joke; very similar was the famous eulogy, written by Seneca and read by Nero, which praised the intelligence of the deceased before a laughing audience (Tacitus *Ann.* 13.3). It is unlikely that such honors were bestowed by people who took the ritual of apotheosis very seriously. Even if we grant that the festive occasion of Claudius's death would have sanctioned humor at the expense of things otherwise taken seriously,[52] the humor of the *Apocolocyntosis* still turns upon the comic portrayal of apotheosis in a work intended for a court audience willing to abuse this tradition in real life.

Suetonius says that Claudius admitted in a number of works that he affected stupidity in order to survive the reign of Caligula (*Div. Claud.* 38); but he was not believed, and a work with the Greek title μωρῶν ἐπανάστασις or "The Elevation of Fools" made the rounds, whose point was that stupidity could not be affected. The *Apocolocyn-*

tosis is not a work with such limited goals of insult and vituperation; it rather allows a moving cipher to reveal a more general Roman corruption. What is fascinating about its place in the history of Menippean satire is that it ultimately asserts the value of the flawed world to which all but Claudius may return. Roman heaven and hell are meaningless. Rather than set us down in the real world with a message from beyond as the *Necyomantia* does, the *Apocolocyntosis* documents the end of a topsy-turvy time, and a return to the way things used to be, a world purged of one great unpleasantness.[53] So does Seneca toy with the Varronian opposition of *tunc* and *nunc*. The *Apocolocyntosis* is prospective: regardless of the nuance to be given to the portrayal of Nero and his coming reign, whether it is hailed as a restoration of Augustan principles or dreaded as a continuation of a vicious system, it speaks of the world that we are to live in despite what we imagine the other world may have to offer. Later Menippean satire will wrestle with this possibility. Does the failure to conquer the Next World make the narrator an inhabitant of an everyday world of greater importance and broader horizons, a theme to be found in the Alexander Romance and in twelfth-century Menippean satire; or does it create a narrator, frustrated by a lack of transcendence, who does not know how to live in this world at all?[54] The greatest representative of the latter position is Boethius, who inherits the considerable late classical Menippean tradition of Martianus Capella and Fulgentius. What will come to full term there is embryonic in the *Apocolocyntosis*.

Chapter Six

PETRONIUS

ALTHOUGH the *Satyricon* is generally admitted in some sense to belong to, or be related to, the genre of Menippean satire, the work's very uniqueness seems to make a generic label unnecessary, if not positively misleading. The term has consequently fallen into some disrepute. The recently discovered papyrus fragments of Greek prosimetric fiction (see Appendix A) have been sufficient for some to claim that Menippean satire is no longer relevant to the discussion; Slater calls the work a novel but follows Bakhtin in denying a generic status to that term.[1] It would be glib to call the *Satyricon* a Menippean satire merely by virtue of its prose and verse; or on the strength of its abundant interest in literary parody (romance, epic poetry, the *Odyssey*, picaresque fiction, Platonic symposium, satire, Milesian tale); or because what Bakhtin calls the genre of the menippea is one of the ancient precedents for his modern polyphonic novel.[2] Perry is not terribly wrong when he assigns to Roman fiction in general an agglutinative tendency, an assembling of scenes, events, anecdotes, and episodes without tremendous interest in their logical coherence.[3] Something of the text's eccentricities may be viewed as the result of the intersection of the Menippean genre and the peculiarities of Roman fiction. Yet the term *Menippean satire* is still a meaningful one. In what follows I make no attempt to summarize either the action of the *Satyricon* or the wealth of perceptive critical opinion upon it, but only to demonstrate how the relatively well-known *Satyricon* belongs to the genre in the sense developed in the previous chapters.[4]

The thematic interests of the *Satyricon*, as laid out by Slater, are absolutely typical of the ends and desires of Menippean satire, and its resistance to coherent interpretation makes sense in specific traditions of this particular genre.[5] What makes the *Satyricon* a Menippean satire is its critical dimension: the narrator, as many have pointed out, is an academic critic, a hypocrite and a fool who passively observes the decadent and fantastic scenes and society around him and who unites them through his wholly inadequate and comic attempts to understand them. Its content is that of Roman satire: understood as a satiric text in the traditional sense, its critical views of literary, religious, and social beliefs and practices of the early Roman Empire have made it a valuable historical document.[6] But its medium is a series of incongruous clashes of low-life characters and the literary models with which they so pompously inflate themselves.[7] If the *Satyricon* parodies any specific literary genre at all (instead of using parody as a means of characterization, a point nicely made by Slater), that genre is verse satire. A useful example of this in terms of plot is found in the *Cena;* if Horace's *Cena Nasidieni* (*S.* 2.8) lies behind Trimalchio's feast, the transformation of the host into a character whose vices are affectionately presented, and the narrator into a character whose vices are never far away from his observations, effectively overthrows Horace's indignation.[8] My suspicion is that this parody of satire has its origin in the innovations of Varro's *Menippeans*. But this is only to restate the primary problem of the *Satyricon's* genre: how have comic criticism and parody of satire been made episodic?

CONTENT AND CHARACTERIZATION

The *Satyricon* is a first-person narrative, related by Encolpius. There is a difference between Encolpius the narrator and Encolpius the actor; in the course of the *Satyricon,* he retains a certain "restrained objectivity" in his comments about the other characters, while becoming rather less rhetorical in his comments about himself.[9] He is at an ironic distance from the other actors, whose actions he can never fully comprehend, in this tale of fraud, deceit, faithlessness, and mind-boggling coincidence; at the same time his opinions of himself are typically amusing, and often self-parodic. Consider the famous elegiac poem at 132.15:

> Ye censors, why do you look at me with furrowed brows and condemn a work [*opus*] of novel naiveté? It is the happy joy of pure speech that laughs, and an honest tongue that tells of what the people do. Who is ignorant of intercourse and the joys of Venus? Who forbids the limbs to warm themselves in a steamy bed? Epicurus himself, the Father of Truth, bids the wise to love, and says that this is the goal of life.[10]

Here, context is everything. Encolpius has just tried to castrate himself, in frustration at his impotence (his actions described in a wonderful parody of Vergilian epic);[11] he declaims against his penis, which refuses, in a cento of Vergilian verses, to respond;[12] he repents of his literary impropriety for speaking of a part of the body which men "of greater moment" ("seuerioris notae," 132.12) never even mention; he argues with himself and indignantly lists the various parts of the body which one can name and curse, wondering why the penis should be any exception; and finally turns to the audience to say that the *Satyricon* records honestly what normal people do. As to the question, "Who is ignorant of intercourse and the joys of Venus?" the answer is clearly Encolpius, who has now twice proved impotent with Circe, and whose homosexual amours (to the exception of a single success with Giton at *Sat.* 11) have known similar difficulties throughout the extant narrative.[13]

It is even more remarkable that the author of the *Satyricon* intrudes here, and here alone in the text as we have it, to identify himself with his narrator.[14] The *opus* can only be the written text of the *Satyricon;* and we are told nowhere else that Encolpius is the author of it. It is not necessarily the case that first-person narratives speak of how the narrator wrote down the words that are before the reader. Whether or not we can read this as Petronius making fun of himself, it is certainly the case that the narrator cannot be trusted with the inter-pretation and understanding of what he sees. We cannot extract from the poem a serious defense of sexual realism or of the Petro-nian style.[15] The sexual matters of the *Satyricon* are prurient and, particularly in the scenes involving children, degenerate, if not actu-ally pornographic; the matters to which the author alludes in the poem can hardly be palliated by a specious citation of Epicurus.[16] Nor do the Vergilian parodies that precede the poem constitute nor-mal discourse. In Sullivan's paraphrase, the question asked by the author/narrator is: "No one is unaware of the important place sex has in ordinary life. Does anyone take a moral stand against harmless and natural sexual enjoyment and comfort?" But where is ordinary life, here or elsewhere in the *Satyricon,* or harmless and natural sex-ual enjoyment?[17] The poem's claim to honest reporting of normal life in the work is at extreme variance with the facts.

Encolpius does not see the difference between his unnatural ac-tions (including his unnatural way of expressing himself, in poetic parody and moralistic epigram) and the theories of life and literature which he expounds. This is a constant source of humor throughout the *Satyricon.*[18] Rather than criticize their behavior or their literary excesses, Petronius allows his characters to clothe immorality in ten-dentious and versified moralizing. The absence of an authorial point of view that would lend some consistency of interpretation to the satirical topics that are constantly to the fore (*captatio,* banquets of the nouveau riche, aggressive women, sexual enormity)[19] goes hand in hand with this. We need not wonder what attitude Petronius has toward his characters;[20] they are chameleons, spouting new theories in new situations in attempts to disguise their own multifarious short-comings. Encolpius is, as Coffey says, "the purveyor of ready-made opinions."[21] Petronius presents the comedy of hypocritical moralists and laughs at their feeble attempts to impose a moral and artistic order upon the facts of experience.

THE GENRE OF THE SATYRICON

The case has been made that it is not necessary to assign the *Satyricon* to one of the particular genres of ancient prose fiction; it can certainly be read and enjoyed as a novel. But the question of genre has an importance beyond the historical question of the development of prose fiction; we should like to know what conventions are invoked, whether parodied or not, in order to gauge its comic devices. I accept Slater's point that the various genres strewn through the pages of the book are there not as parodies per se but as devices for characterization; but the invocation of Bakhtin's heteroglossia and polyphony need not deny that there is a framework in which these voices are heard, and a particular structure of which the characters can make no sense. The romance certainly has its claim on the *Satyricon,* and as the *Odyssey* is the ultimate ancestor of the romance the romance form could serve as a convenient explanation for the explicit presence of the *Odyssey* in the *Satyricon.* We could speak of a parody of the romance, with a substitution of homosexual for het-erosexual love, a triangle for a couple, realism for idealism, a charac-ter like Eumolpus for the wise old man such as Heliodorus's Ca-lasiris, a hero running away from rather than trying to discover his destiny, and so on. Quite a few typical elements of the romance would remain: the immature and weak-willed hero who contem-plates suicide, *Scheintod,* shipwreck, the hero's impending trail for murder. Some elements are not implied, though one can say that fragments make anything possible: for example, the reunion of fam-ily members. But the structure of the *Satyricon* is clearly episodic, the main characters disappearing for long stretches while fools parade across the stage: Trimalchio is the prime example, but Eumolpus's poetry is not to be forgotten.

Whatever the original extent of the *Satyricon,* it is far longer than its Menippean antecedents, and we need an explanation of this. It does not seem to be a serialization of Varronian satires, nor does it follow Seneca's lead in uniting distinct Menippean plots into a coherent Menippean whole. I would appeal to the freely expandable picaresque fiction, to which Apuleius's *Metamorphoses* also belongs.[22] Encolpius is as much an implausible critic of the wide range of the low life as Lucius is, who listens to such amazing things as the story of Cupid and Psyche and who suffers so grotesquely at the hands of the wicked boy driver. Perry's mean suspicions about the *Metamorphoses*—that the redemptive plot that culminates in Lucius's transformation in Book 11 is mere window dressing that cannot obscure the true purpose of the book, to tell a series of funny stories—could explain the *Odyssey*'s presence in the *Satyricon* as well: a grandiose frame that seeks to ennoble the Milesian content.[23] Apuleius too shows how the romance can enter into the picaresque: the romantic view of the world cannot consist with the low-life view, and when elements of the romance obtrude they are disposed of in most unromantic ways (consider the conclusion of the tragic story of Charite and Tlepolemus at *Met.* 8.1–14, the frame that surrounds the tale of Cupid and Psyche). If the picaresque is allied to satire, the romantic view of the world can be one of its targets. And it is certainly distinctive to the *Satyricon* that its narrator and main characters are critics of society, far exceeding Apuleius's Lucius in the extent, frequency, and virulence of their criticism. If the peculiar critical element in the *Satyricon* alienates it from the picaresque, then we may judge the *Satyricon* to be a picaresque novel on which the Menippean genre has been imposed, much as *Daphnis and Chloe* is a romance on which the pastoral genre has been imposed. A debilitated and weak-willed critic is a parodic substitute for the resourceful *picaro,* and the romance is one of the things held up to ridicule.

VARRONIAN MORALIZING IN THE SATYRICON

In his book on humor in the ancient novelists, Anderson makes the excellent observation that in the *Satyricon* moral criticism is closely bound to literary criticism.[24] The heroes of the *Satyricon* are vagabond scholars, always willing and able to unburden themselves of opinions on literature and morals, and these opinions are always contradicted by context and by the lives of those who pronounce them. Agamemnon and Encolpius decry moral degeneration and the decline of literary standards and scholastic education in their discussion of the vices of declamation (chap. 1–5), but both of them are thoroughly corrupt and are seen declaiming against declamation.[25] Trimalchio, in whom the pretensions of learning are most obvious, delivers a poem on the evils of luxurious dining (55.6, said to be from Publilius Syrus).[26] Eumolpus calls for loftier tones and greater moral emphasis in poetry as he prefaces his *Troiae Halosis* (88.2–10) and *Bellum Civile* (118.1–6); but the poems reveal the bankruptcy of his thought as clearly as the scenes in Croton show the bankruptcy of his soul.[27]

Outside of context, such exclamations may seem to be serious commentary, enlivened by the excitement of personal conviction. Consider Eumolpus on the topic of contemporary intellectual and moral decay (88.6–8):

> But we, sunk in wine and prostitutes, dare not even to take cognizance of arts already prepared for us, but, as carpers at antiquity, we learn and teach only vices. Where is dialectic? Where is astronomy? Where that most elevated [?] path to wisdom? Who ever came into a temple and made a prayer for the achievement of eloquence? Who, for the attainment of the font of philosophy? They do not even seek sound mind or sound health, but immediately, before they touch its threshold, some promise a donation, if they could but see a wealthy neighbor dead; others, if they could but dig up a treasure; others, if they attain three hundred thousand sesterces, and live to enjoy it.

All this rings hollow in context, however. Eumolpus is a mediocre poet, superficially educated, and enough in love with money to make any of those final prayers his own. But the rationale of such dyspepsia would seem familiar from Varro: the longing for old-time standards of morality, religion, and education in a thoroughly unworthy preacher. This is not a travesty of Varronian moralizing, as Walsh would have it,[28] but a clear extension of it.

I would explain the *Satyricon* as follows. It is an elaborate joke on the commonplace assertion of the Silver Age (though it is hardly confined to that age) that moral degeneration leads to literary degeneration.[29] Not only does the work feature immoral characters who speak in pompous verse and verse parody, but it is, in and of itself, a degenerate literary form devoted to retailing the immoralities of people who pretend to pass moral judgments on the action. It is inconceivable that Encolpius or Eumolpus would approve of the *Satyricon*, which has none of the loftiness of the ancient greats to whom they turn for inspiration,[30] nor any proper moral tone. Menippean satire, which is fundamentally improper and unfit for the straightforward presentation of an instructive point of view, would be anathema to such moral theorists of literature. Petronius has the last laugh in the *Satyricon*. He has imprisoned his false preachers in a work they would roundly condemn, could they but see that they are a part of it; when Encolpius calls it a work of "novel naiveté," he shows he has no idea of what it is at all.

Running through the *Satyricon* is a parody of Seneca's moralizing pomposity; this has been well documented by Sullivan and has survived skeptical counterarguments.[31] This is not quite as remarkable as it seems at first, given the tragic Seneca's self-parody in the *Apocolocyntosis*. And true to Menippean satire, the *Satyricon* does not comment upon such theories and moralizings in order to suggest other ways of thinking about literature and behavior, but rather concentrates on the incongruity of the life and theories of its preachers. The *Satyricon* is a moralists' brawl; it is not a polemical text and has no pretensions of profundity.[32] In its delicious satire of those who have important things to say, the *Satyricon* shows its Cynic origins, and characterizes preachers as the true social evil.

An adjunct to Petronius's distaste for moralists is his affection for people who have nothing to say. Trimalchio, for example, bears the stamp of Varro's Roman Cynics, the *caue canem* mosaic in his entry hall echoing the placard of the corrupt Cynic host of the *Eumenides* (F 143). Trimalchio seems to have every imaginable vice, and loves to moralize about contemporary degeneration and to parade what passes for learning to him; but he is so obviously gauche and wrong in everything that he says and does that the reader's sympathy is ultimately on his side and not with those hypocritical scholars who eat his food and laugh behind his back.[33] So too the speeches of the freedmen in the *Cena:* in their honest admiration of Trimalchio's wealth, interest in gladiatorial games and drunkenness, love of gossip and complaints about modern times, their words have a much truer ring and a much more sympathetic appeal than the hopelessly structured poses of the intellectuals who overhear them.[34] Coffey calls the *Cena* "a completely negative symposium at which nothing of cultural significance is said."[35] It is a judgment easily extensible to the work as a whole.

IT IS DIFFICULT to speak of the indebtedness of one fragmentary author to another; to claim specific origins for Seneca and Petronius in Varro, especially in the elusive matters of theme and intellectual self-parody, is impossible.[36] Linguistic connections are tenuous.[37] Differences in topic are obvious; Seneca's interests are more personal and political, and Petronius is interested not in the parody of encyclopedic knowledge but in the parody of contemporary moralizing. There are enough verbal parallels between Seneca and Petronius to suggest that Petronius may even have profited by the example of the moralist he toys with in the course of the *Satyricon*.[38] Yet we may certainly speak in general terms about the direct influence of Varro on the Roman Menippean satirists of the first century A.D. Varro's frequent use of a Cynic, comic Hercules is a likely inspiration for Seneca's travesty of the Stoic Hercules; and the various plot elements of the *Apocolocyntosis* can be paralleled piecemeal in the fragments of the *Menippeans*.[39] Petronius fashions a parody of intellectuals, just as Varro did, and the love of the trivial, so obvious in the comic characters of the *Cena*, may owe something specific to Varro. A number of Varro's fragments seem to show less pretentious people speaking of their own interests in matters of cultural and philosophical importance—for example, the man who feared that if everyone was buried in honey, as Democritus was supposed to have recommended, mead would be unaffordable;[40] or the man who complains about the great number of gluttons in Rome because they make it difficult for him to find a decent thrush in the marketplace.[41]

Varro, Seneca, and Petronius form a special triad in the history of Menippean satire. They are not the only practitioners of the form, as the handbooks of Roman satire would have it, but represent a transformation of Menippean satire into a parody of Roman satire. The Cynic parody of preaching found in Menippus has become the parody of authors who presume to attack contemporary social problems. In Seneca, the search for justice has been travestied, and the world has been improved only by the elimination of Claudius; no one is called to improvement. Petronius's distinction, beyond his length and his absence from his narrative (which deprives the reader of the moral satisfaction of hearing an author say that his tongue is in his cheek), is his thoroughgoing insistence on depicting moralists themselves as the primary social evil. In this context, Seneca and Petronius illustrate one path that Varro offered to his followers, one that is, as far as antiquity is concerned, a dead end. Lucian's Menippean satires are not topical but general, and the problems of the nature of true knowledge and where it may be found come increasingly to the fore. But these two texts do have repercussions in late antiquity. Seneca makes clear that the world itself is left behind when heaven fails; and Petronius's experiments in polymetry are nowhere more in evidence than in Boethius, who also combines the Menippean genre and another one (philosophical dialogue) in an attempt to transcend its limits, and to make verse the vehicle for another kind of thought, and other kinds of characterization.

We now proceed from fragments to whole texts and to later authors, both Greek and Roman, who look back over a gulf of time to other traditions of Menippean satire and who interpret them according to the spirit of different ages. Lucian follows the general lead of Menippus himself; Martianus, Fulgentius, Ennodius, and Boethius walk down Varro's other, encyclopedic, path and are sensitive to the nuances and ironic possibilities of the comic genre they inherit and develop still further; Julian manages to combine Greek and Roman traditions. As we come to these later authors, we need not only regret what has been lost of their predecessors but should try to see the influence of great authors in different times and circumstances. The theories that must be questioned and the human behavior that must be seen from some great height have changed greatly from Hellenistic times to the early Roman Empire; and they shall continue to change as we move through the Second Sophistic into late classical times.

III. DIVERGING GREEK TRADITIONS

Chapter Seven

LUCIAN

LUCIAN has recently come back into his own. The Western world grew up with Lucian, and though it may not recapture the love the Renaissance had for him, it now at least takes seriously Lucian's comic fantasies of heaven and hell and their literary forms—novelties and innovations against which Lucian, in deference to the sensibilities of the Second Sophistic, felt compelled to defend his literary propriety.[1] Lucian is a virtuoso, whose commitment to the imitation of the Greek classics may be more properly considered his theme than any actual subject matter.[2] But as Branham contends in his valuable book, we ought to consider why such rhetorical virtuosity had such a contemporary, as well as a lasting, appeal; Lucian is in fact an experimenter, playing with a vast number of traditions.[3] Lucian is not just ringing the changes on well-worn topics to pronounce a predictable moral but is often playing with the idea of conventionality itself, the ability of his narrators to deliver a commonplace truth and of his own text to convey it.[4] Not just a debunker, he appeals to the vitality of the classical tradition to force his audience to see it in different ways; Lucian is the seriocomic author who understands how to use humor to make a subversive point.

Our task here is to assess Lucian's position in the history of Menippean satire. The comic dialogues all betray, to varying degrees, the influence of Menippus, whose provocative use of fantasy, literary impropriety, and parodic preaching has now been established.[5] But we must not confuse what is typical of Lucian as a whole with the peculiarities of his two Menippean satires, the *Icaromenippus* and the *Necyomantia*, the first of our texts to survive entire. I resist the idea that Menippus is a mask for Lucian himself, for although Lucian may understand the use of the Cynic *chreia* as a device for the assault on traditional proprieties, we have no evidence that Menippus himself did so, and Lucian does not characterize him as a Socratic *eiron* in the satires. The possible profundities of Cynicism are replaced by dramatic and fantastic imposture, and Menippus stalks the pages of Lucian as a personification of the abstraction of Cynicism.[6] Further, Lucian makes fun of Menippus: the *Dialogues of the Dead,* to which I shall return, constitutes a Menippean satire broken up into thirty little pieces, and sends Menippus on a voyage to a comic and impossible underworld from which he shall not return and in which his Cynic wisdom ultimately does him very little good. There is I think always an ironic distance between Lucian and Menippus, more than Lucian's typical refusal to be identified with any of the sources of literary tradition and authority with which he capriciously aligns himself: Menippus is a mocker, and Lucian shows us the comedy of the uneasy alliance of mockery of philosophical absurdity and the enthusiastic embrace of fantastic means to prove such things absurd.[7] What follows is an analysis of Lucian's Menippean satires, in which we seek to corroborate the view of Menippus advanced in Chapter 3, illustrate the intricacies of self-destructive fantasies similar to those of the *Apocolocyntosis*, and show Lucian at work refashioning Menippus's *Necyia* according to a good understanding of what is essential to the genre as a whole. It may still seem that I unduly restrict the number of Lucian's Menippean satires; some Menippean satires refashioned and transformed as dialogues will be discussed at the conclusion.

NECYOMANTIA *AND* ICAROMENIPPUS

The *Necyomantia* is commonly regarded as bearing the closest relation of any of Lucian's works to a work of Menippus;[8] in this case, the model is Menippus's *Necyia*. The title in its full form suggests, by its appeal to the Cynic, direct dependence: Μένιππος ἢ Νεκυομαντεία ("Menippus, or The Consultation of the Dead"). On the other hand, the title Ἰκαρομένιππος ἢ Ὑπερνέφελος ("Menippus the New Icarus, or Over the Rainbow") implies a variation on Menippean material, and it is likely that the *Icaromenippus* is Lucian's independent reworking of the motifs of the *Necyia*, here transferred to a heavenly voyage. As a variation on the *Necyomantia*, the *Icaromenippus* draws on a wider range of Menippean motifs and may be seen as the distillation of all those themes and motifs that Lucian considers to be most characteristic of Menippean satire. Menippus's *Letters* may lie behind the decrees read in heaven (and on the moon) against the natural philosophers; and the two-tiered construction of the *Icaromenippus*, with its comic *catascopia* from the moon en route to an interview in heaven, seems closer to the potentialities of the genre (just as the *Apocolocyntosis* is) than is its Menippean source. *Necyomantia* takes pride of place, but *Icaromenippus* shows a sophisticated rethinking and reworking of the genre on Lucian's part.[9]

Both pieces are a fantastic narration delivered by a comic and questionable narrator to a stolid interlocutor who is slow to grasp the import of what he hears.[10] In this Menippean framework may be found many of Lucian's own literary signatures: the insistence on Attic elegance of speech, free play with a wide range of literary traditions, the use of simile, moral pronouncements on the goodness of the simple life, travesty of the Olympian gods, and bitter proclamations of the vileness of human nature. But it is the interplay of Menippean fantasy and earnestness, and the tension between propriety and impropriety, that give these works their brilliance and their point. As the *Necyomantia* and the *Icaromenippus* parallel each other nearly scene for scene, I shall treat them simultaneously. Their variations may be illuminated by their comparison. Their conclusions will be considered separately.

Introduction (**Necyomantia *1–2;* Icaromenippus *1–3*). In both, Menippus is recently returned from a fantastic voyage, from Hades or from Olympus. The interlocutors regard him suspiciously, and he is comically depicted. In *Necyomantia* he is dressed in Heracles' lionskin and Odysseus's cap and carries Orpheus's lyre. This is suggestive of the attire attributed to Menippus by the *Suda* (see Chapter 3). We are told later (*Nec.* 8) that the dress was intended as a disguise, so that Menippus could pretend to be one of those who saw the underworld and returned; had he appeared in his own person or given his true name, he would have been a subject in the realm of Hades. Further, he speaks in verse, and that not in quotations (Lucian's usual practice) but in actual speech made up of bits of the great poets; he explains this as a natural consequence of just having seen Homer and Euripides. Metrical speech overpowers him and has taken control.[11] Both dress and speech establish the narrator as absurd.

There is no verse in the introduction of *Icaromenippus* and in general very little verse throughout. Here, Menippus is identified as comic because he is lost in thought, mumbling about interplanetary distances; he knows that his friend will think that he is speaking nonsense.[12] The interlocutor thinks that Menippus is relating a dream and mocks him, asking if he was a new Ganymede or where he got such a long ladder. Menippus acknowledges the insult: "It's clear you've been mocking me all along." Here too we have a comic narrator and an obtuse interlocutor, but there is much more respectability here than in *Necyomantia:* no obvious physical absurdity, no use of verse, and a narrator who almost seems sympathetic as he answers

barbed and unkind questions. Propriety and fantasy exist side by
side in these Menippean satires, but there is perhaps more of the
former at this point in *Icaromenippus*, and more of the latter in *Necyomantia*.

Decision to Tell of the Entire Journey (**Necyomantia 2, Icaromenippus 3**). In both works, Menippus is about to explain what he learned
in the other world but decides (or is persuaded) to give all of the
preliminary details. In *Necyomantia*, the narrator is going to reveal
the decree passed against the rich in the underworld, but the interlocutor begs him to tell his tale from the beginning; we do not reach
the promised decree until paragraph 19, at which point the narrator
admits that he had lost sight of his true purpose.[13] In *Icaromenippus*,
Menippus stops after telling how he took a vulture's wing and an
eagle's wing for his flight, and prefers of his own accord to tell his
willing audience of all that went before.

At this point, both pieces are trying to set the narrator's adventures
in a comic frame, and thus to call into question whatever knowledge
he may claim to have derived from them. The comic dress in *Necyomantia* and the reference to the bird's wings in *Icaromenippus* are only
a part of this frame. More important is the attempt to justify the
coming morals, to explain by what right and authority Menippus
may make his pronouncements. The corroboration of a fantastic
story by such an appeal to detail and a pretense to reporting is reminiscent of the comic intrusions of the historian/narrator in the *Apocolocyntosis*. But note a difference between the two satires: in *Icaromenippus*, Menippus does not need persuasion to tell his story, but
presents the process by which he gained his information as of equal
importance to the lessons he will learn, which are not yet alluded to.
Here, Lucian is not drawing attention to easily extractable morals so
much as to the means by which such are obtained, and more so than
in *Necyomantia* the humor turns on the implications of fantasy for the
meaning of the story told.

The Reasons for the Journey (**Necyomantia 3–5, Icaromenippus
4–10**). In both pieces, intellectual dissatisfaction with the world and
with the philosophers' contradictory views of it lead to a desire to get
to the truth directly. It is a theme common throughout Lucian;[14]
what distinguishes it are the fantastic means sought to reach this
truth. *Icaromenippus* devotes much more space to this section of the
story than does *Necyomantia* and gives at first the impression that
Lucian is merely trotting out at great length a favorite cliché, the

contradictions of the philosophers. But what is at work here is a greater interest in the comic possibilities of the *proof* of the intellectual advantages of antidogmatism.

In *Necyomantia,* the narrator's confusion is largely moral. After having noted the discrepancies between the poets' stories about the gods and the legal norms of human behavior, he goes to the philosophers to find out how to live. Their disagreements convince him that the life of the ordinary person who minds his own business is best; golden, in fact (4): χρυσοῦν ἀπέδειξαν οὗτοι τὸν τῶν ἰδιωτῶν τοῦτον βίον. All the philosophers differ on the nature of the good life and of the cosmos; further, a satiric commonplace, their lives do not agree with their moral principles. Menippus finally realizes his ignorance; deprived of any means of intellectual satisfaction, he then thinks it best to go to Babylon to find a magus who can take him to the underworld.

In *Icaromenippus,* a similar tale is told of Menippus's confusion about natural philosophy. He tells of how he began to wonder about the cosmos after he had rejected human vainglory. The philosophers whom he selects and pays only lead him to greater uncertainty because of their own contradictory positions and internal disagreements. He comes to view such theorizing about the stars as an impertinence, as they can not see clearly what is at their feet. His distrust of such people grows; their theological and metaphysical opinions are murky and conflicting as well. But he can not disagree with them openly and can find no path to knowledge until he arrives at the idea of putting on wings and flying to heaven.

Menippus has different questions in mind, leading to appropriately different voyages: to Hades to learn about human life, and to Olympus to learn about the gods and the universe. He begins his travels to Hades in ignorance, and to heaven in frustrated silence. Both journeys are shown to be the pursuit of useless knowledge. Menippus in *Necyomantia* knows before he starts that the life of the private citizen is best; this moral will be repeated to him at section 21 by Teiresias, and he will come away no wiser than when he started. In *Icaromenippus,* the voyage is more specifically belittled when Menippus takes heart for his enterprise by remembering the tales of Aesop in which dung beetles, camels, and eagles go to heaven (10). Branham speaks of Menippus's "imaginative capacity for the absurd" in his transcendence of mortal limits, but the point of these satires is that such absurdities are depicted as real.[15] Taking literary authority for a fantastic voyage literally conceived is a nice comic touch and is a device that Lucian elsewhere uses brilliantly.[16] The lowliness of Aesop adds to the emphasis on the fantastic impossibility of the events that will follow, as does Menippus's (I would assert, significant) misquotation; the dung beetle that goes to heaven is found in Aristophanes' *Peace*, one of the major influences on this work.[17]

Preparations for the Voyage (Necyomantia 6–11, Icaromenippus 10–11). Menippus in *Icaromenippus* takes an eagle's wing for his right arm and a vulture's wing for his left and proceeds to give himself flying lessons. He gradually gains confidence and expertise, taking longer and longer flights until he finally decides to fly to Olympus. He grows weak halfway and rests on the moon. Preparations in *Necyomantia* are much more elaborate. Menippus goes to Babylon and persuades one Mithrobarzanes to purify him and be his guide. It is Mithrobarzanes who enjoins the narrator to wear the strange garments described at the beginning of the piece. They offer a sacrifice much like that by which Odysseus raises the spirits of the dead in Homer's *Necyia*, one of the obvious sources of the work (*Od.* 11.23ff.); they see various terrifying creatures and abstractions as they enter the Underworld, much as Aeneas and the Sibyl do in *Aeneid* 6. Charon ferries them over, and they reach the throne of Minos.

These preparatory details are related with a light touch. Menippus throws himself off the Acropolis down into the theater (an omen of things to come) on a first flight in *Icaromenippus;* Rhadamanthys nearly dies of fright to see him in *Necyomantia*. The greater length of *Necyomantia* in this section has a simple explanation. The journey to heaven in *Icaromenippus* will fall into two phases: an interlude on the moon and a final interview in heaven. *Necyomantia* can present sights along the way to the main destination as *Icaromenippus* cannot and proceeds at a leisurely pace; what is preparation in *Necyomantia* corresponds to the first and minor part of the journey in *Icaromenippus*. Further, *Necyomantia* has more descents to Hades to draw on than *Icaromenippus* has ascents to heaven; *Necyomantia* is at this point more of a literary parody, while *Icaromenippus* concentrates on the presentation of the physical theories and their critic. The details of the voyage in *Necyomantia* are essentially a digression (cf. Menippus's admission that he had lost sight of the object of his narration at section 19); *Icaromenippus* deals with physical theories with a much more single-minded insistence.

Survey of Human Folly (Necyomantia 11–18; Icaromenippus 11–19). Menippus is pushing on toward his goal, Teiresias in Hades or heaven itself. He is able to observe en route the follies of humanity, but from a comic and unreliable vantage point.

In *Icaromenippus*, Menippus meets Empedocles, who had been blown there from Mount Etna; this philosopher, a notorious fraud in the pages of Lucian,[18] tells him how to gain eyesight sharp enough to see the actions on the earth below. Menippus puts back on the eagle wing that he had put aside and discovers that he has eagle-keen sight in his right eye; his one-eyed observations from the moon create the now familiar *catascopia*. But note the essential comedy of this convention: Menippus has such a high vantage point that he cannot see and depends upon the ministrations of a false philosopher and the wing of an eagle in his journey to prove the absurdity of philosophers.

In *Necyomantia*, Menippus reaches the throne of Minos and there sees people of wealth and power being arraigned for their evil deeds by their shadows, which, of course, were with their rich masters always. But one sinner is set free; Dionysius, the tyrant of Sicily, is saved from being remanded to the custody of the Chimaera by Aristippus the Cyrenaic philosopher, who points out that Dionysius had often—for a fee—been kind to men of education. Such an unexpected reprieve occurs elsewhere in Lucian[19] and would have its origins in Menippus's own writings, as the conclusion to the *Apocolocyntosis* suggests. But the point here is not the mutability of fortune, but of the influence that philosophers have in the other world for evil. The moral order of Hades, to which Menippus turns for guidance, is a shambles. Menippus next proceeds to the place of punishment, where people of all walks of life are tortured for various human failings; and then to the Acheronian Plain where the heroes lie, although Menippus can not distinguish the bones of Thersites from the bones of Nireus.[20] The fates of those with glorious tombs are considered; we finally hear of the talkative old Socrates, and how Diogenes laughs at the sufferings of Sardanapallus and Midas. Indignation has passed to laughter.

In both works is inserted an extended simile on the nature of life. In *Icaromenippus*, life is first compared to a discordant chorus, and then to an anthill. In *Necyomantia* it is compared to a stage play, in which the goddess Tyche picks the costumes and determines the roles.[21] This a sort of moralizing common throughout Lucian's corpus, and it forms the most serious, or at least the most poignant, section of either work.[22] But there is much irony here. The stage metaphor has particular relevance to *Necyomantia*, considering the bizarre costume that Menippus is himself wearing; the verses he recited at the beginning of the work caused his friend to beg him to stop playing the tragic actor, and Menippus himself in his own *Necyia* probably took on the role of a tragic actor as well. The observer is part of the pomposity and the ridiculousness that he observes.

In *Icaromenippus*, the comparison of life to an anthill follows from the narrator's great height; but when a wealthy landowner is said to farm an area about the size of an Epicurean atom (18), we remember that the narrator's height is impossible and that he is subjecting the world to the sort of absurd scrutiny that is the stock-in-trade of the natural philosophers whom he despises. Perhaps the reference to the discordant chorus reflects a similar joke, calling up theories of heavenly harmonies. The critic belongs to the humanity he condemns, and we begin to see his approach to the solutions of the problems that bother him is, for all of its fantasy, too scientific and dogmatic for us to be convinced of its sincerity.

Council and Consultation (**Necyomantia *19–22*, Icaromenippus *19–34*).** The two works end with Menippus consulting some otherworldly figure about the nature of this world, and with a council of divinities issuing a proclamation. But as the two scenes appear in different orders, I shall treat the two works separately and the two scenes together in each instance.

Necyomantia ends much more quickly than *Icaromenippus*. Menippus's friend reminds him of his promise to tell of the decree against the rich. The narrator tells of how a council was called, and how he worked his way into their number. He hears that after their death the bodies of the rich are to be tortured while their souls are sent back to live in donkeys for 250,000 years, in which form they will be subject to the poor. However plausible the hatred of the rich may be, this punishment is comically unexpected: not only do the rich suffer twice, but the figure of a quarter of a million years must have struck an ancient audience as fantastically long.[23] The punishment does not seem to fit the crime.

Menippus then finds Teiresias, the object of his journey. Teiresias is unwilling to divulge the secret of the happy life, as Rhadamanthys forbids it. He finally yields to Menippus's persuasion and tells our narrator that the life of the private citizen is best, that one should forget inspection of the heavens and contemplation of the beginnings and ends of things, reject the syllogisms of the contradictory philosophers, and consider all their works nonsense. He concludes with a sentiment that echoes not a particular Cynic creed but the archaic poet Simonides: "Above all, pursue only how to put the present in its proper place and run on, laughing at most things and worried about nothing."[24] It is then late and time to leave. Menippus is shown a shortcut to the upper air and with difficulty squeezes through the hole of Trophonius's oracle to find himself in Boeotia. So the piece ends.

This final detail shows the comic status of all that has gone before. As Geffcken notes, the mocker mocks himself, and the moral intent of the work turns to nothing.[25] Lucian mocks Trophonius's oracle elsewhere (cf. *Dial. Mort.* 10); Menippus emerges into the light as a false prophet. But other details cooperate in this travesty of seemingly serious Cynic moralizing. The means by which Menippus sought to find the truth he already knew are explicitly ridiculed by Teiresias: he has contemplated too much the ends of things, and as an enthusiastic prophet takes too seriously the truth not to take anything seriously.[26] Menippus has abandoned the life of a simple and private citizen to show that that life is best. The only extractable moral of *Necyomantia* is that common sense is unprovable and that the champions of common sense transgress, by the very fact of their advocacy, the principles they would preach.

In *Icaromenippus,* before Menippus leaves for Olympus, the Moon herself gives him a message to take to Zeus; she is upset with the conflicting theories that the natural scientists hold about her, and would like all such charlatans destroyed. She has further reasons for hating them as well, for she can observe at night their immoralities. We note here that she is much like Menippus, whose complaints about the lives and theories of the philosophers started the work, and whose *catascopia* provided the first piece of moral commentary. This is a clever sleight-of-hand on Lucian's part. Menippus is no longer bringing his own outrage to heaven, but becomes a messenger for an outraged Moon. He is now dissociated from his original purpose and will in fact ask no explicit questions about the cosmos when he is on Olympus. He becomes the wandering naïf as his original opinions, now the Moon's, are made laughable. The Moon agrees with Menippus, and would go to the extreme of having the philosophers killed. The Moon (who has voice, personality, and inhabitants in the person of Empedocles) is actually possessed of qualities as strange as those assigned to her by the philosophers whom she would see dead. There will be no clear-cut solution to the problems originally raised, as both they and the means of their solution seem increasingly absurd; and Menippus becomes the passive observer of extraterrestrial folly instead of the indignant critic of human folly.

Menippus reaches Olympus and is ushered in; the gods are frightened to see a mortal in their midst, as was Rhadamanthys at *Necyo-mantia* 10. Menippus explains his reasons for coming; Zeus promises to answer his questions tomorrow and to hold a feast in his honor later in the day. He then goes off to his audience chamber to hear the prayers of mortals. This portrait of Zeus is condescendingly amusing. Zeus asks how the weather is on earth (we later learn that he controls it directly); when Menippus tries to assure him that he is still well thought of on earth, Zeus says that he knows that people no longer show him any regard. As he hears complaints and prayers and arranges the day's weather, we see him more as a worker at a thankless job than the Father of Gods and Men.

In a brief scene (27–28), Menippus and Zeus appear at the feast. There is entertainment, and special mortal food is provided for the guest while the gods enjoy nectar, ambrosia, and the blood and smoke of sacrifice. The gods fall asleep, but Menippus sleeplessly wonders how there can be night in heaven, and why Apollo does not yet have a beard. The scene serves to show Menippus in his new role as sympathetic observer; he does not criticize the gods in their presence.

Zeus calls a council the next day, and yet again we hear of the loathsomeness of the philosophers. Contentious and pretentious, they hide under noble exteriors like tragic actors (reminding us of Menippus's similes when observing the earth from the moon) and are revealed as vile when out of costume. They are hypocritical and morally worthless. The complaints of the Moon are judged right and proper; the question remains what to do, and Zeus solicits the gods' opinions. Various suggestions are made as to how to destroy the philosophers utterly, but Zeus remembers that to kill them at such a holy time would be sacrilegious, and concludes the work by promising to exterminate them at the beginning of the spring.

We have heard complaints against the philosophers three times, and it is not Lucian's habit to repeat himself so in a single work without some purpose. Here, we see what became the Moon's indignation transferred again to a higher source, Zeus himself. Zeus now stands in for Menippus, both as moralist and as antidogmatist, but he is powerless to do anything about the problems at issue, and his very existence, as observed through Menippus's eyes, is questionable at best. The fantasy of *Icaromenippus* has taken a human problem and shown it to be insoluble in suprahuman terms. As in *Necyomantia*, the support of the other world has been enlisted in a good cause, but only to the embarrassment of that cause.

At the end of *Icaromenippus,* Menippus tells his friend that he is off to the Stoa Poikile to tell the Peripatetics the good news. But is this news the disapproval of the Moon and the Olympian gods, or of the deferral of the philosophers' punishment? Neither could be calculated to affect a hypocritical philosopher much. At any event, Menippus becomes here, as in *Necyomantia*, a comic prophet, bringing word of a fantastic voyage to people who will be impressed neither by his message nor by his sources. Menippus has engaged fantastic and ineffectual assistants in his campaign against pointless philosophical speculation. The reversion of the narrator to an active rather than a passive role is perhaps unexpected at the end of *Icaromenippus*, but it does bring the work back to the point at which it started, with a comic narrator whose head is too full of absurdity and theory to command our respect.

The Conclusions of Necyomantia *and* Icaromenippus.

Anderson accounts for the variation in the order of the consultation and council scenes in these works by reference to Lucian's models in Old Comedy.[27] Necyomantia patterns itself on Aristophanes' *Frogs:* there "the assembly of the dead is introduced as a digression, and Dionysus resumes the real purpose of his descent as an afterthought." *Icaromenippus* follows Aristophanes' *Peace* and Trygaeus's ascent to heaven where, as the gods have moved away, there can only be a meeting with the lone Hermes; the council scene that follows at the end of the play is not divine. This is true as far as it goes, but Lucian is free to alter Aristophanes' model if he so chooses, and the elements have a particular meaning in context that is not dependent upon the practice or example of Aristophanes.

In *Icaromenippus,* the plot progresses in such a way as to transfer Menippus's original indignation at the vileness of philosophers to ever higher, and ultimately ever further removed and ineffectual, authorities. The nature of the *catascopia* is dramatized: the higher and more inclusive the point of view, the further removed from reality it is. First Menippus, then the Moon, then Zeus, and finally the divine council, capping the progression, take their turn at grappling with the problem of unwarranted speculation. The structure of *Necyomantia* is not nearly as neat, and in this we see one of the ways in which Lucian's adaptation of Menippus is an improvement over the original. Nevertheless, the *Necyomantia* also presents a trivializing progression of authorities. Menippus first sees the judgment of the wealthy dead, which should be his primary interest as he has promised to tell of the fate of the rich. But this is only a station along his way, and it reveals corruption when we learn of the reprieve granted to the tyrant Dionysius. The decree of the council against the rich, which is separated from the scene of judgment by a number of minor interludes and moralizings, lacks the force of an actual judgment: it is purely theoretical and so excessive in its demand for a double punishment that it smacks of the revenge of the poor rather than justice. The machinery of Hades is inadequate to prove the triumph of justice and the rightful exaltation of the poor over the rich, and this underworld is not really much different from that of the *Apocolocyntosis*. The consultation with Teiresias must come last because his lesson, that one should not look too closely at the beginnings and ends of things, is in fact an appeal to Menippus to ignore what he has just seen: there is no truth or salvation in it. Even in Hades, the blind see more than those with eyes; his authority is comically and poignantly asserted over that of Minos and the infernal council; laughter, not judgment, is the proper end of such inquiry.

SOME MENIPPEAN EXPERIMENTS IN LUCIAN'S COMIC DIALOGUES

It is Lucian, not Menippus, who is truly *spoudogeloios*, and Branham provides excellent exemplification of Lucian's serious humor. It may be useful to conclude our discussion of the Menippean Lucian by considering a number of works in which Lucian attempts to adapt the genre of Menippean satire to the nature of comic dialogue for rather more serious, or at least seriocomic, ends. Various restraints are imposed when dialogue pure and simple replaces the dialogue that frames a narrative: there can be no narrator, and it is difficult to imply a fantastic voyage in a conversation. But Lucian's ingenuity in the structuring of his material is great. The thirty works that constitute the *Dialogues of the Dead* are a *necyia* of a person truly dead and who will not return; the individual dialogues serve as occasional resting places as Menippus, who appears in twelve of them, comes to realize that he is just as dead and just as real as all of the underworld fantasies that he meets. Here too Lucian manages to make fun of Menippus as he shatters a Menippean satire to bits; Lucian kills Menippus, does not let him return, and makes him take his place among the bones of Thersites and Nireus, in which there is no distinction accorded to him for his enlightened attitudes about the "real" nature of the Land of the Dead.[28]

Another brilliant adaption of the Menippean genre is *Contemplantes*, whose Greek title ("Charon, or Those Who Look Down from a Great Height") shows its affiliation. In this, Hermes ushers Charon

up from the Underworld so that he may learn what it is that mortals
are so unwilling to leave behind, and their conversation implies a
fantastic voyage—paradoxically, to earth. They need a vantage point;
they pile Parnassus on Oeta on Pelion on Ossa on Olympus in order
to get a good view and an appropriately bizarre *catascopia* (5). It is the
power of language that moves these mountains; Hermes points out
that Homer only needed two lines to put Pelion on Ossa (*Od.* 11.315–
16), so he repeats these lines, and with the same effect. The other
mountains are also jockeyed into position by words alone, to Charon's amazement and the reader's, who scarcely knows how to understand Lucian's point, except to say that power of language and poetry
is clearly held up for ridicule:

> HERMES: Don't worry. Everything will hold steady. Move
> Mount Oeta over! Let Parnassus roll into place!
> CHARON: Would you look at that!

They are soon at an impossible height; Hermes assures Charon that
one cannot be a lover of vision and safe at the same time, and he then
gives Charon sharp vision, just as Empedocles gives it to Menippus in
Icaromenippus, but does so here merely by reciting two more lines of
Homer (7: *Il.* 5.127–28). As in *Icaromenippus,* they have ascended so
high that the objects of their inquiry are nearly invisible, and special,
nonhuman, sight is needed to consider human folly. They observe
the Mediterranean world of Herodotus, so telescoped that Cyrus
and Cambyses can be seen simultaneously. This is due partly to Lucian's desire to grant to his characters universal vision, but it also
serves to call into question the reality of the vision. In this regard,
there is a significant misquotation of Herodotus: Lucian has Solon
tell Croesus (dialogue within a dialogue) that Cleobis and Biton are
the happiest mortals (10), instead of having them yield pride of place
to Tellus of Athens (Hdt. 1.30.3). What Charon and Hermes observe
is not life but a book, the text of Herodotus curiously rewritten.

Its conclusion is Menippean. Charon waxes mordant and, like a
Cynic, prays to Clotho to destroy these foolish mortals (14); he learns
some sympathy from Hermes, who says that no one expects to die.[29]
They moralize about human hopes and passions, and in a simile life
is compared to bubbles (19). Charon is then won over to sympathy,
and wants to shout out a warning (20); now Hermes is Cynical, and
says that it would do no good. Charon then discourses glumly on the
deaths of heroes, and Hermes on the deaths of cities (22–23). They
finally depart, quite literally to mind their own business.

The *catascopia* has had no effect. Inquiry is profitless. Charon's new knowledge about human nature and endeavor only saddens him. The fantasy of the piece underscores the Menippean theme that such speculation and study are impossible, and that the morals derived are like evidence gathered without a search warrant and are not admissible in the court of reason. The end of *Contemplantes* does not so much turn the preceding discussion into a joke (as do the ends of Menippean satires) as suggest that minding one's own business is a lamentable, if necessary, condition for a reasonable life.[30] But it is also important to realize that in *Contemplantes* Lucian finds a way to unite the absurdity of Menippean satire with the literary and thematic propriety that were the normal goals of his literary imitation. I can think of no more moving work in Lucian's corpus; and its essential seriousness, its tearful acknowledgment that this study is a useless endeavor, has little to do with Menippean satire.

Another formal experiment is worthy of notice. *Juppiter Tragoedus* is a fascinating accommodation of limited Menippean resources to the dialogue form: a dialogue on earth is imbedded in a dialogue in heaven, allowing the gods of Olympus to become passive observers of a debate on whether they exist.[31] The parody of the principals of this drama is implicit in the arguments of the atheist who holds that the gods do not exist, and in the inability of the gods to act on their own behalf to prove their existence; the creation of a new sort of *catascopia,* in which the gods themselves observe human folly, replaces the intellectual journey of Menippean satire. They find out too much about themselves by sitting still and listening. The end of *Juppiter Tragoedus* inevitably frustrates the desire for any kind of logical solution to the problem, as the gods are certainly real for the purpose of the dialogue. The gods and the arguments that seem to be able to disprove them are assigned to an uneasy limbo, when Damis the atheist laughingly admits defeat after Timocles argues that gods must exist because altars do. This pulls the rug out from under the reader in good Menippean fashion.

CONCLUSION

The history of the influence of Menippus is more than the history of the influence of the *Necyia* in the genre that we cause to pass under his name. Menippus himself, particularly Menippus the literary character, is another fruitful source of inspiration. Lucian documents a fascination with Menippus the actor: the *Dialogues of the Dead* turns the tables on him and traps him in the underworld; and our two Menippean satires expand his range of activities, so that he is not only a voyager to hell, but also to heaven. It is appropriate that Menippus travels both high and low. Lucian thus makes explicit in the person of the founder of the genre what was implicit in the genre itself and foreshadowed by the voyages of the fool Claudius. Utopian fiction probably reflects this same desire to make a journey to hell only one of a number of possible absurd voyages, and one of the most curious reflexes of this may be seen in a famous passage of the *Alexander Romance,* in which Alexander takes on the role of a Menippean fantastic experimenter and, at the edges of the world, travels to the depths of Ocean in a sort of bathysphere, and flies up to heaven in a basket drawn by birds, only to be warned by talking birds not to attempt the impossible.[32]

I have tried to disentangle Menippus and Lucian. Lucian's is an impish delight in embarrassing those who desire truth and knowledge; he simultaneously proclaims the vigor of traditional literary culture and directs his laughter toward those who look to literature for truth. He is a comic author and master manipulator of stock material; and like P. G. Wodehouse, whom he much resembles, he views his considerable art as nonart, and his considerable meaning as nonmeaning.[33] Yet he does not make himself the narrator of his Menippean satires, and the reticence is telling; Lucian prefers for himself the mantle of the hero of Old Comedy, emerging victorious in the *Piscator* and the *Bis Accusatus,* not as the catechizer catechized in *Necyomantia* and *Icaromenippus.* Menippus exists for Lucian as a personality, and Lucian is inspired by Menippean satire to present Menippus in texts as a comic, rather than a seriocomic, phenomenon. Lucian asserts the Cynical and Menippean distrust of theories, systems, and facile encapsulations of the truth by suggesting that even writing about the failure of logic and comprehension to define the world is a comic waste of time.[34] He can say with Kent in Shakespeare's *Lear:* "I can keep honest council, ride, run, *mar* a curious tale in telling it, and deliver a plain message bluntly" (I.iv).

Satire is a combination of fantasy and morality; Menippean satire embarrasses the intellect through fantasy. In the works just considered, the elements of fantasy have been such as to draw into question the importance of the topics at issue. The topics are intellectual: the theories of philosophers, the nature of the gods, the importance of debate. In each, preaching against theorizing is itself shown to be a vice of presumption and dogmatism. The topic of the Menippean satires in Lucian is not how the perpetuity of debate must be valued over any static theory, or how the human mind must struggle to free itself of the chains of dogma in order to search for the always unattainable truth; Payne's formulation goes too far, including more than our two Menippean satires in her consideration of Lucian.[35] Rather, they show the comedy of trying to find answers by extraordinary means, when the truth was at one's feet all along.

Chapter Eight

JULIAN

AT SOME TIME in his brief reign (361–63 A.D.), possibly just prior to his disastrous march against the Persian Empire, Julian the Apostate wrote a very peculiar work, the Συμπόσιον ἢ Κρονία ("Symposium, or The Saturnalia"), better known as the *Caesars*.[1] Despite its title, it is not generically a symposium,[2] nor is it related to Lucian's Saturnalian pieces.[3] The popular title, "The Emperors of Rome" (at least as old as the Church historian Socrates), reflects its historical content, which is still the focus of most of the modest critical attention which this work receives; and as it must be admitted that Julian is the only one of the Roman emperors to leave behind his personal evaluations of his predecessors, his pride makes this act of self-justification quite interesting.[4] But in claiming the *Caesars* for the genre of Menippean satire, I oppose those interpretations that seek a serious frame for serious matter. The *Caesars* makes fun of all of Julian's predecessors and separates him from them and the silly heaven in which they are to be found: it is neither a Neoplatonic myth,[5] a disquisition on the value of history,[6] nor a piece of political propaganda.[7] In many ways, it is a travesty of political and philosophical notions that Julian elsewhere holds; the comic inconsistency between this work and Julian's personal beliefs is one of the many marks of Menippean satire to be found here. Modern criticism has, quite simply, missed the joke of the *Caesars*.[8] What follows will pay close attention to the dynamics of its plot and the significance of its unexpected details. What will emerge is a literarily sophisticated and personally bitter tale of the absurdities of Roman politics and Roman religion, betraying the influence of Varro and Seneca in its theme and execution, and the influence of Lucian in the externals of its form.

THE MENIPPEAN FRAME

The *Caesars* is not as well known as it deserves to be; I proceed from a summary of its contents.[9]

The narrator (addressed as "Caesar" and to be identified with Julian himself) tells an unnamed interlocutor that he will relate a comic story in keeping with the festal requirements of the Saturnalia, but adds that it will be at second hand, as he is not funny by nature. The disclaimer is disingenuous: he cites the words of Aristophanes in Plato's *Symposium,* and quotes a comic fragment as well; he systematically plays with the interlocutor's expectations of the sort of *mythos* that he will hear (Platonic, Aesopic, or fictional) so that the interlocutor ends their conversation in exasperation.[10] The source of the story is Hermes; its truth the narrator leaves for events to decide (306A–307A).

Romulus is offering a feast on the Saturnalia for the gods and all of the deceased Roman emperors. The scene is the Homeric heaven. Hermes sets the stage by citing the *Odyssey* (6.42): "where they say is the seat of the gods, secure forever." The locations are described (the gods on Olympus, the emperors in the sublunar sphere), as are the thrones of Cronus, Zeus, Rhea, and Hera. A hyperbolic miscitation of Homer then seems to reject the Homeric heaven as the scene of all this, but it is a comic touch that brings it forcefully to mind (308B–C):

> No one was vying with another, but, just as Homer, doing properly, said (evidently having heard it from the Muses themselves), each of the gods had a seat, upon which it was absolutely right to sit fixedly and immovably; even when they rise up in the presence of their father they do not confuse their seats, nor change their order, nor steal them from each other, but they each recognize that which is appropriate to them.[11]

The emperors are led into their banquet hall one at a time and are subjected to the abuse of Silenus, who mocks nearly all of them (307B–316A). The list reveals that Julian has no great knowledge of his predecessors: his knowledge of the third century is very spotty, and his various errors and omissions show that he does not have at hand any of the fourth-century Roman epitomes of imperial history.[12] It is a personal list, with evaluations at times quite incompatible with those of other historians; and the mockery of Silenus is often directed at sexual and other moral delinquencies not elsewhere attested, thus allowing us to suspect that the fantasies of the austere Julian are at work here.[13]

What we have is not a symposium, but a comic contest for deification, whose roots are Hellenistic but which exists for Julian in the form of some of Lucian's dialogues and Seneca's *Apocolocyntosis* as well. It is not a comedy that substitutes emperors for wrangling philosophers, and an obvious source of humor, found for example in

Timon's *Silli*—that the Land of the Dead allows characters separated in time to discover their dislike for each other—is pointedly passed by. The festival of the Roman Saturnalia is the dramatic occasion for this because of its topsy-turvy traditions: it sanctions the mockery of solemn things (as the narrator himself states in the introduction), allows superiors and inferiors a temporary equality at a joint celebration, and may be the occasion of the freeing of slaves.[14] Romulus will follow these customs by inviting the emperors to dine with the gods, and by proposing that one of them rise up to divine status. The *Caesars* is a comic study of the implications of this temporary equality, as the emperors, who are gods for a day, try to gain permanently what they consider to be an exalted rank.

Hermes decides to test the emperors; Quirinus (Romulus) wants one emperor elevated to his divine level to keep him company. Heracles insists that Alexander the Great be allowed to compete, and Quirinus promptly worries whether a Roman will win under the circumstances. Rules are agreed upon: a selection of emperors will be made and the winner among them will be judged the best of all. Hermes has Caesar, Octavian, and Trajan compete, impressed by their prowess in war. Cronus wants a philosopher, and summons Marcus Aurelius to the lists; Dionysus asks that Constantine be allowed to compete, as a votary of sensual indulgence would round out their numbers, and Zeus allows the latter to compete from the threshold of the emperors' hall, to avoid direct contamination. Alexander is the sixth and final contestant; his presence makes the title *Caesars* rather misleading. Hermes makes a formal proclamation of the contest in anapests (316A–319D).

There follow two rounds of competition. In the first, each ruler gives an account of his reign, in the following order: Caesar, Alexander, Octavian, Trajan, Marcus, Constantine. Silenus makes insulting comments only about the last three. Second, each states what was the goal of his life; Hermes here asks the main questions, and Silenus interrogates them on particulars, to their universal discredit (319D–335B). Only the speeches of the first three contain much historical matter; the suspicion is that Plutarch's *Lives* are the main source, including the now lost *Life of Augustus*.[15] The gods vote in secret. Marcus wins, but his victory is not announced. Zeus confers privately with Cronus and then gives orders to Hermes, who announces that all contestants may enter heaven and choose for themselves a guardian god. The joke is that each finds his own level but also that the rules have been changed so as not to respect merit. All choose Olympians except Trajan, who clings to his fellow contestant Alexander;

and Constantine, who catches sight of the abstraction Indulgence and follows her to a place in which Jesus is dispensing absolution to unrepentant criminals. Constantine voluntarily leaves the divine assembly to be with Jesus. Avenging spirits attack Constantine for his shedding of kindred blood (it is not made explicit in the text that the victims are some of Julian's own relatives), but Zeus grants him a thoroughly undeserved reprieve. Hermes then turns away from the action to tell the narrator to follow the commands of Mithras during his life, so as to gain Mithras (and not, we sense, one of these gods or emperors) as a guardian god after his death (335c–336c).

JULIAN casts a wide net in constructing his Menippean satire. Its comic substance is similar to that of Lucian's *Council of the Gods*, itself the inheritor of a long tradition of comic depictions of heavenly examinations and rejections of potential divinities; but Seneca's adaptation of this tradition, involving a single applicant and a burlesque of the specific nature of Roman apotheosis and the sort of heaven implied by it, is perhaps closest to Julian's mind. The introduction is in the manner of Lucian's *Icaromenippus*, in which the narrator plays with a dull interlocutor and frustrates his desire for simple meaning. The conclusion most resembles that of the *Apocolocyntosis*, in which the rules for the heavenly contest are broken and justice is not secured in the other world. In the middle is a brief history of the Roman Empire, a display of learning for comic purposes that announces the influence of Varro's encyclopedism. It is comic not because it gets some of its details wrong, but because it reduces Roman history to a guest list of pretentious emperors who are supposed to be meeting their superiors. Running through it is a use of verse that goes far beyond Lucian's example, and which may again show the influence of the Roman liberties in this regard. It is most unusual to posit the influence of Roman literature on Greek, and critics have always been shy of positing an influence of Seneca on Julian,[16] but Julian is a Roman, and his *Caesars* is in fact proof of the cross-fertilization of Greek and Roman traditions of Menippean satire in the fourth century.[17]

As I have argued elsewhere, the introduction of the *Caesars* is witty and involved, relying on puns and subtle shifts of meaning in various words as the narrator and his not very bright interlocutor discuss what the former's upcoming tale is likely to mean. What is distinctive about this use of a familiar conversational device lies in the caginess of the narrator, as opposed to the simple absurdity of Menippus in Lucian's introductions. We cannot take the narrator at face value and believe that what follows is serious and edifying. The narrator says that he will offer a secondhand comic tale ἐν παιδιᾶς μέρει, a cryptic bit of Greek which admits of two interpretations: "to fulfill the requirement of the comic tale" or "in place of a comic tale." The former corresponds to Aristotle's language concerning appropriate jesting (*Eth. Nic.* 1128a19); the latter suggests outright evasion. It is possible, under the circumstances, that the interlocutor confuses παιδιά with παιδεία, "education"; the words are practically homophonic in Julian's time, and the author may be referring obliquely through them to his genre's seriocomic stance, much as a Latin Menippean satirist can exploit the twin meanings of the term *ludus*. The *mythos* may perhaps be worth hearing, the narrator says; but the interlocutor does not know what to expect.

The introduction and the conclusion of this Menippean satire form a comic frame that denies the importance of the action contained within it. The discussion of the relative merits of the Roman emperors loses its importance when, at the end of the work, the reader discovers that nothing has been accomplished. It is not enough to say that Marcus Aurelius wins the competition, and that his philosophical rule is the model that Julian takes to himself for his own rule. As will be made clear in the following section on the use of verse by the various participants in the *Caesars*, Marcus fares rather badly in the examination. Silenus's castigation of the philosopher-emperor is followed by insults directed against Constantine, and the imperial contest ends on a very sour note.

The conclusion of the *Caesars* is worth special attention. First, the vote (335c):

> There was silence, and the gods in secret brought forward their ballots. It turned out that many of them were for Marcus. But Zeus held a private consultation with his father, and commanded Hermes to make the proclamation. And Hermes was proclaiming: "All ye men who have come to this competition: among us the laws and decisions are such that the victor may rejoice and the loser not be resentful. Go ye now," he said, "whithersoever it be pleasing to each of you, that ye may live henceforward at the feet of your guardian gods. Let each choose for himself his champion and guardian."

Note that Marcus is *not* announced as the winner. The vote is taken in secret,[18] and Hermes' proclamation is based on some unheard instruction given by Zeus after a private consultation with Cronus. No part of the voting is made known to the contestants. Further, all of the emperors, from Marcus Aurelius to Constantine, receive the same prize: to go wherever they please and to pick for themselves a guardian divinity. The phrasing of the end of the proclamation is reminiscent of the end of the *Republic* (617D–E), where the souls pick their own fates; there too there is no distinction among souls before the choice is made.[19] Finally, Hermes' explanation of the law of heaven makes no sense: as the winner is not announced, the rule that the winner may rejoice and the losers may not hold a grudge is irrelevant to the proceedings. Nor does Hermes address the whole body of the emperors here about their relation to the six winners of the contest: the emperors did not come together for the purpose of a contest but for a banquet; the trial among the six was the decision of Hermes and Quirinus (316A–317B). There we learned that the goal of the contest was to find *one* emperor to elevate to Quirinus's rank. The point is that the rules of the game have been changed unexpectedly at the game's end. Hermes' nonsense about fair play among the contestants can only underline the fact that the judges themselves have been unfair and have granted equal honors to all of the participants.

The whisperings between Zeus and Cronus have a sinister air about them, as if they have some vested interest in keeping the results of the voting from being known. We soon see that Zeus must like Constantine, as he intervenes on his behalf; perhaps Zeus himself wants this worst of emperors in heaven. The emperors choose their gods: Alexander runs to Heracles, Octavian to Apollo, Marcus to Zeus and Cronus; Ares and Aphrodite call Caesar, who wanders in confusion, to themselves; Trajan applies to Alexander (335D–336A). So far it is clear that Marcus has not been elevated to a higher rank than his fellow emperors,[20] and all have equal opportunities in heaven.

The narrative then turns to Constantine's choice (336A–B):

> But Constantine, not finding the archetype of his life among the gods, caught sight of Indulgence near by and ran to her; she tenderly took him up and dressed him and adorned him with luxurious and multicolored garments; she led him to Drunkenness; and he found Jesus dwelling there too, and calling to everyone: "Every seducer, every murderer, everyone guilty of pollution and foul, come hither in good hope! For I shall bathe him in this water and make him straightway clean; and should he again be guilty

of the same sins, I shall grant that he become clean, if but he beat his chest and strike his head." Very gladly did Constantine fall in with him, at the same time leading his children out of the assembly of the gods.

Constantine and Jesus are linked by moral hypocrisy; Julian's contempt for Constantine's deathbed conversion to Christianity lies behind this depiction.[21] But Julian's criticisms do not end here. The reader again thinks of the end of the *Republic* as most of the souls make bad choices for their future lives; for all of their similarities, the author seems to imply that Constantine could have made a better choice for a patron god than Jesus. This Jesus is at any event present as a god and not as a mere historical character. In this contemptible heaven the Olympian gods and Jesus are neighbors, and Indulgence and Excess can wander about freely. Even though Constantine voluntarily removes himself and his sons from the divine council, nothing indicates that he is now in a separate region of the skies, or that a great gulf is fixed between the Olympians and Jesus. Rather, just as the evil emperor was allowed to participate in the contests from the doorway of the banquet hall, so too he is merely in a less fashionable region of heaven. Good and bad emperors have ascended to a heaven populated by better and worse divinities and abstractions.

Access to this heaven is so easy because the gods themselves are so poor (336B):

> But the avenging spirits, exacting punishment for kindred blood, were attacking him and them no less for atheism, until Zeus granted them respite, out of respect for Claudius (Gothicus) and Constantius (Chlorus).

Lacombrade believes that Constantius Chlorus's constant pagan faith accounts for the remission of punishment granted to his evil descendant Constantine.[22] This can hardly be true; no religious reason can explain Zeus's motivations here. It is not reasonable for Zeus to forgive Constantine's murder of kin because Constantine himself had good ancestors,[23] for deviance from such sterling examples ought to merit some punishment. Nor can the paganism of an ancestor redeem a man whose conversion to Christianity makes him so loathsome in the author's eyes.[24] And as Constantine has willingly departed from the circle of the gods to go to Jesus, there seems to be no reason for Zeus's intervention, nor any reason for him to care about the emperor who has been despised throughout the *Caesars*. This

rehabilitation of Constantine is absolutely implausible and undeserved, whether viewed from inside the text or without.

The simple fact is that Zeus, like Jesus, has pardoned the unpar-
donable. Both the Olympians, who staged the imperial competition,
and Jesus, who takes Constantine to his bosom, are indifferent to
merit and to hypocrisy. The Menippean device of the unexpected
reprieve has figured earlier in the text, in the exoneration of Aurelian.[25] The plan to raise a single good emperor to the level of
Romulus has been abandoned, and the reader can only suspect that
the gods found it difficult to make a choice. Yet if the gods can find
little to separate Marcus Aurelius and Constantine, it is because the
gods themselves are debased. The *Caesars* is a denunciation of apotheosis: all of the gods that these emperors believe in grant honor
and salvation without demand of effort or devotion. Constantine *is*
worthy of this heaven, just as the fool Claudius is worthy of heaven in
the *Apocolocyntosis;* and just as Claudius was relieved of his torment by
collusion of the good and the bad (Aeacus and Caligula), so too is
Constantine reprieved by Zeus and Jesus.[26]

When Hermes concludes the *Caesars* by telling the narrator about
Mithras, it is made clear that Julian does not look to these emperors
or to any of their religious beliefs as models for his conduct or his
faith, nor does he hope to rise to their morally indifferent heaven
(336c):

> Now speaking to me, Hermes said: "But to you I have
> granted knowledge of your father Mithras. Keep you there-
> fore his commandments, preparing for yourself a mooring
> cable and a safe harbor while you are alive; and, whenever
> you must come away to this place, having established for
> yourself, with Good Hope, a kindly guardian god."

The narrator will not have to undergo a trial, such as his predecessors did. Mithras has not previously figured in the action of the
Caesars,[27] and we see that Julian the author imagines for himself a
separate and superior fate because of his unique faith. He has written of the other emperors not to show how he embodies their superior traits but to emphasize his utter difference from them in religious faith and moral consistency. Their contest is meaningless, and
the honors that they strive for are worthless; the narrator shall, quite
literally, rise above them and their petty gods. As is also true in the *De
Nuptiis,* there are two heavens implied here, and the sublime one
does not figure in the action.

The *Caesars* ends on the same note with which it began, the frustration of a search for moral order within the tale of Hermes. The conclusion is in the best Menippean tradition, and the structural and thematic parallels to the *Apocolocyntosis* are so blatant as to make the emperor's familiarity with that work a certainty. The *Caesars* ends in a puff of smoke; in one sentence, we see that Zeus is like Jesus and that all the contention for honors and divinity has been in vain because the imperial heaven has no respect of merit, being itself corrupt. There is no self-parody in the command that the narrator receives from Hermes, and the narrator is untouched by the humor of the piece. The author's Neoplatonism is abused, largely through the comedy of pretending that Homer's heaven is a philosopher's paradise, a sort of allegorization with which Julian is typically uncomfortable.[28] What remains consistent throughout Julian's works is his pride.

PROSE AND VERSE

If my readings of the introduction and conclusion of the *Caesars* are correct, we see a Julian modifying structures of Menippean satire in general, and the example of Seneca in particular, out of a desire to avoid self-parody, a pose that the *Misopogon* shows he could at least affect when he wanted to. But the *Caesars* has more than a Menippean frame; its use of verse is thoroughly in accord with the genre. Here too Julian has his innovations; although he follows the lead of Lucian in his sparing use of verse, he of all the Menippean satirists is cleverest at finding novel ways to suggest the absurdity of the action, characters, and setting of his work through poetry. Because of his cautious attitude about the relation of poetry and truth, Julian never has verse quoted, parodied, or created to express the truth of a situation, but to show that those who speak in verse are pompous liars. Silenus seems the sole exception, as we are expected to endorse his poetic criticisms of the emperors; but his quotations are merely abusive, and whatever critical content they may have is left unstated, as the reader must remember the context of the work from which the quotation is taken to see Silenus's point. Throughout the *Caesars*, Julian is careful not to preach what he would have us accept as true: poetry is no medium for truth, and the action of the piece is too absurd to be worthy of his righteous indignation.

The humor of the misapplication of Homer has already been noted concerning the seats of the Olympian gods. Marcus Aurelius provides another example. In the second round of the competition, he states that his rule of conduct was to try to follow the gods (333C). Silenus at first has difficulty attacking Marcus on these grounds, and Marcus defends himself well against the strange accusation, founded in Julian's own well-known asceticism, that he did such human things as eat and drink. At 334B, Silenus finally objects that Marcus granted his wife the honor of apotheosis, and allowed his awful son Commodus to rule after him. Again, Marcus insists that he was following the gods. For the first charge, he quotes Homer's verses on Achilles' defense of his love for Briseis (*Il.* 9.341–42): "The good and careful man loves his own wife and cares for her." This is specious and evasive: Achilles is not a god, however divine he may be; though it is proper to love one's wife, apotheosis is not therefore justified. He proceeds (334C, paraphrasing *Il.* 5.897–98): "As to my son, I have the response of Zeus himself. For he said, upbraiding Ares, 'You would have long since been blasted by lightning, had I not loved you because you were my son.'" To answer charges of impropriety he reveals the impropriety of the gods, and these are the gods of Homer.

Marcus is aware of how insufficient these sophistic excuses are and goes on to present a number of ever-poorer supporting arguments (334C–D). He did not know that his son would become so evil; it is normal for fathers to pass their kingdoms on to their sons (hardly true in Rome); he was not the first to honor his wife in such a way; and while it may not have been praiseworthy to start either tradition, it would be practically unjust to deprive his relations of such honors so long established. Marcus couples his defense of having tried to imitate the gods with an admission of moral guilt. At the beginning of his questioning, Silenus flatly labels the emperor a sophist (333C). His apprehensions are justified. The authority for Marcus's behavior is not philosophy, but poetry, and we do not admire his choice. It is clear that the Olympians like Marcus, not least for his desire to be like them; but we see that this is a friendship based on mutual error. It is the disreputable Dionysus who thinks that Marcus will be above Silenus's reproach; he quotes Simonides' famous words on the solid and honest man (333B = Simonides frag. 37.3 *PMG*): "fashioned four-square, without reproach."[29] Dionysus praises Marcus in verse and is proved wrong.

A final quotation apropos of Marcus Aurelius provides perhaps the handiest encapsulation of Julian's view of the status of truth, argument, and poetry. At 328C, Marcus is about to speak for the first time, and Silenus expects to hear Stoic paradoxes and monstrous doctrines from him. Marcus, however, refuses to speak of his ex-

ploits, saying that the gods already know of them; he does not need
to compete, and he expects their just judgment. The narrator adds
that Marcus seemed exceptional in all respects, and very wise as well,
as he seemed to know (328D) "how to speak when necessary and to
keep his silence when appropriate," λέγειν τε ὅπου χρὴ καὶ σιγᾶν
ὅπου καλόν (Euripides frag. 417 Nauck²). Marcus declines in later
debate from the nobility here granted him; we see that in this competition it is never necessary to speak and always advantageous to keep
silent if an emperor wants to gain the reader's respect. Marcus's reservations about the utility of debate are quite correct, but not for the
reasons that he imagines. The contest is pointless not because the
gods know the emperor's deeds, but because they do not care about
them. The poetry quoted to justify an emperor's actions will be
proved wrong by human reason yet will be acceptable to the gods
defined by such poetry, while the poetry of truth (or at least of mockery and contempt) will be shown to be useless.

Silenus is able to quote poetry without making himself foolish, but
the artifice he employs in turning poetry toward moral criticism is a
useful illustration of the general tendency of the *Caesars* not to take
itself very seriously. At 331B, he argues with Alexander as to whether
he deserved the credit for the victory over the Mallians in India,
since a near-mortal wound rendered him incapable of command.
Silenus quotes Euripides, *Andromache* 693–94: "Alas, how pernicious
are the customs throughout Greece whenever an army sets up a
trophy over its enemies!" The quotation seems irrelevant; Silenus's
point lies in those verses of Euripides which follow:

> For they do not think that this is the work of those who
> struggled, but the general gets the credit who, a single man
> brandishing his spear with ten thousand others, does no
> more work than one and has the greater reputation.

Dionysus warns Silenus not to go on, for fear that Alexander may try
to kill him. Alexander hears only the first two lines of the Euripides
passage, then blushes and weeps; he is stung by what Silenus suggests
but does not say.

Julian can thus be very telegraphic in this use of criticism through
silence. A further example is found at 310B: we are told that Silenus
began to sing from the chorus of Aristophanes' *Knights,* twisting it to
make fun of Claudius instead of Demos. The allusion is to *Knights*
1111–20 and is remarkably apt, painting the picture of Claudius familiar from the *Apocolocyntosis,* yet not a word of it is quoted in the
text:

Demos, yours is a pretty rule, when everyone fears you as
though you were a tyrant. But you are easily seduced, and
are happily flattered and deceived, and you are always
openmouthed before a public speaker; but your mind,
though present, is far away.

Not only does Julian spare himself the labor of finding a metrical way
to substitute Claudius for Demos in this passage; he also avoids the
unpleasantness of being an obvious and censorious preacher. Of
course, not all of Julian's citations are this clever, many being examples merely of simple mockery; but this one certainly shows the effort
put into making certain that verse is used to criticize and not to praise
or pronounce eternal truths.[30]

One piece of poetry remains, which is neither quotation nor parody but independent composition. At 318D–319D, Hermes issues a
proclamation in anapestic monometers to summon the six emperors
to the contest. Although the poem takes its inspiration from various
authors and sources,[31] it is no mere cento; and although its verses
may be judged as doggerel,[32] it is not just a concession to the Menippean cliché of the metrical summons.[33] The poem is comic, and fully
integrated into the themes and structures of the *Caesars*:[34] it too
mocks both the attainments of the emperors and the contest that
presumes to judge among them, and provides another example of
verse used not for moralizing or high sentence but for condescend-
ing contempt.

At 317A, athletic rules are established for the competition, and the
opening verses of the poem stress that what is to come resembles an
Olympic game for a glorious prize. Yet Hermes sarcastically describes the battle to come as one of brawn against brains: on the one
side are the mighty in war, enslavers of nations, whose oversubtle wits
are as sharp as their swords; on the other side are philosophers,
people with vulgar notions of justice, and corrupt aesthetes, in de-
scending order. The end of the contest is already in doubt, for where
does our philosopher-emperor belong? And the poem's end reinforces this doubt: Νίκης δὲ τέλος / Ζηνὶ μελήσει ("But Zeus will
decide the winner"). The hierarchy of virtue may not be sufficient to
settle the question of superiority.

This examination of Julian's use of poetry shows that he, like the
other Menippean satirists, does not intend verse to serve the cause of
elegance or the variation of an otherwise colorless narrative. Julian is
perhaps more conservative than the others; it is clear that to him
poetry is lies. Whereas the more genial Lucian uses verse to suggest

the absurdity of the characters who speak it, Julian takes verse to define the corruption of those who rely on its authority. Nor does Julian the narrator himself speak in verse, except perhaps to mislead his interlocutor in the introduction. Julian has Mithras, not Homer, as a guide of life; the special reward envisioned for him at the end of the *Caesars* is part and parcel of the distance he puts between himself and classical poetry, and therefore classical culture as a whole. For all of his education and devotion to things pagan, Julian is at heart a mystic, or at least a believer in his personal virtue in the face of divinity. Like the Christians he grew to reject, Julian here accepts the values of faith over secular culture. His predecessors believed in Homer, and their moral bankruptcy is the joke of the *Caesars;* if Homer is the Greek Bible, then perhaps Julian is twice the Apostate, rejecting pagan and Christian heavens, Zeus and Jesus. Or so he presents himself here; the author's self-presentation in a Menippean satire is allowed to differ from the intellectual ideals in evidence in his other works.

JULIAN AND THE LATIN TRADITIONS
OF MENIPPEAN SATIRE

A number of other structures within the *Caesars* may be dealt with in briefer compass. Julian constructs a novel *catascopia:* the gods on Olympus look down on the emperors in the sublunar sphere. In Menippean satire, the view from a height is an observation of folly; the imperial contest provides sufficient instances of this. Yet there is inherent in the Menippean *catascopia* the idea that the observers are guilty of those same absurdities which they see, and in the *Caesars* the character of Silenus serves to show this equality of divinities and mortals. Not only does Silenus abuse gods as well as emperors during the emperors' entrance (cf. the unkind reference to Zeus's baldness at 308D and to his homosexuality at 311C), but he also champions the cause of justice against the gods' decisions. At 315B, the gods grant to the tetrarchy (Diocletian, Constantius Chlorus, and the two Maximians) preeminence at table, marveling at their unanimity. But Silenus cannot abide Maximian the Augustus, and the goddess Dike (Justice) removes him. As has been shown, Silenus refuses to accept the gods' complacency about Marcus's claim to have followed the gods, and shows Marcus's evil side (333C ff.). The gods are fallible and cannot recognize true merit, and there is a bond of error between gods and men.

Another important Menippean theme in the *Caesars* is the parody of encyclopedic knowledge. If we grant the similarities between the *Apocolocyntosis* and the *Caesars*, the historical material present gives the latter quite a different tone, one not explicable merely as an expansion to include more than one corrupt applicant for divinity. Julian treats his predecessors with contempt; confident of his own capabilities, he has every reason to trivialize theirs. He is superior to their religion and their history. The grand procession of emperors into the banquet hall is punctuated by the mockeries of Silenus, and the reader is assured that no solemn treatment of these emperors will be forthcoming. But the ironic catalog seeks not only the belittling of particulars but also the denigration of the very idea of order among the bewildering facts of the world. The solemnity of the procession is at variance with the nature of the emperors, and their serial ordination and description is similarly out of place in the Homeric fantasy that surrounds them. The attempt to present history in heaven is comic and incongruous, and the *Caesars* makes a mockery of the march of history.

Finally, there is Julian's innovative use of the Menippean theme of the examination of foreign gods. In Lucian's *Deorum Concilium*, Zeus and the other gods decide what to do about the proliferation of barbarian gods on Olympus; like Janus in the *Apocolocyntosis*, they decide to admit no more of such unworthy divinities, but do not effect a general housecleaning.[35] But Julian actually has more unworthy applicants gain godhead. The bitter humor of this detail cannot be overstressed; the lesson that Julian learned from the conclusion of the *Apocolocyntosis*—that the afterworld conspires to deny the emperors of Rome the true reward of their crimes (made explicit in the treatment of Constantine's reprieve)—he makes implicit in the general outcome of the contest. For all their faults, the six contestants are judged worthy of Olympus, and the same double vision of the *Apocolocyntosis* applies here as well: they are not deserving of heaven, but they are deserving of *this* heaven.

JULIAN holds an important place in the history of Menippean satire. He has more in common with the late Roman authors than with Lucian and Menippus, and has more connections with the Latin than with the Greek traditions. He is to some extent the first of Varronian revivalists, and foreshadows Martianus and Boethius in the primacy that he assigns to the simplicities of faith over the complexities of experience and knowledge. Varro was a believer in the value of traditional Roman piety; though presented comically and parodically, religion seems to have been a frequent topic in the *Menippeans*. Some

parallels between Martianus and Julian suggest that Varro lies behind Julian's use of Menippean satire to make a point about religious
belief. Like Julian, Capella presents a comic encyclopedia, though of
the Liberal Arts; the comic frame that surrounds them shows that
such knowledge is not to be taken too seriously. Yet within this is
genuine pagan religious sentiment, as Philology prays in all seriousness to the Unknown Father as the source of true enlightenment,
beyond the reach of, and far more valuable than, any book learning.[36] We also find in Martianus a comic heavenly symposium that is
the scene for the presentation of knowledge of dubious value, and
what is of true worth lies far beyond the Homeric heaven to which
Philology ascends. In both of these authors, mystic faith rejects the
proceedings to look elsewhere, in search of another god and super-
nal truth. Yet in Julian, the Menippean theme of "what you know is
wrong" becomes "what I know is right"; and Julian stands alone in
the personal pride that his Menippean satire attests.

In pointing the way to the future of Menippean satire, Julian
shows a good knowledge of its past and, like Fulgentius, bids the
reader understand his work in the light of a long literary tradition.
The *Caesars* is in a sense an updating of the *Apocolocyntosis*. And for all
of the presence of Varro, it cannot be denied that the influence of
Lucian is great. There is little in the way of verbal correspondence;
the closest parallel is between the beginning of Hermes' metrical
summons at 318D and verses quoted at *Demonax* 65, a work that has
nothing to do with Menippean satire or influence, and whose verses
derive from an Olympic pronouncement in any event. But Julian
owes Lucian much in terms of structure and style. The lack of self-
parody, the sparing use of verse, the construction of the introduction, the fairly Attic purity of the prose: these are all direct importa-
tions from Lucian's brand of literarily proper Menippean satire. The
mocker Silenus derives from the *Deorum Concilium* and the *Juppiter
Tragoedus;*[37] also from the *Juppiter Tragoedus* is the structural device of
the double dialogue, here translated into a heavenly symposium arranged on a higher level, from which to observe the emperors' contest below.

Varro is not the literal source for the fervor of Capella or of Julian.
But what I would like to propose is that Varro, like all Menippean
satirists, recommends between the lines of his comedies the value of
everyday, ordinary life. No doubt, traditional Roman piety was a
large element in the simplicity that Varro, by counterexample, presented for his reader's approval. This, to Varro, was common sense.
But the fourth century, part of that well-known "age of anxiety,"

redefines the nature of common sense. In Fulgentius, Ennodius, and Boethius, it is simple Christianity, a faith that cannot be reduced to the pagan categories of reason and theory, that replaces the common sense of Menippean satire and the pagan piety of Varro. In Capella and Julian, it is a mystic faith.

Yet Capella presents his mysticism as common sense, as though the categories of learning were obviously inadequate, and the inspiration that directed one's learning was not itself apprehensible by calm reason. As such, he is a good teacher, and I shall have much to say in praise of him in the following chapter. But Julian, with a pride that rejects emperors and history and Homer and pagan culture to insist on his own great worth and the superiority of his own unique faith, presents such mysticism as uncommon sense, as something only Julian himself is clear-sighted enough to see. This emotional distance from the self-parodic focal point of his genre is the Menippean Julian's greatest distinction.

Chapter Nine

MARTIANUS CAPELLA

LIKE LUCIAN, Martianus Capella, too, is beginning to come into his own, though he has had a steeper path to climb and is greeted by a smaller circle of well-wishers. Once the definition of the nadir to which classical learning and classical prose had sunk in late antiquity,[1] Martianus now receives some respect for his literary sensibilities, accomplishments as a prose stylist, and achievements as an encyclopedist.[2] Danuta Shanzer, whose commentary on the first book of *The Marriage of Philology and Mercury* is of prime importance, considers the work a "crypto-pagan mystagogic compendium" whose Menippean forms and self-parody provide a good disguise for pagan wisdom under Vandal rule.[3] The heroine Philologia has a name that at first suggests the beatification of the ABCs, but which is better etymologized as "the devotée of the Chaldaean Oracles."[4] Shanzer acknowledges the many parallels between the *De Nuptiis* and other works considered Menippean satires, but is ultimately and appropriately cautious, treating it as a thing sui generis.[5] But this Martianus, who employs bombastic prose for comic effect, who can treat his learned abstractions with a comic touch, and who practices such dissimulation, belongs to a self-parodic genre. Shanzer's commentary regrets that it does not treat the comic Martianus as fully as the Hermetic one; in what follows here I hope to demonstrate, without going too far in the opposite direction, what is the significance of enclosing all of this abstruse learning within a comic frame.[6]

The *De Nuptiis* is a very strange work, an encyclopedia set within an elaborate allegory, whose conclusion, discussed in Chapter 2, requires us to see that the work has failed in its task of being an encyclopedia. We are far beyond the realm of conventional disclaimers of ignorance; this is not the encyclopedia of a Uriah Heep. Philology in the *De Nuptiis*, like Marcus Aurelius in Julian's *Caesars,* will rise to a comic and Olympian heaven in which doubtful merits find a place among indifferent judges. She will join in a symposium in which the learned discourses of the Seven Liberal Arts are that most unwanted of wedding presents, one that impedes and frustrates the consummation of Philology's marriage to Mercury, whose double she seems to be, as descended and undescended aspects of the same soul of

mystic wisdom. I think that the *De Nuptiis* sets out quite purposefully
to establish the mystical lore of Books 1 and 2 as out of "synch" with
the handbook matter in the concluding seven books. Martianus
writes not an encyclopedia but a Menippean satire that parodies encyclopedic knowledge. The allegory provides the framework in
which one is to appreciate the relative value of textbook learning and
mystical revelation, of information and wisdom, of dogma and
truth.[7]

THE ACTION OF THE DE NUPTIIS

   Some details of the plot are now in order. Satura is the narrator of
a fantastic tale, complete in nine lengthy books.[8] To the author, who
presents himself as an old and incompetent scribe, Satura by lamp-
light tells of the apotheosis of Philology (1.2). In Book 1, Mercury
chooses his bride and they are betrothed; in Book 2 Philology pre-
pares for the ascent and is escorted through the spheres to Olympus.
These first two allegorical books, ostensibly concerning the purifica-
tion of the soul and its ascent to the realms of truth, are followed by
the presentation of bridal gifts in heaven from Mercury to his new
wife; and these gifts are the Seven Liberal Arts, goddesses who reveal
their learning to the bride in textbook fashion. First come the trivial
arts (Books 3–5: Grammar, Dialectic, Rhetoric), and then the quadrivial ones (Books 6–9: Geometry, Arithmetic, Astronomy, and Harmony). The work ends abruptly with a brief description of Harmony
humming a lullaby at the door of the bridal chamber (9.996); then
Satura and the narrator exchange insults about the meaninglessness
of what has gone before and who is responsible for it. Each of these
dissertations of the Liberal Arts is enclosed by descriptions of the
goddesses themselves, the reaction of the wedding company to the
goddesses and their learning, details of the heavenly banquet, and,
very important to us here, discussion between the scribe/author and
the narrator of how to relate this tale with propriety.
   Satura reappears four times after the opening pages, and offers a
significant punctuation of the text.[9] The movement of the work is
not just from allegory to encyclopedia, but at various stages we are
asked to consider just what it is that we are reading. Satura is found
at the beginning of the work; at the beginning of the textbook section
(3.221–22, where she is simply called Camena, "The Muse"); at the
beginning of the quadrivium (6.576–79); at the start of the first of
the two concluding, most important, disciplines (8.806–10, Astronomy); and at the end of the work as a whole (9.997–99). In these

encounters, she and the author debate whether the fantastic story serves to promote truth (because mortals cannot accept the naked truth) or to subvert truth.

The debate between author and personified genre is one of the most striking aspects of the *De Nuptiis;* an importation from Old Comedy, it becomes one of the characteristic devices of Menippean satire. There are traces of this in Varro's *Menippeans;* Lucian's debate in the *Bis Accusatus* with Dialogue and Philosophy is nearly parallel; Fulgentius's *Mythologies* learns from Martianus, and has its narrator lose control of his work to Calliope and Satura; even Boethius's debate with Philosophy in the *Consolation* belongs to this tradition. We are witnessing a work in progress. From the beginning, its authorship is uncertain: the opening poem has it that Calliope is singing the song, and that Hymenaeus sponsors it, yet the author's son interrupts to label such a production a silly trifle. The author then tells his son that he will relate a tale that Satura told to him; we seem to have an author changing his mind about what sort of tale he will tell, and to what source he appeals.

The narrator is clearly nervous about Satura's tale; he desires literal truth, and not fictional trappings. He is glad when the allegory is over (2.220):

> So now the myth is over; the Arts begin, which the following books shall document. For true benefit they shall remove all fiction and shall depict sober disciplines, as far as they can, nor shall they forbid the absurd. You have what follows, provided the power of the gods and the Muses and Apollo's lyre support me.

But there immediately follows at the beginning of Book 2 a versified debate in which the Muse (Camena, now a pseudonym for Satura, who evidently moves to counter the narrator's final call for other sources of inspiration) forces the narrator to admit that truth must be told in fictional garb (3.221–22):

> Again, the Muse prepares adornments for this little book and desires that it first of all bear fictions wrapped in lies, reminding me that there comes no application from the cold truth, and that it is a poet's mistake to bear straightforward truths; she gives wantonness to grace and enlivens the page by smearing it with many a color. "But the subscription of the previous book proclaims that myths have been banished from my mouth, and that the Arts, speaking the

Truth, shall compile the lessons of the following books." She said, with a laughing smile, "We shall tell no lies, yet shall the Arts be clothed. Or would you present this band of sisters naked to the wedding couple, and thus have them seek the senate of the Thunderer and the gods? Or if you choose to ignore their fictional clothing, what order can be maintained?" "To be sure, they will speak whatever they have to teach, and their clothing will follow from incorporeal speech." "But this is certainly a figurative expression, and you have deviated from your principle. So why don't you admit that without the images of fiction there can be no understanding?" With these words Camena bested me. "Do you decline?" "I shall join the game together."

The words "I shall join the game together" admit of a wide range of meanings, not all of which Satura would endorse.[10] To join in marriage will remind us of the promise of the opening poem; but as a union of opposites, of fiction and instruction, it will bring back to mind the nature of Menippean satire: a game and an instruction, uneasily joined.

Satura has an opportunity at the beginning of Book 6 to insult the narrator's stupidity. He thanks her for the vision of the trivium, but does not understand what is before him as the quadrivial arts are about to have their turn. She tells him that he is too stupid to discern Philosophia, Paedia, and the mathematician's abacus (6.576–79). She seems to win this part of the exchange, yet we ask what is the value of Satura's fiction if it prevents the narrator's understanding. The narrator then has his turn to embarrass Satura at the beginning of Book 8. She objects to his telling of the drunken slumber of Silenus, and of how Cupid wakes him by hitting him on the head; this should have been edited from the text.[11] In the poem that follows, introducing the discourse of Astronomy in epic hexameters, she upbraids the narrator for preferring fiction to discourse concerning astronomy (8.808.13–14): "tu fingere ludicra perstas / uiliaque astriloquae praefers commenta puellae?" ("Do you persist in inventing ridiculous things, and prefer despicable fictions to a maiden who speaks of the stars?"). The narrator bursts into laughter and labels this for the hypocrisy that it is (8.809):

> While Satura was still singing this, that forbidden laughter, so harshly criticized, was upon me anew. I said, "Well done, Satura! Has anger made you a poetess? Have you begun to thirst for the fonts of the River Permessus? . . . Is there any

> reason why, with your head full of lofty thoughts, you were boiling in mad rage and were, in your haughty way, attacking me with your censorious noise as I laughed at the sleep of Silenus? So I'm to remove fictions, and nothing graceful or comic shall be mixed in and relieve the boredom of the audience? Rather, come to your senses with the verse from the Paelignian poet and, lest you furrow your brow like a tragic actor, 'Laugh, maiden, if you have any sense at all; laugh!'" (Martial *Ep.* 2.41.1, citing Ovid)

The narrator and Satura have now changed positions. The narrator, who has become cleverer in the course of these exchanges with Satura, gleefully pushes Satura's position to the limit by recounting an improper scene, while she comes to see that perhaps the narrator's original idea of unadorned Arts may have been more useful and dignified. Satura's hopes of seriousness have been dashed; the narrator celebrates the triumph of impropriety. The original hopes of neither are satisfied by the work on which they have collaborated; the concluding poem of the *De Nuptiis* abandons it as a hopelessly botched job.

Literary impropriety (as characterized by the alternation of prose and verse, pedantry and mysticism, high and low styles, pathos and bathos, etc.) which goes hand in hand with thematic confusion (typified by a narrator who cannot find the dogmatic truth that he or she seeks) is a hallmark of all Menippean satire; this impropriety, readily enough discernible in the *De Nuptiis*, need not be deplored as proof of the author's imbecility.[12] The conclusion of the *De Nuptiis* states this principle as explicitly as can be expected; discussed in Chapter 2, it is worth summarizing here (9.997–99):

> You have, my son, an old woman's fiction, Satura's playful creation by the lamplight with its hodgepodge flame, while she strove to teach Greek disciplines barely friendly to Attic . . . ; thus does she end after the ninth book. For she, too talkative, piled together the learned on the unlearned, stuffed together the trite and the ineffable, mixed together the Muses and the gods and, undigested, made the Liberal Arts to chatter in a rude concoction. For she herself, shattered by knowledge of this and swelling with gall and bile, said "I could have come forth in a great philosopher's cloak, praiseworthy for my learned elegance, and could have done so decently, as if from the court of Mars himself. But, inspired by Martianus Capella . . . , when am I ever to be able

to drink from a fitting cup the waters of the Muses when he
has created them?"

The author's protestations of ignorance and inability should not be
seen as mere pious noises, insufficient to stop the mouths of critical
readers or ungenerous editors, but should be taken more at face
value and as integral to the work, which concludes: "My son, you
have followed the witness who has revealed my own ineptitude; as
you read, pardon the nonsense."[13]

Thus there is an overall structure that belittles the content. But
what is the content of the *De Nuptiis*? Its theme is the mystical union
of opposites that creates the world. It opens with a poem that sings of
the power of Love to unite the warring and contradictory physical
elements, and Love is invoked to preside over the marriage of
earthly Philology and heavenly Mercury (1.1):

> O beautiful Hymenaeus, who are the greatest concern of
> Venus; you who are said to sing at bridal beds, to be the son
> of a Mother Muse; o holy joining of the gods, who in myste-
> rious chains do coerce the warring seeds of things and in
> your holy embrace nurture unharmonious things as things
> bound together; for you bind the elements reciprocally and
> join the world in marriage and unite the spirit of the mind
> with the body, by which firm treaty nature herself is bound,
> fostering the union of the sexes, and faith in the name of
> love; . . . Calliope, who is composing a tale of the wedding
> of gods, thinks it right that you grant your approval to the
> beginning of her song.[14]

But what begins with a belief in the mystical union of opposites
(earth and heaven, mortal and divine, body and soul) becomes a
comic tale of the incommensurability of the sublime and the ridiculous. Love (Hymenaeus) is called the son of a Muse (Camena, not the
name of a specific Muse[15]) in the first line of the *De Nuptiis;* and
Camena ("my Muse") appears as an alias of Satura herself when she
speaks to the author at the beginning of Book 3, the start of the
textbook portion of the work. The repetition is perhaps significant:
will the union of opposites that the *De Nuptiis* hopes to celebrate, and
which is also at the heart of all Menippean satire, be achieved
through mystic Love of hodgepodge Satura?

We may now turn to some of the details of the actual apotheosis of
Philology. She is an embodiment of earthly wisdom, and it is because

of this that Mercury, in search of a wife, is recommended to her virtues. There is enough Neoplatonic imagery in the first two books to allow us to see Philology and Mercury as the descended and undescended aspects of the soul; Philology is to rise to her true origins.[16] But by this same token she is not perfect; her preparations for marriage are described in the language of the mysteries, and because she qualifies for initiation she stands in need of some vital knowledge.[17] The De Nuptiis possesses the same double perspective of the heavenly world as the Apocolocyntosis or the Caesars: the characters move in and out of their Homeric (comic) and philosophical (serious) characterizations. For example, Philology is Mercury's fourth choice for a wife after Sophia (suggestive of Philosophy, and not marriageable), Prophecy (who belongs to Apollo), and Psyche (snatched away by Cupid; 1.6–7). Shanzer sees these three as three types of soul, each inferior to the theurgic type.[18] But if it is true that theurgy is stressed over Socratic, inward-looking Philosophy, it is most interesting that Psyche is said to be adorned with every gift of the Olympian gods. Mercury loses Psyche because she is snatched away by Cupid, and the marriage of Cupid and Psyche, described by Apuleius in terms similar to that of Philology and Mercury at the end of the De Nuptiis, is in fact present in the De Nuptiis as a parody of the final wedding scene: Cupid and Psyche represent a fall, and Philology and Mercury an elevation.

But Mercury himself in these scenes has his Olympian aspect: he must be dissuaded from his desire for Psyche by Virtue, and the gifts of the gods comport to sensual delight, not spiritual edification. Many of the details of Mercury's passion and courtship are also comic. Virtue bids him consult Apollo for advice (1.8), the god who prevented Mercury's marriage to Prophecy, who adorned Psyche with the mantic arts, and who, in this context, will remind us of the god who is notoriously unlucky in affairs of the heart and hardly one's first choice as a confidant in such matters. It turns out that the Apollo Mercury will find is in fact quite different: he has abandoned all of his earthly haunts for an unearthly grove. Here we meet the Apollo of true heavenly harmonies, although there is a comic touch in that the wind in the branches of the trees (of conveniently varying sizes) makes all possible harmonies, which are, of course, labeled: octave, sesquialtera, sesquitertia, sesquioctava, with semitones in between (1.11). And when she learns that Philology is to be Mercury's bride, Virtue's transports of joy are most probably occasioned by the thought that Philology's sober nature is not likely to result in any sensual indulgence.[19] We are close to Frye's romance pattern of the heroine who belongs in a higher world, rescuing a less impressive male during the time of her descent.

The gods are summoned from every quarter of the sky, occasioning some fascinating Etruscan cosmological lore (1.45–60); though Shanzer suspects that there is here a comic treatment of conventional catalogs of the gods.[20] Jupiter addresses them, and makes formal proclamation of the betrothal. The beginning of Book 2 finds Philology reacting to the news. When she learns that she is to be Mercury's bride, she certainly sings no *Magnificat,* but wonders whether such a marriage would be in her best interests. Her numerological analysis of the names of bride and groom (2.101–9) reveals that his number, 3, is male, and that her number, 4, is female; thus the marriage is auspicious.[21] With magic potions and herbs she smears her body with a heat-resistant substance.[22] Her learning and intelligence are to be seen as comic arrogance. It is Phronesis (Wisdom), Philology's mother, who must strip Philology of the trappings that she would have dared to bring into heavenly society (2.114).

Philology tries by her own unaided efforts to prepare for the ascent. Like Psyche, she does not prosper by the addition of gifts but, rather, by subtraction, and arrogant Philology must learn the *uia negatiua* of mystic faith.[23] Athanasia (Immortality) then appears and bids Philology drink of her cup; the drink is an emetic that will rid Philology of things that would prevent her immortality (2.135–39):

> [Athanasia] said "Unless by a strictly enforced emptying you vomit out these things with which your breast is full and spew them forth, you will in no way gain the seat of immortality." . . . And then in fact that nausea and forced vomiting were transformed into great heaps of literature of every sort. You could see what books, what great rolls, how many works in all languages had poured forth from the maiden's mouth. . . . Yet while the maiden was vomiting forth such things in billows, a number of girls (some of whom were called Arts, and others Disciplines) did thereupon gather up that which the maiden had spilled forth, each of them snatching part away for her own requisite task and competence. . . . Therefore after the maiden had with effort poured forth from her depths that librarial mass, weak with the pallor of exhaustion, she called for the aid of Athanasia, who had been witness to her great labor.

This is more than gnostic/hermetic/mystic rejection of false knowledge in order to see by the true light.[24] Philology, in order to be

worthy of eternal life, must abandon that very learning which ini-
tially had made her desirable. Further, this is not just mystic but
comic; in Lucian *Lexiphanes* 21, we read of a pedant who is given an
emetic and forced to vomit up his pretentious Platonic archaizing
vocabulary.[25] Most remarkable of all, however, is the fact that the
Arts collect such portions of her vomit as are appropriate to them. It
will be necessary that the Seven Liberal Arts speak in the concluding
seven books in their own voices; but this dramatization makes it clear
that the dissertations we are about to hear represent the knowledge
that was a primary impediment to Philology's entrance into the heavenly court in the first place.

Further, after Philology regains her strength, she admits to Juno,
who is her escort through the heavenly regions, that all of her earlier
knowledge was pure conjecture; she begs the goddess to reveal to her
the workings of the universe.[26] Philology still receives a comic treatment: she travels with her three handmaidens Inquisitiveness (Fussi-
ness?), Wakefulness (Insomnia?), and Painstakingness.[27] Further, the
Muses who extol her wisdom at 2.117–26 (in some of Martianus's
nicest verses) and who speak of her as the source of all their activity[28]
do not all speak in the fields of expertise which had become traditional for them by this date, but seem to have attributes assigned to
them for some comic purpose.[29] For example, Calliope, the Muse of
epic poetry, praises her for lyric and prophetic accomplishments
(2.119); Polyhymnia, muse of mime, extols her knowledge of rhythm,
meter, and pronunciation (2.120); Clio, the Muse of history, speaks of
her as an unscrupulous rhetorician, exploiting ambiguous words to
destroy the expected sense (2.122); Erato, Muse of erotic poetry,
speaks of her abilities in the natural sciences (2.123); Terpsichore,
Muse of dance, of her tedious devotion to night-long study (2.124);
Euterpe, Muse of flute music, claims that she knows the prophetic
arts and brings down the will of heaven to inspired minds (2.125);
Thalia, the Muse of comedy, speaks the concluding benediction, describing the wanderings of Mercury, and the superiority of the bride
to the groom (2.126). The Muses figure prominently in mystical initiation in late antiquity, but there is some irony at work here.[30] A
refrain is sung after each Muse has praised some aspect of the learning that Philology will leave behind, suggesting that a single intellectual virtue should be seen as sufficient justification for apotheosis:

> O maiden, climb up to the temples of heaven, worthy of
> such a marriage; Jupiter, your father-in-law, bids you rise
> up to the lofty stars.[31]

The point is that Philology on her own is a comic figure, mistress of mundane study; this knowledge must be replaced by revelation of the Truth.

Menippean satires typically contain a serious passage, whose profundities are strangely out of place in their ludicrous context. Here, Philology perceives that as she rises higher in the company of Juno her guide, she is coming closer to the source of all truth. In impressive hexameters (2.185–93), she prays to the Sun, the first emanation of the Unknown Father, for a glimpse of the true heaven;[32] she soon gets her wish when she reaches the outer wall of heaven. The passage shows Martianus's Latin at its florid best: the following translation is a pale approximation (2.200–6):

> Philology herself leapt down from her palanquin: when she saw the vast fields of light and the springtime of heavenly tranquillity; and now saw the many distinctions and appearances of the decan gods; and was then amazed at how the eighty-four attendants stood in heaven; and saw in addition the blazing spheres of the clustered stars and the meshing of the circles in interdependent connection (yet that very sphere which constrained the outermost orbit was compelled by an awesome whirling, and the poles and the axis, brandished from the height of heaven, passed through the very depths of the earth and set spinning the whole mass and mechanism of heaven); not being unaware that the Father and god of so great a work and so great a design had removed himself even from the perception of the gods (for she had realized that he transcended all supramundane blisses, rejoicing in a certain empyrean and a certain intelligible world), she knelt next to the very wall of the outer orbit and with absolutely concentrated mental exertion prayed for a long time in silence, and in the manner of the ancients called out with the voice of her mind certain words of discordant nations, words varying in rhythm and unknown in sound, sounded within in letters now joined, now in alternation; and in words she adored the guardian gods of the intelligible realm and their ministers (who must be worshiped by the powers of the sensible realm) and the whole universe bounded by the abyss of the Undefinable Father; and she called upon three certain gods and other gods of the day and night, adorned with seven rays. She prayed also to a certain maiden of the source and (accord-

ing to the mysteries of Plato) to the powers Once and Twice
Beyond. When she had prayed with all her heart for a very
long time in these ways to the flower of the flame and to that
truth which exists among things that do not exist, then she
seemed to see that she deserved apotheosis and worship.

It is by virtue of this mystic experience that her apotheosis is justified,
not by virtue of her earthly knowledge. The pinnacle of human intellectual achievement is prayer in silence and in nonsense syllables and
worship of what can never be known at the edge of the universe. At
this point Philology enters the Olympian heaven and the allegory
ends. Book 2 concludes with the author's poem that states his belief
that the myth is over and the Arts will follow, without fiction but with
some entertainment. Satura will soon appear to frustrate these plans
and expectations.

The ascent to the unknowable depends upon a rejection of earthly
knowledge. This is itself hardly a remarkable idea.[33] More remarkable is the fact that Juno's guided tour of the heavenly orders and
harmonies in Book 2 must also be seen as something other than
absolute truth; we learn that knowledge of the Father is withheld
even from the gods. But what is most striking is that Philology, who
has worshiped the Undefinable Father and who has received a
glimpse of ultimate truth, will find herself ushered into the Olympian heaven (2.208ff.). After the description of the transcendence of
the Father, this lets us down with a bump; the grandiloquent description of the abode of the Olympians is ultimately no more serious than
that in Julian's *Caesars*.[34] And even if we were to say that there is no
other heaven that might reasonably be described and which she
might reasonably enter, there remains a further difficulty: the very
information she had to vomit forth in order to reach heaven is now
given back to her when Mercury presents as dowry the Seven Liberal
Arts. Is this to be read as if it were the conclusion of Job, Philology
receiving back the price demanded of her? Or is she like the proverbial dog returning to its vomit?

There are two Philologies in the *De Nuptiis*. The first, the one
jealous of her earthly knowledge and attempting to scale heaven on
her own merits, is the typical butt of Menippean satire, what Frye
could call a *philosopha gloriosa*. She is remarkably transformed into
the second, the passive observer of the place of truth and of an
absurd realm below it, who is the typical Menippean narrator. We are
not told of Philology's reactions to what she sees in Books 3–9, as she
becomes a mute character and is seldom referred to, but hers is the

catascopia and the entry into heaven that allows the old Olympians to reveal why they are unworthy of our respect. We observed a similar transformation of Menippus in his ascent to Olympus in the *Icaromenippus*. Further, there are two heavens in the *De Nuptiis:* Philology perceives the true one when emptied of her learning; but as she gets her learning back she becomes a member of the false one, the traditional comic and Homeric Olympus of Menippean satire, known from Seneca and various dialogues of Lucian. Similarly, the *Caesars* of Julian implies two heavens: the one of the unworthy applicants for apotheosis whose wranglings are the substance of the work, and the special heaven reserved for Julian himself, in the company of Mithras, mentioned at its conclusion.[35] The heaven of the *De Nuptiis* in Books 3–9 is after all the one in which we find the antics of the drunken Silenus. Furthermore, this is also the heaven in which wedding guests and the wedding couple are forced to listen to expositions of textbook learning. The *De Nuptiis* plays frequently on this theme: the longed-for union of Philology and Mercury is delayed by the prolix mistresses of learning. The handbooks come as an anticlimax after the vision of Philology and become a frustration to Mercury, who at one point lets his attentions stray to Venus herself.[36] This learning is not sublime.

What is the meaning of this? Why structure the *De Nuptiis* so that its constituent halves grate so against each other? Note that Martianus in doing so parodies the *Republics* of Plato and Cicero: a vision of eternal truth should follow, not precede, the information that makes the vision intelligible. Imagine how different our reaction would be if the apotheosis of Philology *followed* the description of her learning. Perhaps no reader would have survived to read the apotheosis; but there is more at work here than a pleasant mise-en-scène for the seriousness of the textbook arts. The rejected information is returned to Philology as though it were a sort of ballast necessary to keep her at a lower level than she could otherwise achieve. Or, to borrow an image from Plato, Martianus shows us a Philology who is dragged out of the cave and then dragged back down again. The point, I think, is this: Martianus has so arranged his material to show that there is no *logical* connection between its mystical and its factual content.[37] This is the objection that Satura makes at the end of the work: the presentation has made the learning seem absurd. The *De Nuptiis* makes clear the radical disjunction between learning and mystic truth. Earthly knowledge at its face value qualifies one only for the Homeric heaven.

MYTH AND EDUCATION

But has Martianus just jumbled together the seven books of the Arts as if any order would be sufficient to make this point? I do not think so. Viewed separately, the last seven books do have an order and a logic. The first three, the trivial and trivium subjects Grammar, Dialectic, and Rhetoric, receive the greatest amount of comic detail in the descriptions that frame their discourses.[38] The quadrivial arts deal with the eternal truths of number and proportion; they are more important and are treated with more respect. Geometry and Arithmetic are slightly abused, Astronomy and Harmony hardly at all.[39] In the last two books Astronomy suggests the vastness, and Harmony the unity, of the world.[40] The *De Nuptiis* does end with a wedding: Hymenaeus sings the epithalamium (9.901–3), and Harmony herself sings of the power of Love among the gods (though before her essay on her Art) at 9.911–19; she is also said to hum the lullaby that finally escorts the couple to the marriage chamber (9.996). Although the structure of the *De Nuptiis* denies the possibility of a logical progression to the perception of any logical order in the universe, it does speak of a mystic ascent to a vision of a transcendent order.

The reader is asked at the end of the *De Nuptiis*, as in all Menippean satires, to laugh at the incongruity of the work, and to learn a lesson not so much from anything said as from the defeat of the theorist (here, Satura) who had hoped to put all of life and learning in logical order. Martianus rejects the persona of the instructor-father: whereas a Macrobius may speak of the well-digested material that he has assembled for his son, Martianus insists both in his conclusion and in the scene in which Philology vomits forth the Liberal Arts that this book learning is not a palatable concoction but a revolting hash: the literary (as well as etymological) equivalent of this sort of culinary satura is the farce.[41] We learn that learning is meaningless unless it erects a structure from which we leap into the unknown. In the *De Nuptiis*, Menippean satire, like many genres of Latin literature of late antiquity, has gone back to its preclassical sources: that is, to the *Saturae Menippeae* of Varro.[42] It is not of particular interest here to what extent Martianus draws on or modifies Varro's own textbook of the Liberal Arts, the *Disciplinarum Libri IX;*[43] what is important is that Varro's Menippean form has been so expanded as to include exhaustively a parody of the encyclopedic knowledge that was present in the *Menippeans* embryonically. Martianus's originality lies in transforming the comic and self-parodic essays of Varro the pedant into an ambitious, massive, religious, and philosophical document, whose theme is nevertheless traditional to Menippean satire: the harmony that orders all things is incomprehensible to mortals, and itself includes everything sublime (the Undefinable Father) and everything ridiculous (the drunken Silenus). The improprieties of Menippean satire are emblematic of the incomprehensible and embarrassing details of life itself. While it is foolish to assert that one knows the order of the universe, it is good to believe that there is an order: being incomprehensible, it cannot be reduced to rule, trivialized, or filed away and forgotten. Life, with all of its trivialities and quadrivialities, remains the salutary thorn in the side of the theorist.

It is worthwhile to review here the relation of the *De Nuptiis* to the genre and history of Menippean satire. Martianus's humor is at the expense of a number of academic traditions, being a parody of noble forms of literature and learning (from Plato's *Republic* to the Roman handbook tradition), in a style that abuses all literary standards of propriety. In the tradition of Varro, the author makes fun of his own learning; he doubts his ability to communicate in a meaningful way with his audience, and dramatizes his inability to compose a coherent work. Such serious matters as the *De Nuptiis* wishes to discuss are found by the reader in the contemplation of the failure of theory to comprehend the world. Yet it does participate in the Greek traditions. Philology, like Menippus in Lucian's *Icaromenippus* and *Necyomantia*, becomes a passive observer of all levels of existence, seeing sublimity for an instant but remaining firmly mired in the mundane. As in Julian's *Caesars,* the Hellenistic heavenly ἀγών is transformed into a consideration of just what sort of heaven finds room for earthly imperfections. The *De Nuptiis* demonstrates the change of the tradition of Menippus through time: the Cynic truth, that one should live in this world but not take it too seriously, that one should not pride oneself on philosophical habits that inevitably become hypocritical, becomes a mystic truth, that the things of this world and all of its learning must be transcended in the pursuit of a real world that lies elsewhere, beyond the grasp of reason.

One may sympathize with skeptical reactions to this seemingly fanciful interpretation of what must remain a dull work. It is easier to see the smoke here than to admit to the fire. But Martianus's influence, immediate and profound, leads to works with a similar point of view concerning the value of textbook learning. Within a century or so the three Christian Menippean satirists (Fulgentius, Ennodius, and Boethius) take the *De Nuptiis* as a model for works in which the author contemplates making a synthesis of profane learning and Christian tradition. All three, I shall claim, come to the conclusion that the human attempt to unify such opposites leads only to embarrassment: all three authors reveal a failed synthesis and suggest between the lines that only a higher truth can make sense of the world.

Chapter Ten

FULGENTIUS

TOWARD THE END of the fifth century A.D., Fabius Planciades Fulgentius wrote his *Mythologies,* which sets out in three books a vaguely systematic and superficial account of some basic Greek myths and their allegorical meanings.[1] The exact date cannot be fixed, but it must lie between the publication of the *De Nuptiis,* which Fulgentius refers to in another work (*Serm. Ant.* 45, p. 123. 4–7 Helm)[2] and which is a model for the *Mythologies,* and the composition of Boethius's *Consolation of Philosophy,* which is clearly influenced by Fulgentius's Menippean satire.[3] If we accept the identification of Fulgentius the Mythographer with Fulgentius the bishop of Ruspe (traditional dates, 468–533), as is plausible if not provable,[4] the *Mythologies* could easily be one of a number of the latter's youthful works and may thus belong to the early 490s. The *Mythologies* therefore may have been published soon after the *De Nuptiis.*[5]

The mythographer is revealed by his other works to be a Christian, and it is his Christian claim to higher truth, vaguely hinted at and suitably veiled, which he calls upon in the prologue of the *Mythologies* to justify his reinterpretation of Greek myth. Fulgentius is the first of the Christian Menippean satirists, and his willingness to involve such a serious matter as his own faith in a web of confusion and self-parody makes the *Mythologies* a valuable and overlooked document in the history of the accommodation of Christianity to pagan learning. The narrator will show himself to be a fool as he tries to subject the inanities of mythology to the scrutiny of faith. Like Ennodius and Boethius after him, Fulgentius insists upon a strict demarcation between the pagan and Christian worlds and laughs at the possibility of their coherent synthesis. Like the pagan Martianus, these Christian authors are confident enough of their culture to treat it lightly and not neurotically; a similar point has been made about Lucian and his relation to classical literary culture. These works are at home in the sixth-century revival of literature and learning, a time neither culturally nervous nor complacent; one can no more imagine Augustine writing Menippean satires than Isidore of Seville. For the Christian Menippean satirists, there are certain aspects of human experience which can neither be appropriated by Christianity nor completely ignored, and while such things must seem trivial in comparison with the revelation of faith, they are given their laughing due.

THE BARBARITY of Fulgentius's language, the tortured trivialities of his prose, and the highly erratic nature of his learning and scholarship have proved serious obstacles to a literary appreciation of his works.[6] Yet even though he is neither the thinker nor the stylist that Martianus is, there is no reason to deny him the ability to make fun of himself and his language. The *Mythologies* is certainly notable for its jarring linguistic excess, but only in its prologue. The three books of allegories themselves are written in a fairly sober, if unpleasant, style, and it is clear that Fulgentius, here at least, distinguishes between the calm language of instruction and the extreme language that introduces it, and he follows in the footsteps of the master Martianus.[7] Like the *De Nuptiis,* the *Mythologies* is an ironic encyclopedia; the prologue provides the comic frame into which the allegories are set and which calls into question the importance of the erudition that they contain. However, unlike the *De Nuptiis,* the *Mythologies* seems to forget this comic frame: in the introductions to Books 2 and 3 the author speaks in his own name, and all artifice is set aside. The prologue stands out from the rest of the work, and all that is distinctively Menippean resides within its fifteen pages. What follows is a discussion of the prologue and its implications for the encyclopedic material that follows; the annotated translation in Appendix B allows for some brevity here.

THE SEDUCTION OF THE NARRATOR

In the *Mythologies,* an intellectual with a new theory to preach discovers his own inadequacy and learns that he cannot influence the world and its ineradicable imperfections. This is the Varronian comic contrast of *nunc* and *tunc;* Fulgentius follows Martianus's lead as well, in the device of a debate between the narrator and his suspicious Muse for the control of the writing of this encyclopedia and its interpretation. Here too is a variation: whereas Martianus's narrator worked out a curious compromise with his Satura, the narrator of the *Mythologies* is the unequivocal loser in his contest with Calliope. The narrator claims at 3.16–20 that he invented the myth that follows, and that it will show him to be "no mad poet . . . but an interpreter of dreams who divines meanings from the trifles of sleep." Yet he is not in control of his own myth, and by the end of the prologue he is babbling in his sleep horrible verses, full of mythical allusion, "like an insane poet" (13.18–19). The prologue records the narrator's intellectual embarrassment as the creatures of myth, whom he had hoped to dismiss as outmoded and irrelevant, take the reins of the *Mythologies* and reveal their own idea of the allegorical meanings of Greek mythology. They, not the narrator, preside over the reinterpretation of their own meaning.

The narrator is a polemical preacher who views himself as an anti-Ovid.[8] Not only does he mention the *Heroides* (3.20–4.1) as an example of a way not to write meaningfully about mythology, but in two places he consciously inverts the Ovidian manifesto of *Metamorphoses* 1.1–4 in the name of a new theory of interpretation. Ovid's *Metamorphoses* begins:

> In noua fert animus mutatas dicere formas
> corpora; di, coeptis (nam uos mutastis et illa)
> adspirate meis primaque ab origine mundi
> ad mea perpetuum deducite tempora carmen.[9]

> I intend to tell of shapes transformed into new bodies; gods, inspire my undertakings (for you have changed them as well) and bring down from the first beginning of the world to my own time the eternal song.

The narrator will have none of this. At the end of the first poem the narrator stands the last of these lines on its head (8.4–5):

> ad meum uetusta carmen
> saecla nuper confluant.

> Let the ancient ages flow together in my time for my song.

His song is not to continue through the ages, but all ages are to meet for a new song; the narrator hopes to summarize and end, not perpetuate, the ancient traditions. And when he argues with Calliope and says that he has no interest in the poetic retelling of old myths, he draws a contemptuous reference to Ovid's first two lines (11.12–13): "Mutatas igitur uanitates manifestare cupimus, non manifesta mutando fuscamus." But the narrator's arrogance and contempt are no match for the power of classical mythology. Just as the gods had redirected Ovid's plan at the beginning of the *Metamorphoses* ("nam uos mutastis et illa") so too does Calliope change the narrator's.[10] The interpreter who had hoped to beat Ovid at his own game succumbs to the same fate; the subsequent allegories are not the ones he intended to write. The lines of battle are drawn over what is the proper source of inspiration for the necessary reevaluation of classical mythology.

So much may be said in outline; I turn now to the details of the plot. The narrator and Calliope are both depicted as hopeful refugees: the narrator has escaped the horrors of civil unrest and barbarian invasion, of ruinous taxes and forced confinement, of a world laid waste by the horrors of war (4.6–7.4); Calliope is now an exile from both Rome and Alexandria and is just one step ahead of Galen's vivisectionists (8.22–9.17). The narrator emerges reborn into a new world. He is like a shipwrecked sailor cast up on dry land (an image taken in the *Allegorical Content of Vergil* to signify birth), and learns to walk again after putting off his cloak of stone (5.18–22). The dewy hills and fragrant flowers he finds after crossing the wastelands of infertile fields are allegorical, not real. The advent of "his lord and king, . . . like the dawning of the sun to the world" (5.13–16), speaks of the temporal ruler who put the barbarians to flight, but a Vandal king could not create the *locus amoenus* where our drowsy narrator will find himself.

The narrator's poem shows the scholar's pride; the time of the Muses is past, and there are new sources of inspiration. Their power is prettily enough described, but the poet's derision is obvious when he calls them not the Muses of the *Iliad* and the *Aeneid,* but of the *Batrachomyomachia* and the *Eclogues.* They are also the Muses of Hesiod, notorious for their claim to be plausible liars (*Theog.* 27–28), an association sure to come to the reader's mind since the confrontation of poet and Muse on the hillside in the *Mythologies* is owed, directly or indirectly, to Hesiod.[11] Calliope answers this contemptuous summons, nervous about its implications. When asked to lodge with the narrator, Calliope asks whether it is safe for him to harbor such an exponent of literary culture (9.18–23). He speaks of a rebirth of literature, and his citations of Vergil are proof of the fact; but he concludes with a pointed citation from Terence, designed to show just how much of her student he is (*Eun.* 246):

> Once upon a time and long ago, in an earlier age, there was profit in that sort of thing.

Now poets appropriate the storehouses of Helicon in the name of a higher power and the right of succession (*hereditario iure*). At first blush, a reference to the new poets of the Vandal court; but it will become clear that Calliope is not happy with the narrator's view of his place in Roman literary history.

Calliope now realizes that her own fate hangs in the balance, and she tries to dissuade the narrator from his plans. She praises his poetic abilities, calls him an initiate in her Anacreontic mysteries (a slighting reference to a trivial and drunken poet), strokes him more enticingly than he thinks proper, and reminds him of his love of Satyra; she then begs him to give up dream interpretation and, like Satura to Martianus, speaks of the advantages of literary ornament and lively treatment (10.15–19). Calliope appears dressed for physical seduction; as one of three Muses, she appears for another Judgment of Paris.[12] Her diaphanous garments are wet, and she has gathered up her skirts (8.6–8). The narrator thinks that she has done this merely to keep her gown from being torn on the weeds over which she had passed (8.14–16), but his poem requested that she descend from grassy hills, and the Muses as an ensemble are said to come directly from Helicon. The narrator, the naive observer of Menippean satire, does not notice her wiles and realizes only gradually her seductiveness. Calliope realizes, to her credit, that she will need more than physical charms to argue the narrator out of his proposed plan; Satyra, the enemy of sober instruction, who prefers fiction and delight to edification, will be her most potent weapon.

A direct confrontation follows. The narrator says that his is not a poet's interest in mythology, and that Calliope must have misunderstood the title of his book to suppose otherwise (10.19–11.18). When Calliope asks how he can be certain that he knows what antiquity itself had never known, he claims that knowledge of ignorance is the beginning of learning (11.18–12.2), and concludes: "primum itaque ego scientiae uestibulum puto scire quod nescias" ("And so I think that I know the most important entryway of knowledge, a thing you may not know"). The language is mystical, reminding Calliope of his belief in an ineffable power higher than Helicon which is to transform Helicon. But it is also a paradoxical profession of Socratic ignorance: because the narrator does not know the meaning of myths, he is capable of deciding what they do mean.

Calliope admires the difficulty of the narrator's task and immediately tries to insinuate herself into it (12.9–10): "Therefore we must appropriate Philosophia herself and Urania as assistants for our work." Calliope hopes to change the narrator's goal by making herself and her friends the higher authority that the narrator requires (12.4: "ampliora sunt auctoritatum quaerenda suffragia"). And while Calliope disclaims comedy as an element in this labor, Satyra will be present to refresh the narrator after his intellectual exertions (12.11–13). The narrator is afraid not of the help of the Muses and Philosophia, but of Satyra alone (already a sign of flagging resolve), and begs, out of respect for his jealous wife, that she not be allowed within his house (12.13–20). Yet he fears also for Satyra, whom his wife will attack and send packing back to Helicon. But Calliope points out that all wives and imperious women are afraid of Satyra (12.22–13.5): Satyra is a rival to the narrator's theories, and Calliope implies that the narrator must accept the services of Satyra whether he wants to or not, and will have to satisfy the demands of this mistress, and not of his wife, a figure of something more than literal significance.

The second poem, inspired by the opening poem of the *Apocolocyntosis,* shows that the narrator, under the influence of Calliope's words, is now unable to analyze myths and discover their mystic kernel. He acts as a pagan poet, even though he had boldly claimed that he had no interest in such things (3.20–4.4, 10.19–11.8). His techniques are those of obfuscation, not elucidation. He is under the spell of the pagan night (13.15–16):

> Now phantasms, deceiving the mind with fictitious images,
> were filling soft beds with treacherous signs.

He has become an insane poet, has forgotten the very name of night, and refers to Calliope as "that woman from the country, that guest whom I had seen long ago" (13.19–20). The events of the day seem to have happened in the distant past. The narrator loses control of his own mind, and now he certainly needs the help of Calliope and her crew if he is to make any sense at all of pagan mythology.

The elaborate descriptions of Urania and Philosophia, taken over from the example of the Arts in the *De Nuptiis,* are essentially comic. Urania stubs her toe on the doorjamb while contemplating the heavens (14.12–14); Philosophia seems to have smelled something awful (14.14–20). Only Satyra has powers of observation, and she can see the meanings in drunken writings (14.1–6). These three, the narrator is told, will raise his fame to the stars; and their tools will be those of the philosophers Carneades, Plato, and Aristotle (14.21–15.6). Not by accident are Carneades and his hellebore mentioned first, for hellebore is a cure for madness and Carneades' propaedeutic for the study of philosophy; Calliope's assistants must first cure the insanity of the narrator. This is a hopeful claim, for it is Satyra, the playful wanton who was only to provide entertainment for the narrator, who has become the central member of this committee of interpreters. The narrator's expectations have been utterly confounded, and the creature whom he feared most is now in control.

The prologue of the *Mythologies* is itself a myth and in need of allegorical interpretation. It is also a Menippean satire and in need of Satyra, a personification of the genre, for its understanding. The narrator's comments to Calliope make it clear that he considers the retailers of myths to be fools, and he has become himself a fool in the writing of a myth. The prologue is now the drunken writing that Satyra has the power to analyze, and although she is not the one who dictates the allegorizations that follow (after Calliope explains the origin of idols, she hands the reins of the work over to Philosophia in the second myth of Book 1), she is emblematic of the confusion involved in trying to tell the meaning of mythology in terms of a type of knowledge or belief utterly alien to mythology.[13] She is the mixture of opposites that cannot be reconciled: in the conflict between the narrator and Calliope, between the new world and the old, between truth and lies, there can be no meaningful accommodation, no meeting halfway. Only mythology can understand mythology. Calliope's final words, which attribute the origins of mythology to the error that creeps into the mind of the credulous, seem a last reference to the narrator's presumption and embarrassment (15.12–19):

> "For although there are some who reject the innate nobility of their heads and in their rustic and antique sensibilities are as wise as acorns, and their numbed wits are hidden in an all-too-thick cloud of stupidity, nevertheless, errors never arise in the human senses unless driven in by random impulses, as Chrysippus says in his work *On Fate:* 'Impulses roll on by unpredictable forces.' And so let us abandon this discursiveness and speak of whence idols are derived."

The myth of the prologue would have it that the meanings to be derived from mythology, and from the prologue itself, are trivial in comparison to some sort of higher truth, which debases itself to examine the errors of an earlier age and which would perpetuate these errors by assigning a value to them. Calliope and Satyra live on because the narrator will not leave them alone.

MYTH, ALLEGORY, AND SATIRE

But what is this riddled source of higher truth? It is Christianity, I think, who is the stern wife who brooks no rival; certainly no flesh-and-blood wife is present in the narrator's house at the close of the prologue. What proves the Christian nature of the higher wisdom, I think, is the elaborate set of parallels between it and the *Allegorical Content of Vergil.* To sketch these similarities briefly:

An address to a patron which claims that modern times do
not support literature (*Verg. Cont.* 83.1–9, *Mit.* 3.1–9).

The deprecation of the author's talents (*Verg. Cont.* 84.17–
22, *Mit.* 3.9–20).

Reference to the task at hand as one that requires hellebore
(*Verg. Cont.* 85.2–3, *Mit.* 15.4–5).

Address to the Muses in verse (*Verg. Cont.* 85.59, *Mit.* 7.5–
8.5).[14]

Introduction of a fabulous character (Vergil's ghost at *Verg.
Cont.* 85.11–16; Calliope and the Muses at *Mit.* 8.6–8).

Character(s) drunk from the font of Hippocrene (*Verg.
Cont.* 85.13, *Mit.* 8.6–8).

Character(s) carrying symbolic tools of an appropriate craft
and looking absurd (*Verg. Cont.* 85.13–16, *Mit.* 14.6–20).[15]

Character with a wrinkled brow, smelling something awful
(Vergil at *Verg. Cont.* 85.17–19; Urania at *Mit.* 14.16–18).[16]

The narrator defining for the fabulous character(s) what
the nature of the impending work will be, and receiving
the scorn of his guest(s) because his intentions are unsatisfactory (narrator demands trivialities of Vergil at *Verg.
Cont.* 85.19–86.19; narrator proclaims that he will not re-
tell the old myths at *Mit.* 10.19–11.18).

A fabulous character insults the narrator (*Verg. Cont.* 86.6–
10, *Mit.* 11.18–21).[17]

The narrator dull as a clod (*Verg. Cont.* 86.9; *Mit.* 15.12–15, in
which the narrator is compared to an acorn eater).

Snoring as a sign of the narrator's stupidity (*Verg. Cont.*
86.9–10, *Mit.* 13.25–14.1).

A fabulous character promising to teach what the narrator
may not be able to understand, so that the narrator must
open his ears (*Verg. Cont.* 86.16–19, *Mit.* 15.6–10).

The *Allegorical Content of Vergil* seems to have a prologue that promises a Menippean satire: a mixture of prose and verse, a narrator
whose intelligence is insulted, a comic source of information of
doubtful utility, a fantastic dialogue on the nature of literature and
its interpretation, abuse of literary conventions. For the last point
consider the narrator's admission that the address to the Muses in
verse was a concession to an outmoded literary tradition (85.10–11):

This brief invocation, I think, will satisfy Vergil's Muses.
Now give me the person of the bard of Mantua himself!

But this is not a Menippean satire. What Vergil says will be presented as true; the narrator does not get lost in this fantasy but will continue to ask questions and make observations throughout Vergil's presentation of the secrets of the *Aeneid* without any suggestion that the dialogue is impossible. Most important of all, the narrator will mention in a number of places that Vergil's morals are Christian morals as well (87.6–10, 89.3–10, 96.14–18, 97.18–98.1, 102.18–103.7), a conclusion never reached in the *Mythologies*. Despite the humor of the introduction, the *Allegorical Content of Vergil* has serious things to say; I detect no particular irony in this Dantesque presentation of Vergil's ghost speaking of Christian truth.

The *Mythologies* and the *Allegorical Content of Vergil* form a diptych: pagan sources of wisdom reveal pagan trivialities in the one and Christian truths in the other. For Vergil is the author of the messianic *Fourth Eclogue* and is honored as a prophet by Christian scholars from at least the third century through the Middle Ages. The *Aeneid* is a text that must be defended as acceptable to the Christian community, and Vergil is an author whose integrity must be maintained. No doubt, the *Aeneid* is not the Bible, and the humor of the introduction of the *Allegorical Content of Vergil* prevents the reader from taking Vergil too seriously as a prophet; but Fulgentius writes approvingly of this author as a literary and moral authority. The *Mythologies,* however, has nothing to defend as its myths (with the important exception of Apuleius's *Cupid and Psyche*) have no authors.[18] Mythology is treated as a collection of beliefs, not as a body of literary works; there is no sanctity of the book about them, but only the odor of error. There is no need to accord them any respect, and the author in the prefaces to the other two books makes it clear that he views this treatment of mythology as an inconsequential game that anyone can play.[19]

Pagan mythology is allegorized in the *Mythologies;* if we insist on the force of the prologue throughout the books that follow, Philosophia will allegorize Calliope away at 25.1–27.11, *The Myth of the Nine Muses.* This is important: if the Muses are important figures in the language and practice of mystical initiation in late antiquity, their evaporation here shows Fulgentius, like Boethius after him, rejecting the pagan Muses as sources of wisdom.[20] The allegories they provide yield no Christian secrets: although scripture or liturgy may be called upon to justify an etymology or to supply a detail, they never provide the substance of the interpretations, which are typically and superficially moral.[21] The narrator is a failed apologist, and the *Mythologies* does not subscribe to the specifically Christian theories of pagan myths, that they reflect either the influence of demons or are an adumbration of true revelation granted to the pagan world.[22] Rather, Fulgentius presents a different Christian cliché (a position first fully developed by Plato) that poets are the inventors of the falsehoods of mythology; but the point is made by default, as pagan mythological creatures demonstrate their own allegorical bloodlessness.

So too would Fulgentius pass judgment on the myth of his own prologue. The author who makes up a myth (as the narrator proudly claims that he will do at 3.16–20) confuses the obvious, traffics in lies, and deserves, at best, cursory examination; at worst, contempt. He has presented himself in the guise of Paris, reclining at his ease on the hillside as three goddesses come to him to discover what his choice will be. Because he is a Paris, he will make a bad decision; his attempt to make the good choice (that is, to lead the contemplative life, according to his own allegorization of the myth in Book 2) will come to naught. He is seduced into accepting the fruits of another wisdom, of Philosophia's insights; her trivial wisdom is a mockery of the truth that he imagined he could reveal through his own imagined, Christian contemplation of mythology. The narrator's downfall in the prologue is perfect Menippean self-parody, for it is a comic depiction of a preacher who tries to extract the truth from a body of lies. We applaud the nobility of the attempt but laugh at the misplaced erudition brought to bear on inconsequential material. It is Fulgentius's typical practice to mix learning and lies; the sources he cites, and the authors he claims to have read, can often be proved, and more often be suspected, to be wild impostures.[23] This is true of all the works of the mythographer, and the *Mythologies* is not distinctive in this regard. But here a game is played: literary authority takes its revenge on a cavalier author; but a Christian truth assures that pagan myth produces nothing of value.

The *Mythologies* occupies an important place in the history of Menippean satire. Not only is it the first of the Christian Menippean satires, but it reveals, as the *Caesars* does, extensive acquaintance with the works in the genre that preceded it. The second poem of the prologue shows the influence of the *Apocolocyntosis;* the ironic encyclopedia, the character Satyra, and the debate between the Muse Calliope and the narrator, reflect a close reading of the *De Nuptiis;* the dialogue between a human and a mythical creature on whether that mythical creature exists is in the manner of Lucian. Given the resemblances between the *Caesars* and the *De Nuptiis* we may be fairly certain that there was, by some means, a cross-pollination of Greek and Roman traditions of Menippean satire in the late classical period. Fulgentius also knows Petronius and refers to him frequently and throughout his other works;[24] perhaps his influence is to be seen in Fulgentius's choice of an ironic moral encyclopedia and the comic presentation of wise saws on the nature of morals and learning (the essence of the allegories) through the person of a literary theorist who serves not his wife but his mistress.

But perhaps most surprising of all of the influences on the *Mythologies* is that of Varro himself. Not only is there the underlying opposition of *tunc* and *nunc* in the confrontation of Christian and pagan, and the failure of the academic with a new theory (at some remove from Martianus's narrator, a sleepy scribe); the *Mythologies* also reflects what may be the approximate length of a Varronian satire. As the *Mythologies* keeps its Menippean material to the prologue, it does not attempt, as the *Satyricon*, the *De Nuptiis*, and the *Consolation* do, to draw out a Menippean satire to great length. Whether conscious imitation or happy accident accounts for this resemblance we cannot say, but the *De Nuptiis* does represent a revival of things Varronian in the fifth century, and Fulgentius himself claims to quote from what may be one of Varro's *Menippeans*.[25]

Yet despite the wit of the prologue and the elegance of its construction, the *Mythologies* is a Menippean satire manqué. The structural connections between the prologue and the encyclopedic books are real but tenuous. The Judgment of Paris in Book 2 is central to the meaning of the prologue, and various myths mentioned in the prologue (though by no means all) are later allegorized. But there is no reappearance of a squabbling Muse and narrator as in Martianus, no recurrence of verse; nor can we claim that the lack of connection is used for a thematic effect, as may be claimed in the case of the dissonance between the first two and the last seven books of the *De Nuptiis*. The prologues of the second and third books are in the author's voice, and it is easy to read these concluding allegories as if they were spoken by him and not by Philosophia. Fulgentius seems to abandon his framework to present the allegories; as if his nerve fails him, he decides not to remind the reader of the introduction that mocks the utility of the imperfect, because non-Christian, allegories. And although his view of the function of his allegories is quite salutary (it is good to know there are some authors who do not take such allegorization seriously), he cannot quite lay claim to Martianus's status as a good teacher. The *Mythologies* is ultimately little more than a game: it makes a joke of instruction, but its execution does not satisfy its ambition. Fulgentius certainly makes fun of himself, and deserves credit for this comic treatment of the limitations of Christian thought. He opens the door for Boethius; yet one wishes that he had taken greater liberties with the knowledge that he does present.

Chapter Eleven

ENNODIUS

ENNODIUS, bishop of Pavia in northern Italy from 513 until his death in 521, was born perhaps in 473. He is a Christian rhetorician, an author of abundant letters, rhetorical exercises, poems, and hymns. His panegyric on King Theoderic, his *Life of Saint Epiphanius of Pavia*, and his *Eucharisticon de Vita Sua,* an autobiographical account of his not very profound spiritual life, are his major works. His is not a great mind, and it may be politely said of his works that form triumphs over content; his attempts at artistic sophistication are typically taken to demonstrate the limited literary horizons of his age.[1] His correspondence shows him to be a well-connected toady, currying favor and sitting on fences; he is well at home in the academic world at the end of the fifth and the beginning of the sixth centuries, a culture whose features might find parallels in the modern exchange of scholarly offprints.[2]

Yet Ennodius is an important figure in the history of Christian education and its appropriation of pagan learning, and his frequent references to the lies of pagan poetry and the need for a morally inspired Christian poetry have been read as representing something of an educational program.[3] Riché documents the real dilemma faced by churchmen of Ennodius's time, caught between the models of classical literature and an evangelizing Christianity that sought to reject classical literature and style in order both to avoid moral hypocrisy and to write so as to be understood by the less educated masses who lived outside of the cities, the traditional centers of literary culture.[4] Ennodius can view classical culture in the same way that he can view the rhetoric that is at its (and his own) heart: it is a two-edged sword, and he can proclaim in well-balanced phrases that he despises it.[5]

Among the works of the bishop is a letter on education addressed to two friends Ambrose and Beatus, here styled his sons.[6] Commonly known as the *Paraenesis Didascalica,* or "Educational Address," as it was dubbed by the early editor Sirmond, it was written in 511, two years prior to his elevation. Its most immediate function is that of a letter of introduction, presenting these graduates of the school of the *grammaticus* Deuterius in Milan to the more respectable scholars in

Rome. Ever anxious not to offend, Ennodius recommends scholars
of the two chief, and opposing, families: that of the senator Faustus, a
supporter of Theoderic; and that of the senator Symmachus, a family carefully maintaining ties to the East, and possessing the most
remarkable Boethius.[7] But it is also a pedagogical tract, and it is
usually accounted a serious statement of educational aims by a man
who tried to combine his Christian faith and his pagan learning.[8] Its
particulars, however, have made some throw up their hands:

> The [*Paraenesis Didascalica*] mixes up in a strange way the
> most contradictory points of view: Ennodius recommends
> to his young friends the Christian virtues, *uerecundia, fides,
> castitas*, but also the assiduous practice of the liberal arts,
> especially rhetoric, which at its good pleasure can make an
> innocent man appear guilty, and a guilty man innocent![9]

The work is written in a mixture of prose and verse, but it is not just
an example of the prosimetric epistle popular at this time.[10] What we
have, I submit, is a Menippean satire, whose topic is the incommensurability of faith and pagan learning, making real one particular
answer to the anxieties that our author was perhaps the last to feel so
strongly.[11] The *Paraenesis* aims at spiritual and intellectual improvement, yet it freely admits by and through its verse that its form runs
counter to these aims. The *Paraenesis* is in fact an ironic handbook of
spiritual and scholastic virtues, and its affiliation with Menippean
satire in the manner of Martianus and Fulgentius may now be readily
affirmed.[12] A translation of the work may be found in Appendix C;
the commentary required here will be brief.

THE INCOMPETENT SCHOLAR

After its brief introduction, the *Paraenesis* proceeds to a systematic
exposition of what Ambrose and Beatus ought to pursue. Ennodius
tells first of the Christian virtues (in order Modesty, Chastity, and
Faith), and then of the Liberal Arts, reduced to Grammar and Rhetoric.[13] Each of these receives a prose and a verse treatment. The author speaks first in prose, and then the abstractions speak in verse
about themselves. Yet this systematic treatment is prefaced by a poem
in praise of poetry in the author's own voice, in which poetry is
described as a very doubtful ally of truth; and the order ultimately
breaks down when Rhetoric herself, not the author, speaks of herself
in prose. The work concludes with the author's recommendation of a
number of other teachers who can instruct Ambrose and Beatus

better than he can. Both through this framing and in various details the *Paraenesis* presents gradually, in a number of subtle and comic ways, an author who is not competent to instruct intelligently, who misinterprets the true nature of the abstractions he proposes to praise or blame, and who is himself in thrall to those arts whose enticements he warns of. Rhetoric comes to life, as it were, and refuses to mean what the narrator intends; in this characterization we see a reflex of the expected fantastic action and characters, and the deceptive source, of Menippean satire. Because of this, we may profitably speak of the narrator of the *Paraenesis* as one distinct from the author, even though, unique among Menippean satires, there is no plot or physical action contained within the work. Like Fulgentius's narrator, Ennodius's will fail to teach directly what he intends; it is only through his failure that Ambrose and Beatus may learn of the true relative values of Christian faith and pagan learning.

We may first consider the confusions of the narrator in terms of his description of the Liberal Arts. Grammar is introduced as the most fundamental, and therefore the least objectionable, of the disciplines. Ennodius's description of her is now trivial, now ironically grand: she holds out images of fictitious disasters to create ready-made Ciceros (11); her rudiments make the great quake in fear (12). But it is odd that Ennodius's description is not so much of grammar but of forensic rhetoric;[14] thus he must add the qualification that students ought not fall too much in love with her precepts (13). However, Grammar's poem states her essence rather differently, for she talks only of telling stories to children to improve their minds, while correcting their errors and trying to be pleasant. She begins (13):

> We grant discrimination to the mind while we fashion our
>   fables;
> we are a fair-minded judge, whatever mistakes the little
>   children make.
> Refraining from the hand, I beat in shame by ear and
>   mouth.
> Whatever this art has to be afraid of, the art of speaking
>   mitigates;
> with the young we even joke in the midst of our lessons.
> For the teacher, Strictness, commands that you not be
>   frightening at every turn.

The humor of the teacher's misapprehension of the nature of the subject I shall return to; here it is sufficient to note that the Grammar of the poem is as bland an Art as can be imagined and is the least sophisticated of the Liberal Arts.

If Ennodius stopped here, there would be nothing very much out of the ordinary. But the subsequent discussion of Rhetoric complicates matters. She does not satisfy the expectations created by the earlier description of her consanguinity with Grammar. She is not introduced by the narrator, but introduces herself as a seductress who claims the power of godhead, who can create and change that which has been created (15); like the divine Wisdom of Proverbs, she establishes kingdoms and kings (16). The reader is hardly expected to approve of Rhetoric's proud claim to be the author of truth and of lies and the sole subject of study in the Roman world. Yet the narrator is himself won over by the speech of Rhetoric. For after Rhetoric's poem, he resumes in prose (18): "Therefore, my dearest ones, strive to gain these things and guard them once you have gained them."[15] It is not plausible that Ennodius is seriously recommending the art of Unjust Argument whose flaws have just been revealed at great length. This goes beyond traditional acknowledgments of Rhetoric's twofold powers.[16] This is parody, at the expense of Ennodius's narrator.

We may single out a few more ways in which the narrator's ineptitude is underlined. First, he insists at the beginning that he is a better instructor than a parent because of his profession (4–5), yet concludes with a list of better teachers than himself. This simple fact shows that the *Paraenesis* is not intended per se as a definitive harmonization of pagan and Christian learning but is much more tentative.[17] In this light, the final verses reveal a parody of the conventions of father-son instructional literature, for he has tried to replace the bonds of family affection with those of book learning only to discover that he is neither a teacher nor a parent:[18]

> My illustrious seeds,
> take these words
> from a dry father.
> That is well said
> which points to the truth.

Now Ambrose and Beatus are thought of as children cheated of paternal instruction; Ennodius is the dry father, incapable of procreation.

Second, he singles out Silence (more charitably, perhaps, translated as "Solemn Restraint") as the most salient aspect of the instructive capabilities of Festus and Symmachus (19) and of Barbara (24);

and it is to Symmachus that the *Paraenesis* is ultimately commended. This is not on a par with Philology's prayer to the Unknown Father in silence in the pages of Martianus, and Ennodius throws in the crude joke that he wishes all of the women of Italy would follow Barbara's example and be quiet; but a garrulous author can only recommend the edification of silence out of a desire for self-parody and to suggest that his own words have little in the way of wisdom or truth.

Most important, the framework of the encyclopedia of lessons and teachers stresses something most unscholastic: the value of prayer and simple faith over the intricacies of book learning. The work begins with a weak pun. Ambrose and Beatus have begged Ennodius "multis . . . supplicationibus" to write an instructional work. But a *supplicatio* is a prayer as well as a request, and the author agrees to write "because it is enough for me to be mentioned in your prayers" ("quia . . . sufficit si me in uoto praedicetis"). He returns the spiritual favor by spelling out what grants life ("quod uiuificat"). Section 2 is a completely serious and straightforward recommendation of fidelity to God and to the Golden Rule; these will grant them what they hope for. Ennodius makes prayer and faith the means and end of instruction.

The *Paraenesis* ends with another pun of similar import (26):

> det autem uobis deus quod decet et uelle semper et facere. Ergo si pomposa oratione non ualui, oratione uos memor professionis adiuui.

> And may God grant that you always wish and do what is right. Therefore, if I have not been able to help with a showy oration, I have, mindful of my profession, at least helped you with an orison.

The pompous oration that has preceded has not been useful, he suggests; the pious oration (that is, prayer) is more helpful. The profession of faith, not the profession of rhetoric, is what grants to Ambrose and Beatus the guidance they desire.[19] At section 4 Ennodius claims the right to improve his friends because he is a teacher and well versed in moral precepts, but at the conclusion he proclaims the inadequacy of his learning and the superiority of his faith.

The *Paraenesis* presents the downfall of a preacher and invites the reader to consider how the information there cataloged fails to satisfy. This is the heart of Menippean satire in the tradition of Varro, though at some removes of propriety. And while the reasonable solu-

tion to the problems of dogmatic knowledge and its preaching appears, as expected, between the lines, Ennodius spells out quite
clearly the advantages of faith in the frame that surrounds his account. Ennodius displays neither the wit nor the intelligence of a
Martianus or a Fulgentius. His *Paraenesis* is the least compelling of
Menippean satires, and its affiliation to the genre, while real, is ad-
mittedly weak. But Ennodius has done one remarkable thing: he has
made Faith speak in a Menippean satire and has brought Christianity
directly and unambiguously into his ironic handbook. The poems on
the Christian virtues participate in the narrator's self-parody and
depict his dim wit; to this extent Ennodius is fully a Menippean
satirist. These poems deserve close attention.

PROSE AND VERSE

We can chart through the *Paraenesis* the narrator's decline from
intelligent and plausible theorizing to uncomfortable and hypocritical posturing. The use of prose and verse is an index to his intellectual embarrassment, for he cannot keep the characters who speak in
verse from saying what he wishes they would not. With a single exception, the poem delivered by Faith, the verse passages in the *Paraenesis* are beyond the artistic control of Ennodius's narrator. As in the
Mythologies, there is a reality that proves overwhelming in what the
narrator would seek to encapsulate or dismiss as insubstantial.

He claims at first that the prose passages will contain instruction
and the verse passages relaxation (3). But the poem in praise of
poetry (pointedly obscure in its language) says something more sinister. It claims that verse will be used even though it is seductive, fictitious, and immoral; he will pursue poetry only as far as his "talents
and the strength of truth" ("genius uigorque ueri") will allow, but the
concluding lines suggest that the medium, even when employed as
relaxation, cannot be trusted at all: "We suffer the inborn toughness
of the soldier of Christ to be on guard against effeminate composition."[20] And note that the narrator, once he resumes in prose, immediately proclaims a new theory of the relative functions of prose and
verse (4): "We shall therefore run from the pleasantries of words now
and then and proclaim solid stuff from our own mouth, lest this virile
work suffer the setbacks of impotent speech." Far from offering a
respite in the course of a lesson, poetry actually threatens to undermine what the narrator has to say.

When the narrator proceeds to introduce Modesty he speaks of

her as inhabiting the citadel of the arts and as the mother of good
works. Speaking in her own voice, Modesty has a different message
(5):

> Paint your shining features with rosy purple dye,
>   and show the fidelity of your morals on your face.
> May you be prettier by a scattering of spots about your
>   snow-white mouth
>   when you sweat a little and bear a dewy neck.
> You should not grant yourself more by your tongue than
>   by the nobility of your appearance:
>   from this attract to yourself whatever you want to love.

The elegiacs are in the manner of Ovid and attempt to be a passage
from a Christian *Ars Amatoria* or a *Medicamina Faciei Femineae*. Yet the
transference is not complete; the imagery is of the physical allure of
blushing, and how it can win for its wearer the object of his or her
love. There is no explicit mention of the spiritual value of blushing,
and the narrator proceeds to speak in ironic terms of the maiden's
powers of acquisition (6), observing that "even she who speaks is
crowned with the gift of *profitable* beauty," a gift that seems inappropriate for the mother of good works.

Ennodius then speaks of Shame (*pudicitia*), the relative of Modesty
(*pudor*). But it is *Verecundia* that has just spoken and *Castitas* is in the
wings; again, the speakers' descriptions of themselves do not accord
with the narrator's classifications. Shame, the narrator says, not only
calms the passions of youth and the indulgence of the belly, but she
also "entices the flesh with the savor of holy relations" (6: "carnem
sapore sanctae conuersationis inliciens"). Castitas has no such charms
in her epic verses. She is proud of her haggard appearance, which
broadcasts her virtue; she longs for battle with overeating; she offers
only the promise of a gray-haired old age (7):

> I never hesitate to show at all times my afflicted face,
> so long as the signs of my chaste beauty shine forth.
> For fat flesh chokes the finer senses,
> and a belly, foully stuffed, tramples the mind.
> But the Cross is my spear, the Cross my shield, the Cross
>   my armor;
>   with this I am protected, with this I strike, with this I
>   establish the bonds of peace.
> This is my general in war, so that, with quicksilver youth
>   under my victorious heel,

I may renounce the horrid honies of Cupid's poison.
Hasten to me, stop playing the boy in your actions,
and take from my habits, young men, a gray-haired old
    age.

These hexameters put us in the world of Prudentius's *Psychomachia*.
The assumption of Paul's panoply of faith for the war against overeating is certainly overdone. While Christian moralists connect sexual and sensual indulgence as aspects of the same moral deficiency, it
is curious that no explicit mention is made of the true province of
Chastity beyond the overtones of "fat flesh" and "Cupid's poison."
She is unpleasantly martial and has no pleasing reward.

    The narrator now turns to Faith, which he says is made up of many
things, as are garlands and tiaras. We expect that the preceding virtues will be revealed as aspects of it. The image of Faith as a crown is
conventional enough, but the narrator hastens to add that nothing
can precede Faith, and that it therefore requires our utmost diligence. This is a paradox: is Faith the end and crowning glory of a
composite thing, or is it the beginning of one? The poem that follows
offers a surprising answer. Faith describes herself as simple, not mul-
tiform; and in the contrast between the virtues that it extols and the
acquisitiveness and belligerency of Modesty and Chastity, the reader
sees that nothing really can precede Faith. The author therefore
denies the religious significance of the preceding sections when he
has Faith sing in quite a different spirit. Like the prayer to the Unknown Father in Martianus and the great poem in the *Consolation* at 3
m. 9, unexpected sublimity sneaks into this Menippean satire in the
poem that occupies its center (9):

Whoso wishes to join earth and heaven,
and to abandon the sins of Mother Luxury,
let him seek me, the abiding crown and glory
    of the heavenly gift.

For he does not fear the dread tribunal,
nor does he flit among the city's rich and powerful;
knowing the right, he steers upon the sea
    for the harbor of salvation.

Though the Geloni swell with barbarian rage
and the Morini bark in Parthian wise—
all the grumblings of the mad world
    he loathes and avoids.

> He enters the inner sanctum of the King on High;
> he remains certain of his wealth in disaster;
> he is not subject to the laws of the grave,
>   nor to the evils of life.

The poem is a respectable imitation of and successor to Horace's *Integer Vitae*. These Sapphic stanzas continue the author's program of metrical variety without the poetic parody evident in the preceding poems. The images of separation, searching, and reward stand out in sharp relief from those of adornment and battle lust. The poem marks an end of this first division of the text; no commentary from the narrator's mouth is possible or desirable.

The first half of the *Paraenesis* reveals a narrator whose view of Christianity and its moral virtues is rather different from the opinions expressed by their apostrophied spokeswomen. The virtues are too specific or trivial, and faith itself is too grand, to meet his expectations. There is at work here the Menippean scorn of abstraction and theory; the very act of forcing truth into systems renders it suspicious. Faith transcends such schematization; the central poem breaks the pattern of irrelevance by extolling a simplicity that has no relation to the excesses that preceded it. The second section of the *Paraenesis,* which claims to extol the academic virtues of Grammar and Rhetoric, reinforces the view that the compendious approach to wisdom is futile, for its topic is the hypocrisy of writing about the limitations of written culture.

Faith was a crown, and now the Liberal Arts are an expensive necklace, a gleaming setting for the goods of faith; unfortunately this transitional sentence seems to be corrupt (10). Ennodius has no fascination with or understanding of the quadrivium; his necklace will be composed of two jewels only.[21] The narrator admits to the utility of Grammar, who is the conventional nurse of all the others (11).[22] He counsels against excessive love of it, and describes the virtuous student who displays his true nobility of spirit by allowing the instructor to *curb* his natural love of Grammar (13):

> In this there is need of caution, lest love of the art grow beyond the natural license, as it were, of that immature age, and a spontaneous devotion to this brilliant work spring forth from the constant obligations imposed by their teachers. Nevertheless, a student shows that he devotes himself to good intentions when he allows himself to be so compelled; and he has, as it were, honesty as an art who is not distressed by the nervous concern of his instructor.

The narrator has already referred to himself as a *monitor* (4) and will speak of this work as a pedagogue for Ambrose and Beatus to follow (26); Grammar herself concludes her poem by claiming, as the narrator has already done (5), that she is a teacher superior to a parent because of the lack of carnal lust. What is described here is, in effect, Ambrose and Beatus learning from the example of the *Paraenesis*.

This by itself is not surprising, but the narrator is promptly shown as a teacher who cannot rein in his own appetite for Grammar. Ennodius does not allow his own appraisal of her glories to agree with Grammar's own account. Grammar's poem stresses the simplicity of grammatical instruction through humor; the narrator speaks of the advantages of declamation for creating well-trained orators (11–12). The author has his eye fixed firmly on rhetoric (12): "It is good that the right hands of rhetors and our well-known freedom of speech take up the swords forged in the grammarian's furnace; the often repeated images of slaughter bring it about that they do not fall in open battle." Grammar has simpler objectives, and her verses (quoted in part earlier), trochaic tetrameters in the manner of the gnomic verse of Publilius Syrus, are ideally suited to the humble aspirations that the author advocates in word but not example. The author shows that his own affections, and therefore the writing of the *Paraenesis* itself, goes beyond the simple use of grammar to the love of rhetoric, which abjures instruction to praise the art of lying.

The pattern of the *Paraenesis* breaks down at the introduction of Rhetoric at 15. The narrator does not speak in his own voice except to mention her powers of composition (14); Rhetoric speaks in prose to tell of her duplicity and her pride in concealing the truth (15–17). The author does not introduce the poem; here he has lost control of the plan of his work, and Rhetoric, like Calliope in the *Mythologies*, speaks on the author's behalf to reveal his own questionable intelligence. The author's immoderate love of Rhetoric is here shown by her assumption of the narrator's role, her own grandiloquent descriptions of her utility, and the narrator's surprising acceptance of her in the words that follow her poem. Further, the words by which Rhetoric modulates from prose to verse (discussed above in Chapter 2) would attribute to her a playful nature. Her poem, the "sport of another obligation,"[23] is not different in tone or content from her prose account of herself: if we had expected two natures in Rhetoric, we are frustrated in that expectation and must infer that the *Paraenesis* knows only of Forensic Rhetoric, a rhetoric that corrupts.

Ennodius has led on stage the two Arts responsible for the composition of the present text. Elsewhere Ennodius praises Grammar and

Rhetoric together as being the Christian's shield, but not here.[24] Their descriptions show a narrator who does not follow simple Grammar but who embraces the lies of Rhetoric. The praise of silence as the greatest qualification of the scholars who are the author's betters is pointed.[25] If Ennodius stops short of the Menippean implication that all language is inadequate to transmit true knowledge, he certainly implies that his own language is. Rhetoric obscures truth, and Ennodius does not allow his narrator to escape her clutches. In the embarrassment of the preacher is the lesson for Ambrose and Beatus: do not follow Ennodius's example, for true knowledge cannot be presented in such a cut-and-dried fashion, and faith transcends the attempt to assign it a fixed place in an academic program of study. A Menippean satire, modeled in structure and content on the satires of Martianus and Fulgentius, the work does not instruct according to the narrator's original plans: the narration is taken over by the representative of pagan learning most feared by the narrator, the language of the text serves to parody its narrator, and silence is extolled as a source of true edification.

FAITH AND EDUCATION

Just as a clear conscience is ill-served and rendered suspicious by Rhetoric, so too is Faith.[26] Martianus galvanized the principles of his composition and made them come to comic life in the persons of Periergia, Agrypnia, and Epimelia (2.145–46);[27] Ennodius does the same with Rhetoric. The words that cannot teach are informed by pagan culture and pagan sensibility. This clever display of learned faith concentrates too much on form, and to the detriment of content. The *Paraenesis* takes as its theme the impossibility of forcing Christian belief into pagan categories of analysis or forms of expression: a handbook of moral virtue on the order of a handbook of the liberal arts is ludicrous, and the author who tries to offer a *diuisio* or *partitio* of Christian faith is absurd.

It is possible in the sixth century to call oneself a pagan in terms of culture and a Christian in terms of faith. This spirit informs the works of Sidonius Apollinaris, bishop, poet, and writer of letters of a preceding generation (c. 430–c. 480). Curtius is generally correct to call this a "tensionless coexistence" in late classical times,[28] and after Ennodius and Boethius no one seems to bother with the problem of making the two traditions cohere. But the Christian Menippean satirists do worry about the synthesis of paganism and Christianity; and the *Paraenesis* helps to document that the uncertainty that Ennodius reveals elsewhere about the utility of classical culture can be more than a mere rhetorical ploy. Although he may advocate a Christianized rhetoric, the *Paraenesis* operates on the presumption that such a thing is fundamentally flawed. A lack of consistency in Ennodius's thought is not surprising in any event, but we may allow him to be enough of a scholar to say that here he is, like other Menippean satirists in Varro's line, a scholar at play, abusing a theory otherwise precious to him.

Varro's *Menippeans* present scholastic language as a tool of self-parody; this tradition is still alive in Ennodius. But more interesting is the fact that the *Paraenesis* wonders about its own composition and introduces as hypothetical speakers the abstractions Grammar and Rhetoric, who have presided over the creation of the work. The *Paraenesis* therefore can be seen as a distant descendant of Varro's *Bimarcus,* and as the ultimate ancestor of Alan of Lille's *De Planctu Naturae* ("The Complaint of Nature"), a twelfth-century text in which the perversions of grammar, all abundantly attested in the text itself, are singled out by an angry Nature as analogies for and examples of perversions of morals.[29] Alan will follow Ennodius in making the very act of composition a moral as well as an intellectual affront; one who knows the arts of rhetoric cannot be trusted with the truth. Content rebels against form, and the eager usurpations of rhetoric and the pointless prettiness of poetry are wholly inadequate for the comprehension of faith. Silence is best. The *Paraenesis* shows that Ennodius is capable of introspection and self-parody, and capable of deeper thought about the nature of writing, learning, and literature than his run of letters, poems, and rhetorical exercises suggests.

V. BOETHIUS AND BEYOND

Chapter Twelve

CONCLUSION

ROMANCE and Menippean satire have similar origins, and their histories touch at a number of points. The *Odyssey* is for both genres a thematic starting point, whether as the wanderings that precede the reuniting of lovers and families or as the fantastic adventures of a narrator whose most practiced art is that of lying. But the theoretical first principles that underlie these genres are reactions to, or interpretations of, the literary and philosophical creations of Plato. Gill advances the claim that Plato's Atlantis story is the earliest example of narrative fiction and perhaps the first example of self-conscious fiction in any form in Greek literature.[1] Plato puts forward a theory of fiction in advance of the genre, and in the *Republic* he acknowledges two possible responses of a reader to myths: an emotional reaction in which the reader is deceived into thinking that a story is true; and the reader's willing acceptance of what is not true as true. What Plato desires is the latter's *complicity* in Plato's own philosophical myths, and Gill suggests that Plato is experimenting with the deliberately fictional in presenting what is unreal as real.[2] Gill points out also that most of antiquity misunderstood Plato's intentions: many accepted the Atlantis story as literally true. But we are in a position now to claim that quite a few did understand what Plato was about in writing his myths.

The authors of the romances refused to follow Plato's lead; in choosing to model their fictions on historiography, they sought to involve the reader's emotions directly, not to raise the question of whether the story is literally true.[3] Menippean satirists, on the other hand, see the logical problem in presenting the false as true and, in pointed defiance of Plato, create fictions whose essential theme is that the false cannot teach what is true. Or one may say that they hold Plato's feet to the fire and insist on the doubts that Plato himself expresses in the *Republic,* that language itself is a tool that can only express phenomenal reality and can never describe what is truly real.[4] The reader is invited to disbelieve a provocative mixture of truth and fiction. To the Menippean satirists, Plato's various myths (primarily the Myth of Er, but also the final judgment in the *Gorgias* and the utopian fictions of the *Timaeus* and *Critias*) are paradigms of how not to proclaim the truth. And even Gill notes that while Eu-hemerus and Theopompus understood Plato well enough to make their own attempts at philosophical myth in the Atlantis mold, Lu-cian's explicitly false *True History* belongs to the same tradition.[5]

Plato's place in the history of Menippean satire is not just as the author whose dialogue form and whose *Symposium* are so frequently parodied within it, but as the theoretician who advances the value of falsehood as a heuristic device. It is his literary nature that gets him into trouble; had Plato written like Aristotle, Menippean satire may never have gotten off the ground.[6] We have a few instances in Menip-pean satires in which the question of the utility of Platonic myth is directly raised. Julian's *Caesars* begins with the narrator's claim that he will tell a *mythos* in place of a comic tale; his interlocutor presumes that he will hear a Platonic myth, but it becomes clear that he will get a comic and unedifying myth instead. Fulgentius's *Mythologies* claims that it will resemble the *De Re Publica* of Cicero; in particular, the *Dream of Scipio,* modeled on Plato's Myth of Er. Fulgentius presents himself as an author of a myth he cannot understand. But through-out Menippean satire we have fantastic tales told by comic or self-deprecating figures about a failed search for absolute standards of truth; and this, I think, is in direct response to the authority and practice of Plato, or rather, to be more accurate, Plato's narrator and self-deprecating naïf, Socrates, the most important model for Menip-pus's own literary personality.[7] In short, it is the example of Platonic mythologizing that gives Menippean satire a first push, as it were, and propels it into the realm of self-defeating philosophical fantasy; and the most important of these Platonic myths is the Myth of Er.

Consider how closely the Myth of Er resembles the plot of a Me-nippean satire. Er makes a fantastic journey to the other world (be-ing dead twelve days and then coming back to life); he is an observer of, not a participant in, the other world; the souls that he observes learn of the truth, but it does them no good, as they continue to make bad or foolish choices when the time comes to pick another life; there is a formal proclamation made to the souls which comes just before the conclusion of the work; there is a *catascopia,* a common device of Platonic mythmaking,[8] as well as its attendant Olympian laughter, when Er views from a height the pathetic human comedy of the souls' selection of their new lives (619E–620A):

> For he said that this was a vision well worth seeing, how each of the souls chose its life, for it was pitiful to see, and funny,

and amazing; because, for the most part, they chose according to the habits of their former lives.

And the myth is told at secondhand, by the naive narrator Socrates, who relies on a questionable source, a revivified corpse.

The Myth of Er makes a number of more or less literal and direct appearances in Menippean satire. It is used in a number of dialogues of Lucian and may lie behind the scene in the *Icaromenippus* in which Zeus in his chamber listens to the prayers of mortals.[9] Julian's *Caesars* ends with a group of emperors choosing guardian deities in a manner reminiscent of the souls' choice of lots. We need not conclude that Plato's Myth of Er is a joke, even if it does contain bitter reflections on the ability of humans to perceive the truth and to act upon its. But I do think that it could have appeared to less generous ancient critics as a tale of the futility of the search for truth, and some ancient philosophical critics took Plato to task for his mythologizing in terms reminiscent of the objections of Menippean satire. The most important of these is Colotes the Epicurean, known from Plutarch's essay against him,[10] several papyrus fragments of works directed against specific Platonic dialogues,[11] and responses made to his criticisms of the Myth of Er as preserved in Macrobius's *Commentary on the Dream of Scipio* (1.2) and Proclus's *Commentary on the Republic* (2.105.23–109.3 Kroll).[12] The sources do not give the impression that Colotes was a very intelligent critic, but the need to answer his objections may suggest some legitimate nervousness about them. From a consideration of the objections made and the rebuttals offered we can get a fair idea of the debunker's view of Plato and can also document and explain a curious phenomenon in Menippean satire: namely, the proximity of the ridiculous and the sublime aspects of mythical tales and the ever-present tension in Menippean satire between jokes at the expense of philosophy and jokes in the service of philosophy.

According to Macrobius (*Comm.* 1.1.9), Cicero chose not to repeat the fantasy of the Myth of Er in his own adaptation of Plato's *Republic,* preferring the machinery of a dream vision instead. The Myth of Er, Macrobius states, suffers from unwarranted derision:

> Though Cicero, being himself aware of the truth, was pained that this story was mocked by the ignorant, nevertheless, seeking to avoid this example of stupid criticism, he preferred to wake up the one who was going to tell the tale rather than bring him back from the dead.[13]

Macrobius proceeds from this point to discuss the objections of Colotes and to enumerate the varieties of fictions and those that are
permissible to philosophers (*Comm.* 1.2.7–21): this is the fullest consideration of the varieties and proprieties of fictional discourse extant from antiquity and is of great importance for the understanding
of the revival of Platonic mythologizing in the twelfth century, with
its distinction between meaning and integument.[14]

Proclus too responds to the objections of Colotes in full, and says
that he not only reproduces the arguments of Porphyry (the primary
source for both Macrobius and Proclus)[15] but extends them himself.[16] Colotes objects in particular to Plato's criticism of the fantasy of
poets as regards the horrors of the Underworld, when Plato's own
account is no less fantastic and horrible (Proclus *In R.* 2.105.26–
106.8). More general objections to mythologizing are that it does not
befit a philosopher to tell lies like a poet (105.24–26), and that a myth
is necessarily in vain (106.8–14): the unlearned can never understand
it, and the learned have no need of such fictions. In Proclus's response, Porphyry is quoted as saying that proofs of the immortality
of the soul require a discussion of their life and fortune in Hades,
things that those people must accept who accept also that the soul is
immortal; that Plato only spoke against shameful myths, not edifying
ones; that it is appropriate for fictions to be here employed, for
nature loves to be concealed, as Heraclitus says; and that the spirits
(δαίμονες) who preside over nature often speak to us in dreams and
riddles. To these answers Proclus adds: that it is a reasonable manner
of instruction to speak in myths of this sort about souls that are by
nature in the intelligible realm and not apprehensible by the senses;
that fiction is appropriate for those things which can be visualized
only in the imaginative faculty of the mind; and that the mysteries
make use of myths for holy ends, some of the initiates being merely
compelled by fear, others perceiving the nature of the divinity that
lies behind the stories.[17]

But Macrobius makes the interesting point that the philosophical
myth does not treat the highest level of reality, that of God or the
One (*Comm.* 1.2.14):

> Further, when the essay dares to raise itself to the highest
> and first god of all, who is called by the Greeks The Good,
> or First Cause; or to the Mind, which the Greeks call Nous,
> which contains the original forms of things, which are called
> Ideas, which Mind is born of and descended from the high-
> est god; when, I say, they speak of these things, the highest

god and the Mind, they refrain absolutely from the fictional and, if they attempt to make some definition about these things which pass not only beyond human speech but human thought as well, they take refuge in similes and examples.[18]

Proclus does not speak explicitly of the inappropriateness of myth for discussions of the One, but does speak at length about the advantages of treating the incorporeal and intelligible *souls* by means of the imagination (*In R.* 2.107.14–29). Menippean satire is curiously loyal to this division between fabulous treatments of the lower orders of reality and silence about the ultimate reality. True to the Epicurean objection that words should refer to concrete things,[19] the genre makes fun of the use of fabulous stories to make philosophical points; though in creating this sort of antiphilosophical fiction, the Cynic origins of the genre are evident, as Epicureans do not seem to indulge in popular fictions.[20] But there is silence in Menippean satires about that true and superior realm of truth when such is in fact believed to exist. In general, Menippean satires allow for the triumph of common sense as glimpsed between the lines in the contemplation of the downfall and embarrassment of the fantastic theoretician or dogmatist; but mystic and religious definitions of common sense arise in late antiquity, and Menippean satires point to them. Note how Julian does not describe the heaven that he will rise to by keeping faith with the commands of Mithras; how Philology prays in silence and nonsense syllables to the Unknown Father whose presence she senses beyond the wall of the world; how Fulgentius refers only obliquely to his Christianity; it is remarkable that Ennodius personifies his Christian Faith and lets her speak, but Boethius will not bring his faith to bear in his *Consolation*.

We may say that in the development of the Menippean genre, authors sense more and more the closeness between making fun of dogmatic or fantastic approaches to truth and the profound and Platonic apprehension that what is true lies beyond the realm of human thought. The presence of Plato becomes increasingly explicit in the genre's history, and we can look ahead and say that Menippean satire ultimately comes full circle, starting as a rejection of myth and philosophy and ending in the Middle Ages (if we exclude the *De Planctu Naturae*, being in many ways a parody of the following) with the *De Cosmographia* of Bernardus Silvestris, a poetic and allegorical tale that asserts the incommensurability of the Macrocosm and the Microcosm, and finds in the gap between disordered humanity and

the ordered universe the place of Faith. Bernardus himself, in a
commentary on Martianus Capella that is plausibly attributed to him,
speaks of the ability of a fictional covering (integumentum) to reveal
philosophical truths that cannot be represented by conventional discourse; and Dronke shows this principle at work in the De Cosmographia.[21] It is a principle frequently invoked in the modern studies
of Platonic myth:[22] mythical discourse represents a different and
valuable mode of thought. Menippean satire parodies Plato because
it acknowledges him as the master philosopher; ultimately, the genre
comes to accept the very attitudes that it first rejected.

FROM SUCH a philosophical catascopia we can see the organic unity of
the genre; to include its fortunes after the twelfth-century Renaissance requires a still higher vantage point, toward which I will not
ascend. Some recapitulation is in order. Menippean satire, like verse
satire, has origins in diatribe. The genre teaches commonsense values (the horror of pride and presumption, the folly of dogma and
theory, the joys of the simple life), but only through the example of
the embarrassment of the preacher who tries to establish such common sense logically as ultimate truth. Menippean satire parodies the
diatribist; in it, the catechizer is catechized. One may appreciate the
difference between Menippean satire and verse satire this way: if
verse satire resembles Old Testament prophecy (at least in its Juve-
nalian form, of whom one still reads now and then that he is a Jere-
miah), Menippean satire resembles that literary form which develops
from prophecy: apocalyptic. Menippean satire does not look for
temporal solutions to temporal problems but in fantastic voyages
goes directly to the ends of the earth to find absolute and timeless
answers. Unlike the voyages to heaven and hell in the religious
dream visions that draw their inspiration from apocalyptic, those of
Menippean satire do not find the answers that they look for.

   When Menippus in Necyomantia or Icaromenippus tries to view the
world sub specie aeternitatis, he discovers that folly is the irreducible
factor of mortality, and no logical theory can comprehend it. The
arrogance of those who presume to understand human illogic is the
theme of Menippean satire, and the history of the genre charts a
number of ways of viewing the relation between humanity and the
ordered universe that cannot order it. Varro, Seneca, Petronius, and
Julian primarily present the parody of the satirist who looks for the
moral order of the universe but cannot find it: Claudius and Constantine prove by their incomprehensibility that the categories of
heaven and hell, and the hope of justice in the next life, are silly

notions; Encolpius cannot see that his own life and writing give the lie to his ethical and literary pronouncements. Lucian tells of the desire to get at moral and philosophical truth directly without the intermediary of dogma, by the direct experience of heaven and hell, and of the frustration of this laudable desire because it is fantastic in conception and impossible in fact. The late classical Roman authors turn to a search for the *logical* order in the world, following the lead of Martianus who creates his own vision of the unity of the cosmos, visible not through the efforts of the intellect but through mystic faith. His Christian imitators take Martianus's opposition of inspiration and education and transform it into the conflict of faith and pagan culture: those who attempt to assert the unity of the two traditions, and thus to unite truth and error, suffer for their presumption.

Menippean satire gradually turns from the parody of philosophers to the parody of philosophy, and in this we can see the history of the genre as one of the increasing influence of Plato. The genre plays with Plato's literary forms and techniques of persuasion as its interest in the question of the ability of literature to convey philosophical truth grows. Menippean satire, like many other forms of humor, has certain conservative first principles which it invokes in order to laugh at human pretensions. For the purposes of the genre, poetry is lies and poets are liars; philosophers are obscurantists and hairsplitters; and Plato's mixture of philosophical truth and the fictional apparatus of myth and literary sophistication is not sublime but a doubtful paradox. The Menippean satirists otherwise show healthy respect for poetry, philosophy, and Plato; but the genre is iconoclastic and questions all forms of literary authority, and as Plato becomes through the ages the quintessential philosopher his works are increasingly subjected to Menippean scrutiny. The Menippean theme that the incompatibility of opposites makes humanity and the world incomprehensible finds Plato's mixture of myth and instruction grist for its mill; in this sense we may speak of the importance of the parody of Platonic literary forms, as opposed to their actual philosophical content, for the history of Menippean satire.

The parody is prominent from the genre's inception and grows steadily in importance. Menippus's *Arcesilaus* is probably modeled on the *Symposium*, but the seminal *Necyia* is probably more closely related to Timon's *Silli* than to Plato. Varro too had his comic symposia, leading to Petronius's *Cena Trimalchionis*, but the essence of philosophical parody in the *Menippeans*, as in Lucian's *Symposium, or The Lapiths,* is the discordance between the lives and the beliefs of wrangling pedants, not the expression of philosophy through the medium of a dinner party. Lucian's literary invention, the comic dialogue, is conceived as a parody of the Platonic dialogue; this is of great importance for the history of Menippean satire even though Lucian's comic dialogues are not, strictly speaking, Menippean in form. After Lucian, the abuse of Platonic literary devices is rampant in the genre: the philosophical myth is parodied in Julian, Martianus, and Fulgentius; the *Symposium* in Julian; the *catascopia* of the Myth of Er in Lucian and Julian; the appearance of the spirit of the Laws of Athens to Socrates in the *Crito* in the epiphanies of Fulgentius and Boethius; and the philosophical dialogue of the *Phaedo* and the *Republic* in Boethius. Menippean satire turns Plato's rhetoric of belief into a language of doubt; myth and literary elegance now serve to subvert the truth.

What changes through time is the notion that the collapse of the synthesis attempted is itself meaningful. It is not of any great import that Menippus's journeys are ridiculous, and the failure of supernatural justice in the *Apocolocyntosis* points back uneasily to the everlastingness of the flawed world; but it is very important that Roman history in Julian, textbook learning in Martianus, the accommodation of faith and learning in the Christian authors, all collapse, in order to suggest a *uia media*, a personal way of salvation. The structures invoked increase in size with time. At the end of the classical Menippean tradition, parody of philosophy combines with the parody of encyclopedic knowledge to create works in which the narrator strives mightily to list the elements of the world in some meaningful way and to impose a theory or interpretation upon the erudition thus amassed. At this point in its history, Menippean satire parallels the development in the symposium genre, which has moved away from fascination with personalities (as in Plato's and Xenophon's treatment of Socrates) to fascination with data (as in Athenaeus and Macrobius).[23] In Martianus, Fulgentius, Ennodius (and Boethius as well), the order breaks down under the weight of the sad facts of human knowledge or human experience. The inability of human knowledge to find a logical place in the glorious order of the universe is seen as a philosophical problem and not just a matter for a cynical shrug of the shoulders. The desire to find a logical order in the world, and the human intellect as well that would comprehend this world and find a place within it, exemplify the flawed nature of humanity. The genre in the late classical period reinterprets the original castigation of folly to mean criticism both of the goals of intellectual effort and the intellect itself; nonrational ways of knowing the truth become more important to the genre than the simple advocacy of common sense. In this reinterpretation is the bridge between classical and medieval Menippean satire.

BOETHIUS

When I presented a Lucian who wrote only two Menippean satires, I excluded those works in which Menippean matters had been accommodated to the dialogue form; the *Contemplantes,* whose sad ending seemed so at variance with the Menippean mood, stood as an example of Menippean satire transformed. Yet the *Consolation* is a dialogue, and with a bitter and mordant end; it belongs to our genre because of its content, for it stands in the late classical Menippean tradition of dramatizations of the search for a secure location of human experience within the confines of philosophical abstraction. It is a search that fails, and in asserting this I challenge the usual view of the *Consolation* and its wisdom. A full defense of my position, with an analysis of the *Consolation's* various literary debts and influences, awaits another book: I present here an outline of the *Consolation* as a Menippean text.

The work, like the *Satyricon,* strains the limits of the genre. For all of its Greek wisdom it belongs to the Latin traditions of Menippean satire. It is the most prosimetric Menippean text: the *Satyricon* could have contained more poetry but could not have exploited a more ordered succession of poems or a greater number of meters. The whole of the *Consolation* is structured and ordered by the poems, a constellation revolving about the North Star of 3 m. 9, *o qui perpetua,* the only poem in epic hexameters.[24] No other Menippean satire is as extensive a dialogue: the *De Nuptiis* is more in the manner of a symposium, with seven speakers, as it were, taking it in turns to praise the Liberal Arts. Here we must see the debt to the Roman traditions of philosophical dialogue, as Lerer has set them out.[25] The *Consolation* is at the confluence of a number of traditions; if we may say that the *Satyricon* is a Menippean satire laid on top of a picaresque fiction, we may say that the *Consolation* is a Menippean satire laid on top of a philosophical dialogue. The *Satyricon* abuses the moralist, and the *Consolation* the philosopher; in both cases the Menippean genre is not merely a prosimetric window dressing but is an essential element of the story. Poetry and prose become representatives of two differing types of wisdom, the emotional and the rational; there is a question of the synthesis of the two; the absence of a concluding poem, which in the structure of the work seems so necessary, ends the work with a silence that suggests a lack of reconciliation.[26]

There has been no lack of interest in the literary affiliations of the *Consolation*. But if its theme is identified as the failure, and not the success, of Philosophy to satisfy the needs of the prisoner, then the texts that are seen to lie behind the *Consolation* are necessarily different. The *Phaedo* would seem the prominent philosophical model: the philosopher in prison turns to writing poems in praise of Apollo (as well as composing poetic fictions, versifying some of Aesop's fables) and singing hymns, secure in his decision to remain in prison (*Phaedo* 60c–61c).[27] But Philosophy's promise to take Boethius's narrator to his true home is never kept, and the work cannot be incomplete. The prisoner never leaves his cell. In this light I think that the primary philosophical model is the *Crito:* because the prisoner is a philosopher and only a philosopher he will not leave his prison, even though Philosophy, like Socrates' friends, offers the possibility of escape.

The well-known introduction to Book 1 exploits a Menippean gambit familiar to us from Fulgentius's *Mythologies:* the narrator presents himself as a bad poet and is consequently not in control of the truth. Philosophy therefore manifests herself before an unworthy scribe and needs to change his intended work from elegy to philosophy. But here we have a device of Old Comedy, which may well have found a place in Varro: the personified genre who complains about its author. The ultimate origin of this is the person of Comedy arraigning Cratinus in the *Pytine* for drunkenness; Fulgentius reflects it in his narrator's madness and his allegiance to his (Christian) wife, which Calliope must sever in order to preserve her own integrity. But the Philosophy who appears as an exasperated genre will go on to complain about her ill-treatment at the hands of modern philosophers: her synchronic vision allows her to treat all philosophers between Plato and Boethius at once. Musica in Pherecrates' *Chiron* makes the same complaint; this famous scene of Old Comedy is distantly behind Calliope's complaint in Fulgentius that she is only a jump ahead of Galen's vivisectionists. This is the Philosophy of the tattered robe, who had been dragged off kicking and screaming by the philosophers and who returns with garments blackened by smoke, as death masks are (1.1.3–5, 1.3.7).[28]

A neglected Philosophy does not live in the impassive Epicurean *intermundia*; she returns from the Land of the Dead. She has come to complain and to find a champion, but finds instead our emotionally crippled narrator, whose cure she must then work. She must save him, but she needs him as a philosopher to save her and to prolong her life. Here is a particular bitterness: she describes philosophy as a preparation for death and says that death proves the philosopher. The remedies she will offer are only those of death (1.5.11, 1.4.1, 2.1.7), the stronger potions that he is not yet ready to drink. Therefore, the prisoner must die in order to save Philosophy. The beginning books animate a Philosophy who has traveled to the realms of the light from the world below, and who will snatch the narrator and take him down with her. But she here makes a crucial promise that will not be kept, to make the prisoner aware of who he truly is. His forgetfulness is the root of all his trouble (1.6.14–19), but he will remember, she says, because he is still confident of the providential governance of the world (1.6.20). The prisoner's narrative of the wrongs done him in his political life does not impress her at all, because that life is not real life. Real life is inescapable mortality, and Philosophy's reminders may be more depressing than elevating.

Philosophy claims that the narrator needs careful preparation for her ultimate lessons. She works indirectly. Book 2 begins with a trivialization of Book 1, the surprising claim that the root of his woe is longing for his former fortune (2.1.2). Philosophy attacks Fortune, and by 2 m. 8 achieves the same conclusion that the prisoner had in 1 m. 5, a pious Christian hope that the same peace in heaven may rule on earth.[29] The first half of Book 3 (3.2–9) then repeats the material of Book 2, a critical embarrassment unless the point of the presentation of Philosophy's instruction is that it is trivial, obvious, and repetitive.[30] We then arrive at the central poem (3 m. 9): "O you who rule the world with undying reason, begetter of earth and heaven, who command that time proceed from eternity, who grant motion to all things, yourself immobile. . . ." It is perhaps too easily read as profound, and may strike some as merely platitudinous, but it terminates the first half of the *Consolation*. Philosophy has, by an overly cautious insistence on first steps, repetition, and generally glacial progress led the prisoner to the simple and hopeful conclusion that he already knew: that there is an order to the universe, that the evil may only seem to be happy, that the good are always rewarded.

Book 4 sees a change of plan. The prisoner has not, after all, been thoroughly convinced. Philosophy's instructions make him doubt what he took to be certain before. He interrupts Philosophy because he is still upset and still unsure of her conclusions: he asks about the coexistence of a good God and evil in the world. She will answer, and

will show him the path by which he may return to his homeland; she
will give him wings, so that he may follow her (4.1.9):

> Pennas etiam tuae menti quibus se in altum tollere possit
> adfigam, ut perturbatione depulsa sospes in patriam meo
> ductu, mea semita, meis etiam uehiculis reuertaris.

> I shall attach wings to your mind that it may raise itself up to
> the heights; that fear may be shoved aside and you may
> return intact to your homeland by my lead, by my path,
> even in my vehicles.

This is an uncomfortable enthusiasm. Flight out of prison is reminiscent of Daedalus and Icarus; and Philosophy now arrogates to herself the attributes assigned to ruler of the world at the end of the *o qui
perpetua,* even including the astral body (vehicle) by which the Neoplatonic soul may return to its source (3 m. 9.27–28):

> tu requies tranquilla piis, te cernere finis,
> principium, uector, dux semita terminus idem.

> For the devoted you are undisturbed peace, to see you is
> their goal; you who are at once the beginning, the vehicle,
> the leader, the path, and the end.

It is from this point that we may chart the collapse of the dialogue.
Philosophy hopes to do too much; she will not be able to keep this
promise either. She cannot, after slow first steps, find the speed with
which to raise herself up on her wings. The prisoner, by forcing
Philosophy to address the questions that she had at first hoped to
leave to one side, will clip her wings and ground himself and her.

Book 4 fashions a reasonable answer to the prisoner's question,
and Book 5 again finds Philosophy ready to go on to other topics.
The prisoner now demands an account of the coexistence of human
free will and divine foreknowledge. Philosophy says that she is hurry-
ing to keep her promise; the prisoner's question is worth asking but
the exhaustion its investigation entails in the byways will keep him
from completing the straight homeward journey that he has begun.[31]
He insists; Philosophy agrees to humor him (5.1.8: "Morem, inquit
geram tibi . . ."). In the ensuing discussion, the prisoner is obsessed
by the word "necessity." If things happen by necessity, the bonds
between God and humans break down; this is the tenor of the prisoner's last words, the querulous 5 m. 3. Philosophy enters into the
longest prose section of the work in an attempt to satisfy the prisoner's objections, which concludes the book. She will admit that if the

narrator must have it that what God foresees cannot help but happen, and that what must happen occurs by necessity, then, yes, all happens by necessity, but only a theologian (*diuini speculator*) can understand it.[32] She will end the book by invoking the very thing that the prisoner fears (5.6.48):

> If you [pl.] will not pretend to hide the fact, there is a great necessity of virtuous action imposed upon you, since you act before the eyes of a judge who sees all things.[33]

The silence at the end of the *Consolation* is a powerful thing. The prisoner does not speak in assent, and there is no verse to bring the rational conclusion home to the heart of this philosopher. His enthusiasm for rational truth has prevented Philosophy from supplying the wings that would let him fly away. He never returns to his true home. Death is inevitable for the prisoner; but by clipping Philosophy's wings he is left to stare at death without salvation.

I think that the fifth book demonstrates exactly what Philosophy feared it would at the outset: she yielded to the prisoner against her better judgment, and he, exhausted in travel on the byways, cannot complete the journey home. It is perhaps Philosophy's instructional goal to demonstrate how fruitless such investigations are when transcendence is available by other means. The sixth-century Roman elegist Maximian suggests exactly this. He writes about Boethius in his *Third Elegy*, a curious poem that documents a hostile tradition: after his death, Boethius could be depicted as a philanderer.[34] Maximian writes of his own youth, and how he appealed to Boethius for help in a difficult love affair. Boethius plays the *praeceptor amoris* and, in language specifically modeled on the *Consolation,* bids Maximian reveal his wound so that it can be cured. Boethius's plan is to give Maximian enough rope with which to hang himself; Boethius plays the go-between and bribes the girl's parents. Once the affair becomes possible Maximian finds himself disdainful and impotent: "permissum fit uile nefas, fit languidus ardor" (3.77). The girl leaves in disgust, and Maximian reports back to Boethius, who praises him, ironically, for having overcome his passions and for subduing Venus, Cupid, and Minerva (3.87–90). The poem ends with the poet's moral:

> And so the opportunity granted me stole away from me my desire for such impropriety; my very desire for such things ran away from me. The two of us, equally unsatisfied and

depressed, went our separate ways; the grounds for our divorce was a life of chastity.

Maximian, in other words, invites us to read the *Consolation* as a text in which Philosophy indulges Boethius's desires in order to squelch those desires; in which there is no happy ending but only a pathetic divorce. The prisoner's intellectual rigor is like Maximian's impotence: a failure to take what is offered, and the pretense that this failure is a sign of intellectual or moral superiority.

To say this is not to deny the philosophical content of the *Consolation*. We have here Boethius's considered opinions on the nature of free will, and his discussion will go on to have considerable medieval authority.[35] The works may even be read as a defense of the Seven Liberal Arts, as the prisoner calls on all the disciplines to achieve a final synthesis.[36] The influence of Augustine on Boethius is great, but the conviction that learning aids faith is much more of an Augustinian position: Boethius, at least as evidenced by his *Theological Tractates,* believes that his learning can only help faith in small matters, achieving a logical clarity, perhaps, or resolving ambiguous terms.[37] There is no reconciliation of faith and learning in the *Consolation;* Philosophy is to be seen as correct, but she can only go so far; the point of the *Consolation* is the limitations of learning. The erudition here amassed lacks any authoritative validation and is in the Menippean tradition of the ironic encyclopedia.[38]

If we can reject the view that in the *Consolation* we see the Christian Boethius turning for strength in crisis to love of Philosophy and so exalting rational thought, we can ask why he depicts the failure of Philosophy to satisfy her promises, and why the prisoner's own questions keep him in his cell. A first answer may be purely literary: the small questioner who deflates the grand figure of authority by demanding answers to impossible questions is a staple of Lucianic comedy.[39] We have seen this in the figure of the atheist Damon in the *Juppiter Tragoedus:* his truths about the incompatibility of divine foreknowledge and human responsibility embarrass the gods who overhear him and cannot refute him, but they have no effect. This sort of comedy survives in the sixth century in a poem of the Greek Agathias (*Anth. Pal.* 11.354), which I have argued is in effect a small *Consolation.* Here, an eager student asks the philosopher Nicostratus, who has mastered all of Plato and Aristotle, if the soul is mortal or immortal: the master answers that if the soul has a nature, then it must be one or the other, but the student will have to kill himself to find out the truth.[40]

A second answer may be that two Philosophies are implied, one true and one false. This too is attested in Lucian, where we find a number of animations of Philosophy. In the *Piscator,* Parrhesiades defends himself against the charge of insulting Philosophy in the dialogue *Vitarum Auctio* ("Philosophers for Sale") by saying that the only Philosophy he ever saw was a strumpet; the true Philosophy appears to preside over the trial, at which Diogenes the Cynic speaks for the unsuccessful prosecution. Boethius's prisoner tries to reclaim his status as a true philosopher by staying within the realms of traditional philosophical inquiry; Philosophy herself represents another way in which to be a philosopher, though she is never allowed to reveal it. This too would be in line with the habits of Menippean satire: consider the two heavens implied in Julian's *Caesars,* and the two heavens seen in Martianus's *De Nuptiis.*

But the ultimate answer is that Christianity is to be seen as the way out of the difficulty. The *Consolation* is a Christian text not because it advances Christian truths but because it allows a faith that has been glimpsed here and there to emerge as the victor in a fruitless contest of opposing arguments. The piety of the Lord's Prayer has been detected in the *Consolation,* as has the influence of Latin liturgical language; most important of these quiet Christian presences is the prisoner's delight in hearing the particular words by which Philosophy says that there is a highest good that directs all things forcefully and orders them sweetly (3.12.22: "Est igitur summum, inquit, bonum quod regit cuncta fortiter suauiterque disponit"). The prisoner is surprised to hear an allusion to the Wisdom of Solomon, the Wisdom that "reacheth therefore from end to end mightily and ordereth all things sweetly" (Douay; 8.1: "Attingit ergo a fine usque ad finem fortiter et disponit omnia suauiter").[41] It must be admitted that the *Consolation* is compatible with Christian thought and capable of being interpreted as such in an age in which the gap between Christian and pagan is not always very large.[42]

In this reading, the *Consolation* is still a work in which faith and reason are implicitly incompatible; but we see the inadequacy of reason. It is still a soulful work, but of a man who does not find the answers he seeks. It is still a protreptic and a Platonic remembering, but a protreptic toward something and a remembering of something that the text never reveals. Not only are Augustine's *Confessions* and dialogues behind the literary framework of the *Consolation,* but also Job: the prisoner is the wounded innocent, whose insistence on himself and his virtue is seen as arrogance; and Philosophy, standing in for the trio of accusers, is rebuked for the limitations of her dogmatic visions. Isidore of Seville could read the *Consolation* in this way. In his *Synonyma*, subtitled "The Lament of the Sinful Soul" (*Patrologia Latina* 83:825–68) the defects of the *Consolation* are made up. In the guise of a series of soliloquies, *homo* speaks first to *ratio* and then to *anima* as he complains of his misfortunes and learns to look toward heaven.[43] Ratio tells him, much as Philosophy tells Boethius, about the exempla of other heroic sufferers. But the source of revelation changes from *ratio* to *anima*, there is talk of heaven and hell, and Book 2 begins with an injunction that *homo* remember himself and who he is, the stated goal of the *Consolation* that is never reached. The *Synonyma* is a bipartite *Consolation* that moves from reason's ability to wean the person away from the transience of this life to *anima*'s ability to lead him onward; it does not accept Philosophy's ability to serve in both roles and consciously sets out to answer all of the questions that the *Consolation* leaves unanswered.

APPROACHING THE TWELFTH CENTURY

This reading of Boethius and his tradition allows us to understand medieval Menippean satire. The Renaissance will find Seneca, Petronius, and Lucian congenial as literary models, but the Middle Ages knew primarily of the Menippean satirists from Martianus to Boethius. The Greek tradition was inaccessible, Varro was unrecoverable, and Petronius and the Seneca of the *Apocolocyntosis* (as opposed to the author of the correspondence with Saint Paul and the *Epistulae Morales*) made unseemly reading in a pious age.[44] Not only did they thus reduce the eight hundred–year tradition of Menippean satire to some fifty or sixty years,[45] but the authors that they read were, to the exception of Martianus, Christian. I have already suggested that the Christian Menippean satires of the late classical period constitute a valuable and underunappreciated document in the history of Christian thought. The Christian appropriation of secular knowledge was accepted de facto in the sixth century, but there remained the question of sanctioning it de jure. The sophistication inherent in such comic phrasings of the question of the reconciliation of faith and classical culture is itself a fair guarantee that Christianity would coopt pagan learning as part of the true believer's heritage, but we cannot deny that these works spoke to a real crisis of faith, learning, and tradition in their audience. This problem did not lose its importance or immediacy in the Middle Ages. To the Middle Ages, Menippean satire is a Christian and philosophical genre that considers the relation between Christian faith and secular knowledge in the literate believer, and ponders the place of this believer in the construct of the world.

This allows us to dismiss as facile a number of possible explanations for the long dormancy of Menippean satire in the Middle Ages. It is not a question of the irony of Boethius being too difficult to notice and thus to imitate, or that the encyclopedic attraction of Martianus led to a disregard of his setting, or that the Dark Ages lacked sufficient self-confidence and sense of history to examine the relation between knowledge and tradition. The point, I think, is that Menippean satire would seem to be a philosophical medium for the discussion of the possibility of the synthesis of pagan and Christian knowledge and belief, and it was not until a new synthesis was attempted that Menippean satire was revived. This medieval revival belongs to the twelfth century and the School of Chartres.[46] In the rise and fall of Christian Platonism and its attempts to locate the nature of humanity and human wisdom in a universe defined by Christian faith and Platonic philosophy, Menippean satire once again comes into its own.

Boethius's *Consolation* is the immediate spiritual and formal inspiration for a number of works in the Christian Platonist movement. To be sure, Boethius was of vast influence throughout the Middle Ages as both a philosopher and as a source of learning; together with Martianus, Calcidius, Cassiodorus, and Isidore of Seville, he taught the Middle Ages much of what it knew about classical learning. But it was not until the twelfth century that the *Consolation* inspired other philosophical and prosimetric works affiliated to our genre. Hildebert of Lavardin is the first to revive Boethius's form at the beginning of the century in his *Liber de Querimonia et Conflictu Carnis et Animae* ("The Complaint and the Struggle of Body and Soul"), whose theme is "the tension between a dualistic view of reality and an ultimate affirmation—despite all the forces of dualism—of the value of the physical world."[47] Adelhard of Bath follows with his *De Eodem et Diverso* ("On the Same and the Different," ca. 1116); in this Philosophy champions the Liberal Arts as able guides for the soul to knowledge of the divine order of the universe.[48] But despite the use of prose and verse, the influence of Boethius and Martianus, the supernatural speakers, and the opposed approaches to understanding, these works are estranged from Menippean satire by their seriousness; they prove without irony and over objections that the place of humanity can be logically deduced from a contemplation of the nature of the universe. They are works of confidence, not doubt.

But it is in the *decline* of Christian Platonism that Menippean satire is found intact. First in the *De Cosmographia* of Bernardus Silvestris (between 1130 and 1140?) and then in the *De Planctu Naturae* of Alan of Lille (1160–65?), the system of Christian Platonism is questioned, not advocated. To both authors, the manifest defects in the nature of humanity put it outside the pale of logic and the world order and within the realm of divine plan and special providence; in these satires Theology, not Philosophy, becomes the queen of the Seven Liberal Arts. Bernard is a poet, and the *De Cosmographia*, a truly philosophical contemplation of the incommensurability of the world of human beings and the universe as a whole, rises to the sublime as a cosmological epic that has earned the right to be compared with the *Divine Comedy;* but Alan, the lesser light, writes the comic tale that is a true Menippean satire.

It need not be described here in full.[49] In it, Nature appears to the narrator as Philosophy does to the prisoner, in tattered robes. We are treated to a comic ecphrasis (Prose 1) as all of her garments are described, on which is represented the universe in all its elements and details. She laments that people have abandoned her laws, but we learn that she herself, God's vice-regent, handed the reins of government over to Venus, so that she herself could live a life of ease (Prose 4). Her rules are all the laws of grammar: because people commit solecism, they fall into the vice of homosexuality. Moral virtues are enumerated in the brief Meter 8, a poem that constitutes the relatively unironic and serious center of a Menippean satire. Nature's complaint is to be conveyed by Hymenaeus to Genius, who is an ambiguous figure, seen in the act of writing. From his right hand come good things (Cato and Helen of Troy!), and from his left come the bad (Sinon and the poetry of Ennius); language here too, as in Alan's exuberant purple prose, is a model of moral impropriety. The ending is Senecan. There is an unnamed prodigal, the object of Genius's decree, though the decree is expressed in purely general terms; Generosity is his supporter, though she claims not to be able to intervene on his behalf. The decree is hurried, the narrator wakes up, and nothing has been accomplished.

It is a fitting conclusion to this study. Scholarly writing is emblematic of moral decay. The anatomy of the universe reveals no secure place for human beings, who are outside the realm of both reason and nature, and only theology can take over. The decrees of the gods have no effect, people escape the claims of justice, fantasy reveals absurdity. The Nature who tells a myth about the origins of the universe and the genesis of human corruption cannot understand her own myth, for she is a corrupt element within it.[50] Seneca, Fulgentius, Ennodius, and Boethius exist side by side; most important are Boethius and his Philosophy, whose stories cannot satisfy the inquisitive narrator, or explain the degenerate state of the world. Alan laughs louder, no doubt, and more obviously than does Boethius, but Boethian irony has made Alan's laughter possible.

GREEK PROSIMETRIC
ROMANCES

RECENT DISCOVERIES of two prosimetric papyrus fragments in Egypt, both of the second century A.D., have been brought to bear both on the problem of the "origin" of the novel and on the history of Menippean satire. The fragments are of particular interest here because of the possibility of their reflection of the writings or habits of Menippus himself. The first of these is the so-called Iolaos fragment, first published by Parsons in 1971,[1] and included among the publications of the Oxyrhynchus Papyri in 1974 as P.Oxy. 3010.[2] In it, an unidentified man is initiated into the mysteries of Cybele, in which his friend Nicon plays an instrumental role. The unidentified man then addresses one Iolaos in his new capacity as a gallus; he tells Iolaos that he has become a gallus for his sake and that Iolaos must trust him. Iolaos then submits to this instruction; the fragment ends with a citation of Euripides, on the value of friendship.[3] The remarkable feature about this fragment is that the new gallus addresses Iolaos in verse (lines 14–33), in the unusual Sotadean meter.

The gallus is a comic figure in classical literature, and we seem to have here some sort of mock-initiation. He speaks of Iolaos's intention to have sexual intercourse by means of some sort of trick (line 30: ὅτι δόλῳ σὺ βεινεῖν μέλλεις). Parsons rejected connections with Milesian tales and Menippean satire in his first edition of the papyrus and suggested, tentatively, that we have to do with a Greek *Satyricon.* The general parallels he adduced were the sexual intrigue (Iolaos and the gallus similar to Encolpius and Giton), the vulgar speech to be found in the verse passage (parallel to the linguistic peculiarities of Trimalchio and the freedmen), and the presence of comic verses. *Satyricon* 23.2 has a gallus speaking in Sotadeans (though only for four lines and not really advancing the plot); 80.9 has a similar verse commentary on the value of friendship, also appended without connection or warning.[4] Parsons's evaluation is cautious and sensible; while not insisting too much on the parallels between the fragment and the *Satyricon,* he feels that there is some proof here of a Greek picaresque novel.

In his P.Oxy. 3010 publication, Parsons refers to a reconstruction of the action as proposed by E. R. Dodds as "most ingenious and convincing."[5] Iolaos has convinced his friend to learn about the galli so that Iolaos, dressed in women's clothing and pretending to be a gallus, can gain secret access to the woman he desires. The Sotadeans are thus a mixture of technical jargon and low language. A number of the religious terms would have a comic meaning: νεκρὸν ἄταφον, or "walking corpse," would refer to a real, castrated gallus; τὸν νόθον, "the bastard," would mean a "false gallus," of the sort that would desire illicit sexual intercourse. If the story is merely one of low-life sexual intrigue, as it almost certainly is, then we can leave aside the idea of Merkelbach that this is a satirical initiation scene; this interpretation places too much weight upon the gallus's request that Iolaos "tell all" (line 31): ὥστε μηδὲ ἕν με κρύβε.[6]

This last interpretation would perhaps place the scene within the traditions of the mime or of new comedy; a similar ruse is to be found in Terence's *Eunuch* in the person of Chaerea.[7] But regardless of which particular tack we take, there is little here to cement a connection between the fragment and Menippean satire, as opposed to picaresque or low-life fiction; quotations from Euripides are the common property of the Greek romance, and even the gallus's speech can be explained as in character for a gallus, for whom the Sotadean meter is traditional and appropriate.[8] This could be part of a comic characterization of a religious fraud in the pursuit of immoral behavior and as such could certainly be at home in a comic romance, such as Iamblichus's *Babyloniaca,* or a low-life one, such as the *Phoinicica.* But two things must be admitted that make Menippean satire in the manner of Petronius an attractive generic label here. First, characterization through language is abundantly attested in Petronius but not in Apuleius or the Greek ideal romance; consider Heliodorus, who tells us in the *Ethiopica* that Bagoas spoke bad Greek though he does not reproduce it (8.15.3). Second, Apuleius's *Metamorphoses,* which also makes fun of opportunistic and sexually profligate religious frauds (cf. the eunuch Philebus and the priests of the Syrian goddess, 8.24–9.10), would seem very different if its characters spoke more than their all-purpose oracle in verse (9.8).

I am not convinced by the hypothesis of Cataudella, and he takes pains not to represent it as anything more than that, that P.Oxy. 3010 is a fragment of Menippus himself.[9] The argument is based on resemblances between one of Varro's *Menippeans,* the *Eumenides,* and the Oxyrhynchus text. In Varro we read of the woman's clothing of the galli and how one character puts it on (F 120, F 155), and of rites of the Great Mother (F 132, F 140, F 149, F 150).[10] Sotadean verses, rare in ancient literature, are found in Varro, and only in his *Menippeans;* however, I would point out that the *Eumenides* uses a different, though appropriate, meter for the description of the eunuch priests of Cybele, the galliambic (F 131, 132). Cataudella also points out that Iolaos, as squire of Hercules, may represent a Menippean use of Hercules as a comic character; and many of Varro's *Menippeans* invoke Hercules.[11] But all that this can really demonstrate is that both the *Eumenides* and *Iolaos* make fun of *galli* in appropriate ways; there is certainly not enough evidence to attach the fragment to Menippus's name, nor does any of our evidence for the writings of Menippus indicate that he wrote a work in which such a scene could be appropriate.

The second of these fragmentary works is more compelling, a papyrus published under the name of "Narrative about Tinouphis in Prosimetrum."[12] The plot is difficult to reconstruct: Tinouphis seems to be a magus and a prophet of the goddess Isis; he was condemned on a charge of adultery; he was rescued from some sort of punishment (an executioner figures in the action) by means of a single πλίνθος, possibly a brick in a wall; a builder is praised for his cleverness. Someone has been miraculously set free by a trick; the action could belong to the romance, comedy, mime, or Milesian tale. But what attracts attention is that lines 9–17 are in verse, and of a peculiar sort: they are catalectic iambic tetrameters whose median diaeresis is treated as though it were a verse end. This meter is not otherwise attested in Greek literature, yet may be paralleled in Varro's *Menippeans,* thus leading the editor to the intriguing assumption that the verse form here attested, though not the verses themselves, may well be an invention of Menippus himself. The action itself seems more at home in the romance than in Menippean satire, though a single fragment cannot not tell about the disposition of the whole. Haslam makes a good conjecture: "The Menippean form began life as inherently snook-cocking, repudiating the conventional literary proprieties. Perhaps it here enjoys more innocent application, merely sensationalistic."[13]

Iolaos and *Tinouphis* attest the existence of prosimetric romance. Together with the fragments of the *Phoinicica* of Lollianus, these papyrus finds do what the papyri have always done: force a reevaluation of the origin and nature of the ancient romance.[14] There are low-life and sensationalistic Greek fictions; and it is possible now that Latin fiction is not so divorced from the Greek traditions as it once seemed.[15] They are not necessarily Menippean satires; there is nothing preserved of the intellectual parody or social criticism that marks the *Satyricon*. But it is true that here we have Greek fictions in which original verse is exploited in ways far more suggestive of Roman fiction than Greek romance.[16] But if the *Satyricon* is as I describe it, a Menippean form laid on top of a picaresque fiction, we may conclude that the papyri and the *Satyricon* together suggest a range of possible results of the marriage of Menippean satire and romance. It may seem evasive to claim that *Iolaos* and *Tinouphis* should be assigned to a hybrid genre of "Menippean romance"; but if Achilles Tatius had written his parody of a romance in a mixture of prose and verse, it would not necessarily resemble Menippean satire as it has been defined and explained in this book. Lucian's *True History* (a serial account of impossible adventures, but with Lucian's typically conservative use of quoted and parodied verse) could be then a literarily restrained essay in such a genre.[17] The *Odyssey*, which looms so large behind the *Satyricon,* is an ancestor both of the romance and of Menippean satire; romance and Menippean satire may be viewed, in logical terms at least, as separate entities that recombine to create the Menippean romance. We cannot determine the chronological origins of this genre, as we do not know when the originals of the papyri were written, but the poetic experiments of *Tinouphis* suggest Alexandrian times.[18] The *Satyricon* may well be written against the background of such romances; if so, we may say that Petronius returns the prosimetric romance to its Menippean origins. Or Petronius, the papyri, and the *True History* may all separately document the vitality of Menippean satire in numerous adaptations in the first centuries of the era. In any event, it cannot be maintained that Greek prosimetra require that we separate the *Satyricon* from Menippean satire.[19]

THE PROLOGUE OF
FULGENTIUS'S MYTHOLOGIES

[THE TEXT is that of the Teubner edition of Rudolf Helm. Fulgentius's text is not sound; many divergences are recorded in the notes. An attempt has been made in the translation to suggest the strangeness of the original, not all of which can be ascribed to the corruption of the text.]

MYTHOLOGIES

Although a work that has no effect pursues an ineffectual goal, and where there is no reward for effort the interest behind that effort ceases to be engaged (and for this very reason, that the lamentable misery of our time does not pursue the goal of eloquence but only weeps over the sweatshop of life, nor does it defend the reputation of poetry, but it must look out for the hunger at its doorstep, and thus you would rather weep for what you have lost or look for something to eat than find the right topics to declaim,[1] even though at this time the powerful have the leisure to oppress, the rich to steal, the private citizens to lose all they have, and the wretched to wail); nevertheless, because you are accustomed, my lord,[2] to listen often and graciously to my prattling nothings, coated with satiric charm, when Thalia used to rouse you with absurd epigrams and soothe you with her native charms,[3] and because you have recently seen fit to command me to soothe the seats of your ears (when they are sufficiently free of business) with whatever graceful whisper I could;[4] hear me then awhile as I begin to weave for you a tale wrinkled with an old woman's furrows,[5] which recently I concocted from pungent Attic wit and the midnight guiding lamp,[6] a tale tricked out in the fantasies of dreams in such a way that you will see in me no mad poet, but rather observe an interpreter of dreams who divines meanings from the trifles of sleep.[7] For you ought not to think that the lamps of Ovid's *Heroides* guided my books, or those by which the wantonness of Sulpicia is broadcast or the curiosity of Psyche,[8] nor even that which by force led Phaedra's husband to the grave,[9] nor that which received that swimming of Leander, but that which drew our academic rhetorician so close to the empyrean that it nearly made the sleeping Scipio a citizen of heaven. But let his *Res Publica* attest to what Cicero has accomplished.[10]

[4.6] While I was apart from your presence, lord, when the sloth of rural boredom held me tight, as it were an exile from city business, and while I was avoiding those damnable shipwrecks of disaster which relentlessly upset public affairs, I thought that I would try to get in peace some country quiet; so that, after the gales of anxiety had calmed down after the crisis in the city devolved to mass confusion, I might, like Halcyone,[11] enjoy at ease the quiet serenity of the nest, in the indolence of a country estate. After the blaring trumpets of war had been lulled into the ashes of silence, the trumpets of the barbarian invasions which had so shaken me, I was thinking that I could lead a life made perfect by silence, were it not that the wicked heartache of my grief was following me there as well,[12] and Fate, the stepmother of happiness, who always sprinkles something bitter upon human affairs, was dogging my footsteps like a lackey.

[5.1] For day after day the tax-collecting throng of people treading on my doorstep had worn it down with their feet; they brought new and ad hoc types of indictions, so that had I been transformed from a mortal man into King Midas and the stiff stuff of gold followed my wealthy touch, I believe that I would have dried up the waters of the Pactolus itself because of their frequent assessments.[13] Nor was this alone a sufficient sweatshop of miseries: in addition, the enemy's incursions often compelled us to plant our feet at home, so that no one could see the hinges of our doors, covered as they were with cobwebs. For the barbarians had control of our fields and we of our houses; we could look to our harvest but could not enjoy it; for, in fact, if the barbarians had left any of the fruits unconsumed, they would no doubt have belonged to the barbarians anyway, as we were so shut up.[14]

[5.13] But because no evil is immortal for mortals, finally the glory of my lord and king, coming like the dawning of the sun to the world, cleansed away our fears as the shadows gaped open.[15] And after our sluggish shuffling we could finally go out to the fields which the prohibition of war had covered with rust and could walk around their boundaries; we went out like sailors whom the longed-for shore receives back safe after being crushed by the buffeting of the storm[16] and, as if we had put off a cloak of stone walls after our domestic confinement, we more learned how to walk again than walked,[17] and like the verse of Vergil's finally the horse, free, gains the open plain [*Aen.* 11.493],

we looked on those fields which in the footprints of the warriors bore the seal of their so-called Moorish steps,[18] and as our fear had not yet been wiped clean from our minds,[19] we shuddered at the enemy in their tracks, for the soldiers had left for the heir of their enemy terror to remember them by.

[6.4] Yet like the Trojan women we were showing each other places made memorable by notorious slaughtering or notorious plundering.[20] And finally, in the middle of the thorny shrubs of the forest, which long ago the farmer's hand had abandoned (for due to the disruptive length of fear so pervasive the plows, greasy with smoke, were hanging from the walls, and the muscular necks of the oxen lost the callouses from their yokes in bovine softness), the field, widowed of furrows, lay overgrown, and the olive-bearing treetops were threatened by creeping thorns, for the vines so involved themselves in a tight bond with the wandering weeds that the ground, wrapped in the roots of these weeds, insolently rejected the tooth of Triptolemus.[21]

[6.15] And so, while I was pressing down thorny fields of this sort with an advancing foot, and was measuring out[22] the dewy hills of flowery fleece with a leisurely pace, desire gave birth to exhaustion, and a longing to sit down followed upon my efforts in my desire to get outside. I turned aside and appealed to the aid of a shade tree, that it might protect me by its wandering web of leaves from the blistering glance of Phoebus, and yield to share with me the shade it afforded its own roots with its all-encompassing network of interlocking branches.[23] For a certain native charm of the birds who were giving forth their chirping voices from their instrumental beaks in a sort of brittle sweetness drew me to the following effort, and such an unexpected rest from labor fairly demanded some sort of song and poem:[24]

> [7.5] Daughters of Thespiae,[25] whom Hippocrene bedews with the frothy streams of its garrulous spray, steeped in the Muses' draft, hasten, direct your steps from the grass of the hills, where at dawn the chill dew drops down drops of floral purple, which the stars exude on cloudless nights. Open up your baskets of words, full of flowers. Whatever the rushing stream carries with it through the grass of Tempe, the stream that the horse's hoof created in its journey through the air; whatever the shepherd of Ascra sang upon his ancient rock;[26] whatever your storehouses, emp-

tied of the treasure that you give, have to offer;[27] what
Vergil sang in the forests of rustic Mantua;[28] what the Maeonian poet chortled in the *Battle of the Frogs;*[29] let the Parrha-
sian lyre echo these with a gleaming pick, let the ancient
ages now flow together for my song.[30]

[8.6] And thus this poem attracted by its sacrificial song the Pierian maidens, dripping from the sprinkling of the Gorgon's font and
drunk from the stream of the flying hoof. And so there stood before
me three[31] maidens, translucent in their diaphanous gowns and circled in abundant ivy; one of them, Calliope, my friend, with a playful
touch of her palm warmed my chest and infused it with the sweetness
of the poetic itch; for hers, it seemed, was a pregnant chest, and
disheveled hair which a diadem glorious with pearls held tight. She
was gathering up her ankle-length, twice-dyed gown, which she did,
I think, because of the journey, and lest the barbed spikes of the
weeds somehow rip the borders of such fine material. She stood near
me, so I rose up on my elbow and honored the garrulous maiden
who was once even more clearly revealed to me through poetic evidence, nor was I unmindful for whose garrulous fables did I bear
palms swollen by beatings during my scholastic novitiate; yet because
it was not yet obvious to me who she was, I asked why she had
come.[32]

[8.22] Then she replied: "I am one of the virginal court of the
daughters of Helicon, enrolled in the lists of Jupiter. Once a citizen
of Athens, Roman society took me up to honor me, and there I did so
put forth tender young shoots[33] that I placed their tops in the highest stars. They left as an inheritance such a living fame that they
all the more prolonged their notorious decease. But when the on-
slaught of war widowed me of congress with the citadel of Romulus,
as an exile I gained the assemblies of the city of Alexandria and
prepared the wanton hearts of the Greeks for the various infusions
of instruction; and after the strictures of the Catos, the biting invec-
tives of Cicero and the talents of Varro, for the benefit of the race of
Pella[34] I tickled their effete senses with satire, or amused them with
the fantasies of comedy, or calmed them with tragic piety, or sea-
soned them with the brevity of epigrams. My imprisonment pleased
me, and though my energies were unemployed, my mind would
have found things to laugh at in the midst of its trials had not the
school of Galen, crueler than war, shut me out, even me. The school
had so wormed its way into practically every alleyway in Alexandria
that the butcher stalls of surgical execution outnumbered private

homes. Finally, because of their rivalries, they so remanded people to death that they even claimed that Charon would come all the faster if they were *not* handed over to their schools."

[9.17] A fetching laugh ended her speech, and I begged her therefore to lodge under my roof. She answered: "Aren't you afraid to take the Muses' instruction into your home? For I have heard that barbarian custom so completely rejects trafficking in education that they hale off[35] unheard to the executioner's (examination being rendered obsolete) those who can write the elementary shapes of the alphabet or their own name." I said: "It is not

> as you have heard, but its reputation is no longer [Vergil *Ecl.* 9.11].

For, O Muse,

> our poems have enough power in the midst of the weapons of Mars as [Vergil *Ecl.* 9.11–12]

> a stream of leaping sweet water to slake the thirst [Vergil *Ecl.* 5.47]."

And to make her realize all the more that I was her friend, I added that famous line of Terence:

> "Once upon a time and long ago, in an earlier age,
> there was profit in that sort of thing [*Eun.* 246].

And so it is now that literature preserves its authors for posterity if someone, crafty and by right of succession, transfers whatever Helicon possessed to the pinnacle of power."[36]

[10.8] She was thrilled by my verses, as if she were watching the old Maeonian reciting; she smoothed my hair with the honorific touch of her palm, and after my neck had been stroked more enticingly than was fitting she said: "Aha, my Fabius, you have for some time now been the latest initiate in the Anacreontic mysteries;[37] so lest my recruit lack for anything, accept an equal grace of instruction, and insofar as our Satyra[38] has struck you with her wanton dew of words and keeps you beholden to her through the enticements of love, abandon what you are interpreting from dreams[39] and take into the seats of your ears, free from business, what can be scratched out on Egyptian papyrus;[40] nor will any effect be lacking to whatever tale you ask to be placed in the vitals of."

[10.19] Then I said: "The title of my book deceives you, your noble garrulousness.[41] I have taken up no horned adulterer, nor sung of a maiden deceived by treacherous rain, while a god through his own judgment preferred a beast to himself and deceived by gold the girl whom he could not gain by force. We do not sing of the thigh of the young lover eaten by the boar's bite, nor in my little chapters does childish wantonness hang from a transformed bird; nor do we seek after the adulterer sneaking about in swan's plumage, quickening fowl's eggs in a virgin's womb rather than pouring in human seed; nor after the girls with the lamps, Hero and Psyche, who babble poetic nonsense as the former laments the lamp extinguished and the latter weeps for the lamp lit (for Psyche lost by seeing, and Hero, by not seeing, died). Nor will I tell of the Arcadian maiden deceived by a fictitious maiden, when Jupiter was looking for something that he more desired to be than what he was.[42] Therefore I want to make clear these vanities by transforming them,[43] not to obscure by transformation things already clear, so that an elder god can practice his neighing and the sun can put aside the fire of his brightness and prefer to be furrowed with an old woman's wrinkles instead of his own rays.[44] And so I aim for the real effects of things, so that once the lie of deceitful Greece has been laid to rest we can recognize what the mystic medulla in them ought to mean."[45]

[11.18] Then she said: "How, homunculus, do you come by these things, this great knowledge of ignorance, this so-thought-out ordering of unknowing? For when you seek out things untouched by the ages you show that you in your wisdom know what you do not know."

[11.21] I answered her: "If those who happen not to know something do not even happen to know their own ignorance, how much better would it have been for them not to happen to be born than to come to be so uselessly! And so I think that I know the most important entryway of knowledge, a thing you may not know."

[12.3] To this she replied: "For a lively treatment of matters so hidden and mystical we must seek greater assistance, that of authorities. For this is no laughable thing that we are after, which would have us patch together the metrical profits of words in comic feet. We have need here of the sweat of a grappling genius lest the weighty undertaking of such a glorious work evaporate in the very middle of the momentum of the attempt, stripped of the liveliest treatments. Therefore we must appropriate Philosophia herself and Urania as assistants for our work; nor will your comfort lack a wanton lady-friend, but while the mystical arts make you exhausted by their treatments, your Satyra will safely take you up and make you playful."

[12.13] I answered: "I beg you, your kind beneficence, not to entrust rashly to my home that Satyra of yours, by whose love you proclaimed I have long since been bound.[46] For I have been allotted a marriage so livid with the jealousy of love that if she found this woman in her house like a concubine looking warmly upon the object of her affections, she would have to kick her out back to Helicon, her cheeks so furrowed by my wife's nails that the streams of the Gorgonean font itself would hardly suffice to cleanse her wounds."[47]

[12.20] Then she shattered a brittle laugh and slapped her palm against her thigh once or twice. She said: "You don't know, my Fulgentius, you rustic neighbor of the Pierian maidens,[48] how much wives fear Satyra. Though lawyers yield to the wordy waves of wives and schoolteachers do not grumble against them, though the rhetor falls silent and the town crier hushes his shouting, she is the only one who puts an end to the women's ragings, the example of Petronius's Albucia notwithstanding.[49] For when she plays, the lording of Plautus's Saurea falls asleep, and the garrulousness of Ausonius's little Sulpicia perishes, and the song of the singing of Sallust's Sempronia grows hoarse, despite Catiline's presence."[50]

> [13.6] The driver had released his fire-breathing quadrupeds after he had passed through the region of the world, and he warmed the cool earth with his wheels, and was stripping the horses' necks of their golden reins. Now Phoebus unharnessed his horses, now Cynthia harnessed hers, and the waves that his sister left the brother warmed with his feet. The night, adorned with a starry cape, ordered the world to slow down beneath her dew-bearing wheels, and Luna, glorious with a two-horned, star-bearing crown, had climbed the jeweled heaven with her twin-yoked oxen. Now phantasms, deceiving the mind with fictitious images, were filling soft beds with treacherous signs . . .[51]

[13.17] . . . and, to conclude in as few words as possible, it was night.[52] I had long forgotten the name of night and was going mad in verses like an insane poet,[53] when suddenly that woman from the country, that guest whom I had seen long ago, with a precipitate rush broke through the doors of my chamber by force and, finding me lying there unawares, she assaulted my eyes, which were drooping in the sweet torpor of sleep, with a rapid and most gloriously flashing sort of gleam from her face; for she stood out beyond the normal appearance of mortality.[54] Finally she roused me while I was snoring through my flared nostrils (a sign of slothful quiet up to that point) by a sudden knock on the doorjamb.[55]

[14.1] Before her advanced a comely maiden wanton in floral luxuriance, circled in abundant ivy, with a shameless face and a mouth pregnant with a bundle of insults;[56] her ironic eye darted about with such a penetrating native wit that she could have described even the meanings[57] deeply hidden in drunken writings. Two Muses, one on either side of her, stitched her sides:[58] the one on the right, buoyed up by a certain holy majesty, brandished the brightness of her lofty brow with silver pearls of stars; the horned curvature of the moon pressed down upon her diadem, bejeweled with rare carbuncles; and, adorned with a dark cloak, she held aloft the hollowness of a glass sphere, and spun it with a rod of bone. And so, through the lofty contemplation of this light, her vision was lifted up to heaven,[59] so that she very nearly broke her big toe on the door while looking upward.[60]

[14.14] Her companion on the left side was more withdrawn, and with a sort of retiring contemplation she avoided human gaze by means of a sort of mystic cloak. Her snowy hair shone with white shafts, and her wrinkles (her brow had multiple corrugations) portended that she was smelling something rotten. Her gait was rather slow, and was holy by the mere burden of her weighty thoughts.[61]

[14.20] Then Calliope entered the realms of garrulity and said: "I had promised, Fulgentius, that I would grant you these guardians; if you cling to them they will, in one fell swoop, make you heavenly, not mortal, and they will place you in the stars, not as they did Nero, with poetic praise,[62] but as Plato, with mystic ideas.[63] For you ought not expect of them the effects that a poem tricks out or a tragedy laments or a speech spews forth or a satire cackles or a comedy plays, but those in which Carneades' hellebore sweats,[64] and Plato's golden language and Aristotle's syllogistic pithiness. So now open up the chamber of your mind and take into your mind what you receive from the message heard in the pipes of your ears; but unstring all that is mortal within you, lest the succession of such holy instruction sit uncomfortably in recalcitrant recesses.

[15.10] So now we will speak first of the nature of the gods, and whence so great a pollution of foul credulity has fixed itself in stupid minds. For although there are some who reject the innate nobility of their heads and in their rustic and antique sensibilities are as wise as acorns, and their numbed wits are hidden in an all-too-thick cloud of stupidity, nevertheless, errors never arise in the human senses unless driven in by random impulses, as Chrysippus says in his work *On Fate:* 'Impulses roll on by unpredictable forces.'[65] And so let us abandon this discursiveness and speak of whence idols are derived."

ENNODIUS'S PARAENESIS
DIDASCALICA

[THE TEXT and text divisions are from the standard edition of F. Vogel, pp. 310–15, where it is classified as *Opusculum VI*. The edition of Rallo Freni is hard to come by: its few divergences from Vogel's text are recorded in the notes when they affect the sense; its text divisions are given below in square brackets. The notes otherwise deal primarily with matters of language and translation, and with the identification of the people mentioned in the text. The translation, fairly literal, attempts to respect the strange metaphors of Ennodius's language; see Rallo Freni, edition, pp. xxxiii–xlii.]

TO AMBROSE AND BEATUS[1]

1. [I.1] We obey God when by our counsel we command things that are pleasing to him. There are, therefore, mystical precepts in this my acquiescence, out of desire for your affection, to your request. You have demanded with much pleading that a page with an academic ring to it be fashioned on your behalf, and I have willingly yielded to the will of the majority because (and I have yet to see what weight these words will bear) it is enough for me to be mentioned in your prayers.[2] But at the entryway to my writing I shall not keep silent about what grants life. 2. [I.2] With all the devotion of your minds keep God in your pure vitals; keep him appeased on your behalf with frequent prayers; be separated from him by no fornications of soul, by no duplicity. Furthermore, love those whom your natural association makes your neighbors, and do not rejoice at having done that which would pain you were it done to you. The fruit of this goodness is whatever you pray for.

3. [II.1] However, deliberation and uncertainty as to whether I should offer you my words in a poem or in the form of a letter have kept me confused for some time. I have chosen to reveal my affection for you in both ways of speaking, for strong expression befits an instructor, and the niceties of a gentler pen refresh the minds beset

by good advice. [II.2] So be so kind as to accept that which you have demanded.

In Praise of Poetry[3]

Although whatever the Mother Muse proclaims
is soft with the dew of honey;
although a poem, fashioned with elegant charm,
bewitches the beating of a docile heart;
although virtue does not always befit a poem,
because the rules that ordain the regulation of rhythms
resolve the strong at the insistence of study;[4]
nevertheless, we follow the measure of the chattering
    Muse,
but only so far (at the admonition of caution)
as our talents and the strength of truth allow.
We suffer the inborn toughness of the soldier of Christ
to be on guard against effeminate composition.[5]

4. [II.3] We shall therefore run from the pleasantries of words now and then and proclaim solid stuff from our own mouth, lest this virile work suffer the setbacks of impotent speech. The role of advisor is no stranger to my profession, for correction is the province of those who lead, and just as it is right that a torch be borne before those left behind to ensure their innocence, so too does reason demand that you even show them the road they are to follow by your words. This is in agreement with the divine exhortation,

rebuke a wise man, and he will love thee [Prov. 9.8];

nor is the secular moralist silent:

who wanted a teacher to stand in the stead of the holy parent [Juvenal 7.209–10].

5. [II.4] For he whom the kindness of correction is swifter to prompt than is nature itself is placed on the very brow of affection, and rightly. For fathering a child is but proof of lust, while educating one is proof of devotion. [III.1] Therefore hasten to the citadel of the Arts and love the mother of good deeds, Modesty.[6] She, though virgin, is fruitful and bears the various types of virtue, just as Immodesty, a wanton and corrupt, bears the various types of vice. [III.2] She would urge you on in this voice, to make you come to her:

Modesty[7]

"Paint your shining features with rosy purple dye,
    and show the fidelity of your morals on your face.
May you be prettier by a scattering of spots about your
        snow-white mouth
    when you sweat a little and bear a dewy neck.
You should not grant yourself more by your tongue than
        by the nobility of your appearance:
    from this attract to yourself whatever you want to love."

6. [III.3] It is not right to refuse to give your hand to such holy advice, seeing that even she who speaks is crowned with the gift of profitable beauty and both increases and accumulates the goods of nobility.

[IV.1] Therefore, join always to this Shame her relative Purity,[8] who tempers the natural disposition of youth with her gray-haired moderation; she adds the coolness of her foreign dispensation[9] to years that are swelling with heat, and once she conquers the lust for error she entices the flesh with the savor of holy relations, and makes the zeal for the right seem eager in you and not coerced. 7. [IV.2] Let her be gained by the castigation of the stomach, nor is her enemy to be fed by the vulgar errors of the dinner table. For revelry bought with great expense requires even the loss of one's good merits, and on the same path comes the diminution both of your morals and of others' opinions of you. [IV.3] Were she to approach you, she would make proclamation in words such as these:

Chastity[10]

"I never hesitate to show at all times my afflicted face,
so long as the signs of my chaste beauty shine forth.
For fat flesh chokes the finer senses,
and a belly, foully stuffed, tramples the mind.
But the Cross is my spear, the Cross my shield, the Cross
        my armor;
with this I am protected, with this I strike, with this I
        establish the bonds of peace.
This is my general in war, so that, with quicksilver youth
        under my victorious heel,
I may renounce the horrid honies of Cupid's poison.
Hasten to me, stop playing the boy in your actions,

and take from my habits, young men, a gray-haired old
age."

8. [V.1] Once you have let her in, adorn her with the companion-
ship of Faith, for even as she occupies first place in educated manners, so too is she not retained when stripped of her possessions, nor
is it right that a thing that consists of many parts be pursued as if it
were monolithic. Elegant garlands are not fashioned except with the
varied treasures of meadows; the unified configuration of a tiara
typically derives from various jewels; numerous metallic elements
have given birth to the always awe-inspiring electrum. 9. Further-
more, because there is nothing that can precede Faith, let it be cher-
ished and let it so grow up in the fields of diligence that its milky stalk
of divine food not be cut by an untimely sickle and die. Therefore, let
lame promises be far from your regimen, and let that which you
should follow become second nature through use. [V.2] Yet one
would think that she would call you together with these words:

Faith[11]

"Whoso wishes to join earth and heaven,
and to abandon the sins of Mother Luxury,
let him seek me, the abiding crown and glory
    of the heavenly gift.

For he does not fear the dread tribunal,
nor does he flit among the city's rich and powerful;
knowing the right, he steers upon the sea
    for the harbor of salvation.

Though the Geloni swell with barbarian rage
and the Morini bark in Parthian wise—[12]
all the grumblings of the mad world
    he loathes and avoids.

He enters the inner sanctum of the King on High;
he remains certain of his wealth in disaster;
he is not subject to the laws of the grave,
    nor to the evils of life."

10. [VI.1] Let the absence of diligence for the Liberal Arts be far
from the above-mentioned virtues![13] Through such diligence the
goods of the divine things are glorified as if in the gleam of an expensive necklace; for imperfect beauty is not far removed from ugliness,
and one who has not sufficiently striven for the heights of greatness

has barely left the depths of wretchedness. 11. Nevertheless, these Arts have placed Grammar before their doors as though she were the nurse of all the rest; she entices the minds of the young with the savor of plain and artful elocution[14] and brings them to the heat of a Cicero by the sparks of a well-studied fire. [VI.2] The Campus Martius thus receives a made-to-order soldier[15] who has been roused by the image of false battle and does not shrink from the battle trumpets because he has heard the blare of horns and the offices of war in the midst of the allurements of peace. 12. Virtue grows big when fed on practice, and endurance of trials is born of discipline. First principles have seen men of consummate strength quaking in fear. It is good that the right hands of rhetors and our well-known freedom of speech take up the swords forged in the grammarian's furnace; the often repeated images of slaughter bring it about that they do not fall in open battle. 13. [VI.3] In this there is need of caution, lest love of the art grow beyond the natural license, as it were, of that immature age, and a spontaneous devotion to this brilliant work spring forth from the constant obligations imposed by their teachers.[16] Nevertheless, a student shows that he devotes himself to good intentions when he allows himself to be so compelled; and he has, as it were, honesty as an art who is not distressed by the anxious concern of his instructor. [VI.4] And thus would she speak to her followers:

Grammar[17]

"We grant discrimination to the mind while we fashion our
> fables;
we are a fair-minded judge, whatever mistakes the little
> children make.
Refraining from the hand, I beat in shame by ear and
> mouth.
Whatever this art has to be afraid of, the art of speaking
> mitigates;
with the young we even joke in the midst of our lessons.
For the teacher, Strictness, commands that you not be
> frightening at every turn.
That age, when older,[18] says that we are the best parents,
because we reckon those to be our children by favor
whom the belly swelling of literate seed has given us;
nor has lust overcome the laws of our brilliant hearts."

14. [VII.1] As you make your exit this way, now educated, the Mars of Eloquence calls you back with the trumpets of rhetoric, and just as

one makes mail of links, so does she[19] make the defenses of court speeches of varied and connected parts. She paints a unified image of speeches after forcing the knotty joints of speech into a solid and simple form; in this, diverse elements are so connected in four-square measures that *diuisio* cannot detract from their combination, nor can *partitio*, when the need for it arises, separate the things that have been forcefully assembled.[20] 15. [VII.2] Having sent on before herself the savor of praise, this manly diction, this Latin hauteur of human speech thus addresses you: "After the pinnacle of divinity,[21] I am she who both changes what has happened and causes things to happen. No matter how great the darkness you are involved in in your case, the light I bring by eloquence will suffice. I am she through whom men expect a guilty verdict when I am stormy and innocence when I am calm. Through me, even a dark conscience is suffused in splendor; through me, though it glow with its own brilliance, it is overwhelmed by sudden night, even if it is innocent of shadows: it is a thing that neither innocence can trust nor guilt dare sigh with relief about. 16. Wherever there are Romans, they stay awake over my handbooks. Badges of office, wealth, honors: all are cast aside unless we trick them out. We rule kingdoms and command such things as benefit a ruler.[22] [VII.3] What of the fact that delight in our declamations conquers all things that have any sense at all, and that the opinion which we advise lives forever? Before there were the staffs and robes of the consular order there was mere showy recitation.[23] Only what we wish to be believed about the deeds of brave men is believed; no one values an action that we are silent about; the portentous seeds that we have sown illumine the whole world with the sun of bright perfection. 17. When poetry, jurisprudence, logic, and arithmetic take me as their mother—only when I back them are they worth anything. [VII.4] But now hear a poem, which the sport of another office suggests to us:[24]

Rhetoric[25]

So long as he is ours, no criminal charges will touch
    anyone.
We wipe away the stains of life with the aid of art.
Even if someone has a snow-white record and the senate
    as his witness,
    we compel everyone to say that he was born of Night.[26]
Both the innocent and the guilty are born of our mouth;
    when we speak, the verdict is thought to be locked up.
The wool that is Tarentum's pride, jewels, power—

> what are they next to our grandeur?
> Whoso studies our arts soon rules the world;
> an art that fears nothing as ambiguous has given
> kingdoms to me."

18. [VIII.1] Therefore, my dearest ones, strive to gain these things and guard them once you have gained them. But you will say: "What teachers, what instructors, are we to use for these? By whose example are we to be edified? For happy chance detains in royal councils Faustus and Avienus,[27] the glory of our age and the font of Latin eloquence. While their concerns occupy them, no one can answer; just to approach them in their role as public orators is the same as trying to appropriate for oneself the light of the sun and the power of divinity." 19. [VIII.2] But even while they are sweating it out for the public good, the patricians Festus and Symmachus,[28] who are the very stuff of all the arts and the exemplar of unyielding wisdom, are not absent from this most holy of cities. In them is the noble principate of the lawcourts; to see them is to receive an education. There is in them no speech about trifling matters, no scarcely excusable commemoration of pantomimes. They do not try for the public ear at the expense of modesty; they are pleased to satisfy the upright rather than the majority; they share the good reputation that comes from blameless action. Although their commands are to be obeyed in all matters, there is nevertheless within them the teacher Silence and the exemplar of learned Quiet.

20. [VIII.3] There is also the patrician Probinus,[29] the well-tested brilliance of the seed of Placidus, whom the perfectly polished manners of a family of savants have formed; from the font of his father and his father-in-law he has drunk that which is elegance itself.[30] [VIII.4] There is the patrician Cethegus,[31] Probinus's son; he is a man of consular rank who, though young, has surpassed gray-haired sobriety without the natural inclinations of his age, and has both the savor of maturity and the honey of childhood. 21. [VIII.5] There is the patrician Boethius,[32] in whom you can barely see the years sufficient for his learning, and you understand that his skill in teaching (upon which his selection by the learned has now passed judgment) is now its equal. There is the patrician Agapitus, rich both in reputation and in wisdom.[33] There is Probus, the *uir illustris;*[34] should you follow him, you will have present Faustus and Avienus (whom we have mentioned before) even if they are absent. 22. [VIII.6] Other famous men, whom only rumor has brought to my attention, I leave to silence; learn who they are by yourselves,[35] if you now cherish

your maturity, or from those whom I have just mentioned. For a lover of the good reveals himself by clear signs, nor does any man embrace habits in another which he has not formed within himself.

23. [VIII.7] Or if it pleases you to go to noble women, you will have the lady Barbara,[36] the flower of Roman genius, who by the evidence of her face reveals the brightness of her blood and her discrimination. In her you will find the modest confidence and the confident modesty that come from good action; a speech so spiced with natural and artificial simplicity that neither does the charm of her address grow cold nor its splendor grow stiff with the harsh locutions of women; in whom the desire for what is right has so become second nature that even if she wanted to lie she could not commit the error.[37] 24. Her tongue gives the charm of chaste sweetness, nor is cloudiness of thought covered over by a veil of calm, bright speech; this is as true of her heart as it is of her speech. May she pardon the one who claims for her the crown of women, which I grudge to her Silence; I should wish that imitation of that be held up as an exemplar in all the parts of Italy, so that all of the women who do not yield to her teachings might at least be transformed by her example.

25. [VIII.8] There is also Stephania,[38] a most glorious light of the Catholic Church, the day of whose birth glows with a brighter light once you know her manners, much as the sun, the eye of the world, outshines a torch; and if you set aside the rays of her inborn behavior, nothing will shine brighter than her ancestry. May the heavenly Providence join you to the obedience of all those whom I have just mentioned.

26. [VIII.9] Behold, you now have that page which was hostage for my affection: follow it like a pedagogue. And may God grant that you always wish and do what is right. Therefore, if I have not been able to help with a showy oration I have, mindful of my profession, at least helped you with an orison.[39]

> I beg you, I beg the parents who bore you,[40]
> Symmachus,[41] do not let an unfeeling fate await my
>   writing.
> Give your right hand to my weakness, take me with you
>   over the seas.
> A holy man does not behave according to his habits when
>   he deceives one who believes in him.[42]
> I do not hesitate: behold, I come pleading—have mercy on
>   one who prays to you—
> commending my base words to my wealthy patrons.

My illustrious seeds,[43]
take these words
from a dry father.
That is well said
which points to the truth.

Preface

1. *Bis Acc.* 33.
2. Lewis 1936, 78.
3. Sir Thomas Browne, "To the Reader," in *Pseudodoxia Epidemica* (1646).

Chapter One. Some Modern Approaches

1. My most recent predecessor in this is Riikonen 1987, which may be consulted for a fuller discussion of modern theories of Menippean satire.

2. Some recent works on modern Menippean satire are given in the appendix to Relihan 1987a, 70; add Benda 1979 and Peters 1987.

3. There is now a classical reaction against naming a genre after traditions whose origins are so imperfectly known: cf. Reardon 1991, 49 and n. 5; Astbury 1988, in review of Riikonen 1987, is vitriolic.

4. Frye 1957, 309; further details of Frye's analysis at pp. 308–12.

5. It is interesting for an appreciation of Petronius to note that Frye (1976, 155–57) also discerns many of the essential elements of the romance structure in the Menippean Alice books.

6. Riikonen (1987, 51) quotes with disapproval Fowler's view of Frye's genre: "So many forms are united in the 'anatomy' that it threatens to prove a baggier monster than the novel" (Fowler 1982, 119). For the influence of Frye's theories, see Riikonen 1987, 32–40, discussing primarily Walton's *Compleat Angler* and Joyce's *Ulysses;* Korkowski (1973) takes as his starting point disagreement with later interpreters of Frye, and in a subsequent book (Kirk 1980) he lists over seven hundred works written before 1600 thought to be Menippean satires. Castrop (1982) works with a broad interpretation of Frye's notion of "intellectual satire"; for Frye as applied to utopian literature, see von Koppenfels 1981; Swigger (1975) touches on Frye's concept of anatomy. J. Williams (1966) is unhappy with Frye's inclusion of Boethius and seeks to define Menippean satire purely in terms of Cynic thought and the diatribe; in this she follows the lead of Helm (1906), whose ideas on Menippus were also followed by Scherbantin (1951).

7. Frye 1976, 74–75.

8. At this point (Frye 1957, 310) he refers obliquely to Lucian: "like the *Imaginary Conversations* of Landor or the 'dialogue of the dead.'" Lucian is also invoked (p. 308) as the ultimate ancestor of *Gulliver's Travels* and *Candide*.

9. For such comic content as Athenaeus possesses, see Baldwin 1976. I explore more fully the differences between Menippean satire and symposium literature in Relihan 1992, 228–30.

10. Bakhtin 1984, 132–47; Bakhtin 1981, 25–28, treats the matter in briefer compass.

11. Holland 1979, 36; this study is perhaps the best application of Bakhtin's theories to any field of literature.

12. Holland (1979, 33) goes so far as to say that the genre does not originate with Menippus, but perhaps it is true that authors create their own antecedent traditions: see Frye 1976, 43.

13. For Bakhtin and his theories, see Todorov 1984; Szilárd 1985; Riikonen 1987, 17–31. Clark and Holquist 1984 is an intellectual biography.

14. Riikonen 1987, 41. Bakhtin exalts the unusual *Apocolocyntosis* to paradigmatic status; Nauta (1987, 93–94) objects to Bakhtin's reference to the *Apocolocyntosis* as a truly *popular* and carnivalesque satire, as the work adopts a negative attitude toward the Saturnalia.

15. Payne (1981, 10–11) suggests some additional characteristics: a dialogue between two persons of very different perceptions; a character who is on an endless quest; fantastic elements used to symbolize the joy and horror of mankind's "unsuspendable freedom to think"; characters who agree to talk regardless of events and intellectual concessions; an aura of "unquenchable hope and titanic energy for whatever the problem is"; the lack of any figure of unquestionable authority; obscenity without pornography. These details are drawn primarily from Boethius and Lucian. The first of these is perhaps most important, for it asserts the essential unity of the devices of the *catascopia* and the *catabasis*, or journey to the underworld; the latter is a more dramatic form of the former.

16. Bakhtin 1984, 115.

17. Payne 1981: her Menippean readings of Chaucer have not been widely accepted, but the foundations are well laid, and I have profited much from them. See my Chapter 7, n. 4.

18. Branham 1989b; not as useful is Giangrande 1972.

19. Kirk (1980, x) finds that circularity makes definition impossible; he prefers to speak of "family resemblances" among the various forms of Menippean satire.

20. Though I do not intend to derive from such considerations historical criticism of a given text, by reference, in Jauss's terms, to the "horizons of expectations" that a reader in a certain era may have for a certain work; cf. Jauss 1982.

Chapter Two. A Definition of Ancient Menippean Satire

1. Diomedes (i.485.30ff. Keil): "Satira dicitur carmen apud Romanos nunc quidem maledicum et ad carpenda hominum uitia archaeae comoediae charactere compositum, quale scripserunt Lucilius et Horatius. et olim quod ex uariis poematibus constabat satira uocabatur, quale scripserunt Pacuuius et Ennius."

2. "Probus," *In Verg. Buc.* 6.31 (3.2.336 Thilo-Hagen) is the most important of the testimonia; cf. also Athenaeus 160C; Arnobius *Adv. Gent.* 6.23;

Symmachus *Ep.* 1.4.4. Among the authors in Keil's *Grammatici Latini*, cf. Charisius i.118.8; Diomedes i.371.23–36; Eutyches v.467–68. "Varro Menippeus" means no more than "Varro in his *Menippeans.*"

3. Quintilian 10.1.95: "alterum illud etiam prius saturae genus, sed non sola carminum uarietate mixtum, condidit Terentius Varro, uir Romanorum eruditissimus." I accept as authoritative the translation of Winterbottom 1970, 191: "The other well-known type of satire—one that arose even before Lucilius (i.e., the Ennian satire of varied metre)—was exploited by Varro, but now with a variety given not merely by metrical changes (but by an admixture of prose to the verse)." I take the phrase *alternative convention* from Coffey 1989, 147, where it forms the subtitle for the last division of the book, on Menippean satire.

4. Edited along with the *Sardi Venales* (1612) of Petrus Cunaeus in Matheeussen and Heesakkers 1980.

5. Further discussion of these issues may be found in Relihan 1984a.

6. Reeve (1984), defending Senecan authorship of the *Apocolocyntosis*, argues that *per saturam* means "in prose and verse."

7. "imitatus uidelicet Martianum Felicem Capellam." See Kindermann 1978, 22 and n. 85.

8. van Rooy 1967, 55–59, 78–79.

9. Walsh 1970, 72 and n. 2; Coffey 1989, 181.

10. Macrobius (*Comm.* 1.2.8), speaking of the variety of *fabulae*, or fictions, acknowledges only Petronius's amatory content: "They delight the ear as do the comedies of Menander and his imitators, or the narratives replete with imaginary doings of lovers in which Petronius Arbiter so freely indulged and with which Apuleius, astonishingly, sometimes amused himself" (trans. Stahl 1952).

11. "a societate ingenii, quod is [sc. Menippus] quoque omnigeno carmine satiras suas expoliuerat." Similarly, Apuleius can refer to the Greek Cynic Crates as an author of satires (*Florida* 41.7 ed. Helm); he can also refer to the satirist Lucilius by the Greek term *iambicus* (*Apol.*10). Unfortunately, it is unclear just what works of Crates Apuleius has in mind, or what weight we should assign to these terms.

12. Willis's text; Cristante (1987, 27–29) defends the accepted *senilem*, "old man's," as more in line with the self-parodic depiction of the author in this poem.

13. Willis's text has the misprint *docta doctis.*

14. Scaliger's conjecture of *miscilla* for *miscillo* would yield the superior sense of "hodgepodge Satura"; the reading *creagris*, attested by some manuscripts in place of the meaningless †*cagris*, could yield the meaning "forks" (literally, "fleshhooks"), a culinary image appropriate to *satura:* "making a smorgasbord of liberal arts that Attic diners would not care to taste." Morelli's suggestion, *cathedris*, "seats of learning," is also attractive. Full commentary on this corrupt poem may now be found in Cristante 1987, which supplants Cristante 1978.

15. Compare Horace *Ep.* 1.7.72, in which the overtalkative and indiscreet

Volteius speaks *dicenda tacenda,* "topics both appropriate and inappropriate," at the feast to which he is invited.

16. For the culinary associations of *satura,* see now Petersmann 1986a. LeMoine (1991, 359–63) discusses the metaphors of "digested" and "undigested" learning in the traditions of Roman father-son literary dedications; Martianus is here specifically refusing to offer the sort of digested learning that the son expects and that the tradition requires.

17. Behind the textual corruption lies perhaps a reference to Martianus's vocation as an advocate, in which case such terms may merely express the clichéd metaphor of public life as a barnyard. See Shanzer 1986b, 279, which refers inter alia to F 349 of Varro's *Menippeans:* "praesepibus se retineat forensibus" ("let him keep to his forensic barnyard"). But barking can be an image of futile speech (cf. Boethius *Cons.* 1.5.1: "Haec ubi continuato dolore delatraui . . .") as well as of vicious speech (cf. Lucian *Bis Acc.* 33, in which Dialogue complains of Menippus as a loudly barking dog who bites as he smiles). But as both aspects of such dog-speech seem relevant here (aggressive nonsense), a reference to the Cynic Menippus is quite possible.

18. See Branham 1989a, 160 and n. 6. Further in Chapter 3.

19. τὸ γὰρ πάντων ἀτοπώτατον, κρᾶσίν τινα παράδοξον κέκραμαι, καὶ οὔτε πεζός εἰμι οὔτε ἐπὶ τῶν μέτρων βέβηκα, ἀλλὰ ἱπποκενταύρου δίκην σύνθετόν τι καὶ ξένον φάσμα τοῖς ἀκούουσι δοκῶ. Horace appeals to a similar sort of paradox when he speaks of his *Satires* and their "pedestrian Muse" (*S.* 2.6.17), implying that they are neither prose nor poetry. In the dialogue *Fugitivi* ("The Runaway Philosophers"), Lucian has Philosophy complain in similar language about the fifth-century Sophists (*Fug.* 11): "Like the race of the Centaurs, a hybrid thing and fashioned as a mixture halfway between puffery and philosophy."

20. In two of Lucian's *prolaliae,* the *Zeuxis* and the *Prometheus Es in Verbis* ("Am I a Verbal Prometheus?"), the author speaks of his audience's puzzled reaction to his idiosyncratic comic dialogue: see Branham 1989b, 38–46; and Nesselrath 1990. For the difference between Menippean satire and comic dialogue in Lucian's *Dialogues of the Dead,* see Relihan 1987b.

21. For Stobaeus, see Photius *Bibl.* 167; there is little possibility that the reference is to Menippus the comic poet. Further in Chapter 3. Hense (1902, 185) makes the sensible point that Dialogue is merely exaggerating concerning the presence of verse. Bompaire (1958, 558–59) infers that Menippus is not the source of Lucian's habits in the use of verse; and even Helm, whose principle is that Lucian may be used to reconstruct the works of Menippus from whom Lucian shamelessly borrowed, admits that Lucian is no index to Menippus's use of verse (Helm 1931, 893.9ff.).

22. ". . . florali lasciuiens uirguncula petulantia, hedera largiori circumflua, improbi uultus et ore contumeliarum sarcinis grauido, cuius ironicum lumen tam rimabunda uernulitate currebat quo mentes etiam penitus abstrusas temulentis inscriptionibus depinxisset."

23. Two late texts are of some help here. In the *Paraenesis,* Ennodius has Rhetoric explain her duplicitous arts first in prose and then in verse; when

changing to verse she says: "But now hear a poem, which the sport of another office suggests to us" (17: "audite tamen et carmen, alieni quod nobis suggerit ludus officii"). *Ludus,* with its twin meanings of "joke" and "school," may by itself conjure up associations with things seriocomic; but *alieni officii,* with its overtones of "foreign or unaccustomed obligation/function," suggests that Rhetoric, herself a prose genre (she describes herself in judicial terms), finds it difficult to express herself in verse, as the genre demands. The narrator in Julian's *Caesars* refers to the tale that he is going to tell to his interlocutor on the Saturnalia with a pun on παιδεία (instruction) and παιδιά (play) at 336B. The frustrated interlocutor does not know what to expect but fears (rightly, as it turns out) that it will not be the instructional tale that he wants. For the latter, see Relihan 1989a.

24. The only ancient critic to discuss the art of inserting verse into prose is Hermogenes. At *Id.* 336ff. Rabe, he speaks of achieving sweetness in prose by the apt insertion of verses. At *Meth.* 30, p. 447.5ff., he distinguishes between quotations inserted κατὰ κόλλησιν, in which quotation blends with argument and illustrates it, and quotations inserted κατὰ παρῳδίαν. This latter has nothing to do with the parodied verses of Menippean satire; its sole illustration is Dem. *Fals. Leg.* 245, in which Demosthenes takes a poetic quotation from the speech of Aeschines and intersperses parodied bits of it in a sentence that makes fun of the Aeschines who first used the verse. For philosophers who quote poetry in their prose works, see the good summary of O'Daly 1991, 51–53.

25. The ironic manipulation of literature in the ancient romance is the theme of Anderson 1982a.

26. It is irrelevant whether Menippus's use of prose and verse is inspired by oriental literary forms; the aesthetic that governs their use is classical. For oriental origins, see Immisch 1921. Perry (1967, 206–18) relates prosimetrum to the Arabic *maqamat;* see also Hall 1981, 403–13. The oriental origin of the novel in general is now championed by Anderson 1984.

27. Prosimetrum thus broadly defined is the subject of the series of articles in Czech by D. Bartoňková; see Bibliography.

28. Kindstrand 1976, 97–99.

29. Eckhardt 1983.

30. For Frye's assignment of Macrobius and Athenaeus to the anatomy, see Chapter 1; on verse quotation in the diatribe, see Hense 1909, XCV.

31. Mras (1914, 391) seems to be the first to make that point that action is advanced through poetry in Menippean satire. This article, despite its philosophical focus, remains one of the best treatments of the literary features of the genre, and is a real advance over the theories of Helm 1906.

32. Certainly some other prose works can blur this distinction for specific effects, yet in ways that are essentially different from those of Menippean satire. For example, Tacitus's *Annals* begins (I think deliberately) with a hexameter, and Longus is well known for what his most recent critic calls "prose poetry" (Hunter 1983, 84–98).

33. At the beginning of his *How to Write History,* Lucian speaks of the *comic*

illness that once drove the inhabitants of Abdera, inspired by the *Andromeda*, to speak in Euripidean verse.

34. So also Walsh 1970, 94ff.; Anderson 1982a, 99ff.; as against Sullivan 1968b, 170ff. (*Bellum Ciuile*), 186ff. (*Troiae Halosis*). Unfortunately, Courtney (1991) does not discuss these two poems.

35. As Encolpius says at the end of the *Troiae Halosis* (90.3): "What's with you and this disease of yours? You've spent less than two hours with me, and you've spoken oftener as a poet than a human being." For parody as a device of characterization in Eumolpus's poems, see Slater 1990, 186–99.

36. Boethius would seem to be another. Philosophy at 1.1.7–14 banishes the pagan Muses and offers a different sort of poetry for the narrator's consolation; but we are never offered a programmatic statement as to just how Philosophy's new Muses are going to effect their cure.

37.   iam Phoebus breuiore uia contraxerat arcum
        lucis et obscuri crescebant tempora Somni,
        iamque suum uictrix augebat Cynthia regnum,
        et deformis Hiems gratos carpebat honores
        diuitis Autumni iussoque senescere Baccho
        carpebat raras serus uindemitor uuas.

"puto magis intellegi, si dixero: mensis erat October, dies III. idus Octobris. horam non possum certam tibi dicere. . . ." The passage is imitated by Fielding (*Joseph Andrews*, Book 1, chap. 8): cf. my Appendix B, n. 49. What is practically another imitation of it is the winner of the Tenth Annual Bulwer-Lytton Fiction Contest, submitted by Judy Frazier: "Sultry it was and humid, but no whisper of air caused the plump laden spears of golden grain to nod their burdened heads as they unheedingly awaited the cyclic plunder of their gleaming treasure, while overhead the burning orb of luminescence ascended to its ever upward path toward a sweltering celestial apex for, although it is not in Kansas that our story takes place, it looks godawful like it" (*Chicago Tribune*, Sunday, May 26, 1991, sec. 1, p. 4).

38. Menippean satire mixes together a number of different genres, a fact long noted (for example, see Courtney 1962); Guilhamet (1987, 5–7) is very close to the truth when he speaks of such a mixture of forms in Menippean satire as resulting in nearly no form at all. In Menippean satire, this mixture is inappropriate and polemical.

39. Champlin 1991, 58 n. 55; see his index for further discussion of this piece.

40. Cameron 1984, 220–28. We note a number of Menippean things: Tiberianus is the author of a book in which Diogenes attacks Platonic philosophy; and that he is said to have introduced into some work a letter brought by the wind from the antipodes, beginning "To those above from those below, greetings," a phrase seemingly in hendecasyllables. Willis (1988, 453) dismisses the theory perhaps too brusquely.

41. A good account of all of the fantastic elements imputed to Menippus's writings may be found in Levine 1968, 18–19 and n. 2; see also Shanzer 1986a, 29–44.

42. Mras 1914, 393–95.

43. For example, Christ, Schmid, and Stählin 1920, 89.

44. As in Horace *S.* 2.3 and 2.7. It is my suspicion that the habits of Menippean satire as practiced by Varro interpose themselves in the history of Roman verse satire, and that they account for some of the differences between Horace's satires and Lucilius's model.

45. Lucian mocks the oracles of Trophonius and Amphilochus together in *Dial. Mort.* 10. Plutarch, however, takes them seriously. His *Demon of Socrates* includes an account of the Er-like vision received by the young Timarchus in the cave of Trophonius (590A–592F); *The God's Slowness to Punish* tells of a similar vision received by the wicked Thespesius of Soli when consulting the oracle of Amphilochus, a vision that results in a Scrooge-like metamorphosis (563B–568A). Plutarch's sobriety is a good counterpoint to Lucian's comedy.

46. For this ironic interpretation of the end of the *Necyomantia*, see Geffcken 1911, 474; see also Branham 1989a, 159–60.

47. Anderson 1976a, 211 ("Index of Principal Motifs," s.v. "Surprise intervention") notes this as a commonplace in Lucian.

48. Frye (1957, 224), though not speaking of Menippean satire, makes the following nice definition: "Irony without satire is the non-heroic residue of tragedy, centering on a theme of puzzled defeat." It is a perfect description of the end of the *Consolation*.

49. Especially Payne 1981, 77–79, defining the genre in terms of a conflict of freedom and limitation.

50. See Kennedy 1978.

51. Petronius hides as well, slipping only once at 132.15, in which Encolpius ironically defends the literary virtues of the work before the reader; further in Chapter 6.

52. The function of such contrasts of styles is well documented in the case of Martianus Capella: see LeMoine 1981.

53. For the sublime and the ridiculous in Martianus, see Westra 1981; in the history of Menippean satire, one may say that there is an increasing interest in the later authors, starting with Julian, in the sublimity that refuses to cohere with earthly ridiculousness.

54. Palmer 1961, 147.

55. Astbury's text; Bücheler and Heräus (1922) present an even stranger description for the central phrase: "oculi suppaetuli nigellis pupulis liquidam hilaritatem significantes animi" ("her slightly squinting eyes with their dusky pupils portending an unadulterated gaiety of mind").

56. Varro would certainly have approved of his titles. From Perelman 1981: "No Starch in the Dhoti, S'il Vous Plaît"; "Zwei Hertzen in die Drygoods Schlock" (with the wonderfully named heroine Charisma von Ausgespielt). Theroux in his introduction makes the key observation about this sort of style and humor (p. 14): "He worked hard for *a kind of insane exactitude in his prose* and would not settle for 'sad' if he could use 'chopfallen'" (emphasis added). It should be noted that the essence of the Apuleian or late classical Latin style is not vagueness and diffusion but an academic and com-

pulsive overspecificity and overdescription: the subtleties of polite language, which is content with simple and ambiguous words, do not figure in the humor of Varro and the later Latin Menippean satirists.

57. Sullivan (1968, 90) remarks apropos of Petronius that the Menippean form entails a certain artistic indulgence and formlessness.

58. "si quis mihi filius unus pluresue in decem mensibus gignantur, ii, si erunt ὄνοι λύρας, exheredes sunto; quod si quis undecimo mense κατὰ Ἀριστοτέλην natus est, Attio idem, quod Tettio, ius esto apud me." Cf. F 542: "e mea φιλοφθονίᾳ natis quos Menippea haeresis nutricata est tutores do 'qui rem Romanam Latiumque augescere uultis'" (the quotation is from Ennius's *Annales* fr. 495 Skutsch): "I give you 'who desire that the Roman state and Latium continue to grow' as guardians of those born of my love of envy, whom the Menippean sect has nurtured." Though cataloged among fictional wills in Champlin 1991, 194, it is not discussed.

59. Branham 1989b, 57.

60. *Acad. Post.* 1.8: details in Chapter 4.

61. Reardon 1991, 15–16.

62. Frye 1976, 68–70.

63. N. D. Smith 1989, 155: "Gullibility is anathema to Aristophanes, for his plays—however fantastic their plots and operations may be—always emphasize the ability of his successful characters to find their own ways out of their problems. This is folk wisdom—really, a celebration of common sense—for his characters' successes are never predicated upon special talents or training."

64. These relations are discussed more fully in Relihan 1990c.

65. See Fontaine 1960, 416.

66. Klingner (1921, 115) points out that apocalyptic must have become intertwined with the traditions of Menippean satire at some early date, to account for similarities between Julian, Martianus, and Boethius.

Chapter Three. Menippus

1. Helm 1906 is a monumental attempt to reconstruct Menippus out of Lucian. The thesis was effectively rebutted by McCarthy (1934), who demonstrated that Lucian was not a hack plagiarist but refashioned Menippus to his own ends, and that Menippus did not write dialogues. Helm's book remains, however, a mine of valuable information about Menippus and his relation to Hellenistic literature. For a survey of the minimal conclusions that may be drawn about specific literary debts owed to Menippus by his followers, see Hall 1981, 64–150. Good, brief introductions to Menippus may also be found in Woytek 1986, 316–20; Branham 1989b, 14–28.

2. For details of the first two of these, see Chapter 7; for Lucian's treatment of Menippus in the *Dial. Mort.*, see Relihan 1987b. Helm 1906 operates on the presumption that the true Menippus is not the Menippus of Lucian's works; Piot 1914 goes to the other extreme, that all we know of Menippus is the character in Lucian. I propose a middle way: that Lucian's Menippus is a

plausible literary recasting of a literary personality well established by Menippus himself.

3. Τὰ δ'οὖν τοῦ κυνικοῦ βιβλία ἐστὶ δεκατρία· Νέκυια, Διαθῆκαι, Ἐπιστολαὶ κεκομψευμέναι ἀπὸ τοῦ τῶν θεῶν προσώπου, Πρὸς τοὺς φυσικοὺς καὶ μαθηματικοὺς καὶ γραμματικοὺς καὶ Γονὰς Ἐπικούρου καὶ Τὰς θρησκευομένας ὑπ' αὐτῶν εἰκάδας. καὶ ἄλλα. There is a distinct possibility that there is a lacuna in the text before the evidently corrupt Epicurean references: cf. Crönert 1906, 11, with further references. Other conjectural works have been assigned to Menippus as well: see the index in Helm 1906, s.v. "Menipp"; and Geffcken 1931.

4. Hirzel (1895, 1.358 and n. 2) assumes that the natural scientists, mathematicians, and grammarians received the letters from the gods; while not provable, such a conclusion is suggested by Lucian *Icar.* 21, in which the moon complains to Zeus about natural philosophers and asks him to do something about it.

5. Dörrie (1969) makes this quite plausible assertion, although Menippus is not mentioned in his earlier monumental work on the heroic epistle, Dörrie 1968.

6. Diogenes then tells the crier to call for one who wishes to purchase for himself a master; when not allowed to sit, he says, "Fish are bought no matter how they lie"; he notes that humans for sale are never examined as closely as kitchen utensils; he tells his purchaser Xeniades to obey him, for so he would do if Diogenes were a slave and a doctor or a helmsman. Eubulus's *Sale of Diogenes* is then mentioned for details concerning the education which Xeniades and his sons received from Diogenes; some of these stories are repeated at 6.74 without attribution.

7. "Menippus the Cynic, in his work called the *Arcesilaus*, writes as follows: 'There was a toast as various people caroused, and someone called for a Spartan dessert to be served, and immediately some tiny partridges were passed around, and roast goose and delicate pastries.'" Arcesilaus is the head of the Academy in the middle of the third century and responsible for that school's Skeptic turn; contemporaries and biographers alike dislike him for his acidic personal deportment. Timon mocks him in the *Silli* (frags. 31–34 di Marco 1989), but he eventually wrote a *Funeral Banquet of Arcesilaus*, which, if it did not actually praise him, seems to concentrate on the abuse of philosophers who gather for the feast. See Diogenes Laertius 4.28–45; Kindstrand 1976, 154; Wachsmuth (1885, 29–30) bases this reconstruction of the content of Timon's *Arcesilaus* on Ribbeck's reconstruction of Varro's Ταφὴ Μενίππου. Di Marco (1989, 13–14) thinks the probable model of the *Arcesilaus* is Speusippus's *Funeral Banquet of Plato*.

8. ὁ γοῦν κυνικὸς Μένιππος "ἁλμοπότιν τὴν Μύνδον" φησίν. Fritzsch (1865a, 7) thinks that Athenaeus's quotation may represent an original Μύνδον δ' ἁλμοπότιν; see also Wachsmuth 1885, 80. The epithet is unattested elsewhere, and the neologism, suggestive of the language of Timon's *Silli*, may reflect Menippus's original verse composition; see Coffey 1989, 163. This quotation is preceded in Athenaeus by a reference to the doctor Mne-

sitheus and his opinions on the nature of the various types of wine; as a similar reference to the doctor occurs in Varro's *Menippeans* (F 575), Knaack (1883) argues that Athenaeus's citation of Mnesitheus also derives in some way from the writings of Menippus himself; further in Chapter 4.

9. τίς γὰρ ὅλως οἶδε τὰ μετὰ τὸν βίον; the attribution is made by McCarthy (1934, 12).

10. Mixture of prose and verse: the inference from Dialogue's complaint in Lucian *Bis Acc.* 33; the explicit statement of "Probus" (*In Verg. Buc.* 6.31 = 3.2.336 Thilo-Hagen) that Menippus "polished his satires with verses of all sorts" (see my Chapter 2); the poetic quotation ἁλμοπότιν τὴν Μύνδον; and Photius *Bibl.* 167, who mentions him as one of the poets excerpted by Stobaeus. Further, Haslam (1981, 36–38) makes the plausible argument that the verse form of the Tinouphis fragment, catalectic iambic tetrameters whose median diairesis is so treated as to turn the verse into couplets (unique in Greek but attested in Varro's *Menippeans*), is an invention of Menippus.

11. *Anth. Pal.* 7.417.3–4; 7.418.5–6: "I came forth from Eucrates, I, Meleager, who with the Muses first ran along with the Menippean Graces. . . . Of a select company the Muses glorified me, Meleager, the son of Eucrates, with the Menippean Graces." Athenaeus preserves at 502C a fragment of Meleager's *Symposium;* a *Contest between the Porridge and the Lentil Soup* is mentioned at Athenaeus 157B. The last mentioned sounds more like the sort of fable at home in Roman verse satire; cf. Suetonius *Tib.* 42, in which Tiberius pays a large sum for a literary debate among a mushroom, fig pecker, oyster, and thrush.

12. Diogenes Laertius 6.100: ὡς εὖ δυναμένῳ διαθέσθαι ("as to one quite capable of publishing them"). Fritzsch (1865b, 6) calls attention to the detail but thinks that Laertius here tries to underline, not deny, Menippus's literary excellence.

13. Martin 1931, 211–40, "Menippos und seine Nachahmer"; though the treatment does not distinguish genres so much as particular evidences of Menippean influence, in Horace as well as Menippean satirists.

14. Aulus Gellius 2.18.6–7, copied by Macrobius *Sat.* 1.11.42. Later in this essay (2.18.7–9) Gellius tells the story of Diogenes on the slave block, possibly reflecting but freely rewriting the material of Menippus and Eubulus (see n. 6) on this topic; see Holford-Strevens 1988, 58.

15. Diocles, the source of Diogenes Laertius 6.99, has it that Menippus was the slave of one Baton in Pontus; outside of the life, Laertius calls him a resident of Sinope (6.95).

16. *Dial. Mort.* 1.1, in which Diogenes tells Pollux to summon Menippus; *Dial. Mort.* 4.2, in which Cerberus singles out the two of them for praise for their attitudes toward death; cf. also the similarity of *Dialogue* 10 (Menippus arguing with the oracles Amphilochus and Trophonius, who claim to spend some of their time on earth) and *Dialogue* 11 (Diogenes arguing with Heracles, who claims that his real self is on Olympus). But Diogenes and Menippus are never seen together in these *Dialogues*.

17. Diogenes' adulteration of the coinage of Sinope (Diogenes Laertius

6.20–21), based evidently on a joke concerning his attempts to change the *mores* of the town: both money and mores can be called νομίσματα (6.71). Laertius (6.99) has it that Menippus was a usurer involved in shipping loans, amassing a large fortune which he lost to theft, thus precipitating his suicide by hanging.

18. Diogenes' death: Diogenes Laertius 6.76–77 records that he died by holding his breath, or by eating raw octopus, or by being bitten by a dog (a Cynic fate) while trying to distribute a raw octopus among a pack of dogs. The scholiast at *Dial. Mort.* 1.1 has it that Menippus died after eating raw eggs intended for a "Hecate's dinner"; Laertius's claim that he hanged himself (6.100) is hinted at at *Dial. Mort.* 20.11; both are praised by Cerberus at *Dial. Mort.* 4.2 as coming to the underworld of their own accord.

19. *Dial. Mort.* 1.2: Γέρων, φαλακρός, τριβώνιον ἔχων πολύθυρον, ἅπαντι ἀνέμῳ ἀναπεπταμένον καὶ ταῖς ἐπιπτυχαῖς τῶν ῥακίων ποικίλον, γελᾷ δ' ἀεὶ καὶ τὰ πολλὰ τοὺς ἀλαζόνας τούτους φιλοσόφους ἐπισκώπτει. Cf. Hall 1981, 79; and Relihan 1990c, 188.

20. Donzelli (1960) argues that early versions of the *Life of Aesop* influenced Menippus's *Sale of Diogenes,* and that the *Sale* subsequently influenced the later versions of the *Life of Aesop.* That the popularity of Menippus's work may account for some accommodation of the details of the lives of Menippus and Diogenes, see Donzelli, p. 270.

21. The text seems at first to place Menippus among a group of followers of Metrocles, but see Goulet-Cazé 1986.

22. See Relihan 1987b, 191–92.

23. At *Fugitivi* 11, Philosophy refers to the Cynic succession: Ἀντισθένης . . . καὶ Διογένης καὶ μετὰ μικρὸν Κράτης καὶ Μένιππος οὗτος. But the final demonstrative adjective, derogatory and expressing exasperation ("Antisthenes . . . and Diogenes and after a while Crates and that damn Menippus"), suggests that Philosophy thinks of Menippus as somehow distinct from his Cynic forebears.

24. For example, Laertius does not rebuke Diogenes for his suicide, and mentions without criticism the various versions of the charge that he adulterated the coinage of Sinope (6.20–21); at 6.71 he speaks of Diogenes changing only the customs of society.

25. In an epigram attributed to Lucian but possibly by the emperor Julian, an otherwise unattested Theron, son of Menippus, is attacked as a spendthrift, wasting his inheritance and then the dowry of his wife (*Anth. Pal.* 9.367). This poem may be evidence that Menippus did leave a fortune; but it also suggests that the profligate son was unlike his father. Another poem in the *Greek Anthology* refers to a Menippus as a landowner (9.74), but the land, described in words reminiscent of Horace *S.* 2.2.133–35, actually belongs only to Fortune. This suggests a greedy and unreflective Menippus, which would be consistent with the hostile biographical tradition. Relihan 1989b makes the tentative suggestion that these poems reflect the hostile biographical tradition that attaches to our Menippus; for questions of authorship of 9.367, see pp. 55–56 and nn. 4, 6. Baldwin (1975b, 320–22), discussing the

first poem, is skeptical about its attribution to our Menippus and points to the parallels between it and others in the *Greek Anthology*.

26. Tales are told of such a "dog disease" on the island of Crete; for this interpretation of a very strange phrase, see Relihan 1990b.

27. Diogenes Laertius 6.99: Φέρει μὲν οὖν σπουδαῖον οὐδέν· τὰ δὲ βιβλία αὐτοῦ πολλοῦ καταγέλωτος γέμει καί τι ἴσον τοῖς Μελεάγρου τοῦ κατ᾽ αὐτὸν γενομένου ("Now he has nothing serious, but his books are overflowing with much derision, rather like those of Meleager his [i.e., of Diocles, Laertius's source] contemporary").

28. *Bibl.* 167. Photius's categories of excerpted authors are poets; philosophers and rhetors; historian kings; and historian generals. There is a special Cynic subsection in the philosophers' category, which lists Antisthenes, Diogenes, Crates, Hegesianax, Onesicritus, Menander, Monimus, Polyzelus, Xanthippus, and Theomnestus. Either Menippus is thought of as a poet or is ignored altogether; but it is unlikely that the poet referred to is the comic poet known only from the *Suda:* Μένιππος, κωμικός· τῶν δραμάτων αὐτοῦ ἔστι Κέρκωπες [καὶ Ὄφεις, add. Eudocia] καὶ ἄλλα.

29. *Med.* 6.47: Menippus is one of the αὐτῆς τῆς ἐπικήρου καὶ ἐφημέρου τῶν ἀνθρώπων ζωῆς χλευασταί ("mockers of this fragile and evanescent human life"). Marcus Aurelius, like Lucian in the *Dialogues of the Dead*, thus manages to mock the pretensions of the mocker; see Relihan 1987b, 192–93.

30. *Pisc.* 26: ἔτι καὶ Μένιππον ἀναπείσας ἑταῖρον ἡμῶν ἄνδρα συγκωμῳδεῖν αὐτῷ τὰ πολλά, ὃς μόνος οὐ πάρεστιν οὐδὲ κατηγορεῖ μεθ᾽ ἡμῶν, προδοὺς τὸ κοινόν. Also possible is that Diogenes here contrasts Menippus's adulatory *Sale of Diogenes* and Menippus's more usual habits of antiphilosophical humor.

31. *Bis Acc.* 33: καὶ τοῦτον ἐπεισήγαγέν μοι φοβερόν τινα ὡς ἀληθῶς κύνα καὶ τὸ δῆγμα λαθραῖον, ὅσῳ καὶ γελῶν ἅμα ἔδακνεν.

32. The verb σαίνω, "to wag the tail, to flatter," implies the proverb. Schol. Ar. *Eq.* 1031 and 1068 refer to Sophocles frag. 885 Radt (σαίνεις δάκνουσα καὶ κύων λαίθαργος εἶ) as proverbial. The sentiment parallels Dialogue's description of Menippus's bite at *Bis Acc.* 33.

33. *Demonax* 21, where Peregrinus Proteus, that old fraud, makes the complaint. Demonax does not deny the charge that he is not a dog but replies that Peregrinus is not a human being; cf. Branham 1989b, 62–63.

34. Similarly, the late fourth-century Eunapius denies to Lucian the serious side of the epithet σπουδογέλοιος while adding that he wrote the entirely serious philosophical biography of Demonax.

35. *Anth. Pal.* 7.64.4: νῦν δὲ θανὼν ἀστέρας οἶκον ἔχει. For an extended study of this epigram and its literary and philosophical connections, see Häusle 1989. A literary contrast between Diogenes and Menippus seems to be implied by the Bücheler and Heräus (1922) text of Varro F 517, from the Ταφὴ Μενίππου: "Diogenem litteras scisse, domusioni quod satis esset, hunc quod etiam acroasi bellorum hominum" ("Diogenes knew how to write, but only what would be practical; this one knew it too, but what would also please

refined audiences"); unfortunately, Astbury's text reads: "Diogenem litteras scisse cum usioni quod satis esset, tum quod etiam acroasi bellorum hominum" ("Diogenes knew how to write not only what would be practical but also what would please refined audiences").

36. Hense 1909, XLIII–IV.

37. *Necyia* is the traditional name for Book 11 of the *Odyssey*, as the word denotes a magical ritual by which the shades of the dead are summoned and consulted. Although Menippus's *work* certainly would parody the *Odyssey*, it is not certain that his *title* immediately calls up the association, as we lack evidence that Book 11 was thus known before Menippus's time. It should be kept in mind that *necyia* can also mean "funeral ceremony," and that Lucian uses it in this sense at *Nigrinus* 30: "Then he [sc. Nigrinus] touched upon another sort of production, of those who wallow in funeral ceremonies and last wills and testaments." Menippus's title could therefore imply both a funeral and a journey to the Land of the Dead.

38. *Suda*, s.v. φαιός; see Relihan 1987b, 194–95, for discussion of the attribution of this fragment, which Diogenes Laertius (6.102) assigns to the Cynic Menedemus in the life that immediately follows Menippus's.

39. Helm 1906, 45ff.

40. "saltem infernus tenebrio, κακὸς δαίμων, atque habeat homines sollicitos, quod eum peius formidant quam fullo ululam"

41. *Bis Acc.* 33: τελευταῖον δὲ καὶ Μένιππόν τινα τῶν παλαιῶν κυνῶν μάλα ὑλακτικὸν ὡς δοκεῖ καὶ κάρχαρον ἀνορύξας, καὶ τοῦτον ἐπεισήγαγέν μοι. . . . This is typically taken to mean that Menippus's works were unpopular before Lucian revived them; for some other possible interpretations of the meaning of ἀνορύξας, see Hall 1981, 68–69. I would refer this to the ancient tradition of werewolves trying to dig up corpses, and that Lucian is now behaving as Menippus did, lurking about the tombs; see Relihan 1990b, 223.

42. In Byzantine literature there is little interest in Menippus per se; and in the twelfth-century *Timarion* Diogenes takes over from Menippus the role of the shameless dog, despised by philosophers, who exercises an abusive free speech in Hades (43–44): like Lucian's Menippus, he is a dog to an extreme degree, one that always barks. Menippus's fortunes in later literature are considered in my article "Menippus in Antiquity and the Renaissance," forthcoming.

43. As at the end of the justly famous *Dialogue* 5: the rational Menippus hears from Hermes that the beauty of Helen in the flesh is not denied by the reality of her indistinguishable bones, and Hermes has the last word.

44. An example of this sort of humor is provided by a poem of Agathias Scholasticus which I argue is an approximately contemporary analogue to the plot of Boethius's *Consolation;* Relihan 1990a, 119–29.

45. Di Marco 1989, 23–25.

46. For Philosophy's associations with the Land of the Dead, see Relihan 1990c, 192–94.

47. 30.2: ἰσοτιμία γὰρ ἐν ᾅδου καὶ ὅμοιοι ἅπαντες ("There is democracy in Hades, and we are all equal here").

Chapter Four. Varro

1. For the dates of composition, cf. Woytek (1986, 323–25), who insists on the evidence of Cicero's *Academica Posteriora* (45 B.C.), which has Varro refer to his Menippeans as something written and finished long ago (*in illis ueteribus nostris*).

2. The *Apocolocyntosis* runs to 25 pages, with very full apparatus, in Roncali's Teubner edition; the prologue to the *Mythologies* is 13 pages, with slight apparatus, in Helm's Teubner. A 13-page average would make the corpus of the *Menippeans* nearly 2,000 pages. A curious parallel to Varro's production is recorded by Suetonius (*De Gramm.* 21), who mentions that Gaius Melissus, the inventor of the *fabula trabeata* and possibly also a writer of natural history, wrote 150 books of *Ineptiae*, known in Suetonius's day as *Ioci*.

3. Lucian's works (Menippean and otherwise, but not counting spurious works) total 1,467 pages in MacLeod's Oxford edition; Sullivan (1968b, 34–36) reckons the *Satyricon* to have been of 20 books of approximately 20,000 words each, which would be eight times the length of Apuleius's *Metamorphoses* (51,000 words in 291 Teubner pages in the third edition of Helm [1931]), or approximately 2,300 pages. But this seems to be an impossible length for a single work; cf. the cautious objections of Walsh 1970, 73.

4. It is possible that the *Menippeans* circulated separately, and not as a collection, even in the second century A.D.: Aulus Gellius (13.31.2) refers to his possession of an individual volume of the Ὑδροκύων. At least one of the *Menippeans* survived to the sixth century; see Shanzer 1986b.

5. For a convenient list of the titles, with a discussion (not always reliable), see Alfonsi 1973, 27–32; for a brief outline of the topics of each satire, insofar as they can be guessed, cf. dal Santo 1976a. Astbury's new Teubner edition has a full bibliography, useful for supplementing the information in Cèbe's ongoing edition. For further orientation, see also Woytek 1986, 353–55; Salanitro 1978, 65–66.

6. The first two of these seem to have prologues spoken by mythical characters in iambic senarians (so also the prologues of the Ὄνος λύρας and the *Modius*). Prometheus seems to catalog current vices outside of the prologue (F 432–35). But the praise accorded Prometheus for his creation of (necessarily) old-fashioned humanity is itself comic; cf. F 430, in which he pats himself on the back for the creation of the human buttocks: "retrimenta cibi qua exirent per posticum, uallem feci" ("I made a valley so that food waste could pass through the back door").

7. Though one wonders whether there is a connection between this two-book Περίπλους and that other two-book comic (near) circumnavigation, Lucian's *True History*.

8. This is true of Lucian and, to return to a modern analogue to Varro suggested in Chapter 2, of S. J. Perelman as well. The latter's comic pieces include dramatic fragments, personal reminiscences, fictitious correspondence, and brief dialogues. The same sort of humor and self-parody is to be found within them all, but the particular form his essays take can vary.

9. Alfonsi (1973, 35–41) gives a good review of the problems involved, and presents as an example (pp. 41–57) a reconstruction of the *Endymiones* ("The Moonstruck") which he had analyzed before in Alfonsi 1952.

10. "plurimumque idem poetis nostris omninoque Latinis et litteris luminis et uerbis attulisti atque ipse uarium et elegans omni fere numero poema fecisti philosophiamque multis locis incohasti, ad impellendum satis, ad edocendum parum."

11. Mras (1914, 400–401) suggests that f. 20 of Cicero's *Academica Posteriora*, which describes a fictitious philosophical brawl between Epicurus and the followers of Zeno and Chrysippus, owes something to the example of Varro's *Menippeans* and may have been included out of deference to the dedicatee. And it must also be admitted that Cicero may be somewhat formulaic in his criticisms here; nearly the same objections are made about Lucilius's *Satires* in *De Fin.* 1.3.7.

12. Woytek 1986, 339–45, is a convenient summary of philosophical lore. Consider the following titles: *Andabatae* ("The Blind Gladiators"), *Armorum Iudicium* ("The Judgment for the Arms"), *Caprinum Proelium* ("The Battle of the Goats"), *Endymiones*, Λογομαχία ("The Battle of Words"), περὶ αἱρεσίων ("On Philosophical Sects"), *Aborigines* περὶ ἀνθρώπων φύσεως ("Aborigines, or On Human Nature"), *De Salute* ("On the Eternity of the Universe"), *Dolium aut Seria* (two types of barrels, suggested as rival models for the structure of the universe), Κοσμοτορύνη περὶ φθορᾶς κόσμου ("The World Stirrer, or On the Destruction of the Universe"), *Longe Fugit Qui Suos Fugit* ("Running Away from Home Is Running Too Far," probably on Stoic self-sufficiency), Περίπλους (in two books, the second of which is entitled περὶ φιλοσοφίας), *Virgula Diuina* ("Circe's Wand," on the Stoic transformation of the fool into the sage).

13. Mras 1914, 410, 420; Woytek takes a more positive view of the philosophical material as didactic, addressed to the less learned audience.

14. Mras 1914, 401; Scherbantin 1951, 78–82; Duff 1936, 90, more plausibly attributes to Varro a distrust of all dogmatic systems.

15. Mosca (1937, 49–50) makes the point that philosophical concerns are always secondary to those of old and virtuous Rome and suggests that the philosophical lore may in itself be somewhat self-parodically and ironically intended. See also the analysis of the *Eumenides* in Trilli Pari 1974.

16. Cf. Cèbe 1972, 133, on *Andabatae* F 33: "idque alterum appellamus a calendo calorem, alterum a feruore febrim" ("and so, we call the one 'heat' from the verb 'to be hot,' and the other 'fever' from the noun 'fervor'"); he sees this as professorial speech, though he sees no irony in it.

17. See the introductions to each of the satires in the edition of Riese 1865.

18. The most up-to-date assessment is that of Woytek 1986, 326–39; he also discusses Varro's relation to Menippus (pp. 316–20).

19. Woytek (1986, 320) speaks of Cynicism, admitted to be an enemy of philosophical instruction, as a cloak that Varro can take off when he so desires.

20. So McCarthy (1936), who argues that wherever there is dialogue in the

Menippeans Varro is himself presenting both sides of the argument. Cf. also Scherbantin 1951, 68; Mosca 1937, 53.

21. For modern critics looking in Varro for the social criticism common in verse satire, cf. Duff 1936, 84–91; Knoche 1975, 53–69; Coffey 1989, 149–64 (esp. 158–62); Salanitro 1978, 60–62; Alfonsi 1973, 33–35; Cèbe always associates Varro's habits with those of verse satire; cf. Cèbe 1972, 11 n. 5.

22. The contrast is frequently asserted by Cèbe (cf. Cèbe 1972, 8, 57, 125, etc.). See also Bignone 1950, 334–38; Mosca 1937, 42–46.

23. For the language of the *Menippeans*, see Knoche 1975, 66–67; Coffey 1989, 164. Zaffagno 1976b provides an extensive commentary on the strange mixture of vulgarism and abstraction in the *Menippeans*. See also the studies of Woytek 1970 and 1972; he does not allow himself many comments on the wide range of styles. For the poetics of the *Menippeans*, see the suite of articles of dal Santo 1976a, 1976b, 1978, 1979. For a briefer consideration, see Riposati 1974.

24. Holford-Strevens 1988 discusses Gellius's relation to Varro's works throughout a long and impressive book; but the *Menippeans* find very little space there.

25. Cicero, *Ad Att.* XII 6.1, refers to Varro's general enthusiasm for the style of Hegesias, who founded the Asianic movement in oratory to which Cicero was diametrically opposed.

26. To illustrate the Latin idiom, *Attio idem, quod Tettio* (3.16.13); the Greek idiom τὸ ἐπὶ τῇ φακῇ μύρον (13.29.5); the use of *quadriga* as a singular noun (19.8.17); the vocative *Nerienes* (13.23.4); the meaning of *pedarii* (3.18.5); and the use of *purum putum* (7.5.10).

27. Gellius is fond of recording such embarrassments of would-be scholars; Baldwin 1975a, 48, provides a convenient list of passages.

28. For contemporary Cynic theories of the virtue of simplicity in discourse, see Rawson 1985, 279–81.

29. Aristophanes, whom Gellius also admires (he certainly read *Frogs*), is called not *lepidus* but *festiuissimus* and *facetissimus;* see Baldwin 1975a, 67. For his appreciation of Menander (who is also said to write *facete*, 2.23.11) see Holford-Strevens 1988, 145–48, 175.

30. Coffey (1989, 156) thinks that these remarks were "preliminary to a not entirely serious discourse on the transience of human fortune"; but he adds that Gellius both picked quotations that did not support his judgment that the book was elegant *and* that he overlooked any irony of treatment. Note that Evangelus, the spirit of discord in Macrobius's *Saturnalia* who will insult Vergil and thus inspire the rebuttals that form the body of this symposium, ironically refers to the elegance of the assembled guests by citing F 333 (1.7.12).

31. One thinks of Menippus's *Letters from the Gods* and Lucian's *Saturnalian Letters*. The *Lex Tapula* of Valerius Valentinus (fragments in Bücheler and Heräus 1922) is a set of comic regulations for a *conuiuium*, but it is not necessarily inspired by or related to Menippean satire. For a suggestive modern example of how Varro may have exploited comic regulations in his self-

parodic essays, consider Robert Benchley's "My Five- (or Maybe Six-) Year Plan," "How to Travel in Peace," and "How to Get Things Done," in Benchley 1949; most remarkable is "The Menace of Buttered Toast," in which comic regulations are pronounced in the midst of a self-parodic description of the composition of his own typical essay.

32. "ipsum deinde conuiuium constat, *inquit,* ex rebus quattuor et tum denique omnibus suis numeris absolutum est, si belli homunculi conlecti sunt, si electus locus, si tempus lectum, si apparatus non neglectus." Woytek (1986, 339 n. 125) points to F 151, 236, 298, and 504 for similar plays on compounds.

33. "in conuiuio legi non omnia debent, sed ea potissimum, quae simul sint βιωφελῆ et delectent."

34. "potius ut id quoque uideatur non defuisse quam superfuisse"; Gellius here glosses *superfuisse* as *immodice et intempestiue fuisse,* "to be in excess and out of season."

35. Gellius here also glosses *bellaria* because it is an antiquarian's word (found in Plautus and Terence); this does not prove, however, that the word would have been remote to Varro's contemporaries.

36. "Yet, what do mortals need but two things only, the staff of Demeter and the cup of poured water, which are at hand and are by nature for our nourishment? The fullness they provide is not enough, and in luxury we seek out the devices of other delicacies."

37. As suggested by Riese 1865; cf. also Rötter (1969, 28–32), who thinks it not unlikely that Varro did cite Chrysippus, as Varro often refers to other Greek authorities; but Varro elsewhere in the *Menippeans* only gives the *ipsissima uerba* of Roman authors.

38. From the apparatus of Bücheler and Heräus 1922:

pauo ex Samo, Phryx attagen, grus Melica,
haedi ex Ambracia, pelamys Chalcedonia,
muraena Sicula, aselli Pesinuntii,
ostrea Tarenti, Lesbius pectunculus,
lupus Timaui, helops Rhodi, Cilices scari,
nux Thasia, palma Aegypti, glans Hiberica.

39. That this poem is actually a Petronian effort, put in Trimalchio's mouth along with the false attribution with parodic intentions, see Courtney 1991, 20–22.

40. The shopping list figures prominently in the *Greek Anthology* and in Athenaeus. An excellent modern example of this sort of song (inspired by Gilbert and Sullivan), is Tom Lehrer's "The Elements," in which all of the elements of the periodic table, though in no particular order, are sung to the tune of "I Am the Very Model of a Modern Major-General."

41. Gellius 15.19.2 = F 404: "Had you spent on philosophy only a twelfth of the effort that you expend to make sure that your baker makes a good loaf of bread, you would have already become a good man. But as it is now, those who know him want to buy him for a hundred thousand sesterces, but not a single one who knows you would spend a hundred asses."

42. "sed lepidae magis atque iucundae breuitatis utraque definitio quam plana aut proba esse uidetur." The definitions of *indutiae*, given at 1.25.1–2, equal Varro's *Antiquitates Rerum Humanarum* frags. 1–2 Mirsch. Further on these etymologies in Baldwin 1975a, 80–81.

43. The point made by Woytek (1986, 352), against Wilamowitz and Knoche.

44. Cf. F 551, from τὸ ἐπὶ τῇ φακῇ μῦρον (roughly, "Pearls before Swine"): "legendo autem et scribendo uitam procudito" ("hammer out your life in reading and writing"); and F 219, from the *Gloria* (in choliambics): "tum denique, omnis cum lucerna conbusta est / in lucubrando oliuitasque consumpta est" ("then, finally, when all the lamp is burned in midnight study, and all the oil is spent").

45. Caesius Bassus *De Metris*, 6.261 Keil (= F 230): "Varro in Cynodidascalico phalaecion metrum ionicum trimetrum appellat." Bücheler and Heräus 1922 in the apparatus suggests that this satire is the same work as the *De Compositione Saturarum*, mentioned by Nonius p. 67: "pareutactae assunt, mulier quae mulier, Venus [caput]" ("nubile women are present, each one of them the soul of Venus"). This is a hazardous conjecture, though attractive.

46. Cèbe 1975, 374ff., thinks that if the subtitle is to be kept, it should refer to the necessity for Varro, as a man of letters, to keep himself as supple as a trick horse. But, dissatisfied with such an interpretation, he emends the subtitle to περὶ τοῦ τρέφειν "On Upbringing," the subject of the satire being an attack on the Roman passion for wild horses.

47. Mosca (1937, 43) draws a distinction between Varro's *opposition* to modern times and Lucilius's *polemic* against them. This is preferable to the theory of L. Robinson (1974), who concludes that Varro was "forced into inactivity and silence" (p. 483) by politicians upset by the nature of his criticisms in the *Menippeans*.

48. For text, see Chapter 2, n. 58.

49. Bibliography on the relation between Menippus and Horace may be found in Salanitro 1978, 65–66.

50. Cf. esp. F 250, 252, 253, and F 265–66.

51. Livy 40.29 refers to casks of Numa's writings being dug up under the Janiculum by plowmen; the writings had a decidedly Pythagorean cast. Fulgentius in the *Expositio Sermonum Antiquorum* 14 (p. 116 Helm) seems to refer to one of these texts through one of Varro's writings, *In Pontificalibus*. Livy 25.12.3–15 refers to the similar promulgation of the prophecies of Marcius in 212 B.C., which attempted to influence the conduct of the Punic Wars. The buried manuscript is also a device of prose fiction: cf. the prologue to the *Diary of the Trojan War* of Dictys, and *The Wonders beyond Thule* of Antonius Diogenes 111b.

52. The Ὄνος λύρας is introduced by the personification "Voice Training" (F 348): "Phonascia sum, vocis suscitabulum / cantantiumque gallus gallinaceus" ("I am Voice Training, the stimulant of the voice and the dung hill cock of singers"). F 379, from the Papia Papae, περὶ ἐγκωμίων: "ille ales gallus, qui suscitat †aitharum† Musarum scriptores? an hic qui gregem rabu-

larum?" ("Is that the true cock which awakens the authors of the (Attic?) Muses, or this one which awakens the crowd of lawyers?").

53. As reported by Plutarch in *Quaest. Conviv.* 5.1 (674B); I have not seen Geller 1966.

54. "pudet me tui et Musarum †agnosceret. piget currere et una sequi." Vahlen posited a lacuna between *Musarum* and *agnoscere*, to which he supplied "dolet enim meam amusiam agnoscere" ("for I am pained to acknowledge my own lack of inspiration").

55. "poema est lexis enrythmos, id est, uerba plura modice in quandam coniecta formam; itaque etiam distichon epigrammation uocant poema. poesis est perpetuum argumentum ex rythmis, ut Ilias Homeri et Annalis Enni. poetice est ars earum rerum."

56. Cf. Diogenes Laertius 7.60; Mras 1914, 416 and n. 1. Such discussion is also to be found in Lucilius Book 9, frags. 376–85 K (338–47 Marx); cf. Krenkel's bibliography there.

57. F 399: "in quibus partibus, in argumentis Caecilius poscit palmam, in ethesin Terentius, in sermonibus Plautus" ("in these respects, Caecilius takes first place for his plots, Terence for his characters, and Plautus for his language").

58. Cèbe 1974, 211–13, argues that the *Bimarcus* involves Varro and an imaginary critic with whom Varro discusses the necessary subjugation of stylistic to satiric concerns.

59. As Astbury points out in the introduction of his edition (pp. XVII–XX), the so-called *lex Lindsay*, which allows us to make some conclusions from the order of citations in Nonius about the logical order of the fragments, yields the following paltry information: F 59 precedes F 54, and F 50 precedes F 56.

60. Cf. *Sexagesis* ("After Sixty Years") F 505: "erras, inquit, Marce, accusare nos; ruminaris antiquitates" ("You're wrong, Varro, to accuse us; you are chewing the cud of your *Antiquities*").

61. More Greek learning at F 62: "κατάχρησις est enim uera cum in candelabro pendet strigile" ("for *true* catachresis occurs when a strigil hangs from a candelabrum"). The analogy in F 62 is comic by its distance from the ordinary uses of the technical term, which should refer to the analogical use of a word (Quintilian *Inst. Or.* 8.6.34). But it seems that the pedant misunderstands the word to mean the juxtaposition of incongruous elements rather than the application of a word to a thing that has no proper term to describe it.

62. In senarians: "τρόπων τρόπους qui non modo ignorasse me / clamat, sed omnino omnis heroas negat / nescisse." *nescisse* makes a double negative; Skutsch (1964) suggests *me scisse*.

63. Priscian's *Partitiones Versuum XII Aeneidos Principalium* gives a good idea of just how long a grammarian can discuss the purely formal aspects of the first line of an epic poem.

64. "cum Quintipor Clodius tot comoedias sine ulla fecerit Musa, unum libellum non 'edolem' ut ait Ennius." This Clodius may be the comedian who

is contemptuously referred to in F 51: "scaena quem senem Latina uidit derissisimum" ("the most ludicrous person that the Roman stage has ever seen"). Cèbe (1974, 234) rejects the theories that see personal references behind this and takes it as a description of the stock character Pappus of Atellan farce.

65. Cf. F 189, citing Ennius to support a desire not to have children.

66. Cèbe (1974) offers some interesting emendations: for F 58 (= frag. 54 Cèbe), he reads: "mihique diui, cum stilo nostro papyri euolui scapos, capite annuont partum poeticon" ("and as I unroll the sheets of papyrus with my pen, the gods, with a nod, inaugurate my poetic birth"). For F 57 (= frag. 55 Cèbe): "ne me pedatus ⟨iste⟩ uersuum tardor / refrenet arte, comprimo rhythmon certum" ("lest that metrical slowness of verse hold me tight, I suppress regulated rhythm"). I do not agree that this demonstrates a rejection of neoteric poetry in favor of moral earnestness and emotional force (pp. 240 ff.).

67. F 63: "Even though their words smelled of garlic and onions, our grandfathers and great-grandfathers were nevertheless men of the greatest spirit."

68. Lerer (1985, 14–93) makes the interesting point that frequently in Roman dialogue the goal of discussion is the creation of another text out of a preexisting one; his examples are Cicero's *Tusculans*, Augustine's *Soliloquies* and *De Magistro*, Fulgentius's *Allegorical Content of Vergil*, and the *Consolation* as well as others of Boethius's works. One wonders then in what proportions Varro's dramatization of the difficulty of composition derives from Old Comedy and from a parody of Roman philosophical tradition. Similarly, Boethius's distress in the *Consolation* about how to write may draw on both traditions; see O'Daly 1991, 106–9, for traditions of Roman poetry and of Neoplatonism in Boethius's opening poem.

69. As claimed by Mras, who makes much of Varro's eclecticism. For Varro's philosophical associations, see Mras 1914, 410ff.; Long 1974, 222–29; Woytek 1986, 339–45.

70. Mras 1914, 393–410.

71. Mras 1914, 410–11, 419–20.

72. Rawson 1985, 322. Woytek (1986, 320) speaks however of Cynicism as not an organic growth but as something grafted onto (and therefore detachable from) Varro's protreptic and didactic aims.

73. F 220: "Varro . . . equites quosdam dicit 'pedarios' appellatos" ("Varro says that certain of the knights were called *pedarii*").

74. From the simple title *Cynicus* we can deduce nothing; from Κυνίστωρ ("The Cynic Historian"), little.

75. The *caue canem* mosaic in the house of the Tragic Poet at Pompeii is well known.

76. Mosca 1937, 58.

77. Although I would not deny the point made by Mosca 1937, 56–57, that the topic of the conversation is the contrast of old-fashioned Cynic ways and those of modern Cynics, I would modify it by suggesting that the host him-

self is an example of the modern Cynic tendencies that he decries. The guests call him a drunk (F 137; cf. Mosca 1937, 57) in order to protect themselves from the force of his criticism, but it can hardly be that such an accusation does not carry with it some truth. Thus the narrator is susceptible to his own criticism, in the manner of Menippean ambiguous preaching.

78. Cèbe 1975, 455; the text of the end of the fragment is not secure.

79. For this opposition throughout the *Menippeans*, cf. Mras 1914, 398–99 and his discussion there of F 210 (from the Γνῶθι σεαυτόν ["Know Thyself"]): "age nunc contende alterum genus φιλοθέωρον, ne quid ibi uideris melius" ("come now, set against it another philospeculative type, and see if you see anything better there").

80. Weinreich (1941) adduces a parallel between this fragment and Dio Chrysostom *Or.* 10.5 ("Diogenes, or On Servants") to prove a Menippean model for Varro: "And do you think that more people have been injured by bad dogs or by bad men? They say that only one man died by dogs—Actaeon, and those dogs were mad. But one cannot say how many private citizens, how many kings and entire cities have been lost at the hands of worthless men." Of course, many unpopular authors are said to be killed by dogs, such as Heraclitus, Euripides, Diogenes, Menippus, and Lucian; see Baldwin 1975a, 67.

81. F 535: "non uides in publico ante tabernas, qua populus ambulando, proinde ut in arato, porcas reddit" ("don't you see in public, in front of the taverns, where the people walking about look exactly like pigs in a field . . ."); F 536: "non uides in magnis peristylis, qui cryptas domi non habent, sabulum iacere †a pariete aut et† xystis, ubi ambulare possint" ("don't you see how, in the great courtyards, those who do not have covered walkways throw sand along the walls or in the porticoes, so that they can walk?"). Cf. also the alliterative F 209, from the Γνῶθι σεαυτόν: "non animaduertis cetarios, cum uidere uolunt in mari thunnos, escendere in malum alte, ut penitus per aquam perspiciant pisces?" ("Don't you see that when fishmongers want to see tuna in the sea they climb high up the mast so that they can catch sight of the fish deep in the water?").

82. Pliny, *N.H.* praef. 24.

83. Varro himself may be the object of such seductions, as someone asks him why he has gotten himself all dressed up (F 175): "quare, o Marce, pransum ac paratum esse te hoc minume oportet" ("Why, Varro? It so little behooves you to be ready, willing, and able").

84. Cf. the title of Aristophanes's Τριφάλης, a play attacking Alcibiades.

85. Another example is F 384: "nasturcium [indige] non uides ideo dici quod nasum torqueat, ut uestispicam quod uestem spiciat?" ("Don't you see that a nasturtium is so called because it twists the nose, just as a wardrobe mistress is so called because she looks at the clothes?").

86. "non uides apud Mnesitheum scribi tria genera esse uini, nigrum, album, medium, quod vocant κιρρόν, et nouum, uetus, medium? et efficere nigrum uirus, album urinam, medium πέψιν? nouum refrigerare, uetus calefacere, medium esse prandium caninum?"

87. Knaack 1883; see my Chapter 3.

88. ὁ μέλας οἶνός ἐστι θρεπτικώτατος, ὁ δὲ λευκὸς οὐρητικώτατος καὶ λεπτότατος, ὁ δὲ κιρρὸς ξηρὸς καὶ τῶν σιτίων πεπτικώτερος.

89. From the Γνῶθι σεαυτόν ("Know Thyself," the Delphic Motto), whose title should indicate the presence of true Cynic concerns, F 204: "non uidetis unus ut paruulus Amor ardifeta lampade [arida] agat amantis aestuantis" ("Don't you see how the one tiny Love with his torch, pregnant with flame, drives on the burning lovers?"). Cf. also the Ὄνος λύρας, on the power of music, F 364: "non uidisti simulacrum leonis ad Idam eo loco, ubi quondam subito eum cum uidissent quadrupedem galli tympanis adeo fecerunt mansuem, ut tractarent manibus?" ("Haven't you seen the statue of the lion near Mount Ida, in the place where once, when the eunuch priests of Cybele suddenly saw the four-footed beast, they made it so tame with their drums that they could even pet it?"). Given the bad press that the galli receive elsewhere in the *Menippeans* (and especially in the *Eumenides*), it is very hard to believe that Varro the author would want us to accept a tale of their power and a vindication of their music, though it is possible that he expresses the sort of fascination that Catullus does in the *Attis*. In this example the thing referred to is rather more concrete than in the fragments just cited, but it is effectively as invisible (being in Phrygia) as the gods and Love.

90. As McCarthy (1936) and Cèbe have it. Cèbe is very schematic, and presumes that most of the satires are so arranged that a fictive interlocutor poses all of the objections, and that a Varronian narrator or Varro himself comes on to refute all charges in the name of the decent and the good.

91. The high proportion of poetic fragments among the remains of the *Menippeans* (more than a third of the whole) indicates primarily that verse features to a great degree the grammatical oddities necessary for preservation. But the meters go far beyond the hexametric and iambic quotations of Lucian's practice. The verse does not rely heavily on direct parody of other authors; cf. Scherbantin 1951, 89–92; Courtney (1962, 87–90) points more to parody of genres than to parody of specific authors and passages in the *Menippeans*. For Menippus's possible poetic experiments, see Haslam 1981, 36–38 (my Chapter 3 and Appendix A).

Chapter Five. Seneca

1. Riikonen (1987, 41–42) points out that while Bakhtin does not discuss the *Apocolocyntosis* in detail, it is the prime example for Bakhtin's claim that the menippea offers a three-leveled construction. Bartoňková (1976, 67 and 80) takes the *Apocolocyntosis* as the perfect Menippean satire by virtue of its poetic parodies, though the independent verses are considered non-Menippean. The parodies are worth listing here, but my own concerns in this analysis are more structural. 1.2 = Vergil *Aen.* 2.724; 3.2 = *Georg.* 4.90; 4.2 = Euripides *Cresphontes* frag. 449 Nauck[2]; 5.4 = *Od.* 1.170, 9.39–40; 9.3 = 2 epithets from Homer (ἀρούρης καρπὸν ἔδουσιν and ζείδωρος ἄρουρα); 11.1 = *Il.* 1.591; 11.6 = Catullus 3.12; 13.3 = Horace *Carm.* 2.13.34; 13.4 = part of

an Isis cult ritual; 13.6 = a parody of Thales (Diels–Kranz A22), πάντα θεῶν πλήρη; 14.1 = a Homeric phrase, ὅσα ψάμαθός τε κόνις τε; 14.2 = a fragment of Hesiod (Μεγάλα Ἔργα frag. 286 Merkelbach–West; cf. Aristotle, *Eth. Nic.* 1132b).

2. Eden's edition, 8–13, offers a convenient overview; Bringmann 1985, 892–900, is fuller; Wolf (1986, esp. 152–55) bitterly concludes that the *Apocolocyntosis* expresses a disgust with Roman imperial politics in general. Eden adopts a moderate position, that the work is "obliquely didactic," showing Nero how not to govern. This seems a minimalist revival of the theory of Marti 1952, that the *Apocolocyntosis* is a sort of negative "mirror for princes." When viewed as an attack on Claudius the person, the work is judged anywhere from mild to tasteless and savage.

3. Nauta 1987.

4. The Irish *Voyage of St. Brendan* comes closer than the *True History:* its Atlantic sailors find both the earthly paradise and the volcanic hell where they have a chance to talk to Judas Iscariot, currently enjoying a little time off. But there would seem to be no historical connection between classical texts and the native Irish literary tradition of the *imram*.

5. A translation of the *Visio Pauli* may now be found in Gardiner 1989, 13–46; *The Voyage of St. Brendan* is included at 81–127.

6. As Alexander relates in his letter to Olympias, 2.32–44.

7. Markus 1990, 204, citing the *Life of Caesarius of Arles* 2.6.

8. Possibly the oddest incarnation of this idea is Aristophanes' *Peace*, when Trygaeus's attempt to compel the gods to create peace becomes a strange attempt to rescue Peace herself from wherever is the heavenly cave in which she is imprisoned; a harrowing of heaven, as it were.

9. Reeve (1984) effectively counters a growing trend to deny Senecan authorship; Bringmann (1985, 885–89) summarizes some of these arguments.

10. The translations are my own. The reader is referred also to Eden's edition (equipped with a facing translation), and the annotated translation in Sullivan 1986, 207–42.

11. See the laborious commentary on this passage in Weinreich 1923.

12. Seneca's language is conceivably ambiguous: *ad deos isse* could be a euphemism for dying, but context is against this, and we will meet Augustus in heaven soon enough.

13. The proverb is Greek: μωρῷ καὶ βασιλεῖ νόμος ἄγραφος, Porphyrion ad Hor. *S.* 2.3.188.

14. Duff (1936, 93) holds that the *Apocolocyntosis* is a satire on the very notion of apotheosis; so also Taylor 1930, 240–41.

15. Cf. *Jupp. Trag.* 15, *Bis Acc.* 26, *Necy.* 2. For discussion, cf. Weinreich 1923, 31–32; Helm 1906, 150–54, 277ff.

16. The source cannot state conclusively whether Claudius messed his toga when he died (4.3); the author refuses to tell of the events on earth as being too well known and proceeds to tell of what happened in heaven with an ironic insistence upon his stature as a reporter (5.1: "in caelo quae acta sint audite: fides penes auctorem erit" ["Hear what happened in heaven; its au-

thority lies in my source"—that is, Livius Geminus]); before the speech of Janus at 9.2 the source states that the court clerk could not catch all of Janus's speech and therefore he does not himself reproduce it, lest he put words in Janus's mouth, and then proceeds to create an entire speech of his. Weinreich (1923, 96–97) sees the humor in the excessive concern over the historical commonplace of the fictitious speech, but also thinks that the intrusion serves to make the importance of the speech that follows it more obvious. These intrusions come before two of the scenes that abuse Claudius fairly severely, the scene at the gate of Olympus and in the heavenly council; I think that they can only serve to blunt the force of the criticisms there expressed.

17. Parallels between Lucian and Seneca seem to assure the affiliation of the *Apocolocyntosis* to Menippus and Menippean satire, but the temptation to posit common sources or to downgrade the significance of the parallels is strong. Suetonius (*Div. Aug.* 70.1) proves that Romans could parody an assembly of the gods: he mentions a scandalous banquet at which Augustus (as Apollo) and his guests dressed as the twelve Olympians. Coffey (1989, 175) is typical in seeking other sources for "Menippean motifs" in the *Apocolocyntosis;* see also Coffey 1961, 266ff. Similarly Bompaire (1958, 266) sees Seneca's originality as an argument against proof of Menippean influence. Bringmann (1985, 900–5) rarely brings Menippean satire into the discussion of the work's literary background.

18. Roncali (1973) offers an interesting history of the dramatic divisions of the text offered by the printed editions since the Renaissance. The article favors a simple scheme: prologue and three scenes (earth, heaven, hell).

19. We infer a rapprochement from chaps. 8–9, in which we see that Hercules has gained entrance for Claudius into the gods' council chamber and is actively petitioning on behalf of Claudius's godhood, whereas in chap. 7 Hercules is Claudius's enemy and belittles him.

20. Weinreich believes, I think rightly, that the presence of Hercules outside of the council is a Senecan innovation. As he points out, Heracles does show up in the heavenly councils in Lucian (cf. *Jupp. Trag.* 32) as a buffoon who tries to solve delicate problems by brute strength (Weinreich 1923, 61ff.). But Heracles does not appear at the entrance to Olympus in Lucian, nor does he make friends with anyone. Weinreich rightly opposes Helm's contention that Menippus gave to Heracles a role that Lucian rejected and Seneca retained. Weinreich also notes that the travesty of Heracles is a Menippean motif but that the pairing of the hero and Heracles as heavenly idiots is not. The funeral dirge that the deceased himself hears is at best only vaguely Menippean; Lucian in *Dial. Mort.* 20.10 tells of a tyrant who hears his own dirge but who does not, as Claudius does, see it as well. Finally, the *exchange* of punishments is Seneca's own, even though the unexpected reprieve is a motif of Menippean satire. The satiric possibilities that Claudius's life offered and which Seneca overlooked (his fondness for women, the question of incest with his niece; cf. Sullivan 1966, 380) reveal not only the courtier's rather than the satirist's bias, but also a willingness to treat Claudius more sympa-

thetically than he deserved. Sullivan is certainly right (p. 381) to point out that the tone is essentially mild, not harsh as is so often alleged; and that Seneca, with such limited goals, is being neither cruel nor offensive.

21. Cf. Dobesch 1975.

22. Weinreich (1923, 36–48) takes the poem as being perfectly serious; Coffey (1989, 173) considers the flattery "gross but relevant" in defining a contrast between the deceased and his successor; in his edition Eden (p. 75), speaking of the poem's "facile elisionless flow," claims the author achieves his ends not by parody but by "holding up a mirror to uninventive mediocrity." The funeral oration that Seneca wrote for Nero to read over the dead Claudius (Tacitus *Ann.* 13.3) exploits a similar difference between superficial praise and essential fatuity.

23. Binder (1974) takes this scene as a parody of the Hercules-Cacus scene in *Aen.* 8; for further connections with the *Aeneid*, see below, n. 36.

24. As Eden points out in his commentary, the most remarkable event in Claudius's reign was this beginning of the subjugation of Britain; but the Brigantes were not subjugated until the 70s A.D., and Eden suspects here an ironic reference to the suppression of an internecine rebellion, which led to the installation of Cartimandua as a Roman client-queen. For the seriousness of this passage, cf. Weinreich 1923, 115–18.

25. "So tell us now, what sort of god do you want him to become? He can't be an Epicurean god; such a god experiences no difficulties, nor offers any to anyone else. A Stoic god? But how can he be 'spherical,' as Varro says, 'having neither head nor foreskin'? But there is something of the Stoic god in him, I see it now: he has neither heart nor head." This passage is as close as Seneca comes to parodying his own Stoicism; the author's self-parody lies largely in the sphere of drama, not philosophy.

26. 8.2: "illum deum ⟨induci⟩ ab Ioue, quem, quantum quidem in illo fuit, damnauit incesti!" ("Can he be deified by Jupiter, whom, as far as he could, Claudius convicted of incest?").

27. 9.3: "ne uidear in personam, non in rem dicere sententiam" ("Lest I seem to express an opinion based on personality rather than the case at hand").

28. It is worth noting that the *Metamorphoses* ends with the deification of Julius Caesar, who is (pointedly, perhaps) not in Seneca's heaven.

29. Weinreich 1923, 84–106 (esp. 97–98), compares Janus's speech and that of Momus, the mocker of the gods, in Lucian *Deor. Conc.* 15; cf. also Helm 1906, 161.

30. Skutsch (1964) conjectures that the line "Romulus in caelo feruentia rapa uorare" was a popular joke at the expense of the deified emperors: "even in heaven, Romulus eats boiled beets."

31. 9.6: "noli mihi inuidere, mea res agitur; deinde tu si quid uolueris, in uicem faciam: manus manum lauat" ("Don't begrudge me; the outcome is my concern, too. And if you ever want anything, I'll return the favor; one hand washes the other").

32. Weinreich (1923, 82) points out that the comic Hercules here is a

parody of the tragic Hercules; cf. also Eden in his edition at 7.1. Varro too may have offered a precedent for this presentation of Hercules. His comic use of Cynicism makes us suspect a comic use of the Cynic exemplar of self-sufficiency in such titles as *Columna Herculis* ("The Pillars of Hercules"), *Hercules Socraticus* ("The Socratic Hercules"), *Hercules Tuam Fidem* ("Hercules, Help!"), and Ἄλλος οὗτος Ἡρακλῆς ("Hercules the Second").

33. Eden, ibid., 115–16, notes that the speech is framed by the two long poems, the praise of Nero and Claudius's dirge. Wolf (1986, 42ff.) discusses Augustus's self-absorption and concern with his family (as opposed to the Roman state) at length.

34. "incipit patronus uelle respondere. Aeacus, homo iustissimus, uetat et illum, altera tantum parte audita, condemnat et ait: αἴκε πάθοις τά ἔρεξας δίκη εὐθεῖα γένοιτο. ingens silentium factum est. stupebant omnes nouitate rei attoniti, negabant hoc umquam factum."

35. Eden in his commentary on the funeral dirge (12.3.19–22) points out that the reference to Claudius's rendering of justice after only one side had been heard is a distortion of his laudable practice of awarding decisions in favor of those who show up for a hearing, against those who are, for whatever reason, absent.

36. Binder (1974–75) argues that Claudius here resembles Catiline on Aeneas's shield in *Aen.* 8.666–70. Discussion in Bringmann 1985, 903–4; on the basis of such associations with the *Aeneid,* Nero may be seen as a new Augustus. In a well-known passage Suetonius mentions that Claudius wrote a book on dice playing (*Cl.* 33.2); but Suetonius also has it that his enemies objected to Augustus's dice playing during the difficulties of the Sicilian War (*Div. Aug.* 70.2, where also is mentioned Augustus's banquet that parodied the heavenly banquets of the gods; see earlier n. 17). Augustus too could be said to ape divinity; and Wolf (1986) makes the repeated point that Augustus in heaven is primarily concerned not with affairs of state but with private and family matters.

37. Eden reads "adiudicatur. C. Caesari illum Aeacus donat. is Menandro liberto suo tradidit . . ."; the usual text, accepted in Roncali's edition, makes Menander Aeacus's freedman, which is improbable: "adiudicatur C. Caesari. Caesar illum Aeaco donat," etc.

38. As Sullivan (1986) in the note to his translation would have it. Weinreich (1923, 131) takes the second punishment as a wholly new one, designed in its very Romanness to supersede the original one, which was too Menippean and mythological.

39. Knoche 1975, 105; Coffey 1989, 166: ". . . and so, having been the dupe of freedmen in his lifetime, he becomes the slave of a freedman in the underworld and is compelled to work as a lawyer's clerk. His degradation is thus complete."

40. See n. 13.

41. Cf. Heinze 1926, 49–50.

42. Ball (1902, ad loc.) is off the mark, as Heinze (1926) points out, but he comes close to emphasizing the *advantages* of stupidity that are implied:

"Claudius was not born a monarch, but by being *fatuus* he had of course the luck to become one."

43. Not a pumpkin. The authoritative treatment of this is Heller (1985), who makes the interesting suggestion that the point of the word *Apocolocyntosis* (which he considers to be not the work's real title but an offhand characterization of it by its author some time after its composition, when his rancor against Claudius had cooled, being tempered by the unpleasant reality of Nero) is that the dull Claudius is transformed into something vaguely useful, providing humble service in the underworld just as the gourd provides flower, shade, and storage.

44. This is a parodic application of Catullus 3.12, the lament for the death of Lesbia's sparrow.

45. For these, see Riikonen 1987, 45–46. Hoyos (1991) argues that the colocynth could refer to a nickname of Claudius, gained because of his intestinal troubles and the colocynth's connection with good health; thus, the title refers to the passing of the Colocynth, "The Departure of Our Gourd." Other theories are summarized in Bringmann 1985, 889–92.

46. Consider too that, early on in the text, when Mercury urges Clotho to end Claudius's life, he refers to Vergil's description of the struggle between king bees in the hive: "hand him [i.e., the weaker of the two] over to death, let the better one rule in an empty hall" (3.2 = *Georg.* 4.90: "dede neci, melior uacua sine regnet in aula"); yet if this quotation is a parody as well, "kill him and let him be a better ruler in an empty hall" is a possible translation; and it is more appropriate for Claudius than for a new king to rule over emptiness.

47. Bringmann (1985, 892–900) surveys various interpretations. I agree with the argument developed in Wolf 1986, but reach similar conclusions by different routes.

48. For Claudius as the Saturnalian lord of misrule, see *Apoc.* 8.2: a god in the assembly complains that Claudius celebrated the Saturnalia all year long. Nauta (1987, 90–96) describes how the *Apocolocyntosis,* read at a Saturnalian festival, would function to release the pent-up fears of those who had reason to be terrified of the live Claudius.

49. Bringmann (1971) sees Seneca's frustration with lack of political freedom in subtle stylistic ironies.

50. Wolf 1986, 152–55.

51. More than any other Menippean satirist (and I am not forgetting Boethius and the *Consolation of Philosophy*) Seneca presents his work in the trappings of drama. For example, at 7.1, Hercules demands to know the truth of Claudius's origins and threatens to beat the truth out of him; he then makes himself even more imposing by adopting a tragic pose: "et quo terribilior esset, tragicus fit et ait. . . ." There follow fourteen paratragic senarians, "a superman confronting a monster" (Eden's edition, 93). Weinreich (1923) demonstrates the parallels between them and various passages from Seneca's *Hercules Furens.* He also notes the similarity between the *Apocolocyntosis* and drama (p. 19): "Eine komodie hat er nicht geschrieben, die *Apocolocyntosis* aber ist gleichsam ein Satyrspiel nach einer Praetexta. Seneca hatte

zum Tragöden wie zum Buffo." At 12.3, Claudius hears his funeral dirge: "When Claudius saw his exequies, he realized that he was dead. For in a great dramatic chorus a funeral dirge was being chanted [in anapests]" (Claudius, ut uidit funus suum, intellexit se mortuum esse. ingenti enim μεγάλῳ χωρικῷ nenia cantabatur [anapestis]). Cf. Weinreich 1923, 114–15, on the funeral dirge as a parody of the great *nenia* in *Hercules Furens* 1054–1132. As Eden comments on the excision of the word *anapestis*, which seems to be a grammarian's gloss: "If kept, the word must be taken as a gesture of self-mocking pedantry."

52. Coffey (1989, 171) notes that there was no official *damnatio memoriae* of Claudius; his deification was accepted as a matter of policy, and this tale was "to be enjoyed as part of the frivolity."

53. Nauta (1987, 93–94) opposes Bakhtin's view that the *Apocolocyntosis* celebrates the Saturnalian world and argues (correctly, I think) that the work is much more conservative and rejoices that the Saturnalia are now over.

54. I make the suggestion that the fantastic voyages of Alexander in the *Romance* are influenced by the fantastic voyages of Menippus in my "Menippus in Antiquity and the Renaissance," forthcoming.

Chapter Six. Petronius

1. Slater 1990, 234.

2. Two spirited defenses of the *Satyricon*'s Menippean status on the basis of its literary parodies are Courtney 1962 and Adamietz 1987. The latter includes the novel as one of the parodied genres; Anderson (1982a, 65–73) argues that the *Satyricon* is not a parody of the novel but an extreme example of its inherent tendencies: inflated rhetoric not appropriate to the action or to the characters; allusions to great classical works in perverse contexts; the incongruity of style and scene; ironic moralizing; and the general perversion of literary topoi and techniques by characters who reveal comic claims to our sympathy by their emotional and linguistic excesses; see also Sullivan 1968b, 214–31.

3. Perry 1967, 321–24, speaking of Apuleius and *Apollonius, King of Tyre*, though including Petronius's interest in fairy tale and folklore. More to the point (p. 209): "In short, Petronius has just about everything. . . . It is not emulative of any literary tradition but is shaped by the author's need . . . for a safe place in which to experiment artistically with various types of poetry, rhetorical declamation, and criticism." Perry assigns the work to a genre he calls burlesque novel, "the most contemptible and least respected of all possible literary forms."

4. Slater 1990, 27–133, is a careful reading of the text as a whole; Sullivan 1968b, 34–80, attends more to the problems of reconstruction. M. S. Smith 1985 provides an impressive analytical bibliography of recent Petronian scholarship.

5. Slater (1990) does a good job of rereading the *Satyricon* as an account of a man who tries to impose a meaning on events (Slater's words are theatrical,

to put a frame around them) but who never gets "more than a temporary foothold" (p. 241). The work "evoke[s] expectation of meaning—and then refuses to supply it" (p. 239).

6. A thorough orientation in these matters is found in Petersmann 1986b.

7. Slater (1990, 211) speaks of "the failure of characters or incidents to measure up to their literary paradigms," and locates realism in Petronius in this contrast, which "grounds" them.

8. See M. S. Smith 1975, xix–xx.

9. Cf. F. Jones 1987. Beck's theory that Encolpius the narrator is older, presenting a detached view of the activities of the younger Encolpius, is discussed by Slater (1990, 46–47).

10. "quid me constricto spectatis fronte Catones / damnatisque nouae simplicitatis opus? / sermonis puri non tristis gratia ridet, / quodque facit populus, candida lingua refert. / nam quis concubitus, Veneris quis gaudia nescit? / quis uetat in tepido membra calere toro? / ipse pater ueri doctos Epicurus amare / iussit et hoc uitam dixit habere τέλος." Sullivan (1968b, 98–99) offers a fantastic paraphrase ("A translation . . . would not be very helpful . . ."), which takes Encolpius and his literary and moral theories much too seriously.

11. 132.8 (the meter is sotadean): "ter corripui terribilem manu bipennem, / ter languidior coliculi repente thyrso / ferrum timui, quod trepido male dabat usum. / nec iam poteram, quod modo conficere libebat; / namque illa metu frigidior rigente bruma / confugerat in uiscera mille operta rugis. / ita non potui supplicio caput aperire / sed furciferae mortifero timore lusus / ad uerba, magis quae poterant nocere, fugi" ("Three times with my hand I snatched up the awful ax; three times, more limp than a plant stem, I quickly feared the blade, which would render sad service to my terror. Nor could I accomplish what I had just decided to do, for it, colder than the stiffening frost, retreated in fear into my guts, covered with a thousand wrinkles. Thus, I could not by entreaty reveal its head, but, frustrated by the mortal fear of my private crucifixion, I took refuge in words, which could do more harm").

12. 132.11: "illa solo fixos oculos auersa tenebat, / nec magis incepto uultum sermone mouetur / quam lentae salices lassoue papauera collo" ("It turned away and held its eyes fixed on the ground, and its appearance was no more changed by the speech I had started than a pliant willow would be, or poppies on a drooping stem"). The first two lines are *Aen.* 6.469–70, in which Dido in the underworld rejects Aeneas's pleas for sympathy; the second half of the last line is *Aen.* 9.436, from a simile describing the death of Euryalus.

13. His failures with Circe are implied at 128.1–2 and 132.6. See also Slater 1990, 165–67.

14. Raith (1963, 44) points out that we cannot disentangle three possible speakers of these verses: Encolpius the actor, Encolpius the fictive author, and Petronius the actual author. Raith also notes that part of the parody of this complex of narrators is the misunderstanding of Epicurus's doctrines on pleasure (pp. 45–46).

15. As does Sullivan 1968b, 99–100.

16. Even if we grant to the Romans a liberal view of homosexuality and promiscuity (cf. Sullivan 1968b, 234–36), Encolpius's actions are hardly normal. His inclinations may be lightly thought of but his behavior is extreme. The relations in the triangle Encolpius-Ascyltus-Giton are compounded of jealousy, violence, and hysteria, and serve the comic delineation of our main characters, all of whose other actions arouse some sort of laughter. That Epicureanism in the *Satyricon* which consists of the praise of a sound mind in a sound body (cf. 61.1 and 88.8, the latter quoted subsequently) is in the mouths of people unsound in both respects; for the Epicurean *bona mens* as praised by Eumolpus and Agamemnon, see Raith 1963, 31. For the distasteful sexual scenes involving children, see the episode with Giton and Pannychis at *Sat.* 25–26; Eumolpus's story of the son of his Pergamene host at *Sat.* 85–86; Eumolpus with the children of Philomela at *Sat.* 140. Sexual matters are almost entirely absent from the *Cena*, a fact that underlines their use in comic characterization elsewhere.

17. Arrowsmith (1966, 328–29) takes the story of the Widow of Ephesus as the sole example of healthy sex and honest vitality. Against Arrowsmith's view of the *Satyricon* as a moral work, see the elegant rebuttal of Sullivan 1985, 1672–75.

18. Cf. Walsh 1970, 80: Encolpius and Giton "represent wandering scholars at large in the world, and their reactions are invariably and exaggeratedly scholastic; but this comedy of rhetorical foibles is affectionately represented."

19. Witke (1970, 166–67) points out that for all of this the *Satyricon* is *not* a satire in the ancient sense of the term.

20. Coffey (1989, 201), speaking of the relation between the guests at the *Cena* and our heroes, says: "The attitude of Petronius to his characters is, as so often, elusive and baffling." He also suggests (p. 187) that Petronius may or may not agree with his characters' opinions and that his stance may have been intended to "baffle his contemporaries."

21. Coffey 1989, 192.

22. Another text that seems to defy generic labels; Winkler (1985) shies away from such questions altogether.

23. Perry 1967, 242–43; I do not agree with this assessment of the *Metamorphoses*, however. Kenney (1990, 6–11) points out that the spiritual and salvific conclusion has been prepared for, though it takes a fine eye to see it. Winkler (1985, 292–321) will allow an Isiac interpretation of the book as one of a number of possibilities.

24. Anderson 1982a, 99–102.

25. Kennedy 1978; Soverini 1985, 1706–38, is an exhaustive analysis of the scene. Despite the characterizations of the speakers, the views expressed on Asianism and Atticism correspond in some ways to the artistic nature of the *Satyricon* itself.

26. The poem is most reasonably seen as Petronius's creation, and Tri-

malchio attributes his own moralizings to an esteemed moralist: see Courtney 1991, 20–22.

27. For these poems as artistic failures, see Anderson 1982a, 100–102, and
Walsh 1970, 95, against Sullivan 1968b, 170ff. (*Bellum Ciuile*) and 186ff. (*Troiae
Halosis*).

28. Walsh 1970, 22.

29. Williams (1978, 6–51) provides a good discussion of the various theories of Petronius and his contemporaries for the decline of literature in the
early Empire; he cites the classic formulation of Seneca, *Ep. Mor.* 114.11:
"quomodo conuiuorum luxuria, quomodo uestium aegrae ciuitatis indicia
sunt, sic orationis licentia, si modo frequens est, ostendit animos quoque, a
quibus uerba exeunt, procidisse" ("In the same way as extravagance in dress
and entertaining are indications of a diseased community, so an aberrant
literary style, provided it is widespread, shows that the spirit [from which
people's words derive] has also come to grief"); trans. Campbell 1969, 216.

30. Cf. Encolpius at 2.3–8, as he invokes Sophocles, Euripides, Pindar, the
lyric poets, Plato, Demosthenes, Thucydides, and Hyperides against the corruption of contemporary Asianism. Slater (1990, 28–29) notes that these are
all Greek authorities, though the topic is the decline of Latin rhetoric.

31. See Sullivan 1968b, 186–213. His arguments are further developed in
Sullivan 1968a; 1977, 139ff. M. S. Smith (1975) is overly cautious, though it is
true that for any given parallel other sources or parallels are possible. Sullivan (1985, 1679–86) responds convincingly to his critics.

32. Sullivan (1968b) argues throughout that the *Satyricon* must be a defense of new literary principles; but as Anderson points out (1982a, 99),
Petronius can be an opportunist when it comes to criticism, and not advocate
anything at all. Various current attempts to turn Petronius back into a moralist (by Arrowsmith, Zeitlin, and Cameron) are efficiently disposed of by Anderson 1982a, 95–97; Sullivan 1985, 1670–75.

33. Sullivan 1968b, 152; M. S. Smith (1975, xx) merely points out that the
fact that Encolpius narrates the events directs some of the criticism away
from Trimalchio and the freedmen; either is preferable to Walsh (1970,
111ff.), who defends the *Cena* as a thorough attack on the manners of the
nouveau riche after the habits of traditional Roman satire.

34. For a good discussion of the speeches of the freedmen, see Sullivan
1968b, 139–51. Boyce (1991, 76–102) gives an excellent analysis of their language, and points out the linguistic details that serve to characterize each
one; but the literary implications of such details are of secondary importance
in this study. It is also worth noting that Petronius's characterization through
use of language (a thing not found in Greek romance) extends to prose
rhythm: Petronius's narrative is rhythmic, but the speeches of Trimalchio
and the freedmen are not (see the edition of Müller and Ehlers, 449).

35. Coffey 1989, 200–201; M. S. Smith (1975, xix–xx) is too quick to dismiss the presence of Plato in the *Satyricon*.

36. Astbury (1977) claims that there is no connection at all between Petro-

nius and Varro or Menippean satire, and looks to Greek prosimetric romance (see Appendix A) as the true generic predecessor of the *Satyricon*.

37. Zaffagno (1976b) tentatively suggests a relationship between Varro and Seneca (pp. 197–200) and between Varro and Petronius (pp. 200–205). This study is bitterly criticized by Puccioni (1976) and adequately answered by Zaffagno (1976b).

38. See Altamura 1959.

39. Varro may have written of an ascent to heaven in the *Marcipor*, of a council of the gods in the *Pseudulus* Apollo περὶ θεῶν διαγνώσεως ("The False Apollo, or How to Tell True Gods from False"; cf. Mras 1914, 396–97, on the Cynic and Menippean bias against poor substitutes for gods in heaven), of funeral exequies in the *Manius* and Ταφὴ Μενίππου, and of a necyia in the περὶ ἐξαγωγῆς and the *Epitaphiones* περὶ τάφων ("Collectors of Epitaphs, or On Burial"), but it is most unlikely that he combined all of these motifs in a single *Menippean*. Seneca's relation to Varro is typically minimized because Varro did not offer an example for the critique of contemporary politics; cf. Weinreich 1949, XLVII, LXXII. The Τρικάρανος, on the First Triumvirate, though included in Astbury's edition, is probably a separate political pamphlet and not one of the Menippeans; cf. Coffey 1989, 153. The appeal of Seneca's narrator to the untrustworthy source to make a point about contemporary decadence resembles the plot of the *Manius*, with the narrator's involvement in the discovery and interpretation of a cache of (Numa's?) writings at F 255–56.

40. F 81, from the *Cycnus* περὶ ταφῆς ("The Swan, or On Burial"). Burial in honey is the topic of a fascinating page in Hamilton-Patterson and Andrews 1978, 61.

41. F 529, from the Ταφὴ Μενίππου. Given the prominence of death and burial in Varro's *Menippeans*, the fascination with death so evident throughout the *Satyricon*, and especially in the *Cena*, may betray generic affiliations more than social observations. The matter deserves further study: for the importance of death in ancient symposium literature, and for a brief treatment of the *Cena* as a parody of Plato's *Symposium*, see Relihan 1992.

Chapter Seven. Lucian

1. C. Robinson 1979 is a serviceable introduction to the Renaissance Lucian; see also Vives Coll 1959, Mattioli 1980, Mayer 1984, Lauvergnat-Gagnière 1988; Zappala 1990 is highly recommended and includes a discussion (pp. 1–10) of the merits and defects of his predecessors. For Lucian's defense against the charges brought by Rhetoric and Dialogue in *Bis Acc.* 30–32 and 34 and by Philosophy in *Pisc.* 29–37, and for his claims to originality (*Zeuxis* and *Prometheus Es in Verbis*) see now Branham 1989b, 28–57, a good literary treatment with full bibliography. C. Robinson (1979, 1–63) summarizes what is known of Lucian's life and what is thought about his works; he draws heavily and to good effect from the two crucial monographs, Anderson 1976a and 1976b. See also Anderson 1982b.

2. Bompaire 1958 is the seminal work for the study of literary imitation as the motive force in Lucian. C. Robinson (1979, 44) pithily sums up the prevailing attitude: "The theme of the satires is not, in a sense, their ostensible subject matter, but the fact of imitation itself." A thorough treatment of Lucian's topicality in his satires is provided by Baldwin 1973, and C. P. Jones 1986; but I do not think that the topical Lucian intrudes in his Menippean satires.

3. Branham 1989b, 5: "Lucian offers a series of rhetorical experiments in the contemporary significance—or comic inappropriateness—of the cultural types and codes evolved by the Greeks over many generations to evoke and define their most characteristic qualities." It should be added that Lucian's "contemporary appeal" is not universal; he is excluded from Philostratus's *Lives of the Sophists* (early third century). Korus (1984) rightly distinguishes Lucian's humor from the merely satiric: all things false, ugly, or contrary to common sense are laughable, and all are bound up in the world of human action (p. 312). Korus (1986a), on the seriocomic in Lucian's comic dialogues, is less successful, speaking of pleasant poetry and useful prose, and denying particular significance to the mixture of genres.

4. This is the theory put forth by Payne (1981, 38–54), in a discussion of Lucian. I differ, for reasons made clear in Chapter 1, from the criteria there given for defining a work of Lucian's as a Menippean satire (p. 38: the use of prose and verse, the appearance of Menippus as a character, Menippus having written on a similar topic, the presence of Cynic philosophy, all together or in significant combinations). Payne's approach to the thematic essence of Menippean satire I find congenial though sometimes too philosophically profound for the playfulness that I detect in these texts; and while I disagree on the specifics of her interpretations of Lucian, we are more or less in accord on the nature of fantasy in Lucian.

5. We can no longer be certain that all of the Menippean pieces, however they are defined, belong to a single chronological period. Anderson (1976a, 149) speaks of Lucian as a "literary Procrustes"; he can reuse his material at any time, and his works are essentially undatable. C. Robinson (1979, 13ff.) goes even further than Anderson to talk of the uniformity of technique throughout the corpus as making almost all groupings of works within it arbitrary. The fullest attempt at Lucian's chronology is Schwartz 1965; see also Korus 1986b, which speaks of a development, the last phase of which is truly comic and satiric and includes the *Piscator*, though our Menippean satires are not specifically dealt with.

6. Branham (1989b, 105 and elsewhere) takes Menippus as one of Lucian's voices.

7. Branham (1989b, 19–20) notes that we are to see the absurdity of Menippus's costume in the *Necyomantia*, and to note a difference between the sophisticated author who speaks through him and Menippus's own fantastic uncouthness. The scholiast at *Icaromenippus* 1 makes a truer observation, I think, about Lucian's preservation of propriety by refusal of self-parody. Cf. Rabe 1906, 98.10ff.: . . . διὰ δὲ τὸ μεγαλόπραγμον καὶ περίεργον καὶ φασμα-

τῶδες εἰς Μένιππον τὸν Κυνικὸν φιλόσοφον ἁρμοζόμενος, ὃς Πατάρων ὑπάρ-χων τῆς Λυκίας καὶ τὴν Ἀντισθένους δόξαν ὑποποιούμενος γενναῖος ἦν καὶ συγκεκροτημένος τὸ σῶμα καὶ οὐκ ἀδόκιμος (". . . because the character forms grandiose designs, is overly inquisitive, and is fantastic, the author cast him as Menippus the Cynic philosopher who, coming from Patara [an error for Gadara] in Lycia, affected even the glory of Antisthenes; he was noble, well disciplined in body, and not without renown"). The scholiast confuses Menippus the Cynic with the Lycian Menippus found in Philostratus's *Life of Apollonius of Tyana* 4.25ff.

8. Tackaberry 1930, 8–40; and Anderson 1976a, 139–40, give the hand-iest bibliographic orientations in the matter.

9. C. P. Jones (1986, 51) calls the *Necyomantia* a "pendant to the *Icaromenip-pus*."

10. Branham (1989b, 105) notes that the dialogue framing a narrative which is Lucian's *Symposium* is the same structure as Plato's *Euthydemus;* but what is framed in the Menippean satires is a journey, not a symposium.

11. 1: Μὴ θαυμήσῃς, ὦ ἑταῖρε· νεωστὶ γὰρ Εὐριπίδῃ καὶ Ὁμήρῳ συγ-γενόμενος οὐκ οἶδ᾽ ὅπως ἀνεπλήσθην τῶν ἐπῶν καὶ αὐτόματά μοι τὰ μέτρα ἐπὶ τὸ στόμα ἔρχεται ("Don't be surprised, my friend. I was just with Euripides and Homer and I can't say how but I was infected by their words and verses just come to my mouth of their own accord").

12. 1: Μὴ θαυμήσῃς, ὦ ἑταῖρε, εἰ μετέωρα καὶ διαέρια δοκῶ σοι λαλεῖν ("Don't be surprised, my friend, if it seems to you that I'm speaking of things ethereal and meteoric").

13. οὐ γὰρ οἶδ᾽ ὅπως περὶ τούτου λέγειν προθέμενος παμπόλυ ἀπεπλανή-θην τοῦ λόγου ("I intended to talk about this but somehow or other I strayed far from my topic").

14. C. P. Jones (1986, 52) gives a number of examples. Winkler (1985, 257–70) describes five fictional narratives (inter alia, the romances of Iambli-chus and Antonius Diogenes) of the type he calls "I went in quest of secret wisdom," and assigns the *Necyomantia* to the same format, along with other works of Lucian (pp. 270–71).

15. Branham 1989b, 16.

16. Cf. *Cont.* 5 and the climb of Hermes and Charon up an impossibly high stack of mountains to observe the world below; this is discussed later.

17. Anderson 1976a, 140; *Peace* 179ff.

18. Cf. Empedocles' tacit admission of fraud at *Pisc.* 2, where he says that Parrhesiades (one of Lucian's *noms de plume*) ought to be thrown into a vol-cano for his blasphemy against philosophers.

19. Cf. Anderson 1976a, "Index of Principal Motifs," svv. "Patron protects cultured criminal," and "Surprise intervention." Branham (1989b, 19–20) sees the reprieve more as an in-joke, Lucian's delight in the powers that patronage can bring. Branham acknowledges that the scene breaks the illu-sion of text, inviting the reader to enjoy a literary game; but I think that the moral implications are to the fore.

20. A pathetic and poetic detail found also in *Dial. Mort.* 30.1.

21. Branham (1989b, 24–25) discusses this simile, noting that here, as elsewhere in Lucian, the theatrical implies both "participation and detachment"; actors ought not confuse themselves and their roles.

22. Cf. Anderson 1976a, "Index of principal motifs," s.v. "Similes of life."

23. Especially as the Greek philosophers tended to view time cyclically; the time between conflagrations in the Stoic great year was a mere 24,000 years. This sort of unjust justice was found in Seneca (*Apoc.* 14.2), when Claudius is condemned after Aeacus hears only one side of the case against him.

24. ... μόνον ἐξ ἅπαντος θηράσῃ ὅπως τὸ πάρον εὖ θέμενος παραδράμῃς γελῶν τὰ πολλὰ καὶ περὶ μηδὲν ἐσπουδακώς. See Branham 1989a, 159–60; and Branham 1989b, 25. Simonides' fragment (frag. 646 *PMG*): "In life, play, and be perfectly serious about nothing."

25. See Chapter 2.

26. Branham (1989b, 25) claims that "Menippus returns eager to inform the powers that be of the reversals that await them."

27. Anderson 1976a, 140.

28. See Relihan 1987b.

29. Cf. his role in *Dial. Mort.* 5.2, in which he almost convinces Menippus that Helen was worth dying for.

30. Tackaberry (1930, 91) romantically assigns this work to a late period in Lucian's Menippean phase, at a time in which his "venom was spent."

31. Branham (1989b, 163–77) provides an extended analysis of this dialogue, which allows my comments to be brief. He notes its uniqueness (p. 167): it "is formally closest to the hybrid of dialogue and comedy that lands the Syrian in court in *The Double Indictment*" (*Bis Acc.* 33). But *Juppiter Tragoedus* in structure resembles Julian's *Caesars,* in which an assembly of Olympian gods hears an imperial contest for deification in the sublunar sphere.

32. 2.38.5ff., recension A; see Stoneman 1991, 118–25, which includes material from other recensions.

33. I make this comparison between these two authors more fully in Relihan 1987b, 186 n. 6.

34. Branham (1989b, 57) is right to point out that Lucian can proclaim the conundrum: "He hesitates to let us take even his own serious efforts with unqualified seriousness"; cf. also p. 25.

35. Payne (1981, 39) makes the point that Lucian here criticizes the idea of the norm itself; but her theories about the hero on an endless quest who champions "man's unsuspendable freedom to think" (pp. 10–11), while defining a very commendable intellectual attitude, fail to take into account the humor had at the expense of those who dare to find out anything.

Chapter Eight. Julian

1. Lacombrade (1962, 65–67) argues for the December of 362, when Julian was in Antioch and may have had some respite from affairs of state; the arguments are repeated in his edition, pp. 27ff. But there is no reason why

the dramatic date of the *Caesars*, the December Saturnalia, must correspond to the date of composition; cf. the sensible objections of Baldwin 1978, 450–51.

2. A number of critics have tried, without great success, to align the *Caesars* with the tradition of the Platonic symposium: cf. Ullrich 1909, 65–68; Martin 1931, 230–40; and Gallardo 1972, 282–96, largely a representation of Lacombrade's views. While they have little difficulty in compiling lists of symposiac motifs and borrowings from the *Symposia* of Plato and Xenophon (the latter is of greater importance, the lengthy chapter 4 presenting a series of speeches on the utility of those aspects of his character in which each speaker takes the greatest pride), the *Caesars* still does not satisfy expectations: Ullrich notes the lack of attention to physical detail, and finds its indulgence in fantasy distressing (p. 68); Martin is so disturbed by the lack of a meal proper (such as is found in Horace *S.* 2.8, Petronius, and Lucian, all of whom are supposed to be writing under the influence of a Menippean symposium) that he posits the *Arcesilaus* of Menippus as Julian's model, even though this work too is said to have had a meal, which Julian left out (pp. 234ff.). The thesis of Alonso-Nuñez 1974, that the *Caesars* is a symposium whose topic is politics, not love, similarly fails to gain conviction. But just as Plato's *Symposium* anticipates Socrates' death, so does Julian's anticipate his own, and in the implications of this death-centeredness we may assert a real generic link. See Relihan 1992, esp. 236–38.

3. The *Saturnalia* is an ambitious collection of short pieces in various genres, but none of them relates to a fantasy taking place in heaven. There is a dialogue between a priest and Cronus on why the latter is glad to be rid of the rule of heaven; an address by one Cronosolon, the prophet of Cronus, in which he reveals two sets of convivial rules told to him by Cronus; and an exchange of letters between a poor man and Cronus. Geffcken (1911, 477 n. 6) denies any dependence between Lucian and Julian on this score, as against the claim of Helm (1906, 74 n. 1).

4. Kaegi 1964, 29ff. For "self-justification," see Bowersock 1982, 171–72.

5. Pack (1946) attempts to show that the heaven of the *Caesars* is like that of his other philosophical works, particularly of *To the Mother of the Gods* and of *Hymn to King Helios;* but even he is forced to admit that there are only vague resemblances. Further, Pack identifies the *Caesars* and the Κρονία, which Julian says he dedicated to the Neoplatonist Sal(l)ustius or Salutius (the author of the Neoplatonic *On the Gods and the Universe;* see Bowersock 1978, 125) at the end of the *Hymn to King Helios;* this thesis is adequately refuted by Baldwin 1978, 452.

6. Kaegi 1964, 29–38.

7. Baldwin (1978, 466) concludes that the purpose of the work is to convince his audience that he combined all of the virtues of his predecessors and could thus be expected, with the aid of the gods, to win further victories in the East. Or, as Alonso-Nuñez (1974, 319) has it, his self-propaganda is designed to show that all of Roman history converges on him. Athanassiadi-Fowden (1981, 199–201) offers useful connections between the *Caesars* and

Julian's political aims and personal beliefs, even as it misses the irony of the piece. She notes how the *Caesars* contains Julian's vision of a peaceful and universal Roman Empire to which the empire of Persia could be joined; she adds, however, that Tyche is present throughout the work, expressed as a worry that Julian may not be as fortunate in his enterprise as Augustus was; and an atmosphere of piety as well, expressed through the victory of Marcus Aurelius in the heavenly contest as Julian's pledge to continue to imitate the gods.

8. Rostagni (1920, 112–14) sees the *Caesars* as a farce and a burlesque at the expense of Julian's predecessors, but finds very little to say about it on the literary level. He much prefers the humor and the satire of Julian's *Misopogon*. Witke (1970, 163–65) deals harshly with Julian's low intent, lack of detail, and lack of universality; the *Caesars* is not amusing, and is just a predictable series of criticisms of ancient emperors according to modern, enlightened, standards. Hirzel (1895, 2.345) similarly condemns Julian for the absence of real life in the *Caesars*.

9. The only translation of the *Caesars* into English is the Loeb edition of Wright 1913. Baldwin (1978, 457–66) provides a lengthier synopsis, but one focusing on the historical matter.

10. Details of this in Relihan 1989a. The introduction ends with the interlocutor exclaiming, "And this prologue of yours has already been tricked out in mythical and rhetorical colors! Come now, relate the story itself, whatever it is."

11. This is thought to be a dig at the Homer of Lucian and the heaven that the latter compiled from scandalous passages in the *Iliad* and *Odyssey;* Julian is said to be defining heaven in terms of his own faith (cf. Helm 1906, 74 n. 1; Martin 1931, 233). But there is no passage in Homer which speaks of the gods' separate thrones and of immovable seats. Closest to this idea is *Il.* 1.533–35, speaking of the gods all rising as Zeus comes into their presence; and passages such as *Il.* 1.605ff. and 11.76, which refer to the gods' individual homes. If Julian wanted literary authority for a non-Homeric heaven, he could have quoted Plato *Phaedr.* 247A, which speaks of the gods in order following the lead of the heavenly Zeus who presides over the zodiac (Lacombrade notes the parallel in his edition).

12. For the theory that he did, see Alföldi 1944, 60–80; Levine (1968) seeks to prove this thesis, noting (p. 28) the simple fact that almost all of Julian's historical allusions are to be found in the *Caesars* (summarizing the arguments of Kaegi 1964, 29ff.).

13. Bowersock 1982, 164–70, supplies the details: Julius Vindex is considered an emperor; there is a leap from Severus Alexander to Valerian and Gallienus; and Julian omits Tacitus between Aurelian and Probus, makes Probus suffer at the hands of Christians (probably by confusion with another Probus), and has quite eccentric evaluations of Titus, Antoninus Pius, Severus Alexander, and Septimius Severus. As for the prurient sexual interest in his predecessors' behavior, Bowersock observes (p. 162): "The *Caesars* betrays a taste for erotica that goes well beyond the requirements of the Menip-

pean genre." His examples are the characterizations of Trajan as a pederast, Hadrian as a homosexual sophist, and of course Constantine.

14. For details of the festival and ancient sources, see Lovejoy and Boas 1935, 65ff. Pack (1946, 153–54), contending that as the Saturnalia is a festival of the winter solstice it is appropriate for the tale of the migration of a soul to heaven, takes the piece too seriously. Remember that the *Apocolocyntosis* is also a Saturnalian piece: Nauta 1987.

15. Bowersock 1982, 171. Baldwin (1978, 453–57) looks to an amalgam of Plutarch, Suetonius, and the *Historia Augusta,* and wonders whether the phil-hellene Julian actually read a Roman work.

16. Geffcken (1911, 478; and 1914, 8off.) speaks of a Hellenistic ἀγών involving princes in the other world as a common source; Martin (1931, 238) is similar. Pack (1946, 151 n. 1) rightly says that Geffcken is "non-committal" on the question of influence. Both Ball (1902, 78) and Levine (1968, 17–18) consider the case unprovable despite the parallels. Eden points out in his edition that the *Apocolocyntosis* was known to Ausonius in the fourth century (*Ep.* 23), but briefly dismisses the possibility of Seneca's influence on Julian (pp. 18–19).

17. Similarities among Julian, Martianus, and Boethius are acknowl-edged. Klingner (1921, 115) explains this by saying that the tradition of apoc-alyptic became entwined with that of Menippean satire at an early date in its history.

18. In Xenophon *Smp.* 5.9–10, there is a secret ballot taken on whether Socrates or Critobulus is the more beautiful. But in Xenophon, the results of this balloting are announced (Critobulus wins). If there is a parallel between the two texts, it lies in the corruption of the vote, as Socrates immediately claims that Critobulus's money has unfairly affected the outcome.

19. "The divinity shall not choose you, but you shall choose a divinity. Who has the first lot is first to choose the life that is his of necessity. But virtue has no master; each shall have more or less of her as each honors or dis-honors her. The blame is his who chooses; the god is blameless." Julian would agree that, as far as the emperors are concerned, "virtue has no master," although he may wish to reserve himself as an exception. The importance of the Myth of Er in the history of Menippean satire is discussed in Chapter 12.

20. As, for example, Lacombrade claims in the note in his edition.

21. Rostagni 1920, 234 n. 3; Lacombrade, edition, p. 25.

22. Lacombrade 1962, 54–55.

23. Constantine had murdered his son Crispus and his second wife Fausta, though through the machineries of government; Fausta herself was responsible for the false charges brought against Crispus.

24. Christianity singles Constantine out for attack in the *Caesars.* Further-more, Julian loathed his Christian cousin and predecessor on the throne, Constantius II, for his slaughter of Julian's father and eight others of Julian's family in 337, and this may have helped turn Julian toward apostasy (cf. Bowersock 1978, 21–32). The murder of family by a Christian relative is hardly an act that Julian was prepared to palliate.

25. At 313D-314A the emperor Aurelian enters the banquet hall and is pursued by those who hate him to the court of Minos, now located on Olympus. He defends himself badly against the many charges of murder his prosecutors bring, and Helios, whom the narrator calls "my master" comes to his aid as he had often done before. Quoting the same Hesiodic proverb that Aeacus pronounced over Claudius in the *Apocolocyntosis* (14.2: "Should he suffer what he himself has done, it would be straight justice"), he brings the episode to an abrupt close. Because Aurelian restored the cult of Sol Invictus, and because of the honor paid elsewhere by Julian to Helios, critics typically interpret this passage to Aurelian's and Helios's credit. But Lacombrade (edition, p. 16) notes that the praise of Aurelian has some reservations; Baldwin (1978, 464) observes that Helios concedes Aurelian's guilt, and that elsewhere (*Or.* 4, 155B) Julian minimizes Aurelian's importance in the cult of Helios. Aurelian suffered what he did in that he was murdered by the military conspiracy that put Tacitus in power; but just before this scene (313B), we see Silenus condemning to punishment those who killed Severus Alexander even though he did not think much of that emperor's attainments. Helios's reference to death by conspiracy may only serve to remind the reader of Aurelian's complicity in the death of his predecessor Gallienus, well known to fourth-century historians (cf. Aurelius Victor *Caes.* 33.20–21).

26. It is pleasant, though unlikely, to think that the vaguely named Claudius for whose sake Constantine is forgiven is Seneca's Claudius, more apropos than Claudius Gothicus as Zeus's justification for pardoning an unforgivable emperor.

27. The god Helios is mentioned at 314A as the patron god of a morally compromised Aurelian. Although Helios is referred to as "my master" by the narrator, we need not presume that Helios is Helios-Mithras; none of the participants has anticipated the nature or object of Julian's faith.

28. For Julian's general distrust of the allegorization of Homer, see Lamberton 1986, 134–39: "Julian himself emerges as the champion of a misconceived and unexamined literalism" (p. 139).

29. An allusion to Simonides figures prominently at the end of Lucian's *Necyomantia;* see Chapter 7, n. 24.

30. For example, Silenus implies much more than he says when he quotes *Il.* 3.55 in an attack on the manners of the emperor Constantine at 335B: " 'Your locks and your looks' made one suspect this, but now it is your opinions that convict you." The quotation does nothing to add to the charge unless its original context is remembered. With these words, Hector condemns Paris's womanizing.

At 309D, Tiberius turns around to reveal a back covered with welts from scourging. Silenus quotes *Od.* 16.181: Ἀλλοῖός μοι, ξεῖνε, φάνῃς νέον ἢ τὸ πάροιθεν ("My friend, you seem different to me now than before"). This is originally spoken by Telemachus after witnessing Odysseus's transformation. Silenus's is a small joke, depending upon our understanding of πάροιθεν, "before," in a spatial rather than a temporal sense: Tiberius from the front is different from Tiberius from the back.

At 313C, Silenus greets Valerian, who carries the chains he wore as a prisoner of the Persians, and his son Gallienus, who has an effeminate manner of walk and dress, with two quotations: "Who is this man with the white crest, who leads in the front of the army?" (Euripides *Phoen.* 119–20); and "Who in gold is every way effeminate, just like a girl" (adapted from *Il.* 2.872). The first was originally spoken by Antigone, who asks her tutor who Hippomedon is. Silenus is merely being sarcastic; seeing a king in chains, he asks who is this haughty leader of armies. The second is the only example in the *Caesars* of a quotation that is a literal parody. Homer speaks of one Nastes, leader of the Carians, at the end of the catalog of the ships: "who in gold went off to war, like a girl, the fool, nor did it keep dismal death away from him."

31. The opening verses (*Carm. Pop.* 863 *PMG*) may be found in a slightly different form in Lucian *Demonax* 65 (*Carm. Pop.* 865 *PMG*); Julian may be drawing upon both a genuine Olympic pronouncement and Lucian's version of it. Cantoclarus in Heusinger's edition, ad loc., suggests the possibility of other influences; Lacombrade's edition gives only the one parallel to the *Demonax*.

32. So Baldwin 1978, 449.

33. Cf. the address of Hermes at *Jupp. Trag.* 6; after Julian the device is found in Fulgentius's *Mythologies* 7.5–8.5 (the narrator summons the Muses) and in Ennodius's *Paraenesis didascalica,* as Modesty, Chastity, Grammar, and Rhetoric are imagined as calling the learner to what they have to offer.

34. Cf. Rostagni (1920, 206 n. 1), who takes the poem as one of the elements of the parody of the comic mime performances held at the funerals of emperors, in which the bad habits of the deceased are recounted for fun.

35. *Deor. Conc.* 14–19; *Apoc.* 9.2–3.

36. *De Nuptiis* 2.200–206.

37. So Helm 1906, 74 n. 1. Baldwin (1978, 449) thinks reasonably that we are to be reminded of Socrates in the descriptions of the bald Silenus (cf. Plato *Symp.* 215a4ff., Alcibiades' comparison of Socrates to satyrs). Martin (1931, 232), considering the only connection between Momus and Silenus to be the freedom of abusive speech, sees in the pair Dionysus/Silenus a parallel to Aesop/Solon in Plutarch *Symp.* 150A and 152C.

Chapter Nine. Martianus Capella

An earlier version of this chapter (Relihan 1987a) is here substantially modified.

1. As Richard Johnson says in his description of the opening fictional frame of the *De Nuptiis,* "The long wintry nights and the senility of the author we may see as portending the Dark Ages." (Stahl, Johnson, and Burge 1971, 231). This work, while accessible, is not sympathetic to Martianus as an author (except perhaps as a poet) nor does it provide an accurate translation. More recent discussion of the influence of Martianus's encyclopedic matter may be found scattered through Wagner 1983.

2. Its literary and structural qualities are nicely examined by LeMoine 1972b; summarized in LeMoine 1972a. See also two other recent editions of individual books of the *De Nuptiis:* Lenaz 1975 (Book 2); Cristante 1987 (Book 9).

3. Shanzer 1986a, 43. See the review of this study by Baldwin 1988b.

4. Shanzer 1986a, 67: "one might boldly guess that the word is partially a Martianean neologism for a female personification who is imbued with the discipline of the *Chaldaean Oracles,* the Julianic λόγια δι' ἐπῶν."

5. Shanzer 1986a, 29–44 ("The *De Nuptiis* as a Menippean Satire"). She notes the following themes: heavenly voyage, heavenly council, petition for deification (she considers Seneca an influence here), personifications, parody of mystery religions, *necyia,* the thirteenth labor of Heracles, the doxographical characterization of philosophers in the afterlife. She considers Varro and Lucian to be direct influences on Martianus.

6. Shanzer 1986a, 44; see also p. 4: "Perhaps the greatest insensitivity that one encounters in Martianean criticism is lack of a sense of humor and ear for parody." Lenaz 1972 provides a convenient summary of modern literary and religious opinions on Martianus but does not mention its humor. LeMoine 1972b in fact goes a long way toward rectifying the situation; the current chapter extends this study in this respect.

7. A rough contemporary analogue to this sort of framework is suggested by the volumes of the Neoplatonist Iamblichus, an encyclopedist who discourses on philosophy, mathematics, science, and mysticism, but whose teachings are all to be related to and understood in the light of the introductory book, the *Life of Pythagoras.*

8. At 9.891, Apollo suggests that, although Medicine and Architecture stand waiting to speak, their mundane topics are inappropriate and that Philology may interrogate them at her leisure. Thus Varro's nine disciplines are whittled down to what will become the canonical Seven Liberal Arts. The discourses of the Prophetic Arts are delayed until the day after the wedding, at the insistence of the Moon, who may not tarry any longer (9.897). This is a comic detail: Luna thinks that the audience should come to such discourses fresh (i.e., they are now weary after listening to so much talk); and that the Moon should express an opinion on what doctrines are proper to discourse upon reminds us of the speech of the Moon in Lucian *Icar.* 20–21.

9. Shanzer 1986a, 38, referring to the two central encounters: "Martianus and Satura perform a comedy routine which intrudes in the main *fabula* of the *De Nuptiis* in two places."

10. Cf. LeMoine 1972b, 121–22.

11. At 8.806, Satura seems to imply that the narrator invented the scene on his own: " 'ne tu' ait 'Felix, uel Capella, uel quisquis es non minus sensus quam nominis pecudalis, huius incongrui risus adiectione desipere uel dementire coepisti?' " ("She said, 'Don't tell me, Felix, or Capella [sc. little goat], or whoever you are, beast no less in sense than in name, that by adding this discordant laughter you have started to abandon your intelligence, or maybe your mind?' "). But she cannot shift the blame so easily; he is still her scribe.

12. See in particular Westra 1981.

13. 9.1000: "testem ergo nostrum quae ueternum prodidit / secute nugis, nate, ignosce lectitans." Janson 1964 is a good catalog of such programmatic possibilities; Shanzer (1986a, 50) notes the use of "winter vigil, midnight oil, food metaphors, modesty topoi." But Janson notes two unusual things about Martianus's use of traditional material: Martianus and Boethius counter, by prefacing a mainly prose work with a poem, the habit of prefacing verse with prose (p. 116); and Martianus so extends the use of the nocturnal study image as to have its personification, Agrypnia, inhabit his "strange mythical world" (p. 148).

14. For the theme of the opening poem as the union of opposites under divine Love, see LeMoine 1972b, 21–29. I follow Shanzer's alteration of Willis's text at v.12, *qui* for *quae*.

15. Shanzer 1986a, at 1.4.

16. Martianus's knowledge of Iamblichus has been proved: see Turcan 1958, and the chapter on Martianus in Gersh 1986, 2.597–646. Ferrarino (1969) insists that Philology and Mercury are essentially the same person; in agreement with this view is Lenaz (1975, 101). This view is opposed to that of Nuchelmans (1957), who sees Philology as *studiosa rerum* and Mercury as *studiosus uerborum*. Nor can we forget that Mercury can be seen as the psychopomp, leading Philology to her new home. Gersh (1986, 2.597–605) interprets Mercury and Philology as symbolizing the divine and human intellect, and their marriage as the deification of humanity through intellect.

17. For an analysis of the language of the mysteries in Philology's preparations, see Lenaz 1975, 23–25.

18. Shanzer 1986a, 65–67.

19. Virtue's approval is expressed at 1.23; yet at 1.35ff., when Jupiter wonders whether Philology's attentions will make Mercury forget his job as messenger of the gods, Juno points out that she will not allow Mercury to sleep and reminds Jupiter of Philology's "peruigilia laborata and lucubrationum perennium . . . pallorem" (1.37); Mercury's likely reaction will be to take wing and seek the farthest corners of the universe (1.38): "ut commotis ab eadem suscitatisque pennis extramundanas petere latitudines urgeatur." This is clearly ironic.

20. Shanzer 1986a, 4 and n. 11.

21. For the importance of numerology in late antiquity and its function as a structural principle in the *De Nuptiis,* see LeMoine 1972b, 215–30, which does not, however, note the comic aspect of this passage. See also Hadot 1984, 140–42.

22. Her magical preparations at 2.110 are to remind us of Medea; in a corrupt passage we read of "Colchica . . . fiducia."

23. The rejection of earthly knowledge and the wordless vision of Truth in ignorance becomes very influential after Martianus (though not unknown before) in the writings of pseudo-Dionysius, whose thought leads to such works as Nicholas of Cusa's *De Docta Ignorantia.* Nicholas devotes chapter 1.10

to Philology, which begins: "Nunc inquiramus, quid sibi uelit Martianus, quando ait Philosophiam ad huius trinitatis notitiam ascendere uolentem circulos et sphaeras euomuisse" ("Now let us ask what Martianus means when he says that when Philosophy [an error for Philology] wanted to rise to the notion of this Trinity, she vomited forth circles and spheres").

24. As it is according to Lenaz 1975, 23–25.

25. Lenaz (1975, 23–25) claims that Philology vomits all of her learning; Turcan (1958) argues that Philology vomits only her false learning. In the passage from the *Lexiphanes,* the pedant is forced to vomit a number of archaizing expressions that run counter to the Atticist movement of the second century: μῶν, κᾆτα, ἢ δ' ὅς, ἀμηγέπῃ, λῷστε, δήπουθεν, ἄττα: a similar list of pedantic terms may be found in Gregory Nazianzen *Or.* 4.105. Further, in Lucian's *Charon* 7, Charon claims to be able to speak Homeric Greek because Homer was seasick while being ferried across the river Styx and vomited forth verses; for the possible Cynic (Menippean) origins of this joke, see Helm 1906, 172–73.

26. 2.149: "da nosse poscenti, quid haec aeria latitudo atque atomis perlucentes concurrentibus campi animantum gerant" ("Please tell me, for I do desire to know it, what living things do this ethereal expanse and these fields flashing with colliding atoms sustain").

27. 2.145–46: Periergia, Agrypnia, Epimelia. The first two of these are mentioned at 2.111–12 as well; see n. 13. Johnson, Stahl, and Burge (1971, 39 n. 27) miss the joke, wondering why terms often pejorative seem to be held here in great esteem.

28. 2.119: "o lux nostra" ("you who are our light"); 2.121: "spes atque assertio nostri" ("you who are our hope and the guarantor of our freedom"—i.e., our status as *Liberal* Arts); 2.123: "caput artibus" ("you who are the source of all the Arts").

29. Bie (1894–97) concludes a discussion of the artistic representations of the Muses by pointing to Martianus Capella's extraordinary combinations of Muses and functions as a good reason not to assign the names of the Hesiodic Muses automatically to any given depiction: "Selbst in dieser spätesten Zeit findet man noch vereinzelte Spuren fruherer Willkür . . . bei Martianus Capella."

30. Shanzer 1986a, 40–41, but without an acknowledgment of any comic aspect of Martianus's Muses; Hadot 1984, 146–48, also discusses the significance of these poems in terms of mystical initiation, but does not deal with the attribution of particular fields of study to particular Muses.

31.   scande caeli templa, uirgo, digna tanto foedere;
         te socer subire celsa poscit astra Iuppiter.

32. The poem concludes: "da, pater, aetherios superum conscendere coetus / astrigerumque sacro sub nomine noscere caelum" ("Grant, O Father, that I may rise to the ethereal assemblies of those above, and know, by virtue of your holy name, the heaven that bears the stars"). The poem is also one of the inspirations of the great pivotal poem in the *Consolatio,* 3 m. 9, *O qui*

perpetua. For an analysis of that poem and discussion of its debts to Martianus, see Klingner 1921, 38–67; also the relevant portions of the commentary of Gruber 1978.

33. For example, the topic of Augustine's *De Ordine* is that the study of the arts exists only to lead to an irrational leap of faith; on the pagan side, Porphry *Ad Marc.* 9 makes the point that education is not a function of polymathy but is a rejection of diseases of the soul.

34. 2.208; cf. *Caesars* 307Bff.

35. *Caesars* 336c.

36. 9.889, after Venus speaks and reclines, to everyone's admiration, in the arms of Pleasure: "As a matter of fact, a longing of such ardent desire shook the very son of Atlas that he wanted to abandon the careful preparations he had made for the wedding celebration; so much was it worth to him not to displease Venus." The scene is reminiscent of Demodocus's song of the adultery of Aphrodite and Ares in *Od.* 8.266ff.; cf. especially Hermes' words to Apollo (338–42), expressing his desire to lie, even in chains, next to Aphrodite.

37. Hadot (1984, 154–55) observes that Martianus does not write a work that leads from the sensible to the intelligible, such as Augustine attempts in the *De Ordine*. The Neoplatonic orientation of his learning is occasional, not thoroughgoing; I suggest that the lack of such a progression is at the essence of the *De Nuptiis*.

38. Dialectic is attacked by Mercury's serpent as one "fraudulenta semper argumentatione uersutam" ("ever well versed in deceitful argument," 4.331), and Bacchus, playing here as at Julian *Caesars* 338c the role of soothsayer, calls her a sorceress; Rhetoric kisses Philology's head rather noisily, and the scribe remarks that she couldn't do anything silently, even if she wanted to (5.565); Grammar, the first of the three, is introduced in honorific terms (3.223–28), but Minerva cuts short her discourse when she launches enthusiastically into a discussion of anomaly (3.325–26).

39. Geometry at the end of her discourse takes as praise of herself praise given to Euclid for his constructions, and she jealously snatches his books away from him (6.724); Arithmetic stops herself before she bores the audience (7.802) and so comes off in a decent light.

40. See LeMoine 1972a. LeMoine (1972b, 88) notes also that the descriptions of the heavens in Books 1 and 2 of the *De Nuptiis* (1.42–61, 2.150–67) evoke "a vision of the tremendous distance, vastness, and yet carefully arranged pattern of the heavens." Barthelmess (1974) advances the intriguing idea that the frame story resembles the Diotima story of Plato's *Symposium* and is an allegorical correction of Apuleius's Cupid and Psyche story, having as its goal a more nearly Platonic view of a well-ordered universe accessible to mortals (summarized in *DA* 36 [1975]: 3669A).

41. For food metaphors in father-son dedications and Martianus's play with them, see LeMoine 1991, 361–63.

42. Shanzer (1986a, 42) correctly labels a common definition of the *De*

Nuptiis as an attempt to combine Varro the satirist and Varro the academic as a "partial truth."

43. Hadot (1984, 137–55) discusses Martianus's encyclopedic and mystic tendencies and, arguing that Neoplatonism has much to do with the creation of his and other courses of the Seven Liberal Arts, and that Martianus uses a wide variety of sources, concludes that Varro's encyclopedia cannot be reconstructed from late sources.

Chapter Ten. Fulgentius

1. With a fair amount of confusion, the pattern of the three books is as follows: Book 1 tells of the major gods, goddesses, and abstractions (e.g., Saturn, Neptune; Proserpina, Ceres; Furies, Fates, and Muses); Book 2, goddesses, heroes, and love affairs (e.g., Judgment of Paris, Hercules, Ulysses, Scylla, Leda, Endymion); Book 3, heroes and mortal love affairs (e.g., Hero and Leander, Cupid and Psyche, Myrrha and Adonis, Orpheus and Eurydice). The matter of the organization of the myths deserves further attention. Certainly crucial is the placement of the important Judgment of Paris at the beginning of Book 2.

2. "Placuit Mineruae pellere celibatum," misquoting *De Nuptiis* 1.5: "constituit [sc. Mercurius] pellere caelibatum."

3. Helm 1899, 119–21. Verbal similarities in the two texts include the appearance of Philosophy to Boethius at *Consolation* 1.1 and the appearance of Calliope to Fulgentius at 8.6ff. and 13.19ff. His arguments have convinced Courcelle (1969, 296 n. 8). Gruber (1969, 167 n. 6) prefers not to speak of a direct dependence of Boethius on Fulgentius but quotes approvingly Reichenberger (1954, 7), who speaks of the epiphany of Philosophy in the *Consolation* as an elevation of common late literary possibilities.

4. Helm (1899) argues convincingly for their identity. So also the latest full discussion, Langlois 1964. Stevens (1982, 328 n. 5) allows that the two are probably the same, though without discussion. Further bibliography may be found in Préaux's bibliographical "Addenda" in Helm's edition of Fulgentius, in which all works discussing the matter are marked with an asterisk.

5. Shanzer (1986a, 5–28) argues for a date in the 460s or 470s for the *De Nuptiis*, opposing Cameron (1986), who prefers a date not long after Alaraic's sack of Rome in 410. See also Barnish 1986.

6. Courcelle (1969, 220–23) attempts a balanced appraisal of Fulgentius's output against traditional criticisms, but does so largely to illustrate the narrow confines of literary production in the early sixth century.

7. In the introduction to the *Sermones Antiqui* (111.1–6), the author desires simplicity and clarity: "non faleratis sermonum studentes spumis quam rerum manifestationibus dantes operam lucidandis" ("Not longing for a bejeweled spray of speech as much as taking seriously the illumination of the appearances of things"); cf. *Mit.* 11.12–13 for a similar thought in the mouth of a confused narrator. What follows is all matter-of-fact, being brief defini-

tions of sixty-two obscure words. On the other hand, the *De Aetatibus Mundi et Hominis* ("The Ages of Human History") is a clearly playful lipogrammatic showpiece: the first chapter, an account of the creation according to Genesis in which the letter A and therefore the names Adam and Eva do not appear, is a particularly recommended piece of desperate periphrasis.

8. For a fuller treatment of Fulgentius as an anti-Ovid, see Relihan 1984b.

9. The text follows Lejay's emendation of the end of verse 2, *illa* for *illas;* for a defense of this, see Kenney 1976.

10. Kovacs (1987) makes the convincing point that what the gods have changed in Ovid is his genre, and that the second line of the *Metamorphoses*, a hexameter and not an elegiac, shows that he has been made to write epic.

11. Fulgentius may have learned this mockery of Hesiodic Muses and their inspiration from Persius's prologue (1–3): "I don't recall wetting my lips in the nag's fountain, or having napped on twin-peaked Parnassus, so as to emerge that way instantly as a poet." The later appearance of the Muses, drunk from Hippocrene (8.6–8), also recalls Persius.

12. The Judgment figures prominently in the *Mythologies,* and is described at length at the beginning of Book 2. Fulgentius's idiosyncratic allegorization of this myth is destined to have a great medieval vogue; though the three goddesses were often said to represent three ways of life (intellectual, active, sensual), Fulgentius is the first to condemn the active life and recommend only the intellectual, contemplative life. For the importance of this, see Ehrhart 1987, 23–28, 75–121.

13. For an extended analysis of Satyra as the principle that would unite the opposite worlds of pagan and Christian cultures, see Relihan 1986.

14. Parallels given in Appendix B.

15. *Verg. Cont.*: "quales uatum imagines esse solent, dum adsumptis ad opus conficiendum tabulis stupida fronte arcanum quiddam latranti intrinsecus tractatu submurmurant" ("as the representations of poets customarily are, in which they take up their tablets to write something and, with a stupid look on their face, mutter some secret thing under their breath, their thoughts barking something inside of them").

16. *Verg. Cont.*: "Cui ego: Seponas quaeso caperatos optutus, Ausonum uatum clarissime, rancidamque altioris salsuram ingenii iocundioris quolibet mellis sapore dulciscas" ("I beg you, most illustrious of Italian poets, away with that furrowed brow, and sweeten that foul-selling ill-humor of your lofty mind with some honey-sweet savor").

17. *Verg. Cont.* 86.7, *Mit.* 11.18–19: "homuncule" ("miserable little mortal"); *Verg. Cont.* 86.6–7: "creperum aliquid desipere" ("to be stupid in some obscure way"); *Mit.* 11.18–20: "Unde . . . tantam ignorantiae scientiam, unde tam ratum ordinem ignorandi?"

18. Despite the great debt which Fulgentius owes to the *Metamorphoses* both in style and in various matters of detail (some similarities are given in nn. 4, 31, and 40 to the translation, Appendix B; Psyche and her lamp are referred to twice in the prologue [3.20–24.12, 11.6–10]), the myth of Cupid and Psyche (66.19–70.2) is treated very contemptuously. It is given great

space, but the narrator moves from the remarkable opinion that it is simply told (66.19–20) to boredom with its details (he refuses to give specifics of Psyche's labors, 68.16–20), and he quickly accuses Apuleius of amassing lies (68.21–69.2). We may consult the probably fictitious Aristophontes of Athens if we want more of this (Baldwin [1988a, 41] expresses no particular opinion on the historicity of this author). He proceeds to give only an outline of the allegory, describing the relation of Psyche (Soul) to Venus (Lust) and Cupid (Desire). He concludes (69.28–70.2): "But those who read the story itself in Apuleius will understand the remaining things that I did not say from the substance of my discussion here." Fulgentius (speaking through Philosophia, though the name of the allegorist has not been repeated since first mentioned in the second myth of the first book) accuses Apuleius of muddling a story that should have been obvious, dismisses him, and proceeds to the next allegory.

19. Prologue to Book 2, 35.20–24: "Therefore, if you know more than these, praise that most unscheming mind that did not withhold what it possessed; if you had not known of them before, you now have the arena of my inquiries in which to exercise the wrestling of your intelligence." Prologue to Book 3, 58.20–24: "I have commended the labor of my naiveté to your most unbiased judgment, confident that you will not out of jealousy demean what has been poorly comprehended, but will, in your great wisdom, correct it." Much of this has the ring of the clichéd protestation of ignorance and of the *captatio beneuolentiae,* but is not without its thematic significance in the whole of the work.

20. Shanzer 1986a, 40–41 and n. 80, where she suggests "the lewd Muses of Fulgentius' *Mythologiae* would repay a close examination."

21. Fulgentius alludes at 25.5–6 to Psalm 32.2, "sed et lex diuina decacordum dicit psalterium"; at 36.6–8 he quotes Psalm 1.1; at 39.4 Solomon (Ecclesiasticus 11.29); at 41.21–22 Ezekiel 16.4. Further, he mentions without any introduction at 60.17 the phrase "initium sapientiae timor est" (cf. Proverbs 1.7, Psalm 110.10, Ecclesiasticus 1.16), and at 59.18–20 illustrates the meaning of the prefix ἀντι- by *antichristus.* The Judgment of Paris (36.1–37.20) also mentions bishops, priests, and monks as exponents of the contemplative life, which in pagan times was the province of philosophers. Gersh 1986, 2.762–65, distinguishes the four types of interpretations of myth: metaphysical, physical, astronomical, and moral.

22. For example, Athenagoras *Legatio* 24–27: cf. Appendix B, n. 65.

23. Baldwin 1988a is a complete treatment.

24. Fulgentius preserves a dozen unique fragments of Petronius. For a full treatment of Fulgentius's place in the history of Petronius's text, see Ciaffi 1963; Baldwin (1988a, 50–53) has his doubts.

25. *Serm. Ant.* 115.8–10: "Varro in mistagogorum libro ait: 'Semoneque inferius derelicto deum depinnato orationis attollam alloquio'" ("Although Semo has been abandoned down below, I shall raise up the god by means of the winged address of speech"). Astbury denies in his apparatus to this fragment (*Fragmenta falso uel temere Menippeis adscripta* II) that Fulgentius's au-

thority carries any weight. At least one of Varro's *Menippeans* survived entire into late antiquity; see Shanzer 1986b.

Chapter Eleven. Ennodius

1. One example will suffice (de Labriolle 1924, 490): "his writings consisted of little else than uttering mere trifles in harmonious and well-balanced phrases, or in verse formed on Vergilian *recipes*. His 297 letters are of an elegant turn, and incredibly void of ideas. . . . Most of his productions . . . betray the superficial and entirely academic character of the culture with which he was enamored." A more sympathetic account of his work may be found in Alfonsi 1975, which describes him as a defender of faith and learning in the face of barbarism. Current appraisal of Ennodian studies in Carini 1987; see also the valuable introduction and bibliography of Cesa 1988.

2. Riché (1976, 24–32) discusses Ennodius's correspondents and their educational careers.

3. Rallo Freni 1978.

4. Riché 1976, 86–95.

5. Riché (1976, 95–97) discusses Caesarius of Arles, Sidonius Apollinaris, and Ennodius as three examples of nervousness about the function of pagan literature for the faithful that prove the existence of an injunction against bishops reading such works. Some passages concerning Ennodius's distrust of pagan poetry are collected and discussed in Rallo Freni 1978, 834–41; some examples of the antirhetorical topos are collected in Alfonsi 1975, 308: "ego ipsa studiorum liberalium nomina iam detestor" (*Ep.* 9.1: "now I despise even the words 'Liberal Arts'"); "cessent anilium commenta poetarum, fabulosa repudietur antiquitas!" (*Ep.* 1.9: "The lies of the old women poets must stop; antiquity with its mythology must be rejected!"). The latter dates after his elevation to the episcopate. See also Riché 1976, 96 and nn. 110–13.

6. Cf. the concluding poem (26): "Germina clara / sumite sicci / uerba parentis." Ennodius adopts the pose of a father in imitation of the Latin tradition of father-son instructional literature; Ennodius was never married.

7. Details in Riché 1976, 26–28.

8. Rallo Freni 1971; this summarizes conclusions drawn in her edition, pp. xxv–xxxi. See also Couvreur 1933–34.

9. De Labriolle 1924, 490. In the fundamental article of Fontaine 1960 (see the praise and reservations accorded it in Carini 1987, 328–31), this shameful praise of the unjust argument is not assigned merely to the influence of traditional school exercises but is seen in the light of Aristophanes' presentation of the λόγος ἄδικος in *Clouds* 889ff. (col. 416).

10. Cf. Sidonius Apollinaris *Ep.* 2.10, 4.8, 4.11, 4.18, 5.17, 7.17, 8.9, 8.11, 9.13, 9.14, 9.15, 9.16.

11. Succinctly put in Cross and Livingstone 1974, 459, s.v. "Ennodius, St., Magnus Felix": "His work is probably the last serious attempt to combine a fundamentally pagan culture with the profession of the Christian creed."

12. Fontaine (1960, 402) notes that the plan of study advanced in the *Paraenesis* is practically pagan in a number of points; and Fontaine sees in the mixture of prose and verse, in the personifications of Virtues and Arts, and in the exaltation of the power of Rhetoric, a *De Nuptiis* writ small.

13. Critics often despair of Ennodius's general ignorance of the quadrivium, and this reduction of the trivium to rhetoric. See Fontaine 1960, 404–12, for a discussion of Ennodius's education; see also the neat summary of this in Carini 1987, 330–31.

14. Certain preliminary exercises in composition could be the province either of grammatical or of rhetorical instruction, but not speeches before popular assemblies or in courtrooms; see Curtius 1953, 442. For the blurring of the distinctions between grammaticus and rhetor in Ennodius's time, see Riché 1976, 23–25.

15. "Haec ergo, dulcissimi, et adsequi contendite et adepta custodite."

16. See n. 9.

17. A point made by Carini 1987, 335 n. 21, in response to the description of its educational goals in Rallo Freni 1971.

18. Martianus similarly presents himself as an inept teacher of a (real) son; he tells, as Macrobius does in the *Saturnalia*, a tale told by others in the hopes of instructing his son. For Martianus's subversion of the topoi of father-son instruction, see LeMoine 1991, 360–63; Ennodius is not included in this valuable discussion. Martianus and Ennodius prove to teach well because they show the ways in which they cannot teach; but Ennodius deserves credit for the thoroughgoing parody of father-son instructional literature. There is something of Varro here. In the *Satyricon*, Echion the freedman tells his son to pursue education because it pays off: it puts bread on the table (46.7) and is a treasure-house (46.8). But Echion aims in fact to crush the independence of the son he tries to instruct, and his language reveals a number of errors that arise from affectations of education and hyperurbanisms (Boyce 1991, 81–85). It is, however, unlikely that Ennodius learned of the self-parodic possibilities of such instruction from Petronius.

19. Riché (1976, 96 n. 110) refers to Ennodius's *Ep.* 2.6.4 (Vogel 38.19–21, to Pomerius) as containing a similar contrast between the *pompa* of rhetoric and the profession of faith.

20. "Christi militis insitum rigorem / elumbem patimur cauere ductum." Fontaine (1960, 412) notes the small connection between this poem and Ennodius's earlier descriptions of the nature of poetry and suggests the development of a Christian theory of poetry here. Carini (1987, 331 n. 7) speaks of the presentation of the two aspects of poetry as an example of the superficiality born of Ennodius's ideological "hybridism."

21. Riché (1976, 49) notes that Ennodius was frankly baffled by Boethius's love of advanced study (*Ep.* 7.13).

22. Riché (1976, 40 and n. 158) discusses Cassiodorus's similar sentiments (*Var.* 9.21).

23. 17: "audite tamen et carmen, alieni quod nobis suggerit ludus officii."

24. *Dictio* 12: "uestris umbonibus directa ab aduersariis tela repelluntur" ("the weapons cast by the enemy bounce off of your shields") (example from Alfonsi 1975, 308).

25. Though for Boethius he reserves true praise of learning (21).

26. 15 (Rhetoric speaks of conscience): "Through me, even a dark conscience is suffused in splendor; through me, though it glow with its own brilliance, it is overwhelmed by sudden night, even if it is innocent of shadows: it is a thing that neither innocence can trust nor guilt dare sigh with relief about."

27. See Chapter 9, n. 27.

28. Curtius 1953, 443 and n. 30. His example is the Christian Priscian, whose book of rhetorical exercises, the *Praeexercitamina*, advocates, among other things, the use of pagan mythological detail as appropriate adornment. Curtius considers Ennodius a somewhat similar case in the West.

29. *De Planctu*, prose 5. The intellectual background of Alan's moral use of grammatical metaphors is provided by Ziolkowski 1985.

Chapter Twelve. Conclusion

1. Gill 1979, 64 and n. 1.

2. Gill 1979, 76-77.

3. For the relation of Plato and Gill's thesis concerning Plato's understanding of fiction to the nature and history of the romance, see Reardon 1991, 62-69.

4. Coulter (1976, 21-22) discusses Neoplatonic reactions to the "doubts which Plato expressed in the 10th Book of the *Republic* about the very *possibility* of literature representing anything but phenomenal reality."

5. Gill 1979, 77.

6. I speak of the esoteric Aristotle; the dialogues of the exoteric Aristotle, whose style was held in wide acclaim, are almost completely lost to us.

7. Of course, we do not need to accept Socrates' claim to ignorance and believe that in Plato's dialogues his is an open mind in disinterested pursuit of the truth; see Dover 1980, viii, for an eloquent rejection of this. But as a literary motif, Socratic ignorance has great influence, and the accounts of Socrates' dissatisfaction with philosophy are the direct models for Menippus's in Lucian's *Icaromenippus* and *Necyomantia*. Lucian's descriptions of Socrates are not uniform, but at *Dial. Mort.* 6.5, Socrates complains to Menippus that everyone called it irony when he said that he knew nothing; Menippus, of course, took Socrates at his word all along. For the fortunes of Socrates in later philosophy, see Long 1988.

8. Anderson (1982b, 64 and n. 10) speaks of the *catascopia* in Lucian's works as an extension of an Old Comedy device, filtered through Plato's *Phaedo*. In the *Phaedo* (108E ff.), Socrates describes the world, imagined from above (110B: εἴ τις ἄνωθεν θεῷτο), as a series of depressions on a great sphere, each unable to communicate with the other. This could also be a starting point for Menippean satire, as Socrates can easily be seen as describ-

ing an even greater marvel with which to replace the marvelous physical theories of the philosophers whom he followed in his youth but later rejected (such as Anaxagoras: 97D ff.). Menippus in *Icaromenippus* 5–9 would represent a parody of this: his account of his intellectual growth also has him rejecting the theories of the natural philosophers only to embark on a ridiculous journey that implies a universe far more absurd. But not that the *Phaedo* describes no fantastic journey; for this we look to the Myth of Er.

9. Anderson 1980.

10. See in particular the exhaustive work of Westmann 1955.

11. Crönert 1906, 5–7, contains fragments of the works against Plato's *Euthydemus* and *Lysis*.

12. Colotes' criticisms are discussed as part of the Epicurean reaction against the habits of Stoic allegorization of myth in Pépin 1958, 137–38. Coulter (1976, 45–60) does not discuss this passage from Proclus's *Commentary* but does treat related passages in which Proclus defends both Homeric poetry and Plato's criticism of it.

13. "hanc fabulam Cicero licet ab indoctis quasi ipse ueri conscius doleat irrisam, exemplum tamen stolidae reprehensionis uitans excitari narraturum quam reuiuescere maluit." Cf. the similar statement in the *Commentary on the Dream of Scipio* by Favonius Eulogius, 1.1 (Scarpa 1974): "non fabulosa, ut ille, assimulatione commentus est sed sollertis somnii rationabili quadam imaginatione composuit uidelicet scite significans haec quae de animae immortalitate dicerentur caeloque, ⟨non⟩ somniantium philosophorum esse commenta nec fabulas incredibiles quas Epicurei derident, sed prudentium coniecturas" ("He did not create whole cloth, as the other did, by means of a fictional representation, but wrote using a certain rational, imaginative faculty of a wise man's dream, evidently making the clever point that these things which are asserted of the immortality of the soul and of the heavens are not the lies of dreaming philosophers nor fictions unworthy of belief [such as the Epicureans mock], but are the conjectures of reasonable people").

14. Dronke (1974, 13–78) prefaces his discussion of medieval fiction with a discussion of a commentary of William of Conches on the *Commentary on the Dream of Scipio*.

15. Brief analysis of the two treatments is found in Westmann 1955, 34–38; Whittaker 1923, 58–59; and the notes on Macrobius *Comm.* 1.2 in Scarpa 1981. For Porphyry as the primary source for Macrobius's *Commentary*, see Stahl 1952, 23–39.

16. 106.14–16: Ἡμεῖς δὲ πρὸς τοὺς τοιούσδε λόγους οὐχ ὅσα μόνον ὁ φιλοσοφώτατος κατέτεινεν Πορφύριος ἔχοιμεν ἂν ἀπαντῶντες λέγειν.

17. I interpret the phrase at 107.14, προσθετέον δὲ τούτοις καὶ ὅτι κτλ., to mean that Proclus's additional arguments begin at this point. But there is some overlap between Proclus at this point and Macrobius's reply to Colotes at *Comm.* 1.2.3–6, which would point to Porphyry as a common source.

18. "ceterum cum ad summum et principem omnium deum, qui apud Graecos τἀγαθόν, qui πρῶτον αἴτιον nuncupatur, tractatus se audet attollere,

uel ad mentem, quem Graeci νοῦν appellant, originales rerum species, quae
ἰδέαι dictae sunt, continentem, ex summo natam et profectam deo: cum de
his inquam loquuntur summo deo et mente, nihil fabulosum penitus at-
tingunt, sed siquid de his adsignare conantur quae non sermonem tantum
modo sed cogitationem quoque humanam superant, ad similitudines et exempla confugiunt."

19. Westmann 1955, 38.

20. De Lacy (1948, 20–23) makes the point that Epicurus himself rejected
the use of poetry and all the forms of popularization; later Epicureans found
room for poetry and the popular discourse, but De Lacy makes no reference
to the use of popular *fictions* by Epicureans.

21. Dronke 1974, 119–43: the commentary is edited by Westra (1986).

22. To name some recent examples: J. E. Smith 1982, Zaslavsky 1981, and
Hirsch 1971. Rosen (1987, 1–2) makes the nice observation that as both recol-
lection and myth seek "to transcend history in a return to the origins," all
Platonic writings are myths in a very important sense.

23. Plutarch's *Banquet of the Seven Wise Men* occupies an intermediate position. Julian and Martianus show how Menippean satire and symposium can
overlap; I prefer not to follow Frye in assigning an author like Athenaeus,
through the designation "anatomy," to the Menippean genre. The relations
between the two genres are discussed in Relihan 1992, 228–30.

24. See Gruber 1978, 16–24, and the diagram between pp. 16 and 17.
O'Daly (1991) demonstrates the Romanness of the themes and the functions
of the poetry.

25. Lerer 1985, 4–93.

26. Tränkle (1977) argues that the lack of a poem, among other things,
means the *Consolation* is unfinished and that a sixth book is missing; O'Daly
(1991, 28–29) accepts with Gruber the work's completeness. Lerer (1985,
235–36) suggests that in the prisoner's silence the authority of God is asserted over that of Philosophy's articulated speech. Janson (1964, 116) notes
that Boethius shares with Fulgentius a reversal of an opening convention:
one expects a prose preface to a verse work, not a verse preface to a prose
work; Boethius's concluding lack of poem is similarly striking. Scheible
(1972, 10) argues that poetry becomes less important in the course of the
work, but this ought not make a concluding poem irrelevant.

27. Shanzer 1984, 362–66.

28. For these arguments, see Relihan 1990c, 187–88.

29. 2 m. 8.28–30 ("O felix hominum genus, / si uestros animos amor / quo
caelum regitur regat!) echoes 1 m. 5.46–48 (Rapidos, rector, comprime fluc-
tus / et quo caelum regis immensum / firma stabiles foedere terras). For the
overtones of the Lord's prayer here, see Klingner 1921, 5–6.

30. See Klingner 1921, 83–84. Gibbon's famous words are apposite (*Decline and Fall,* chap. 39): "Such topics of consolation, so obvious, so vague, or
so abstruse, are ineffectual to subdue the feelings of human nature."

31. 5.1.4–5: "Festino, inquit, debitum promissionis absoluere uiamque tibi
qua patriam reueharis aperire. Haec autem etsi perutilia cognitu tamen a

propositi nostri tramite paulisper auersa sunt, uerendumque est ne deuiis fatigatus ad emetiendum rectum iter sufficere non possis."

32. 5.6.25: "Hic si dicas quod euenturum deus uidet id non euenire non posse, quod autem non potest non euenire id ex necessitate contingere, meque ad hoc nomen necessitatis adstringas, fatebor rem quidem solidissimae ueritatis, sed cui uix aliquis nisi diuini speculator accesserit." Philosophy has admitted before that there are higher sources of wisdom than herself. At 4.6.8 she would seem to speak so of Hermetic wisdom: cf. Shanzer 1983b.

33. "Magna uobis est, si dissimulare non uultis, necessitas indicta probitatis cum ante oculos agitis iudicis cuncta cernentis."

34. See Shanzer 1983a; parallels between the *Elegy* and the *Consolation* are noted both in Agozzino 1970 and Spaltenstein 1983; an English translation of the *Elegies* may be found in Lind 1988, 307–36. Barnish (1990) argues that all six of the *Elegies* reflect the *Consolation;* we differ in our evaluations of the character of Boethius in the *Third Elegy.*

35. See Chadwick 1981, 244–47.

36. So Uhlfelder 1981.

37. See Chadwick 1981, 251.

38. Frye 1957, 312: "Boethius' *Consolation of Philosophy,* with its dialogue form, its verse interludes and its pervading tone of contemplative irony, is a pure anatomy, a fact of considerable importance for the understanding of its vast influence." It would seem unlikely, for example, that the otherwise skeptical Chaucer would be so devoted to a dogmatic text; Payne (1981, 77–79) describes the action of the *Consolation* that Chaucer admires as an initial gaining of freedom, when the prisoner realizes that his old theories cannot account for his current situation, and an ultimate loss of freedom, as Philosophy duns into him lessons and constructs that overlook embarrassing reality.

39. In the *Juppiter Confutatus,* Cyniscus questions Zeus on the relation of the gods to fate, and on the irreconcilability of divine Pronoia with free will; he wonders also why the guilty go free, and Zeus ends the discussion in disgust. See also *Dial. Mort.* 24, in which Sostratus the thief escapes his punishment by pleading Fate and Necessity. Further connections between Boethius and Lucian in Kirk 1982.

40. Discussed in Relihan 1990a; for the poem as an analogue to the *Consolation,* see pp. 127–29.

41. For this and other possible biblical allusions, see Chadwick 1981, 237–38.

42. Chadwick (1981, 249) calls the *Consolation* a non-Christian work by a Christian author; for similarity of Christian thought and Neoplatonic learning in Boethius, see Wallis 1972, 167–68; Gersh (1986, 2.647–54) speaks of Christianity as playing only a subordinate role in the *Consolation,* accounting for the absence of certain un-Christian Neoplatonic ideas, such as henads. O'Daly (1991, 24–26) argues nicely against seeing the *Consolation* as a work whose Christianity is "just beneath the surface."

43. Job is present on every page; but surely due to Boethius is the complaint at the beginning that the narrator is the victim of corrupted officials

and bribed magistrates, and that the world around him shows unmistakably that there is no justice. For a general discussion of the work, see Fontaine 1965.

44. Seneca the philosopher and Paul's fictive correspondent saved Seneca the satirist to some extent. There is one medieval commentary on the *Apocolocyntosis* (Clairmont 1980) which may belong to the beginning of the fourteenth century.

45. Reckoning eight hundred years from 275 B.C. to A.D. 525; the second range of figures follows Shanzer's arguments for a publication date in the 460s or 470s for Martianus.

46. The Menippean satires of this period and their background are accessible and understandable thanks to a number of recent excellent and useful works: Wetherbee 1972 and 1973; Stock 1972; Dronke 1974, 1978, and 1988. The translation of Alan of Lille's *Complaint of Nature* (Sheridan, 1980) needs to be used with caution. The recently discovered prose prologue to the *Complaint* has been edited by Hudry 1989.

47. Dronke 1978, 8.

48. Wetherbee 1973, 9.

49. Sheridan 1980, 35–54, is a detailed summary of argument and interpretation.

50. So too is Fulgentius's narrator an incompetent teller of myths. For the importance of Nature's lack of understanding of the myths by which she is to be kept veiled from mortals, see the analysis of the *De Planctu* in Wetherbee 1972, 188–211, esp. 196–97.

Appendix A. Greek Prosimetric Romances

1. Parsons 1971.

2. Parsons 1974. The remains are translated with an introduction by Gerald N. Sandy in Reardon 1989, 816–18.

3. Lines 39–44 = *Orestes* 1155–57: οὐκ ἔστιν οὐδὲν κρεῖσσον ἢ φίλος σαφής, / οὐ πλοῦτος, οὐδὲ χρυσός· ἀλόγιστον δέ τι / τὸ πλῆθος ἀντάλλαγμα γενναίου φίλου ("There is nothing better than a certain friend, neither money nor gold. The multitude is a valueless thing, compared with a noble friend"). The texts of Euripides read οὐ τυραννίς ("nor kingship") for οὐδὲ χρυσός. It is uncertain whether this is a genuine variant, a free adaptation, an error, or an intended misquotation (by the author or another speaker). The quotation lacks any sort of introduction.

4. Parsons 1971, 65–66.

5. Parsons 1974, 35 n. 1.

6. Merkelbach 1973. See the sensible objections of Reardon 1976, esp. 90–98.

7. As pointed out by Parsons 1974, 35.

8. Parsons 1971, 65 and n. 58; further on the meter of the piece, see Merkelbach 1973, 90–92, "Exkurs über das Sotadeum."

9. Cataudella 1975a; the argument is presented in modified form in Cataudella 1975b. The suggestion is opposed by Astbury 1977.

10. Further on Cybele in Varro in Romano 1974.

11. Cataudella (1975a, 42 n. 3) refers in particular to Varro's *Hercules Socraticus*.

12. Haslam 1981.

13. Haslam 1981, 39.

14. For Lollianus as sensational fiction, see Winkler 1980; fragments translated by Gerald N. Sandy in Reardon 1989, 809–12. The text there translated needs to be modified in the light of emendations and criticisms offered in Browne 1982 and Browne 1989, 239.

15. Reardon (1991, 42–45) discusses briefly the associations of Roman and Greek fiction.

16. Bartoňková (1985) notes that *Iolaus* is closer to Roman than Greek habits of verse insertion in prosimetra; but elsewhere Bartoňková (1988) argues that *Iolaus* and *Tinouphis* taken together suggest either Greek authors influenced by Varro's example or an otherwise unattested tradition of Greek, Hellenistic prosimetric writing.

17. The *True History* used to be regarded as a parody of Antonius Diogenes, but a wide range of literary parody is involved: see Morgan 1985, and C. P. Jones 1986, 53–54, whose arguments are cautiously approved in the introduction to Reardon's translation of the *True History* in Reardon 1989, 619 and n. 1. Lucian's narrator claims the *Odyssey* (*Ver. Hist.* 1.3) as the ultimate precedent for his literary play. For the *True History*'s relation to the tradition of parody of Platonic mythmaking, see Gill 1979, 77.

18. Reardon (1991, 166–67) is tempted by *Iolaus* and *Tinouphis* to suspect that important aspects of the romance form may be as old as the third century B.C.

19. As argued by Astbury (1977).

Appendix B. The Prologue of Fulgentius's Mythologies

1. "quod edas inquiras quam quod dicas inuenias": *edas*, "eat," may suggest *edas*, "publish, narrate": "you search for words but do not find proper expression."

2. Identified in the incipits as one Catus (or Cantia) *presbiterus Cartaginis*. He is not noticed in *PLRE* II.

3. Salmasius here and at 7.1 (but not 14.5) emends *uernulitate* to *uernilitate*, "coarse jesting"; and Souter (1957) defines *uernulitas* as "talkativeness, saucy or blunt wit." I prefer to preserve *uernulitate* in all three places in the meaning "native wit, homebred charm," the word being derived from *uerna*, "homeborn slave, native."

4. "ut feriatas affatim tuarum aurium sedes lepido quolibet susurro permulceam"; cf. Apuleius *Met.* 1.1: "auresque tuas beniuolas lepido susurro permulceam." For a similar adaptation of Apuleius, cf. 10.16–17.

5. "rugosam sulcis anilibus . . . fabulam"; cf. Martianus Capella *De Nuptiis* 9.997: "Habes anilem, Martiane, fabulam." *anilem* is Willis's conjecture for *senilem.*

6. This contrast of wit and boring study (as typified by burning the midnight oil) is also found in the *De Nuptiis* 1.2 and 9.997; cf. also Varro's *Menippeans*, F 219, F 573. Fulgentius's *commentus sum* is reminiscent of *Satura comminiscens* in *De Nuptiis* 1.2: in different ways, both mean "concocted," or better, "pulled out of thin air."

7. In Lucian's *True History* (2.33) we read of a similar function assigned to the pre-Socratic Antiphon, the dream interpreter. He is the prophet in charge of the oracle on the Island of Dreams, near the temples of Truth and Deceit, established as such by Sleep himself. Fulgentius mentions Antiphon as one of a number of dream interpreters at *Mit.* 24.17.

8. "Sulpicillae procacitas": the immediate source is Ausonius *Cento Nuptialis* 218.11 Peiper: "prurire opusculum Sulpiciae, frontem caperare." Ausonius's Sulpicia is named again, specifically, at 13.3. Ausonius, like Martial (10.35, 10.38), seems to refer not to the Augustan poet but to a later namesake. Psyche derives from Apuleius's *Metamorphoses*, which Fulgentius attempts to allegorize in Book 3, 66.19–70.2.

9. "neque illam quae ui maritum Fedriam in tumulum duxit": corrupt. Meleager's death through the agency of Althaea's torch seems to lie behind this; Phaedra (if she is meant by Fedria) does not cause Theseus's death (or Hippolytus's, for that matter) by means of a torch. One is forced to emend for the sake of grammar, if not of sense; my translation reflects *Fedrae.*

The word *ui* (by force) is strange, and Muncker's two suggestions are at least interesting: "illam quae privignum Phaedrae in tumulum duxit" (the stepson of Phaedra is Hippolytus, identified by this phrase at *Priapea* 19.6); "illam quae bimaritum Phaedrae in tumulum duxit" (Phaedra's husband Theseus could be described as twice-married; perhaps the story reported in Plutarch [*Thes.* 35.7–8] that Theseus died by a fall from a cliff once involved a deceptive light).

10. Fulgentius speaks of the *Somnium Scipionis*, no doubt known to him through Macrobius's *Commentary*, whose introduction also discusses philosophical and unphilosophical myths. There is, however, no torch in Cicero's work, unless "torch" now is a metaphor for "guiding principle." It is appropriate to reject the *Dream of Scipio* here, as its *catascopia* is not a Menippean one, and Scipio sees eternal verities.

11. Halcyone was transformed into a seabird along with her husband Ceyx after his death and her sympathetic suicide (Ovid *Met.* 11.410ff.).

12. "memorum angina improbior": *memorum* ("of mindful things/people") seems to be an error; I follow the manuscripts and read *merorum*, "of griefs."

13. An illogical hyperbole. The Pactolus is supposed to be a gold-bearing river because Midas washed his hands in it when he wanted to be rid of his golden touch. With his power intact, Midas could pay any tax. Fulgentius deals with this myth in Book 2, p. 50.5–24.

14. "merces quippe gentilis fuerat, si uel ad manendum clausos relin-

querent." I take *fuerat* as equivalent to *fuisset,* and *si uel* here as equivalent to *si quid;* for *relinquo* with two accusatives, cf. 6.3–4: "terrorem . . . miles hostis heredem relinquerat" ("the soldiers left behind terror for the heir of their enemy"). The passage may be corrupt.

15. Probably referring to the Vandal king Gunthamund, no great patron of the arts, ruling from 484–96; it is not clear which barbarian invasion Fulgentius has in mind. It is evidently Gunthamund who restored land to some who had lost it to the repressions of Gaiseric, as implied in the *Tablettes Albertini;* cf. Bright 1987, 12–13.

16. In *Verg. Cont.* 91.6ff. Fulgentius has the very plausible idea that the shipwreck in *Aen.* 1 is a symbol of rebirth, and that Aeneas's actions at Carthage mirror the stages of infant development; a similar idea is at work here.

17. In the *De Aetatibus Mundi et Hominis* 174.25–175.3 there is a cripple cured by Paul (Acts 3) who is described in similar terms: "iam aetate prouectus gressu pererrare didicit libero"; here too the image is one of rebirth.

18. "mauricatos quod aiunt . . . gressus": Souter (1957), citing this passage, takes *mauricatus* as "timid," but the adjective *Maurus* can be a poetic expression for "African," which seems better to suit the context here. Yet *mauricatos* seems to be a comic formation in this sense; the adjective as derived from *murex,* the sharp seashell from which purple dye comes, can also mean "blood-red" or "sharp"; cf. Pliny *N.H.* 20.262.

19. "formidine menti nondum extersa"; this despite the fact that the coming of the narrator's lord and king removed all terror from the world (5.16: "pauores abstersit"). Perhaps this helps to characterize the narrator as one of weak resolve, as he will prove to be in his meeting with Calliope and Satyra.

20. As Aeneas, speaking to Dido, says the Trojans did (*Aen.* 2.27–30).

21. "Triptolemicum . . . dentem": the plow. Triptolemus is said to have brought the arts of agriculture to humans.

22. *meterem,* "I was reaping," seems inappropriate; "I was traversing" is the expected meaning, for which *metirem, metarem* (Ellis), or *metarer* would suffice.

23. This overdone description of the *locus amoenus* and its intertwining greenery strangely resembles some sophistic excesses of the comic romance of Achilles Tatius (1.1.3, 1.15.2–4).

24. The poem, twenty-eight lines in Helm's edition, consists of fourteen trochaic tetrameters in the manner and mood of the *Peruigilium Veneris.* Cameron (1984, 223), who attributes the *Peruigilium* to Tiberianus, notes that Fulgentius twice quotes (I think the resemblance is more general) another poem which Cameron assigns to Tiberianus, an address to the Muses preserved and discussed by Augustine (*De Musica* 3.2.3 = Morel *FPL* 184–85, number 86 of the *Incerti*). In some of its details, the poem here is comically reprised in the Vergilian pastiche at the beginning of the *Allegorical Content of Vergil* (85.5–9):

> Vos, Eliconiades, neque enim mihi sola uocanda est
> Calliope, *conferte gradum,* date praemia menti.
> Maius opus moueo; neque enim mihi sufficit una.

> *Currite, Pierides,* uos enim mea ⟨maxima cura,⟩
> *Parrasias niueo conpellite pectine cordas.*

Cf. *Mit.* 7.9: "ferte gradum properantes"; 8.2–3: "Pharrasia candicanti / dente lyra concrepet."

25. A city at the base of Mount Helicon, where also is found the font of Hippocrene, which sprang up where Bellerophon's hoof struck the ground. The belittling of the Muses here recalls the beginning of the prologue of Persius's *Satires.*

26. Hesiod; the reference is pointed, as his Muses claimed to tell lies as well (*Theog.* 27–28). Baldwin (1988a, 46) notes that Fulgentius's one attempt to cite Hesiod (*Mit.* p. 60.1–2) is spurious (frag. 381 Merkelbach–West).

27. "quicquid exantlata gazis / uestra promunt horrea." Plasberg would emend *gazis* to *Grais,* "emptied by the Greeks."

28. Referring only to the *Eclogues,* not to his other works.

29. Homer was often assigned to Maeonia, in Lydia; cf. *Mit.* 10.8–9. The work referred to is the comic *Bactrachomyomachia,* or "The Battle of the Frogs and Mice," attributed to Homer in antiquity.

30. "ad meum uetusta carmen / saecla nuper confluant"; cf. Ovid *Met.* 1.4: "ad mea perpetuum deducite tempora carmen."

31. *ternae:* Barth emended to *ter ternae,* or nine, the proper number of the Muses. But what we have here is another Judgment of Paris; cf. Apuleius's description of it, and Venus's transparent beauties, at *Met.* 10.30–33. For Fulgentius's interpretation of the Judgment of Paris at the beginning of Book 2 (*Mit.* 36.1–37.20), in which both the active/kingly and the sensuous life are rejected in favor of the contemplative, see Ehrhart 1987, 23–28.

32. The logical connection here is difficult. Perhaps it is the seductive aspect of Calliope's appearance and actions, something the narrator never saw before, that makes him seem both to know and not to know who she is. As much is made of the narrator's reclining position (reprised later in the prologue, when he is discovered at night in his bed), we should perhaps relate it to the allegorization of the Judgment of Paris, in which the contemplative, active, and sensuous ways of life are associated with the three actions of Psalm 1.1: *stetit, abiit, sedet* (stood still, went away, sits).

33. "novellos . . . frutices": *frutex* usually means "shrub," or, more rarely, "trunk (of a tree)."

34. Home of the royal court of the Macedonians; Calliope speaks obliquely of Hellenistic literature and Alexandria in particular. Is Fulgentius speaking of the rise of Alexandrian literature in the period between the sack of Rome in 410 and 500? The allegory of the myth of Hero and Leander in Book 3 (63.6–23) may point to a knowledge of Musaeus (late fifth century) even if we do not insist that Fulgentius read him in Greek.

35. *reptarent:* Helm in his Preface (p. VII) thinks that due to a confusion of *pt* and *ct* in Fulgentius this is a form of *rectare,* defined in DuCange as "bring a charge" or "bring to court." It could also be a corruption of *raptarent,* "they seize," which in context would mean roughly the same.

36. The sentence is corrupt: "preserves its authors for posterity" attempts

suos . . . extendunt; "if someone" fills a lacuna; "crafty" is *catus,* for which Scriverius suggested *cados,* from κάδος, "bucket, urn"; "pinnacle of power," *ipsis potestatum culminibus,* suggests the literary fame to be won by a Vandal court poet.

37. "Anacreonticis iamdudum nouus mistes initiatus es sacris": Baldwin (1988a, 39) observes: "Fulgentius may as often be deliberately perverse in here solemnising a poet best remembered as libertine and drunkard." He adds that the Greek-Coptic glossary of Dioscorus of Aphrodito defines Anacreon as "the drunkard that sings, the poet."

38. I read *Satyra* for *satyra;* Calliope seems to refer to the person who will later appear to the narrator.

39. "redde quod deuerbas sipnotico": difficult and probably corrupt. *deuerbo* seems to refer to interpretation; and as the narrator set out to be an interpreter of dreams (3.20) I take *sipnotico* as reflecting *hypnoticon,* "dream book." Souter (1957) takes *sipnoticon* to mean "writing"; Helm thinks it a corruption of *ipnotice,* "dreaming."

40. Adaptation from Apuleius *Met.* 1.1: "modo si papyrum Aegyptiam argutia Nilotici calami inscriptam non spreueris inspicere." Egypt has associations of fantastic fiction here, not of Hermetic wisdom as it does in Martianus.

41. The references in the next two sentences are to the stories of Zeus and Europa, Zeus and Danae, Venus and Adonis, Zeus and Ganymede, and Zeus and Leda. Of these, only the last two are treated at any length in the *Mythologies:* Ganymede at 31.10–24, Leda at 54.1–55.13. Hero and Psyche were paired earlier at 4.1–4; Hero and Leander are allegorized at 63.6–23.

42. For *Aricinam* I read *Nonacrinam,* "Arcadian," referring to Callisto, whom Jupiter seduced after taking on the form of a maiden (cf. Ovid *Met.* 2.401ff.). The last clause, "dum quareret Iuppiter quod magis esse uellet quam fuerat," echoes Ovid's description of Jupiter's decision to become an eagle in order to steal away Ganymede (*Met.* 10.156–57: "et inuentum est aliquid, quod Iuppiter esse, / quam quod erat, mallet"). Details in Relihan 1988.

43. "mutatas . . . uanitates manifestare cupimus." Here, Fulgentius opposes himself to Ovid *Met* 1.1–2: "in noua fert animus mutatas dicere formas / corpora." Cf. also Apuleius Met. 1.1: "figuras fortunasque hominum in alias imagines conuersas et in se rursum mutuo nexu refectas ut mireris."

44. The elder god in the form of a horse may be Poseidon pursuing Demeter; the second of these stories refers to Helios, who took on the appearance of Eurynome, mother of his beloved Leocothoe, in order to gain access to her (Ovid *Met.* 4.190–255). Neither myth is treated in the *Mythologies.*

45. Cf. also *Mit.* 74.8–9, discussing the myth of Apollo and Marsyas: "Nunc ergo huius misticae fabulae interiorem cerebrum inquiramus" ("So now let us investigate the inner medulla of this mystic tale"). For Satyra's ability to see deeply hidden meanings ("mentes etiam penitus abstrusas"), see *Mit.* 14.4–6.

46. At 10.14–15.

47. If the narrator speaks of a real wife, we would have to deny the identity of the mythographer and the bishop, who was by all accounts celibate. But no physical wife appears in the final scene of the prologue, and Fulgentius here playfully personifies his new approach to ancient learning.

48. We are to think of the Muses' contemptuous address to Hesiod at *Theog.* 25–28: ποιμένες ἄγραυλοι. Hesiod's Muses were in evidence at 7.21–22.

49. Petronius, frag. 6. Unfortunately, nothing more about this Albucia is known. Baldwin (1988a, 51) suggests this may not be genuine Petronius, but could be inspired by the Albucilla of Tacitus *Ann.* 6.47.

50. The references are to Plautus's *Asinaria* (though Saurea is only a slave, the wife being Artemona); Ausonius *Cent. Nupt.* 218.11 Peiper (Sulpicia has appeared before at *Mit.* 4.1); and Sallust *Cat.* 25 (where singing is described as one of the vices of this sometimes charming friend and ally of Catiline).

51. This hexameter poem is an epic parody modeled on the poem in Seneca *Apoc.* 2.1–2; both are bombastic descriptions of the time of day, followed in prose by a comic disclaimer. Seneca's deflationary tactic is adopted by Ausonius as well (*Ep.* 23 Peiper). Baldwin (1988a, 47) notes parallels to Lucan *Phars.* 1.45ff. (the praise of Nero); and points out that Fulgentius alludes to this borrowing in his reference to Nero at 14.23.

52. Cf. Fielding's *Joseph Andrews*, chap. 8: "Now the rake Hesperus had called for his breeches, and, having well rubbed his drowsy eyes, prepared to dress himself for all night; by whose example his brother rakes on earth likewise leave those beds in which they had slept away the day. Now Thetis, the good housewife, began to put on the pot, in order to regale the good man Phoebus after his daily labours were over. In vulgar language, it was in the evening when Joseph attended his lady's orders."

53. "ut insanus uates": Fulgentius plays with the two meanings of *uates*, "prophet" and "poet." No longer able to herald a new interpretation of mythology, he has become a poet instead of a prophet. For the parody of the divine frenzy of poetic composition, see Curtius 1953, 474–75.

54. In its general outlines, this scene is borrowed by Boethius *Cons.* 1.1.

55. As Calliope has already broken through the doors (*fores*), I take *ostii* at 14.1 to mean "doorjamb"; but the author may just be confused in his details, or trying to suggest the confusion of the scene and his fogged apprehension of what is happening to him.

56. Satyra resembles the Muses as they first appeared at 8.6ff.: "hedera largiori circumflua" (8.8: "edera largiore circumfluae"); her pregnant mouth suggests Calliope's pregnant chest (8.12); and there is the general suggestion of seductiveness.

57. *mentes*: this recalls the narrator's claim that he sought the *misticum . . . cerebrum* of Greek myths at 11.17–18.

58. "Musae autem latera sarciebant altrinsecus duae": a very odd phrase. The verb *sarciebant* recalls the patchwork (*sarcinis*) of insults visible on Satyra's face at 14.4; but the import of the sentence is difficult to grasp. Perhaps the three of them together are a sort of crazy quilt of analytical powers.

59. Deleting *intuitus*, following the suggestion in the apparatus.

60. "quo pene foribus . . . pollicem inlisisset": *pollicem foribus inlidere* should mean "to stub the big toe"; *pene* and the pluperfect subjunctive have no meaning unless this action is only potential. To almost stub the toe seems not as to the point as almost to come to serious injury by stubbing the toe. While the comic and allegorical details of Urania owe something to the introductions of the Seven Liberal Arts in Books 3–9 of Martianus's *De Nuptiis*, note that Urania resembles Calliope herself (8.13, diadem of pearls), and Luna and Night (13.11–14, horned diadem, dark cloak).

61. "ipsa ponderationis grauidine uenerandus": a pun. Philosophy is holy either because of "the pregnancy of her weight," or "the weight of her thoughts."

62. Cf. the praise of Nero in Lucan *Phars.* 1.45ff.; see n. 51.

63. "misticis . . . rationibus": it is uncertain whether this refers to Plato's forms in particular or to his thought in general.

64. At *Verg. Cont.* 85.2–3, Fulgentius describes hellebore (the traditional cure for madness) as characteristic of Chrysippus.

65. "conpulsationibus lubricis uoluuntur incursus": Chrysippus, *SVF* 2.927 von Arnim. Gould (1970, 56 n. 3) accepts the fragment as genuine and translates: "Impulses are turned about by uncertain and fleeting compulsations." It is significant that this Stoic view of the origin of individual perversions of the god-given mind is readily accepted by Christian apologists, who assign pagan religion and its idols to the influence of demons in the minds of the weak (cf. Athenagoras *Legatio* 24–27). The first allegory related in the *Mythologies,* on the origin of idols, most decidedly does not accept this Christian approach. A Euhemeristic account of the gods is offered instead as a suitably contemptuous frame of reference for the understanding of the allegorizations to come, which are related by Philosophia and not by Calliope.

Appendix C. Ennodius's Paraenesis Didascalica

1. *PLRE* II, Ambrosius 3: a student in Rome in 511, the addressee of Ennodius's *Dictio* 19 in 507, when Ambrose was a student in Milan. He became *quaestor palatii* in 526–27. *PLRE* II, BEATUS: known only from Ennodius's writings as a young man of noble family, a student in Rome 509–12.

2. "sufficit si me in uoto praedicetis": a pun. Ennodius refers to the pleadings of Ambrose and Beatus as a prayer in a religious sense; a similar pun concludes the prose part of the *Paraenesis*.

3. Meter: Hipponacteans. Rallo Freni, edition, p. 2, reasonably takes this and all subsequent poem titles to be interpolations.

4.   Quod lex praecipiens tenere fluxum
         Resoluat studio iubente fortes.
Possibly corrupt. Otherwise, a pun suggesting that the laws that allow for the resolution of long (*fortes*) into short syllables will debilitate strong minds.

5. "Christi militis insitum rigorem / Elumbem patimur cauere ductum." I

take *ductus* here as a noun, meaning "composition," and implying versifica-
tion; *elumbem ductum* would parallel *eneruati sermonis* of the following prose
section. The phrase could also mean: "We suffer the inborn toughness of the
soldier of Christ to beware lest it be considered effeminate," with *ductum* for
ductum esse.

6. "ad disciplinarum arcem": cf. Philosophy's citadel from which her general defends the philosophers in Boethius's *Consolation* (1.3.13): "nostra quidem dux copias suas in arcem contrahit."

7. Meter: elegiacs in the manner of Ovid's *Ars Amatoria*. The topic is blushing.

8. The *Verecundia* of the previous poem is now called *Pudor,* or approximately Shame. The addresses are asked to join this *pudor* to *pudicitia* or
purity, a virtue that shall deliver the next poem in the person of Castitas. As
Professor Shanzer points out to me, *pudor* is, as it were, naked and beautiful,
while *pudicitia* is clothed.

9. "peregrinae frigus dispensationis": in this context *frigus* suggests both
heavenly peace (*refrigerium*) and the absence of the ardor of passion; *peregrinae dispensationis* has the overtones of the Providence which looks after the
pilgrim or sojourner.

10. Meter: epic hexameters in the manner of Prudentius's *Psychomachia*,
the tone of which can be heard throughout the preceding prose passage.

11. Meter: Sapphic stophes modeled in form and content on Horace's
Integer Vitae, Odes 1.22.

12. The Geloni and Morini are found together at *Aen.* 8.725–27, the former a Scythian, and the latter a Gaulish, tribe. "In Parthian wise," *Par-
thica . . . figura,* probably means "like barbarians"; Parthians are otherwise
known in poetry only for shooting arrows backward from their retreating
horses.

13. "De praefatis uirtutibus facessat studiorum liberalium deesse diligentiam": as Professor Shanzer communicates to me, the passage is very likely
corrupt. *facessat* with a nominative noun is common in Ennodius in the sense
of "away with it!" and some manuscripts read *diligentia,* inviting the meaning
"Away with diligence for the Liberal Arts!" though this leaves no plausible
construction for *deesse,* and elsewhere in Ennodius *ab* rather than *de* expresses the thing from which the subject of the sentence should flee. One
passage in Ennodius is close to this sense, however: "facessat philosophiae in
nostrorum nota conventibus" ("in our associations let the stigma of philosophy be far away!") (*Ep.* 9.1.4, Vogel 292.18–19, to Arator). The subject of
facessat can be an infinitive: "facessat stimulare currentem" ("far be it from
me to whip on someone who is already running") (*Ep.* 8.40, Vogel 290.29–30,
to Boethius); "facessat ab studiis meis negare testimonium" ("let the denial of
this evidence be far from my studies") (*Ep.* 9.3.3, Vogel 294.26, to Mero-
baudes). But *facessat deesse diligentiam,* "away with the absence of diligence!"
seems a very awkward phrase.

14. "sapore artificis et planae elocutionis": cf. the "naturali et artifici sim-
plicitate" of the Lady Barbara at 23.

15. "fabricatum . . . militem": "pre-fab" would better render the sense, though with some violence to the tone.

16. "de continua per pedagogos et indicta necessitate." Vogel would prefer to transpose *continua* et *indicta*. He may well be right.

17. Meter: trochaic tetrameters catalectic, in the manner of the moralist and writer of mimes, Publilius Syrus.

18. "nos parentes dixit aetas illa maior optimos": *maior* is confusing. I take it to mean "when grown up," the *aetas* referring to the young wards of Grammar.

19. The *Mauors eloquentiae* will turn out to be the female abstraction Rhetorica. The text is neuter at this point; the translation anticipates the gender of the speaker.

20. *diuisio* and *partitio* are synonymous, and refer to the division of a judicial speech into its several components. The joke is weak and obvious.

21. "post apicem diuinitatis ego illa sum": this ought to mean that Rhetoric is next in power after God, a brazen enough statement; but it is possible that her arrogance is complete and that she styles herself next in line *beyond* divinity.

22. "nos regna regimus et inperantis salubria iubemus": Rallo Freni's edition points to Proverbs 8:15: "per me reges regnant, et legum conditores iusta decernunt." A less compelling parallel is asserted between the previous sentence ("fasces diuitia honores si non ornamus, abiecta sunt") and Proverbs 8:19: "melior est enim fructus meus auro et lapide pretioso, et genimina mea argento electo."

23. "ante scipiones et trabeas est pomposa recitatio": cf. the reference to the *Paraenesis* itself at 26: "pomposa oratione."

24. "carmen, alieni quod nobis suggerit ludus officii": for the implications of this passage for an understanding of the role of verse in Menippean satire, see Chapter 2.

25. Meter: elegiac couplets, suggestive here not of Ovid's amatory verse (as in the poem of Modesty) but perhaps of funerary inscriptions.

26. "Born of Night": *nocte satum.* Rallo Freni's edition notes the parallel to Vergil *Aen.* 7.331, where Juno addresses Allecto as "uirgo sata nocte." Rhetoric's Unjust Argument threatens to confound heaven and hell.

27. Father and son: *PLRE* II, (Anicius Acilius Aginantius) Faustus iunior (albus) 4; (Rufius Magnus Faustus) Avienus iunior 2. They were consuls in 483 and 502 respectively.

28. *PLRE* II, (Fl. Rufius Postumius) Festus 5, consul in 472 and not attested after 513, a year after the *Paraenesis;* (Q. Aurelius Memmius) Symmachus iunior 9, consul in 485 and father-in-law of the Boethius of the *Consolation.* This Symmachus is addressed in the penultimate poem of the *Paraenesis.* Festus and Symmachus are heads of opposing families in Rome; details in Riché 1976, 26–28.

29. *PLRE* II, (Petronius) Probinus 2, consul in 489.

30. The father is *PLRE* II, (Fl. Rufius) Placidus 6; the father-in-law is unknown. "Has drunk that which is elegance itself": "hausit . . . quod mun-

dum est," following Rallo Freni's emendation. Vogel's text reads "quod mundus est" ("that which is the world").

31. *PLRE* II, (Fl. Rufius Petronius Nicomachus) Cethegus, consul in 504,
still alive in the early 560s.

32. The famous Boethius, *PLRE* II, (Anicius Manlius Severinus) Boethius
iunior 5: son-in-law of the Symmachus named previously and consul in 510,
two years before the writing of the *Paraenesis*. Ennodius is not always so kind
to Boethius; *Carm.* 2.132 refers to Boethius in an obscene context. Shanzer
(1983) uses Ennodius and the *Third Elegy* of Maximian to document Boethius's reputation as a philanderer.

33. *PLRE* II, Fl. Agapitus 3; consul in 517 and an old acquaintance of
Ennodius.

34. *PLRE* II, Fl. Probus 9, consul in 513.

35. "By yourselves": reading, with Rallo Freni, *per uos* for *per hos*.

36. Barbara is known only from the works of Ennodius (*PLRE* II, BAR-
BARA). Her literary interests may have led to her being appointed as tutor to
Theoderic's daughter in 510.

37. I retain Vogel's *uellet . . . posset* in this contrary-to-fact clause, against
Rallo Freni's *uelit . . . possit*.

38. Like Barbara, Stephania is known only from Ennodius (*PLRE* II,
STEPHANIA). She is the aunt of the Avienus already mentioned, and was
widowed in 511 or 506.

39. "ergo, si pomposa oratione non ualui, oratione uos memor profes-
sionis adiuui." The pun on the two senses of *oratio* (rhetorical production and
prayer) reminds us of the introduction, in which Ennodius took the pleadings of Ambrose and Beatus as a prayer in the religious sense. Ennodius
elsewhere contrasts love of prayer (*orandi*) and of rhetoric (*perorandi*): see
Opusc. 5.7, Vogel 301.25–26, translated in Laistner 1957, 112 (with an error in
reference). See also Vogel's index s.v. "oratio," p. 399.

40. Meter: dactylic hexameters. The first line reproduces *Aen.* 10.597, the
beginning of Lucagus's unsuccessful plea that Aeneas spare his life.

41. The same Symmachus mentioned previously (19) as a model of learning and eloquence.

42. Rallo Freni (edition, p. 2) considers this verse a later accretion to the
poem. I retain Vogel's text ("non facit ad mores credentem fallere sanctus");
Rallo Freni reads *sanctos*. (My copy of Rallo Freni's edition, on loan from the
University Library at Messina, seems to have the editor's own corrections
inserted; the original text took the entirety of both concluding poems to be
later additions.)

43. Meter: anapaestic monometers. The sons referred to are Ambrose
and Beatus. There is an obvious oxymoron: the seeds (*germina*) cannot come
from a father incapable of procreation (*sicci parentis*).

Journal abbreviations follow the conventions of L'Année Philologique.

Adamietz, Joachim, ed. 1986. *Die römische Satire.* Darmstadt.

———. 1987. "Zum literarischen Charakter von Petrons *Satyrica.*" *RhM* 130: 329–46.

Agozzino, Tullio, ed., comm. 1970. *Massimiano: Elegie.* Bologna.

Alföldi, Andreas. 1944. *Zu den Schicksalen Siebenbürgens im Altertum.* Budapest.

Alfonsi, Luigi. 1952. "Intorno al Menippee di Varrone." *RFIC,* n.s. 80: 1–35.

———. 1973. "Le 'Menippee' di Varrone." *ANRW* 1.3: 26–59.

———. 1975. "Ennodio letterato (nel XV centenario della nascita)." *StudRom* 23: 303–10.

Alonso-Nuñez, J. M. 1974. "Politica y filosofia en 'Los Caesares' de Juliano." *Hispania Antiqua* 4: 315–20.

Altamura, D. 1959. "*Apokolokyntosis* et *Satyricon.*" *Latinitas* 7: 43–54.

Anderson, Graham. 1976a. *Lucian, Theme and Variation in the Second Sophistic. Mnemosyne* Supplement 41. Leiden.

———. 1976b. *Studies in Lucian's Comic Fiction. Mnemosyne* Supplement 43, Leiden.

———. 1980. "Some Sources of Lucian, *Icaromenippus* 25f." *Philologus* 124: 159–61.

———. 1982a. *Eros Sophistes: Ancient Novelists at Play.* American Classical Studies 9. Chico, Calif.

———. 1982b. "Lucian, a Sophist's Sophist." *YClS* 27: 61–92.

———. 1984. *Ancient Fiction: The Novel in the Graeco-Roman World.* London.

Arrowsmith, William. 1966. "Luxury and Death in the *Satyricon.*" *Arion* 5: 304–31.

Astbury, Raymond. 1977. "Petronius, P.Oxy. 3010, and Menippean Satire." *CP* 72: 22–31.

———. 1988. Review of *Menippean Satire as a Literary Genre,* by H. K. Riikonen. *CR* 38: 417.

Athanassiadi-Fowden, Polymnia. 1981. *Julian and Hellenism: An Intellectual Biography.* Oxford.

Bakhtin, Mikhail. 1981. *The Dialogic Imagination.* Edited and translated by Michael Holquist and Caryl Emerson. University of Texas Slavonic Series 1. Austin.

———. 1984. *Problems of Dostoevsky's Poetics.* Edited and translated by Carolyn Emerson. Theory and History of Literature 8. Minneapolis.

Baldwin, Barry. 1973. *Studies in Lucian.* Toronto.

———. 1975a. *Studies in Aulus Gellius.* Lawrence.

————. 1975b. "The Epigrams of Lucian." *Phoenix* 29: 311–35.

————. 1976. "Athenaeus and His Work." *AC* 19: 21–42.

————. 1978. "The *Caesares* of Julian." *Klio* 60: 449–66.

————. 1988a. "Fulgentius and His Sources." *Traditio* 44: 37–57.

————. 1988b. Review of *A Philosophical and Literary Commentary on Martianus Capella's* De Nuptiis Philologiae et Mercurii, *Book I*, by D. Shanzer. *Mittellateinisches Jahrbuch* 23: 309–12.

Ball, A. P., ed. 1902. *The Satire of Seneca on the Apotheosis of Claudius*. New York.

Barnish, S. J. B. 1986. "Martianus Capella and Rome in the Late Fifth Century." *Hermes* 114: 98–111.

————. 1990. "Maximian, Cassiodorus, Boethius, Theodahad: Literature, Philosophy and Politics in Ostrogothic Italy." *Nottingham Medieval Studies* 34: 16–32.

Barthelmess, Jane J. 1974. "The Fictional Narrative of *De Nuptiis Philologiae et Mercurii* of Martianus Capella as Allegory." Diss., University of Washington, Seattle.

Bartoňková, Dagmar. 1969. "Prédmenippovské pošátky prosimetra, smíšeného stylu, v řecké literatuře." *SPFB* E 14: 59–71.

————. 1971. "Střídání prózy a verše v díle Lúkiánově." *SPFB* E 16: 253–61.

————. 1972. "Mišení prózy a veršu v antické románové literatuře." *SPFB* E 17: 83–102.

————. 1973. "Prosimetrum, the Combined Style, in Boëthius' Work *De Consolatione Philosophiae*." *GLO* 5: 61–69.

————. 1973–74. "Prosimetrum, smíšený styl, y díle Julianově." *SPFB* E 18–19: 225–40.

————. 1976. "Prosimetrum, the Mixed Style, in Ancient Literature." *Eirene* 14: 65–92.

————. 1977–78a. "Prosimetrum v Seneky (*Apocolocyntosis* a *Epistulae*)." *SPFB* E 22–23: 216–37.

————. 1977–78b. "Prosimetrum v díle Martiana Capelly *De Nuptiis Philologiae et Mercurii*." *SPFB* E 22–23: 205–15.

————. 1979. "K pošátkum římské menippské satiry." *SPFB* E 24: 41–46.

————. 1980. "Daréz Fryžský a Diktys z Kréty a jejich místo v antické literatuře." *SPFB* E 25: 223–34.

————. 1985. "Prozimetrické pasáže v starořeckých románech, zvláště fragmentárních." *SPFB* E 30: 125–32.

————. 1986. "K žánrovému zařazení díla Antonia Diogena." *SPFB* E 31: 159–65.

————. 1988. "Prozimetrický zlomek o Tinúfiovi." *SPFB* E 33: 41–45.

Benchley, Robert. 1949. *Chips Off the Old Benchley*. New York.

Benda, Frederick Joseph. 1979. "The Tradition of Menippean Satire in Varro, Lucian, Seneca and Erasmus." Diss., University of Texas, Austin.

Bie, O. 1894–97. "Musen." In *Ausführliches Lexicon der griechischen und römischen Mythologie*, edited by W. H. Roscher, 2.2: 3238–95. Leipzig.

Bignone, E. 1950. "Le 'Satire Menippee' di Varrone." In *Studi di Filosofia Greca*, edited by V. E. Altieri and M. Untersteiner, 321–44. Bari.

Billerbeck, M. 1978. *Epiktet: von Kynismus*. Philosophia Antiqua 34. Leiden.

Binder, Gerhard. 1974. "Hercules und Claudius: Eine Szene in Senecas *Apocolocyntosis* auf dem Hintergrund der *Aeneis*." *RhM*, n.s. 117: 288–317.

———. 1974–75. "Catilina und Kaiser Claudius als ewige Büßer in der Unterwelt: Eine typologische Verbindung zwischen Vergils *Aeneis* und Senecas *Apocolocyntosis*." *ACD* 10–11: 75–93.

Bompaire, J. 1958. *Lucien écrivain, imitation et creation*. Bibliothèque des Écoles Françaises d'Athènes et de Rome 190. Paris.

Bowersock, G. W. 1978. *Julian the Apostate*. Cambridge, Mass.

———. 1982. "The Emperor Julian on His Predecessors." *YClS* 27: 159–72.

Boyce, Bret. 1991. *The Language of the Freedmen in Petronius' Cena Trimalchionis*. *Mnemosyne* Supplement 117. Leiden.

Branham, R. Bracht. 1989a. "The Wisdom of Lucian's Tiresias." *JHS* 109: 159–60.

———. 1989b. *Unruly Eloquence: Lucian and the Comedy of Traditions*. Cambridge, Mass.

Bright, David. 1987. *The Miniature Epic in Vandal Africa*. Norman, Okla.

Bringmann, K. 1971. "Senecas *Apocolocyntosis* und die politische Satire in Rom." *A&A* 17: 56–69.

———. 1985. "Senecas 'Apocolocyntosis': Ein Forschungsbericht 1959–1982." *ANRW* 2.32.3: 885–914.

Browne, Gerald M. 1982. "Ad Lolliani Phoinicica." *ZPE* 46: 135–43, and plates 5–7.

———. 1989. "Notes on Literary Papyri." *ZPE* 76: 239–40.

Bücheler, F., and G. Heräus, eds. 1922. *Petronii Saturae et Liber Priapeorum . . . adiectae sunt Varronis et Senecae saturae similesque reliquiae*. 6th edition. Berlin.

Cameron, Alan. 1984. "The *Pervigilium Veneris*." In *La poesia tardoantica: Tra retorica, teologica, e politica*: 209–34. Messina.

———. 1986. "Martianus and His First Editors." *CP* 81: 320–28.

Campbell, Robin, trans. 1969. *Seneca: Letters from a Stoic*. Harmondsworth.

Carini, Mario. 1987. "Recenti contributi alla critica Ennodiana (1960–1983)." *QC* 9:327–42.

Casaubon, Isaac. 1605. *De Satyrica Graecorum Poesi & Romanorum Satira*. Paris. Reprint New York, 1973.

Castrop, Helmut. 1982. "Die varronische Satire in England, 1660–1690." Diss., Heidelberg.

Cataudella, Quintino. 1975a. "Ultime da Oxyrhynchos." *C & S* 54: 41–48.

———. 1975b. "Un frammento di Menippo di Gadara?" *Sileno* 1: 143–54.

Cèbe, Jean-Pierre, ed. *Varron, Satires Ménippées*. Collections de l'École Française de Rome 9. Rome. In progress.
1972. I. Aborigines—Andabatae.
1974. II. Ἀνθρωπόπολις—Bimarcus.
1975. III. Caprinum Proelium—Endymiones.
1977. IV. Epitaphiones—Eumenides.
1980. V. Εὖρεν ἡ λοπὰς τὸ πῶμα—Γεροντοδιδάσκαλος.

1983. VI. Γνῶθι σεαυτόν—Κυνορήτωρ.

1985. VII. Lex Maenia—Marcipor.

1987. VIII. Marcopolis—Mysteria.

Cesa, Maria, ed., trans. 1988. *Ennodio: Vita del beatissimo Epifanio vescovo della chiesa pavese.* Biblioteca di Athenaeum 6. Como.

Chadwick, Henry. 1981. *Boethius: The Consolations of Music, Logic, Theology, and Philosophy.* Oxford.

Champlin, Edward. 1991. *Final Judgements: Duty and Emotion in Roman Wills, 200 B.C.–A.D. 250.* Berkeley.

Christ, W. von. 1920. *Geschichte der griechischen Literature,* 2.1. 6th edition, revised by W. Schmid and O. Stählin. Berlin.

Ciaffi, V. 1963. *Fulgenzio e Petronio.* Torino.

Clairmont, Richard E., ed., trans. 1980. *A Commentary on Seneca's* Apocolocyntosis Divi Claudii *or* Glose in Librum de Ludo Claudii Annei Senece. Chicago.

Clark, Katerina, and Michael Holquist. 1984. *Mikhail Bakhtin.* Cambridge, Mass.

Coffey, Michael. 1961. "Seneca, *Apocolocyntosis,* 1922–1958." *Lustrum* 6: 239–71, 309–11.

———. 1989. *Roman Satire.* 2nd edition. Bristol.

Coulter, James A. 1976. *The Literary Microcosm: Theories of Interpretation of the Later Neoplatonists.* Columbia Studies in the Classical Tradition 3. Leiden.

Courcelle, Pierre. 1969. *Late Latin Writers and Their Greek Sources.* Translated by H. E. Wedeck. Cambridge, Mass.

Courtney, Edward. 1962. "Parody and Allusion in Menippean Satire." *Philologus* 106: 86–100.

———. 1991. *The Poems of Petronius.* American Classical Studies 25. Atlanta.

Couvreur, W. 1933–34. " 'n Paedogogisch traktaat uit het beginn der VIe eeuw: Paraenesis didascalica van Magnus Felix Ennodius." *PhS* 5: 122–33, 215–26.

Cristante, L. 1978. "La σφραγίς di Marziano Capella (σπουδογέλοιον: autobiografia e autoironia)." *Latomus* 37: 679–704.

———, ed., trans., comm. 1987. *Martiani Capellae* De Nuptiis Philologiae et Mercurii *Liber IX.* Medioevo e Umanesimo 64. Padua.

Crönert, Wilhelm. 1906. *Kolotes und Menedemos.* Studien zur Palaeographie und Papyruskunde 6. Leipzig.

Cross, F. L., and E. A. Livingstone, eds. 1974. *The Oxford Dictionary of the Christian Church.* 2nd edition. Oxford.

Curtius, E. R. 1953. *European Literature and the Latin Middle Ages.* Translated by Willard R. Trask. Princeton.

Dal Santo, L. 1976a. "I Frammenti della Musa Varroniana, I." *RSC* 24: 263–77.

———. 1976b. "I Frammenti della Musa Varroniana, II." *RSC* 24: 434–60.

———. 1978. "I Frammenti della Musa Varroniana, III." *RSC* 26: 405–33.

———. 1979. "I Frammenti della Musa Varroniana, IV." *RSC* 27: 247–89.

De Labriolle, Pierre. 1924. *History and Literature of Christianity from Tertullian to*

Boethius. Translated by Herbert Wilson. London. Reprint New York, 1968.

De Lacy, P. H. 1948. "Lucretius and the History of Epicureanism." *TAPhA* 79: 12–23.

Di Marco, Massimo, ed., comm. 1989. *Timone di Fliunte: Silli*. Texts and Commentaries 10. Rome.

Dobesch, G. 1975. "Eine Vergilreminiszenz in Senecas *Apokolokyntosis*." *Publik. aus dem Archiv der Univ. Graz, Beitr. zur allgem. Gesch.* 4: 1–10.

Donzelli, G. 1960. "Una versione Menippea della Αἰσώπου Πρᾶσις?" *RF* 38: 225–76.

Dörrie, Heinrich. 1968. *Der heroische Brief: Bestandsaufnahme, Geschichte, Kritik einer humanistisch-barocken Literaturgattung*. Berlin.

———. 1969. "Menippos (4)." *Der Kleine Pauly* 3: 1217.

Dover, Kenneth J., ed. 1980. *Plato: Symposium*. Cambridge.

Dronke, Peter. 1974. *Fabula: Explorations into the Use of Myth in Medieval Platonism*. Mittellateinische Studien und Texte 9. Leiden.

———, ed. 1978. *Bernardus Silvestris: Cosmographia*. Textus Minores 53. Leiden.

———. 1988. *A History of Twelfth Century Western Philosophy*. Cambridge.

Duff, J. Wight. 1936. *Roman Satire: Its Outlook on Social Life*. Berkeley.

Eckhardt, Caroline D. 1983. "The Medieval Prosimetrum Genre (from Boethius to Boèce)." *Genre* 16: 21–38.

Ehrhart, Margaret J. 1987. *The Judgement of the Trojan Prince Paris in Medieval Literature*. Philadelphia.

Ferrarino, P. 1969. "La prima, e l'unica, 'Reductio omnium artium ad philologiam': Il 'De Nuptiis Philologiae et Mercurii' di Marziano Capella e l'apoteosi della filologia." *Italia Medioevale e Umanistica* 12: 1–7.

Fontaine, J. 1960. "Ennodius." *RAC* 5: 398–421.

———. 1965. "Isidore de Séville auteur 'ascetique': Les énigmes des *Synonyma*." *Studi Medievali*, 3rd ser. 6: 163–95.

Fowler, Alastair. 1982. *Kinds of Literature: An Introduction to the Theory of Genres and Modes*. Oxford.

Fritzsch, F. V. 1865a. *De Scriptoribus Satiricis*. Index Lectionum in Academia Rostochiensi. Specimen Tertium: Apr. 18: 3–10.

———. 1865b. *De Scriptoribus Satiricis*. Index Lectionum in Academia Rostochiensi. Specimen Quartum: Oct. 16: 3–8.

Frye, Northrop. 1957. *Anatomy of Criticism: Four Essays*. Princeton.

———. 1976. *The Secular Scripture: A Study of the Structure of Romance*. Cambridge, Mass.

Fuhrmann, M., and J. Gruber, eds. 1984. *Boethius*. Wege der Forschung 483. Darmstadt.

Gallardo, M. D. 1972. "Los Simposios de Luciano, Ateneo, Metodio y Juliano." *CFC* 4: 239–96.

Gardiner, Eileen, ed. 1989. *Visions of Heaven and Hell before Dante*. New York.

Geffcken, J. 1911. "Studien zur griechischen Satire." *NJahr*. 27: 393–411, 469–93.

————. 1914. *Kaiser Julianus*. Leipzig.

————. 1931. "Menippus περὶ θυσιῶν." *Hermes* 66: 347–54.

Geller, H. 1966. "Varros Menippea 'Parmeno.'" Diss., Cologne.

Gersh, Stephen. 1986. *Middle Platonism and Neoplatonism: The Latin Tradition.* 2 vols. Notre Dame.

Giangrande, L. 1972. *The Use of Spoudaiogeloion in Greek and Roman Literature.* Studies in Classical Literature 6. The Hague.

Gill, Christopher. 1979. "Plato's Atlantis Story and the Birth of Fiction." *Philosophy and Literature* 3: 64–78.

Gould, Josiah B. 1970. *The Philosophy of Chrysippus*. Albany.

Goulet-Cazé, Marie Odile. 1986. "Une liste de disciples de Cratès le Cynique en Diogène Laërce 6, 95." *Hermes* 114: 247–52.

Gruber, Joachim. 1969. "Die Erscheinung der Philosophie in der *Consolatio Philosophiae* des Boethius." *RhM* 112: 166–86.

————. 1978. *Kommentar zu Boethius* de Consolatione Philosophiae. Texte und Kommentare 9. Berlin.

Guilhamet, Leon. 1987. *Satire and the Transformation of Genre*. Philadelphia.

Hadot, Ilsetraut. 1984. *Arts libéraux et philosophie dans la pensée antique*. Paris.

Hall, Jennifer. 1981. *Lucian's Satire*. New York.

Hamilton-Patterson, James, and Carol Andrews. 1978. *Mummies: Death and Life in Ancient Egypt*. Harmondsworth.

Haslam, M. W. 1981. "Narrative about Tinouphis in Prosimetrum." P. Turner 8. *Greco-Roman Memoirs* 68: 35–45, and plate IV. London.

Haüsle, Helmut. 1989. *Sag mir, o Hund—wo der Hund begraben liegt: Das Grabepigramm für Diogenes von Sinope: Eine komparative literarisch-epigraphische Studie zu Epigrammen auf theriophore Namensträger*. Spudasmata 64. Zurich.

Heinze, R. 1926. Review of *Senecas Apocolocyntosis*, by O. Weinreich. *Hermes* 61: 49–78.

Heller, J. L. 1985. "Notes on the Meaning of Κολοκύντη." *ICS* 10: 67–117, with eight figures.

Helm, Rudolf. 1899. "Der Bischof Fulgentius und die Mythograph." *RhM* 54: 111–34.

————. 1906. *Lucian und Menipp*. Leipzig.

————. 1931. "Menippos 10)." *RE* 15.1: 888–93.

Hense, Otto. 1902. "Zu Lucian und Menippus." In *Festschrift für Th. Comperz*, 185–96. Vienna.

————, ed. 1909. *Teletis Reliquiae*. 2nd edition. Tubingen. Reprint Hildesheim, 1969.

Hirsch, Walter. 1971. *Platons Wegen zum Mythos*. Berlin.

Hirzel, R. 1895. *Der Dialog, ein literarhistorischer Versuch*. 2 vols. Leipzig.

Holford-Strevens, Leofranc. 1988. *Aulus Gellius*. London.

Holland, Philip H. 1979. "Robert Burton's Anatomy of Melancholy and Menippean Satire, Humanist and English." Diss., University College, London.

Hoyos, Dexter. 1991. "Gourd God! The Meaning of *Apocolocyntosis.*" *LCM* 16.5: 68–70.

Hudry, Françoise. 1989. "Prologus Alani *De Planctu Nature.*" *Archives d'Histoire Doctrinale et Littéraire du Moyen Age* 63: 169–85.

Hunter, R. L. 1983. *A Study of* Daphnis and Chloe. Cambridge.

Immisch, Otto. 1921. "Über eine volkstumliche Darstellungsform in der antiken Literatur." *NJahr.* 24: 409–21.

Janson, Tore. 1964. *Latin Prose Prefaces: Studies in Literary Conventions.* Acta Universitatis Stockholmiensis 13. Stockholm.

Jauss, Hans Robert. 1982. *Toward an Aesthetic of Reception.* Translated by Timothy Bahti. Introduction by Paul de Man. Minneapolis.

Jones, C. P. 1986. *Culture and Society in Lucian.* Cambridge, Mass.

Jones, F. 1987. "The Narrator and the Narrative of the *Satyrica.*" *Latomus* 46: 810–19.

Kaegi, W. E. 1964. "The Emperor Julian's Assessment of the Significance and Function of History." *PAPhS* 108: 29–38.

Kennedy, George. 1978. "Encolpius and Agamemnon in Petronius." *AJP* 99: 171–78.

Kenney, E. J. 1976. "Ovidius Prooemians." *PCPhS* 22: 49–52.

———, ed. 1990. *Apuleius: Cupid and Psyche.* Cambridge.

Kindermann, Udo. 1978. *Satyra, Die Theorie der Satire im Mittellateinischen: Vorstudie zu einer Gattungsgeschichte.* Erlanger Beitrage zur Sprach- und Kunstwissenschaft 58. Nuremberg.

Kindstrand, J. F. 1976. *Bion of Borysthenes.* Uppsala.

Kirk, Eugene. 1980. *Menippean Satire: An Annotated Catalogue of Texts and Criticism.* New York.

———. 1982. "Boethius, Lucian, and Menippean Satire." *Helios* 9: 59–71. [See also Eugene Paul Korkowski.]

Klingner, F. 1921. *De Boethii Consolatione Philosophiae.* Philologische Untersuchungen 27. Berlin.

Knaack, G. 1883. "Menipp und Varro." *Hermes* 18: 148–50.

Knoche, Ulrich. 1975. *Roman Satire.* 2nd edition. Translated by E. S. Ramage. Bloomington, Ind.

Korkowski, Eugene Paul. 1973. "Menippus and His Imitators: A Conspectus, up to Sterne, for a Misunderstood Genre." Diss., University of California, San Diego. [See also Eugene Kirk.]

Korus, Kazimierz. 1984. "The Theory of Humor in Lucian of Samosata." *Eos* 72: 295–313.

———. 1986a. "Funktionen der literarischen Gattungen bei Lukian." *Eos* 74: 29–38.

———. 1986b. "Zur Chronologie der Schriften Lukians." *Philologus* 130: 96–103.

Kovacs, David. 1987. "Ovid, *Metamorphoses* 1.2." *CQ* 37: 458–65.

Lacombrade, Christian. 1962. "Notes sur les 'Cesars' de l'Empereur Julien." *Pallas* 11: 47–67.

Laistner, M. L. W. 1957. *Thought and Letters in Western Europe*, A.D. 500 to 900. Revised edition. London.

Lamberton, Robert. 1986. *Homer the Theologian: Neoplatonist Allegorical Reading and the Growth of the Epic Tradition.* Berkeley.

Langlois, P. 1964. "Les oeuvres de Fulgence le Mythographe et le problème des deux Fulgences." *JAC* 7: 94–105.

Lauvergnat-Gagnière, Christiane. 1988. *Lucien de Samosate et le lucianisme en France au XVIᵉ siècle.* Geneva.

LeMoine, Fannie J. 1972a. "Judging the Beauty of Diversity: A Critical Approach to Martianus Capella." *CJ* 67: 209–15.

———. 1972b. *Martianus Capella: A Literary Re-evaluation.* Münster Beiträge zur Mediävistik und Renaissanceforschung 10. Munich.

———. 1981. "The Precious Style as Heuristic Device: The Function of Introductions to the Arts in Martianus Capella and Boethius." In *Boethius and the Liberal Arts: A Collection of Essays,* edited by Michael Masi, 51–65. Berne.

———. 1991. "Parental Gifts: Father-Son Dedications and Dialogues in Roman Didactic Literature." *ICS* 16: 337–66.

Lenaz, L. 1972. "Marziano Capella." *C & S* 44: 50–59.

———, ed., trans. 1975. *Martiani Capellae:* De Nuptiis Philologiae et Mercurii *Liber Secundus.* Padua.

Lerer, Seth. 1985. *Boethius and Dialogue: Literary Method in the Consolation of Philosophy.* Princeton.

Levine, N. A. S. 1968. "The *Caesares* of Julian: An Historical Study." Diss., Columbia University.

Lewis, C. S. 1936. *The Allegory of Love: A Study in Medieval Tradition.* Oxford.

Lind, L. R., trans. 1988. Gabrieli Zerbi, Gerontocomia: *On the Care of the Aged; and Maximianus, Elegies on Old Age and Love.* Memoirs of the American Philosophical Society 182. Philadelphia.

Long, A. A. 1974. *Hellenistic Philosophy.* London.

———. 1988. "Socrates in Hellenistic Philosophy." *CQ* 38: 150–71.

Lovejoy, Arthur O., and George Boas. 1935. *Primitivism and Related Ideas in Antiquity.* Reprint. New York, 1965.

Markus, Robert. 1990. *The End of Ancient Christianity.* Cambridge.

Marti, B. M. 1952. "Seneca's *Apocolocyntosis* and *Octavia,* a Diptych." *AJP* 73: 24–36.

Martin, J. 1931. *Symposion, die Geschichte einer literarischen Form.* Studien zur Geschichte und Kultur des Altertums 17. 2 vols. in one. Paderborn.

Matheeussen, C., and C. L. Heesakkers, eds. 1980. *Two Neo-Latin Menippean Satires.* Textus Minores 54. Leiden.

Mattioli, Emilio. 1980. *Luciano e l'Umanesimo.* Naples.

Mayer, C.-A. 1984. *Lucien de Samosate et la renaissance française.* La Renaissance Française 3. Geneva.

McCarthy, Barbara P. 1934. "Lucian and Menippus." *YClS* 4: 3–55.

————. 1936. "The Form of Varro's *Menippean Satires*." *University of Missouri Studies* 9.3: 95–107.

Merklebach, R. 1973. "Fragment eines satirischen Romans: Aufforderung zur Beichte." *ZPE* 11: 81–100.

Morgan, J. R. 1985. "Lucian's *True Histories* and the *Wonders Beyond Thule* of Antonius Diogenes." *CQ* 35: 475–90.

Mosca, B. 1937. "Satira filosofica e politica nelle 'Menippee' di Varrone." *ASNP,* 2nd ser. 6: 41–77.

Mras, Karl. 1914. "Varros menippeische Satiren und die Philosophie." *NJahr.* 33: 390–420.

Nauta, R. R. 1987. "Seneca's *Apocolocyntosis* as Saturnalian Literature." *Mnemosyne* 40: 69–96.

Nesselrath, H. G. 1990. "Lucian's Introductions." In *Antonine Literature*, edited by D. A. Russell, 111–40. Oxford.

Nuchelmans, G. 1957. "Philologie et son mariage avec Mercure jusqu'à la fin du XIIᵉ siècle." *Latomus* 16: 84–107.

O'Daly, Gerard. 1991. *The Poetry of Boethius*. Chapel Hill.

Pack, R. 1946. "Notes on the *Caesares* of Julian." *TAPhA* 77: 151–57.

Palmer, L. R. 1961. *The Latin Language*. Corrected edition. London.

Parsons, Peter. 1971. "A Greek Satyricon?" *BICS* 18: 53–68 and plate 7.

————, ed. 1974. "Narrative about Iolaos." P.Oxy. 3010. *Greco-Roman Memoirs* 42: 34–41 and plate I. London.

Payne, F. Anne. 1981. *Chaucer and Menippean Satire*. Madison.

Pépin, Jean. 1958. *Mythe et allegorie*. Aubier.

Perelman, S. J. 1981. *The Last Laugh*. Introduction by Paul Theroux. New York.

Perry, Ben Edwin. 1967. *The Ancient Romances: A Literary-Historical Account of Their Origins*. Berkeley.

Peters, Sigrid. 1987. *Ludwig Holbergs menippeische Satire: Das 'Iter subterraneum' und seine Beziehungen zur antiken Literatur*. Frankfurt am Main.

Petersmann, Hubert. 1985. "Umwelt, Sprachsituation und Stilschichten in Petrons 'Satyrica.'" *ANRW* 2.32.3: 1687–1705.

————. 1986a. "Der Begriff 'Satura' und die Entstehung der Gattung.' In *Die römische Satire*, edited by Joachim Adamietz, 7–24. Darmstadt.

————. 1986b. "Petrons 'Satyrica.'" In *Die römische Satire*, edited by Joachim Adamietz, 383–426. Darmstadt.

Piot, Henri. 1914. "Un personnage de Lucien, Menipp." Diss., Rennes.

Puccioni, C. 1976. "Varrone Menippeo modello di Seneca e di Petronio?" *ASNP,* 3rd ser. 6: 35–52.

Radermacher, Ludwig. 1939. "Der Reisepass des Menipp." *WS* 57: 165–69.

Raith, Oskar. 1963. *Petronius ein Epukureer*. Erlanger Beiträge zur Sprach- und Kunstwissenschaft 14. Nuremberg.

Rallo Freni, Rosalba A. 1971. "Le concezioni pedagogiche nella Paraenesis didascalica di Magno Felice Ennodio." In *Umanità e storia: Scritti in onore di Adelmi Attisani*, 2: 109–26. Naples.

————. 1978. "Attegiamenti topici nel programma poetico di Magno Felice Ennodio." In *Scritti in onore di Salvatore Pugliatti*, 5: 831–58. Milan.

Rawson, Elizabeth. 1985. *Intellectual Life in the Late Roman Republic*. Baltimore.

Read, M. Ch., ed. 1876. *La Satyre Ménippée ou La Vertu du Catholicon*. Paris.

Reardon, B. P. 1976. "Novels and Novelties, or, Mysteriouser and Mysteriouser." In *The Mediterranean World: Papers Presented in Honor of Gilbert Bagnani*, 78–100. Petersborough.

————, ed. 1989. *Collected Ancient Greek Novels*. Berkeley.

————. 1991. *The Form of Greek Romance*. Princeton.

Reeve, M. D. 1984. "Apotheosis . . . per saturam." *CP* 79: 305–7.

Reichenberger, Kurt. 1954. *Untersuchungen zur literarischen Stellung der* Consolatio Philosophiae. Kölner Romanistiche Arbeiten, Neue Folge 3. Cologne.

Relihan, Joel C. 1984a. "On the Origin of 'Menippean Satire' as the Name of a Literary Genre." *CP* 79: 226–29.

————. 1984b. "Ovid *Metamorphoses* 1.1–4 and Fulgentius' *Mitologiae*." *AJP* 105: 87–90.

————. 1986. "Satyra in the Prologue of Fulgentius' *Mythologies*." In *Studies in Latin Literature and Roman History*, vol. 4, edited by C. Deroux, 537–48. Collection Latomus 196. Brussels.

————. 1987a. "Martianus Capella, The Good Teacher." *Pacific Coast Philology* 22: 59–70.

————. 1987b. "Vainglorious Menippus in Lucian's *Dialogues of the Dead*." *ICS* 12: 185–206.

————. 1988. "Fulgentius, *Mitologiae* I.20–21." *AJP* 109: 229–30.

————. 1989a. "A Metrical Quotation in Julian's *Symposium*." *CQ* n.s. 39: 566–69.

————. 1989b. "Menippus the Cynic in the Greek Anthology." *Syllecta Classica* 1: 55–61.

————. 1990a. "Agathias Scholasticus (*A.P.* 11.354), the Philosopher Nicostratus, and Boethius' *Consolation*." *C&M* 41: 119–29.

————. 1990b. "Menippus, the Cur from Crete." *Prometheus* 16: 217–24.

————. 1990c. "Old Comedy, Menippean Satire, and Philosophy's Tattered Robes in Boethius' *Consolation*." *ICS* 15: 183–94.

————. 1992. "Rethinking the History of the Literary Symposium." *ICS* 17: 213–44.

————. Forthcoming. "Menippus in Antiquity and the Renaissance." In *The Cynics: The Cynic Movement in Antiquity and Its Legacy for Europe*, edited by Marie-Odile Goulet-Cazé and R. Bracht Branham.

Riché, Pierre. 1976. *Education and Culture in the Barbarian West from the Sixth through the Eighth Century*. Translated by John J. Contreni. Columbia, S.C.

Riese, Alexander, ed. 1865. *M. Terenti Varronis Saturarum Menippearum Reliquiae*. Leipzig.

Riikonen, H. K. 1987. *Menippean Satire as a Literary Genre with Special Reference to Seneca's* Apocolocyntosis. Commentationes Humanarum Litterarum 83. Helsinki.

Riposati, B. 1974. "Sul alcuni aspetti technici e formali delle Menippee di Varrone." In *Poesia latina in frammenti,* 45–55. Geneva.

Robinson, Christopher. 1979. *Lucian and His Influence in Europe.* Chapel Hill.

Robinson, Laura. 1974. "Marcus Terentius Varro, *Sexagesis* or Born Sixty Years Too Late." In *Atti del Congresso Internazionale di Studi Varroniani* 2: 477–83. Rieti.

Romano, Domenico. 1974. "Varrone e Cibele." In *Atti del Congresso Internazionale di Studi Varroniani* 2: 495–506. Rieti.

Roncali, R. 1973. "Partizione scenica della satira di Seneca." *Belfagor* 28: 425–29.

Rosen, Stanley. 1987. *Plato's* Symposium. 2nd edition. New Haven.

Rostagni, A. 1920. *Giuliano L'Apostata: Saggio critico con le operette politiche e satiriche tradotte e commentate.* Torino.

Rötter, Ingeborg. 1969. "Varros Menippea ΠΕΡΙ ΕΔΕΣΜΑΤΩΝ." Diss., Cologne.

Salanitro, M. 1978. "Varrone Poeta Satirico." *C & S* 66: 58–66.

Scarpa, Luigi, ed. 1974. *Fauonii Eulogii: Disputatio de Somnio Scipionis.* Collectanea Accademica 5. Padua.

———, ed. 1981. *Macrobii Ambrosii Theodosii Commentariorum in Somnium Scipionis Libri Duo.* Padua.

Scheible, Helga. 1972. *Die Gedichte in der Consolatio Philosophiae des Boethius.* Bibliothek der klassischen Altertumswissenschaften, n.s. 46. Heidelberg.

Scherbantin, Alexander. 1951. "Satura Menippea, die Geschichte eines Genos." Diss., Graz.

Schwartz, J. 1965. *Biographie de Lucien de Samosate.* Brussels.

Shanzer, Danuta. 1983a. "Ennodius, Boethius, and the Date and Interpretation of Maximianus's *Elegia* III." *RFIC* 111: 183–95.

———. 1983b. " 'Me quoque excellentior': Boethius, *De Consolatione* 4.6.38." *CQ,* n.s. 33: 277–83.

———. 1984. "The Death of Boethius and the 'Consolation of Philosophy.'" *Hermes* 112: 352–66.

———. 1986a. *A Philosophical and Literary Commentary on Martianus Capella's* De Nuptiis Philologiae et Mercurii, *Book I.* Classical Studies 32. Berkeley.

———. 1986b. "The Late Antique Tradition of Varro's *Onos Lyras.*" *RhM* 129: 272–85.

Sheridan, J. J., trans. 1980. *Alan of Lille: The Plaint of Nature.* Medieval Sources in Translation 26. Toronto.

Skutsch, Otto. 1964. "Studia Enniana VI." *CQ* 14: 89–91.

Slater, Niall W. 1990. *Reading Petronius.* Baltimore.

Smith, J. E. 1982. "Plato's Use of Myth as a Pedagogical Device." Diss., University of Toronto.

Smith, Martin S., ed. 1975. *Petronii Arbitri Cena Trimalchionis.* Oxford.

————. 1985. "A Bibliography of Petronius (1945–1982)." *ANRW* 2.32.3: 1624–65.

Smith, Nicholas D. 1989. "Diviners and Divination in Aristophanic Comedy." *ClAnt* 8: 140–58.

Souter, Alexander. 1957. *A Glossary of Later Latin to 600* A.D. 1st edition, corrected. Oxford.

Soverini, P. "Il problema delle teorie retoriche e poetiche di Petronio." *ANRW* 2.32.3: 1706–79.

Spaltenstein, François. 1983. *Commentaire des Élégies de Maximien.* Bibliotheca Helvetica Romana 20. Vevey.

Stahl, William Harris, trans., comm. 1952. *Macrobius: Commentary on the Dream of Scipio.* Records of Civilization: Sources and Studies 48. New York.

Stahl, William Harris, Richard Johnson, and E. L. Burge. 1971. *Martianus Capella and the Seven Liberal Arts,* vol. 1. Records of Civilization: Sources and Studies 84. New York.

————, trans. 1977. *Martianus Capella and the Seven Liberal Arts,* vol. 2. Records of Civilization: Sources and Studies 84. New York.

Stevens, S. T. 1982. "The Circle of Bishop Fulgentius." *Traditio* 38: 327–41.

Stock, Brian. 1972. *Myth and Science in the Twelfth Century: A Study of Bernardus Silvester.* Princeton.

Stoneman, Richard, trans. 1991. *The Greek Alexander Romance.* Harmondsworth.

Sullivan, J. P. 1966. "Seneca: The Deification of Claudius the Clod." *Arion* 5: 378–99.

————. 1968a. "Petronius, Seneca and Lucan: A Neronian Literary Feud?" *TAPhA* 99: 453–67.

————. 1968b. *The Satyricon of Petronius: A Literary Study.* London.

————. 1977. "Petron in der Neueren Forschung." *Helikon* 17: 137–54.

————. 1985. "Petronius' 'Satyricon' and Its Neronian Context." *ANRW* 2.32.3: 1666–86.

————, trans. 1986. *Petronius:* The Satyricon; *and Seneca:* The Apocolocyntosis. Revised edition. Harmondsworth.

Swigger, R. T. 1975. "Fictional Encyclopedism and the Cognitive Value of Literature." *Comparative Literature Studies* 12: 351–66.

Szilárd, Lèna. 1985. "Menippus and Modern Literature." *Russian Literature* 17: 61–70 (in Russian).

Tackaberry, W. H. 1930. *Lucian's Relation to Plato and the Post-Aristotelian Philosophers.* University of Toronto Studies, Philological Series 9. Toronto.

Taylor, L. R. 1930. *The Divinity of the Roman Emperor.* American Philological Association Philological Monographs 1. Middletown, Conn.

Todorov, Tzvetan. 1984. *Mikhail Bakhtin: The Dialogical Principle.* Translated by W. Godzich. Minneapolis.

Tränkle, H. 1977. "Ist die 'Philosophiae Consolatio' des Boethius zum vorgesehenen Abschluss gelangt?" *VChr* 31: 148–56. Reprint with author's afterword in Fuhrmann and Gruber 1984, 311–19.

Trilli Pari, Lilia. 1974. "Alcune precisazioni sulle Eumenides di Varrone." *Atti del Congresso Internazionale di Studi Varroniani*, 2: 565–70. Rieti.

Turcan, R. 1958. "Martianus Capella et Jamblique." *REL* 36: 235–54.

Uhlfelder, Myra. 1981. "The Role of the Liberal Arts in Boethius' *Consolatio*." In *Boethius and the Liberal Arts: A Collection of Essays*, edited by Michael Masi, 17–34. Bern.

Ullrich, F. 1909. *Entstehung und Entwicklung der Literaturgattung des Symposium: II. Teil, Das literarische Gastmahl von Aristoteles bis Methodius und Julianus Apostata*. Progr. Wurzburg.

Van Rooy, C. A. 1967. *Studies in Classical Satire and Related Literary Theory*. Leiden.

Vives Coll, Antonio. 1959. *Luciano de Samosata en España (1500–1700)*. Valladolid.

von Koppenfels, W. 1981. "Mundus Alter et Idem: Utopiefiktion und menippeische Satire." *Poetica* 13: 16–66.

Wachsmuth, C., ed. 1885. *Corpusculum Poesis Epicae Graecae Ludibundae Fasciculus Alter: Sillographorum Graecorum Reliquiae*. Leipzig.

Wagner, David L., ed. 1983. *The Seven Liberal Arts in the Middle Ages*. Bloomington, Ind.

Wallis, R. T. 1972. *Neo-Platonism*. New York.

Walsh, P. G. 1970. *The Roman Novel: The "Satyricon" of Petronius and the "Metamorphoses" of Apuleius*. Cambridge.

Weinreich, Otto. 1923. *Senecas Apocolocyntosis*. Berlin.

————. 1941. "Varro und die Geschichte des Pantomimus." *Hermes* 76: 96–100.

————. 1949. *Römische Satiren*. Zurich.

Westmann, Rolf. 1955. *Plutarch gegen Colotes: Seine Schrift "Adversus Colotem" als philosophiegeschichtliche Quelle*. Acta Philosophica Fennica 7. Helsingfors.

Weston, Arthur H. 1915. *Latin Satirical Writing Subsequent to Juvenal*. Lancaster, Penn.

Westra, H. J. 1981. "The Juxtaposition of the Ridiculous and the Sublime in Martianus Capella." *Florilegium* 3: 198–214.

————, ed. 1986. *The Commentary on Martianus Capella's De Nuptiis Philologiae et Mercurii Attributed to Bernardus Silvestris*. Pontifical Institute of Mediaeval Studies, Studies and Texts 80. Toronto.

Wetherbee, Winthrop. 1972. *Platonism and Poetry in the Twelfth Century: The Literary Influence of the School of Chartres*. Princeton.

————, trans. 1973. *The Cosmographia of Bernardus Silvestris*. Records of Civilization: Sources and Studies 89. New York.

Whittaker, Thomas. 1923. *Macrobius, or Philosophy, Science and Letters in the Year 400*. Cambridge.

Williams, Gordon. 1978. *Change and Decline: Roman Literature in the Early Empire*. Berkeley.

Williams, Juanita S. 1966. "Towards a Definition of Menippean Satire." Diss., Vanderbilt University.

Willis, J. 1988. Review of *A Philosophical and Literary Commentary on Martianus Capella's* De Nuptiis Philologiae et Mercurii, *Book I*, by D. Shanzer. *Gnomon* 60: 451–53.

Winkler, John J. 1980. "Lollianos and the Desperadoes." *JHS* 100: 155–81.

———. 1985. *Auctor & Actor: A Narratological Reading of Apuleius' Golden Ass.* Berkeley.

Winterbottom, Michael. 1970. *Problems in Quintilian. BICS* Supplement 25. London.

Witke, Charles. 1970. *Latin Satire, The Structure of Persuasion.* Leiden.

Wolf, Sonja. 1986. *Die Augustusrede in Senecas* Apocolocyntosis: *Ein Beitrag zur Augustusbild der frühen Kaiserzeit.* Beiträge zur klassischen Philologie 170. Meisenheim.

Woytek, Erich. 1970. *Sprachliche Studien zur Satura Menippea.* Weiner Studien, Beiheft 2. Vienna.

———. 1972. "Stilistiche Untersuchungen zur Satura Menippea Varros." *Eranos* 70: 23–58.

———. 1986. "Varro." In *Die römische Satire,* edited by Joachim Adamietz, 311–55. Darmstadt.

Wright, Wilmer Cave, ed., trans. 1913. *The Works of the Emperor Julian,* vol. 2. London.

Zaffagno, Elena. 1976a. "Ancora su Varrone Menippeo." *ASNP* 3rd ser. 6: 799–811.

———. 1976b. "Commento al lessico delle 'Menippee.'" *Studi Noniani* 3: 195–256.

Zappala, Michael O. 1990. *Lucian of Samosata in the Two Hesperias: An Essay in Literary and Cultural Transmission.* Scripta Humanistica 65. Potomac, Md.

Zaslavsky, Robert. 1981. *Platonic Myth and Platonic Writing.* Washington, D.C.

Ziolkowski, Jan. 1985. *Alan of Lille's Grammar of Sex: The Meaning of Grammar to a Twelfth-Century Intellectual.* Speculum Anniversary Monographs 10. Cambridge, Mass.

Index

Note: Authors' names are used as shorthand for their Menippean works when there is no possibility of confusion (e.g., in Boethius, in Julian). Appendixes B and C are selectively represented.

299

Designed by Susan Bishop

Composed by Village Typographers, Inc.,
in Linotron Baskerville text and display

Printed by The Maple Press Company, Inc.,
on 50-lb. Glatfelter Eggshell Cream
and bound in Holliston Kingston Natural

DATE DUE